1ℒ   54.95
6 5ℬ

DARK EDEN

Selected books in the series:

CHARLES ALTIERI, *Painterly Abstraction in Modernist American Poetry:
The Contemporaneity of Modernism*
DOUGLAS ANDERSON, *A House Undivided: Domesticity and Community
in American Literature*
STEVEN AXELROD AND HELEN DEESE (EDS.), *Robert Lowell: Essays on the Poetry*
SACVAN BERCOVITCH AND MYRA JEHLEN (EDS.),
Ideology Classic and American Literature
PETER CONN, *The Divided Mind: Ideology and Imagination in America, 1898–1917*
MICHAEL DAVIDSON, *The San Francisco Renaissance: Poetics and Community at Mid-Century*
GEORGE DEKKER, *The American Historical Romance*
STEPHEN FREDMAN, *Poet's Prose: The Crisis in American Verse*
ALBERT GELPI (ED.), *Wallace Stevens: The Poetics of Modernism*
RICHARD GRAY, *Writing the South: Ideas of an American Region*
ALFRED HABEGGER, *Henry James and the "Woman Business"*
DAVID HALLIBURTON, *The Color of the Sky: A Study of Stephen Crane*
SUSAN K. HARRIS, *19th-Century American Women's Novels: Interpretive Strategies*
JOHN LIMON, *The Place of Fiction in the Time of Science: A Disciplinary History
of American Writing*
JOHN McWILLIAMS, *The American Epic: Transformations of a Genre, 1770–1860*
MARJORIE PERLOFF, *The Dance of the Intellect: Studies in Poetry in the Pound Tradition*
ERIC SIGG, *The American T. S. Eliot: A Study of the Early Writings*

For a complete listing of books available in the series, see the pages following the Index.

DARK EDEN

THE SWAMP IN NINETEENTH-CENTURY AMERICAN CULTURE

DAVID C. MILLER
Allegheny College

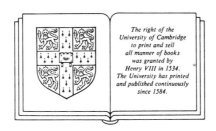

The right of the
University of Cambridge
to print and sell
all manner of books
was granted by
Henry VIII in 1534.
The University has printed
and published continuously
since 1584.

CAMBRIDGE UNIVERSITY PRESS
Cambridge
New York   Port Chester   Melbourne   Sydney

Published by the Press Syndicate of the University of Cambridge
The Pitt Building, Trumpington Street, Cambridge CB2 1RP
40 West 20th Street, New York, NY 10011, USA
10 Stamford Road, Oakleigh, Melbourne 3166, Australia

© Cambridge University Press 1989

First published 1989

Printed in the United States of America

Library of Congress Cataloging-in-Publication Data
Miller, David Cameron.
Dark Eden : the swamp in nineteenth century American culture /
David C. Miller.
p.   cm. – (Cambridge studies in American literature and
culture)
Bibliography: p.
ISBN 0-521-37553-3
1. American literature – 19th century – History and criticism.
2. Swamps – Social aspects – United States – History – 19th century.
3. Swamps in literature.   4. Eden in literature.   I. Title.
II. Series.
PS217.S95M55   1989
810.9′32169–dc20   89-32631
                                                             CIP

British Library Cataloguing in Publication Data
Miller, David C.
Dark Eden: the swamp in nineteenth century American
culture. – (Cambridge studies in American literature
and culture)
1. English literature.   American writers, 1800–1915 –
Critical studies
I. Title
810.9

ISBN 0-521-37553-3   hard covers

To my mother and father,
for their endless encouragement,
support, and help

Contents

List of Illustrations   *page* ix

Acknowledgments   xi

Introduction   I

Part One: The Matrix of Transformation   21

Chapter One   To the Lake of the Dismal Swamp: Porte Crayon's
Inward Journey   23

Chapter Two   The Elusive Eden: The Mid-Victorian Response to
the Swamp   47

Chapter Three   Mid-Victorian Cultural Values and the Amoral
Landscape: The Swamp Image in the Work of William
Gilmore Simms and Harriet Beecher Stowe   77

Part Two: The Phenomenology of Disintegration   105

Chapter Four   Frederic Church in the Tropics   107

Chapter Five   The Penetration of the Jungle   118

Chapter Six   American Nature Writing in the Mid-Victorian
Period: From Pilgrimage to Quest   125

Chapter Seven   A Loss of Vision: The Cultural Inheritance   132

Chapter Eight   A Loss of Vision: The Challenge of the Image   151

Chapter Nine   Infection and Imagination: The Swamp and the
Atmospheric Analogy   184

CONTENTS

Part Three: The Circuit of Death and Regeneration   205

Chapter Ten   Immersion and Regeneration: Emerson and Thoreau   207

Chapter Eleven   The Identification with Desert Places: Martin
Johnson Heade and Frederick Goddard Tuckerman   224

Chapter Twelve   Religion, Science, and Nature: Sidney Lanier and
Lafcadio Hearn   241

Conclusion: Katherine Anne Porter's Jungle and the Modernist
Idiom   255

Appendix: "Wading in a Marsh" by David Wagoner   269

Notes   271

Selected Bibliography   313

Index   317

Illustrations

I.1 William H. Buck, *Louisiana Swamp*   page 7

I.2 James Smillie, engraving after Thomas Cole's *Garden of*
     Eden   12

I.3 Martin Johnson Heade, *The Great Florida Marsh*   14

1.1 David Hunter Strother, *The Barge*   24

1.2 David Hunter Strother, *Lake Drummond*   27

1.3 John Gadsby Chapman, engraving after *View of the Dismal*
     Swamp   31

1.4 James Hamilton, *Bayou in Moonlight.*   33

1.5 Henry Inman, engraving after *The Great Dismal Swamp*   33

1.6 Flavius Fischer, *The Dismal Swamp*   39

1.7 Anonymous, *Lake Drummond*   40

2.1 A. R. Waud, *Cypress Swamp on the Opelousas Railroad,*
     Louisiana   58

2.2 A. R. Waud, *On Picket Duty in the Swamps of Louisiana*   59

2.3 Harry Fenn, *A Sudden Turn in the Ocklawaha*   61

2.4 Harry Fenn, *Ascending the Ocklawaha River at Night*   62

2.5 Harry Fenn, *Waiting for Decomposition*   63

2.6 Harry Fenn, *A Florida Swamp*   64

2.7 Harold Rudolph, *Bayou Sunset*   65

2.8 Meyer Strauss, *Bayou Têche*   66

2.9 Granville Perkins, *Florida Landscape*   67

2.10 Joseph Rusling Meeker, *Bayou Têche*   69

2.11 Joseph Rusling Meeker, *Swamp on the Mississippi*   70

2.12 Anonymous, *My Saurian's House*   71

2.13 Norton Bush, *Misty Day in the Tropics*   73

2.14 Fortunato Arriola, *Tropical Landscape*   74

3.1 Rodolphe Bresdin, *Eclaircie dans la Forêt*   82

3.2 John Adam Houston, *The Fugitive Slave*   91

ix

3.3   David Hunter Strother, *Osman*   93
3.4   Thomas Moran, *Slaves Escaping Through a Swamp*   94
4.1   Frederic Church, *The Heart of the Andes*   108
4.2   Frederic Church, *Morning in the Tropics* (1876)   114
4.3   Frederic Church, *Morning in the Tropics* (1856)   115
4.4   Frederic Church, *Deep Jungle Foliage*   116
4.5   Frederic Church, *Jungle Scene*   117
5.1   A. R. Waud, *Bear Hunt in a Southern Canebrake*   123
7.1   Thomas Cole, *Landscape with a Dead Tree*   137
7.2   William Trost Richards, *In the Woods*   147
7.3   David Johnson, *Brook Study at Warwick*   148
7.4   William Trost Richards, *Ferns in a Glade*   149
8.1   Martin Johnson Heade, *Orchids and Hummingbird*   155
8.2   Caspar David Friedrich, *Oak Tree in Snow*   156
8.3   Eadweard Muybridge, *Las Nubes, Delia Falls*   164
8.4   Martin Johnson Heade, *Brazilian Forest* (1864).   165
8.5   Martin Johnson Heade, *View from Tree-Fern Walk, Jamaica*   166
8.6   Frederic Church, *Evening in the Tropics*   167
8.7   François Regis Gignoux, *Sunset in a Swamp*   168
8.8   Jacob van Ruisdael, *Oak by a Lake with Water-Roses*   169
8.9   Asher B. Durand, *The Beeches*   170
8.10   Asher B. Durand, *In the Woods*   170
8.11   Worthington Whittredge, *The Old Hunting Grounds*   171
8.12   Martin Johnson Heade, *South American River Scene*   173
8.13   Herman Herzog, *Moonlight in Florida*   174
8.14   Frederic Church, *Tropical Scene at Night*   175
8.15   Fortunato Arriola, *Moon over Lake Nicaragua*   176
8.16   Anonymous, *A Louisiana Swamp*   182
11.1   Martin Johnson Heade, *Lake George*   226
11.2   Winslow Homer, *Homosassa Jungle*   229
11.3   Winslow Homer, *In the Jungle, Florida*   229
11.4   Martin Johnson Heade, *Approaching Storm: Beach near
       Newport*   234
11.5   Martin Johnson Heade, *Salt Marshes, Newport, Rhode Island*   235

Color plates follow page 114

Acknowledgments

I owe the most to my teacher Barton L. St. Armand, without whose example my own journey into the swamp would no doubt have been far different. Professor St. Armand is a rare soul who still takes the organic metaphor seriously. His unique sensitivity to the culture of nineteenth-century America remains a constant spur and rebuke to my own efforts to imaginatively inhabit the past. I am deeply grateful as well to Sherman Paul, who kindly consented to serve as an outside reader for this project in its dissertation phase and whose own work has been an inspiration; to John L. Thomas, whose enthusiasm alone could have kept me going against all odds; to Donald M. Scott and William G. McLoughlin, for their sensitive and encouraging readings during the early stages of writing. Angela Miller was my toughest critic and made wonderful contributions and suggestions all along the way. My cohorts and colleagues, in graduate school and beyond, who helped me sharpen and reassess my ideas are far too numerous to mention by name. But without the stimulation from Susan Donaldson, Peter Balakian, Jan Emerson, David Green, Mark Asquino, Linda Lomperis, David Lubin, Allan Wallach, and Charlotte Wellman, this book would have been much fuzzier and much thinner than it is. What there is of art historical sensitivity simply would not be here without the abiding efforts of my father, Dwight C. Miller, who, with a truly infectious enthusiasm, trained me to look at paintings. I would like to give special thanks to Elizabeth McKinsey and Jay Fliegelman for offering thoughtful responses to the manuscript at key stages in its development. A Melon post-doctoral fellowship in the humanities at Stanford University enabled me to extensively revise the manuscript as well as to turn to other interests. A grant from Allegheny College helped subsidize the cost of the color plates. Finally, I would like to thank my editor Albert Gelpi for his patience and encouragement.

The yarns of seamen have a direct simplicity, the whole meaning of which lies hidden within the shell of a cracked nut. But Marlow was not typical (if his propensity to spin yarns be excepted), and to him the meaning of an episode was not inside like a kernel but outside, enveloping the tale which brought it these misty halos that sometimes are made visible by the spectral illuminations of moonshine.

Joseph Conrad, *Heart of Darkness*

Generally speaking, a howling wilderness does not howl: it is the imagination of a traveller that does the howling.

H. D. Thoreau, "Allegash and East Branch"

Crispin knew
It was a flourishing tropic he required
For his refreshment, an abundant zone,
Prickly and obdurate, dense, harmonious,
Yet with a harmony not rarefied
Nor fined for the inhibited instruments
Of over-civil stops.

Wallace Stevens, "The Comedian as the Letter C"

Introduction

In the 1850s and 1860s Americans began turning to new landscapes to express their changing perception of nature. Whether faraway places – tropical forests, ice-bound vistas, desert islands – or the swamps, marshes, and uninhabited beaches closer to home, landscapes previously neglected were seized upon. Such imagery posed an alternative to high Romantic iconography, associated, for example, with the Hudson River school and to the moral allegory and aesthetic criteria that underlay it. The new resonance that natural images assumed just before the Civil War reflected both the self-consciousness and cosmopolitanism of an emerging middle class and a deep-seated cultural strain. In keeping with the deflation of Romantic ebullience – the loss of faith in the boundless capacity of unaided intuition occurring at this time[1] – nature was becoming less a source of moral insight and more a sanctuary from an increasingly urbanized and technological environment. This development helped set the stage for the rise of such late nineteenth-century trends as tourism, naturalism, and social Darwinism. But it is especially important in its own right. Severe cultural conflict and change led to a resourceful new symbolic mode.

Interest in the new landscapes coincided with a renewed apprehension of the natural image in its often startling immediacy, a retreat from the didactic tone and "picturesque" conventions canonized by the preceding generation of writers and artists. Even more important than the growing emphasis on the scientific accuracy of observation, however, was the way in which the new landscapes were likely to present an altogether indifferent or hostile face to the world of human enterprise and social concern. It is in this respect that they fall under the age-old rubric of "desert" places. The term at once recalls the wilderness of the Old Testament and designates wasteland. Its old-fashioned usage referred to "any wild, uninhabited region, including forest land . . . deserted, forsaken, abandoned" (Oxford English Dictionary). Swamps, in particular, had been characterized as desert places from the earliest years of English settlement in North America.

1

Yet by the mid-nineteenth century the associations of these waste places were changing, gaining in nuance and sometimes actually reversing in value. Articles in such magazines as *Harper's Monthly*, *Putnam's*, and *The Atlantic* (to name only the most significant to begin publishing in this period) not only expressed but also largely shaped the attraction of the new reading public to exotic and even alien experiences. Such periodicals were filled with accounts of travel and adventure in faraway places, especially Latin America. *Harper's*, especially, contained numerous illustrations that brought the world all the more vividly into middle-class parlors and libraries. The theme of immersion in the unknown became standard popular fare and was adopted and refined by a number of writers and artists.

The novel description provided metaphors through which to explore the inner self and to expand the horizons of culture. Remote from the arena of public meaning, desert places had always alternated uncertainly between outer world and inner. With growing dissatisfaction over the course of civilization in the years before the Civil War, this subversive ambiguity began to offer the means for developing a world apart from civilization or at least for bringing about a significant adjustment in the traditional relationship between nature and culture. As civilization came to seem burdensome, nature tended to be progressively interiorized and relativized.

If the outlines of this development appeared on the European scene as well – the dialectical counterpart, ultimately, of the reification of the material world wrought by capitalism – its American nuances were molded to the peculiarities of the American environment. The shift in the attitudes of Americans during the Mid-Victorian period from moralistic preoccupations to a concern with psychic fulfillment and self-exploration was effected to a surprising extent by attention to landscapes that – unlike mountains or waterfalls, lakes, or forests – had never before been awarded particular notice, much less positive value.

The way in which a landscape is represented pertains not only to its physical shape but also to what artists and writers project on it, owing on the one hand to their professed values, hopes, and ideals and on the other to their implicit fears, prejudices, and needs. Hence, given the orientation to nature that we find in America during much of the nineteenth century,[2] descriptions of landscapes can be a revealing index of both the culture's inner life and its professed worldview. Psychic projection is especially evident in desert landscapes that, by definition, are untrammeled by conventions that reflect conscious aspirations to the exclusion of other kinds of meaning. Regions of the unknown have often provided open fields for the projection of unconscious material. But the invitation to psychic projection was never more imperative than in the case of the swamp, an image whose complexity and elusiveness, as I hope to show, could lure awareness through an endless array of dissolving surfaces and shifting dimensions.

To reconstruct the traditional associations, basic beliefs, empirical observations, and metaphoric suggestions that comprised the cultural profile of the swamp image during the nineteenth century affords an organic basis for comparing the responsiveness of various levels of culture to new experiences. Indeed, to study the response of various nineteenth-century Americans to this multiplex and multivalent image is to peer through a keyhole into the inner sanctum of the culture where reside some of its most furtive but urgent motives. However delimited the perspective, we may glimpse there what is simply not to be encountered in the breezy hallways and sunny verandahs at the culture's more accessible levels. Even though it never did so, the image of the swamp might well have provided some writer with an organizing metaphor – like Herman Melville's white whale and the whaling industry – for the most profound and poignant problems of American culture at mid-century. As it was, Harriet Beecher Stowe, in her second novel, *Dred, A Tale of the Dismal Swamp* (1856), came closest to making it such, though she too fell sadly short.

In any case, response to the swamp, as well as to such related landscapes as jungle and marsh, was not merely symptomatic of underlying cultural issues. This study rests on the assumption that images play an instrumental role in the evolution of cultural sensibility. It argues for the partial autonomy of images in shaping new cultural forms and styles and thereby influencing basic attitudes and values. And the claim for such autonomy is philosophically justifiable when applied to an age that still assumed an "objective" nature.

During the 1850s the swamp overcame, in the minds of many thoughtful Americans, its age-old stigma. Rather than evoking stock responses, it began to be confronted with fresh awareness and even to be inhabited imaginatively. Its associations had been traditionally tied to theological and folkloric contexts: It was the domain of sin, death, and decay; the stage for witchcraft; the habitat of weird and ferocious creatures. These associations remained current, at least in the popular mind, right up to the present. But this scrutiny of the swamp, through exploration and advancing scientific knowledge, led to a number of unforeseen implications. The image, realized more and more as an environment as well, illuminated emergent attitudes and half-repressed emotions and also gave shape to the moods and insights being engendered by a changing economic and social reality. These novel moods and insights in turn imparted mystique to a landscape hitherto shunned.

At the most visible levels of American culture, artists and writers discovered the distinctive "imagistic" features of the landscape: the arabesques of its vines and tendrils, the shifting patterns of light that played about its fastnesses, the surprising prospects offered at almost every step. This aestheticization of the swamp image revealed an ever-closer and more widespread engagement with the landscape in the years around the Civil War. Even more significantly, characteristics long noted – the sultry atmosphere, the treacherous mire, the bewildering vegetation – were granted a new, more positive perspective. The immersion in the unknown that desert places had always represented came to be embraced by many as not only a dangerous but also an exhilarating and self-renewing experience.

At the deeper levels of the culture, the swamp emerged as a metaphor of newly awakened unconscious mental processes. Here, the ongoing dialectic between image and meaning became synthesized. As the anthropologists Clifford Geertz and Victor Turner argued, cultural evolution pertains to metaphor. Metaphor is a way of grappling with the unknown, of understanding complex and contradictory experiences not amenable to logical analysis. Geertz sees metaphors as the creative aspect of ideologies and as equivalent to maps through unfamiliar socioeconomic terrain for which established cultural norms fail to provide direction.[3] Turner views metaphor as "a certain kind of polarization of meaning in which the subsidiary subject is really a depth world of prophetic, half-glimpsed images, and the principal subject, the visible, fully known (or thought to be fully known component), at the opposite pole of it, acquires new and surprising contours and valences from its dark companion."[4]

How does this metaphoric function intersect with the social milieu? Alterations in the socioeconomic climate of the mid-nineteenth century – most of all its heightened freedom, variety of life, and quickened pace – opened up new areas of human interaction and disclosed previously unfathomed aspects of consciousness that lay on the fringes of thought and behavior but sank roots deep into the cultural ferment. A developing self-awareness lay behind the quickened interest in the metaphoric possibilities of the swamp that, owing to its own recent emergence from the realm of social taboo, could embody heretofore-unsanctioned types of experience and feeling.

But for this very reason, the image left its imprint on what it had come to express. As Turner put it, in metaphor, the "dark companion" of the image also falls under the influence of the association; because "the poles are active together the unknown is brought just a little more into the light of the known."[5] Accordingly, such elements of Modernist consciousness as a feeling for the portentous, ambiguous, or ambivalent or for the animistic or the insidious (representing to some extent a recrudescence of primitivistic sensibility within a more self-conscious awareness) could be experienced and explored through swamp and jungle imagery, which thus fulfilled its metaphoric potential. Although all these states of mind, whether challenges to the norms of morality or displacements of spiritual essence, became increasingly salient features of people's experience in mid-nineteenth-century America, they were most strenuously exercised in the presence of swamps and jungles.

Its character complicated and enriched by the engagement with both its material and expressional aspects, the image of the swamp developed as an ever more potent metaphor. The core of my study is consequently an analysis of swamp and jungle images from what I call a *phenomenological* perspective. I shall examine the image of the swamp, as perceived in contemporary descriptions and representations, in relation to the prevailing epistemological and aesthetic criteria, in order to show how it came to challenge the Romantic-realist iconography. For instance, whereas the Romantic approach to landscape stressed dramatic contours (as shown in relatively distant prospects) and pastoral or instructive associations, the energy and intricacy of jungle vegetation tended to undermine these inherently moralizing conventions.

By the same token, the more the perspective entered the actual landscape (as with the depiction of lowland scenery it inevitably did), the less well the image could transmit an unequivocal message and so serve a didactic purpose. Gaston Bachelard's concern with "the onset of the image in the individual consciousness"[6] is relevant here. As he contended, "Some might insist on speaking of symbol, allegory, metaphor, and ask the philosopher to designate moral lessons before images. But if images are not an integral part of moral thought, they would not have such life, such continuity."[7] Indeed, it is the subtle, endlessly variable reverberations that the image stirs in the individual consciousness before the imposition of stable patterns of conceptualization that constitute the dynamic aspect of moral thought. A phenomenological approach, in Bachelard's terms, thus highlights the way in which images and moral thought interacted dialectically to determine cultural boundaries.

Bachelard's distinction between images and moral thought corresponds to the difference that another French philosopher, Jean-Paul Sartre, drew between *meaning* and *signification*, using a terminology with even wider ramifications: "By *signification* I mean a certain conventional relationship which makes a present object the substitute of an absent object; by *meaning* I denote the participation of the being of a present reality in the being of other realities, whether present or absent, visible or invisible, and, eventually, in the universe."[8]

In other words, meaning refers to the image per se, with its potential for forming relationships, whether physical or imagined, between itself and the rest of the universe. Meaning therefore underlies and subsumes the total range of significations, those conceptual relationships that define a cultural identity and that, because they are concerned with questions of value, limit the chances for making connections among distinctly perceived entities. This is not to suggest that the image lies beyond the social construction of meaning; it simply distills itself at a level of the self that is relatively free of the accretions of such constructions and thus is energized by the instinctive response.

We may think here of Samuel Coleridge's famous distinctions between allegory and symbol, fancy and imagination. Coleridge, too, assumed "a sort of participation mystique" linking us with the symbol, as Angus Fletcher noted.[9] It is intriguing to consider in this light the reappraisal of landscapes like the swamp in relation to the flowering of American symbolism during the 1850s. I argue that the probing of the texture, contours, and associations of surfaces by American writers (especially Herman Melville, Walt Whitman, and Henry David Thoreau) was a way of awakening wonder and realizing a reality that represents a fulfillment of Coleridgean theory never rivaled by the English Romantics themselves, inheriting as they did the idealizing temperament and diction of the eighteenth century. Once liberated from the grasp of the Ideal, the symbol could become a more effective medium for metaphysical truth, psychological insight, and social reality.

The idea that meaning involves the "participation of the being of a present reality in the being of other realities" is instrumental in understanding not only the shift in the recreation of the swamp in America but also the way in which we conceive of this shift. In adopting a phenomenological approach, we naturally are less concerned with the significations that Americans imposed on the landscape, given their preconceptions, than with those meanings of the phenomenology of the images themselves that tend to subvert the adequacy and authority of the conventional symbols.

This is a subtler distinction than it might first appear, as the act of perception is itself so interpretive. We are in effect simply shifting to a level of interpretation at which there is less of a bifurcation between subject and object. To intuit meanings at this level demands our empathy for both the subject represented (the landscape) and the mind behind the representation. We might speculate on the impact of the representation on the public it addressed; yet this question lies largely outside the scope of this book, as it seeks to indicate only generally the currency of swamp, jungle, and marsh images in the United States during the Victorian period, while suggesting what impacts such images had on basic values and assumptions.[10]

Still, this book is less a chronicle of American encounters with the swamp and other desert places than an examination of evolving literary and cultural sensibility. I have chosen to concentrate on the cultural transformation of the 1850s and 1860s as the matrix for the most important alteration to occur in literary, artistic, and even popular conceptions of such landscapes. The symbolic potential of an image must always be weighed against those factors that determine the culture's ability to exploit it.

To clarify further the relationship between imagery and cultural sensibility, it is useful to draw a parallel between Sartre's notions of signification and meaning and what the art historian Erwin Panofsky defined as *iconography* and *iconology*.[11] Panofsky isolated three levels of meaning above the formal basis of any image, which apply equally to painting and to real life (and, by extension, to literature). The first level consists of "primal" or "natural" meanings, including the recognition of facts and expressions (a level generally mistaken, says Panofsky, for the formal level). We see something – a collection of sense data – as a manifold, a "man" or a "tree," and we may also apprehend a complex of emotions. The second level is that of conventional meaning, of signification. This is the iconographic level, involving the connection of motifs with themes and of concepts with images.

Turning to nineteenth-century representations of the swamp, we could point here to common motifs like the moss-draped oak or the lone bird, an egret perhaps, as discrete iconographic elements. Of the lone bird, for instance, consider the description by the eighteenth-century naturalist William Bartram: "The solitary bird . . . stands alone on the topmost limb of tall dead cypress trees, his neck contracted or drawn in upon his shoulders, and beak resting like a long scythe upon his breast. In this pensive posture and solitary situation, it looks extremely grave, sorrowful and melancholy, as if in the deepest thought."[12]

There is a suggestive pictorial analogue to this description in a work entitled *Louisiana Swamp* (Figure I.1) by William Buck – an artist working in New Orleans during the latter part of the nineteenth century – suggesting how persistent Bartram's conception was. Painters of the swamp generally place the bird not in a tree but (obviously for the sake of composition and to give it prominence) somewhere in the lower foreground. In any case, the point is that the bird, though entirely naturalistic in appearance, exemplifies the pathetic fallacy; it commands a consistent, conventionalized emotional response. The same is true of the oak, no less melancholic with its "funereal" trappings. Both motifs focus the mood of the landscape as a whole, offering a kind of shorthand for its overall meaning. The remainder of the composition falls into place around this unitary pattern. Like the bird or the tree, everything seems suffused with the air of pensiveness and dejection.

Motifs like the melancholy oak or the sentinel bird might best be classified as emblematic; their function relates them to the long-standing tradition (ul-

Figure I.1. William H. Buck (American, born in Norway, 1840–1888), *Louisiana Swamp* (oil on canvas, 18 × 24 in., c. 1880). Acquired through the Ella West Freeman Foundation Matching Fund, New Orleans Museum of Art.

timately medieval) of allegorical pictures or heraldic devices accompanied by a label and usually a verse relating a moral truth.[13] Such emblems referred to certain topics or master narratives – the pilgrimage or life journey, the *psychomachia,* the chain of being – that organized society's values and sanctioned modes of behavior according to the Christian theological framework. We think immediately of John Bunyan's Slough of Despond. Emblems functioned as codes through which cultural concerns could be communicated and enforced.

In emblems, as in allegories (in Coleridge's definition), vehicle and tenor remained distinct. Ideally, in their schematic pictorialism and rigid meaning, emblems were meant to intrude between artist, reader, or viewer and the world of ideas to prevent any exchange that might generate dispute. The web of semantic and semiotic possibility in a visual image was mediated by conventions that proscribed its ambiguities, substituting a linear pattern for the normal visual continuum.[14]

Panofsky's third level of meaning, the "intrinsic," pertains to iconology. Intrinsic meaning is "a unifying principle which underlies and explains both the visible event and its intelligible significance, and which determines even the form in which the visible event takes shape."[15] We move away, in other words, from the text or painting itself into culture viewed as a gestalt, a complex of interacting forces. Iconology refers to the interpretation of symbolic values "which are often unknown to the artist himself and may even emphatically differ from what he intended to express."[16]

Hence, although the swamp's conventional meaning (or iconography) clearly reflects larger cultural interests and problems, its implicit meanings help open up the deeper workings of the culture. With the dissolution of centralized authority and social hierarchy, traditional codes continued to carry meaning, but because they were detached from any fully coherent system of values, their individual formulations took on new inflections and often surfaced in new contexts. Similarly, an alteration in the usual composition of a landscape (in itself a cultural paradigm) impinges on the signification of that image, throwing it off balance in revealing ways. Stable patterns of experiencing and understanding something can yield to dynamic patterns. A quality of strangeness, or otherness, may eventually pervade the image, transforming it from a conventional symbol into an object of considerable subjective fascination, ready to displace the culture's most enduring touchstones.

It is difficult to miss the feminist implications of such otherness for certain trends in American culture with which the emergence of the swamp as metaphor is associated. Indeed, the aura of prohibition that traditionally surrounded the landscape may be attributed to the predominance well into the nineteenth century of Protestant (especially Puritan) patriarchal values.

In the growing fascination for the swamp during the middle of the century, we witness firsthand the erosion of patriarchal patterns of culture, motivated by an urge to control or suppress a "female" nature as the source of heretical and potentially anarchic meaning. We also detect the concomitant fabrication of alternative versions of America, associated not only with women and matriarchy but also with blacks (later we shall examine the popular image of the escaped slave hiding in the swamp) and with manifestations of the savage or precivilized. Above all, the swamp became a symbol for Southern civilization, whether positively or negatively conceived. Even the Cavalier figure so closely identified with the antebellum South shared many affinities with the connotative world of the swamp. The ambivalence with which all such figures and concepts were invested attests to the struggle for repression in Victorian culture, which is what makes them so revealing.

My view of what Ann Douglas called the "feminization of American culture" does not include her negative judgment of the trend.[17] Surely, some of the most creative aspects of American thought derived from the matriarchal and feminist perspectives of nature's meaning. Metaphors can be associated with one another, often linking diverse areas of experience; this process was begun during the Mid-Victorian period. Consider, for example, the etymology of the word *mother* offered by Noah Webster in the *First American Dictionary* (1828). It includes such associations as "matter," "mold," "mud," "stuff, the material from which anything is made," "womb," "cause," "origin," "root," "spring," "matrix," "the bed of a river, a sink or sewer," "pus," "purulent discharge," "vagina," "stark naked," and "hysterics."[18]

The list suggests one important set of connotations that the swamp can provoke and helps locate that landscape on the underside of patriarchal culture, dominated by the body, materiality, corruption, infection, sexuality, and irrationality – but also origin and creativity. What prompts these associations in the case of the swamp is the resistance of nature to the values of the dominant industrial-capitalist order.

The relationship of swamp imagery to the hegemonic values of capitalism is, however, two edged. As I have already suggested, swamp imagery would not have flourished without the aid of capitalist expansion and class formation. First, the shift of much of the population from producing to consuming goods and enjoying increased leisure time led to the relaxation of strict moral codes that was necessary before a taste for the "wayward" environment could be cultivated. Second, the rise of tourism, particularly in exotic locales like the swamps of Florida, was part of a growing cosmopolitanism that helped inculcate the self-consciousness of the new bourgeoisie. Cultural forms were generated from the new sensations confronting the average person, but such forms could easily be appropriated by the stereotyping processes that empowered the expanding and ever-more tyrannical market. It is crucial at every point to try to determine the role of imagery in interacting with the forces of modern life. To a large extent, it was simply compensatory, a symbolic antidote to the rigors and depredations of the new system. No wonder that this interest in the swamp came at a time when the new market economy was finally being accepted by the American public (at least in the northeastern part of the country). The vogue for the swamp following the Civil War, I believe, was part of the consumerism that seemed to be overtaking every aspect of American life. But there are nonetheless examples of the swamp's truly creative and subversive potential.

To assess the alterations in the conception of an image we must consider the various forces at work in the culture as a whole. Knowledge of the cultural background also helps explain why such motifs as the sentinel bird or moss-draped oak lose prominence or disappear altogether at a particular time, making room for other less familiar, more ambiguous features and a different feeling. Panofsky pointed out that iconology is as much above the sphere of conscious volition as expressional meaning is beneath it. Potential meaning – both phenomenological and iconological factors – thus surrounds intentional meaning, the expressional and the intrinsic interacting dialectically from different directions on the area of the known.

This configuration confirms the dynamic of cultural evolution as I see it: image and interpretation working together to inject traditional meaning into new forms that in turn influence what is perceived.[19] Despite the dichotomy that I am suggesting between image and interpretation, the connection between them is indissoluble. Accordingly, language, literature, and art must be given the same status as productive forces that we give to the manufacture of goods and services. Underlying my methodology is the assumption that no real distinction can be drawn between matter and spirit. Far from being ontological categories, matter and spirit are human constructs whose changing relationship reveals its evolving social and cultural orientation.

Given this dialectical view of cultural unfolding, the changing response to the swamp and its related images offers some clues to understanding the movement out of the sentimental ethos in the 1850s and 1860s that took place largely beyond the realm of articulate values. Even if this transition was finally only a prelude to the proliferation of genteel platitudes in the postwar period, it does indicate a period of searching and reevaluation in which some Americans took a plunge into the whirlpool of the primitive self.

The psychological repercussions of the swamp were most pronounced in its peculiar ecology. Mid-Victorian nature writers observed that the swamp lives off its own decay and produces so much vegetation that it can actually be seen to strangle itself. Contemplation of this mingling of forces normally thought to be opposed – life and death, good and evil – undercut the fundamental assumptions connected with the sentimentalist quest for purity and flight from death and both prefigured and later affirmed the Darwinian struggle for survival. To polarize life and death had been a way of closing off the physical and unconscious aspects of life that might interfere with the economic enterprise and the moral crusading implicated in it. To merge life and death opened up new avenues for culture to move in.

It is no accident that this shift in sensibility occurred during a period of increasing sectional divisiveness culminating in the Civil War. Sensitivity to the more radical implications of the swamp may be viewed as a by-product of the failed compromise that had been pressed by conservative Whigs like Daniel Webster. In talking about the prospect of disunion in a speech at Capon Springs, Virginia, in 1851, Webster used swamp imagery: "But secession and disunion are a region of gloom, and morass and swamp; no cheerful breezes fan it, no spirit of health visits it; it is all malaria. It is all fever and ague. Nothing beautiful or useful grows in it; the traveller through it breathes miasma, and treads among all things unwholesome and loathsome."[20] Webster's use of the swamp as moral emblem here contrasts the ideal of union with an imagery of dispersal, infection, corruption, and death that unveils the one-sided hegemonic and patriarchal prejudices at stake in his political culture.

The increasingly positive aura the swamp assumed in the 1850s indicates a reconfiguration of notions of the self and its relation to the body politic that contradicted the assumptions behind Webster's devotion to the shibboleths of union, constitution, and compromise. Moreover, much of the imagery we shall examine represents a departure from the aesthetic desiderata of the American picturesque tradition with its ideological conservatism as well as its adherence to a Burkean organicist political theory and to oratorical strategies that assumed the "sublime" universal appeal of the spoken word. Like the conservative Whigs of Massachusetts – where this political culture found its purest form and staunchest advocacy – the promoters of the picturesque and the sublime guarded elitist values emphasizing unity and hierarchy, collective continuity with the past, and the priority of history and property over nature in determining social status and taste.

The aesthetic equivalent of such an ideology stressed the distant prospect (with its natural hierarchy of elements running from inhabited foreground to the heavens above), the massing of forms to ensure their rational disposition, the harmony of parts, and the presence of human associations – all of which turned the natural prospect into a facsimile of social and political harmony, in the case of the picturesque, and into an expression of divinely instituted authority, in the case of the sublime.[21] In Chapters 7 and 8 we shall discuss how the phenomenology of the swamp challenged these criteria, acting instead as a conduit for subjective responses and newly released energies that spelled the demise of any spirit of union or compromise parochially conceived, just as it undermined any sense of paternalistic hegemony.

But for some Americans, the reach of nature's influence went even farther. As the relatively conservative and controlled version of nature represented by the picturesque tradition gave way to the anarchistic implications of the swamp, the interpenetration of nature and the self was intensified, amplifying the possibilities for regeneration but also inviting psychic disintegration. Thoreau's celebration of the swamp in "Walking, or the Wild" is a testimonial to the power of the landscape to reintegrate and refresh the self. The "dank tarn" of Edgar Allan Poe's "The Fall of the House of Usher" is a symbol of the swamp's insidious influence, of the dangers of the irrational. This central dichotomy reflects the paradox of the swamp experience and mirrors the opposition in American literature of the antebellum period between the regenerative propensities of the symbol pursued by the Transcendentalists and the "gnostic" suspicion of a prison-house world shared by the authors of *The Narrative of Arthur Gordon Pym* and *The Confidence-Man: His Masquerade,* in which are encountered the "slippery, sliding" surfaces of reality. Immersion in the unknown, if taken too far, as Pym discovers, can become suffocating rather than enlivening.

A second and related division derives from the contrasting associations with the swamp, as opposed to those of the tropical ideal. If swamps had long appeared sardonic and mysterious, sirens whose call must not be heeded, the tropical image had distinctly Edenic overtones. In the highly stylized works of such American artists as Thomas Cole (for example, *The Garden of Eden,* Figure I.2, or the first panel of the *Voyage of Life*) and Erastus Salisbury Field, tropical imagery stands, in its immodest profusion, for unfallen nature. As David Huntington and Katherine Manthorne showed, this approach is used in the work of such artists as Frederic Church and Louis R. Mignot, who appropriated the Latin American jungle as their usual subject matter.[22]

Although unself-conscious sensuality and fecundity denote the paradisal state, it is noteworthy that any suggestion of danger or seduction is eliminated by the controlled way in which the tropical growth is disposed. Manthorne, for instance, focused on the palm tree, which functions in an emblematic way. This unilateral or emblematic approach is disrupted, however, when the tropical image is portrayed more naturalistically, taking on the visual density of

Figure I.2. James Smillie, engraving after Thomas Cole's *Garden of Eden*. Frontispiece, *The Holy Bible*, vol. 1 (Boston: Gray and Bowen, 1831). General Research Division, New York Public Library, Astor, Lenox, & Tilden Foundations.

an actual jungle. With more faithful observation, the close visual affinities between tropical and swamp images emerge, and the ambiguities of each image now serve to strengthen the link.

Eventually, swamp and tropical images, along with the opposing moral values for which they stood, were merged. In fact, a number of artists in the latter part of the century (most notably Martin Johnson Heade) found themselves equally at home in the highland jungle of Latin America and, say, the bayou country around New Orleans or the swamplands of Florida. Just as a single image could visually unite sensual gratification and the energy of tropical growth with a sense of brooding mystery attached to the swamp (to witness this we need only look at one of Heade's late Florida landscapes, Figure I.3), so positive and negative connotations could spring simultaneously to mind. The ambivalence of modern awareness developed along just such lines.

The darkest of all the implications of the swamp metaphor emanate, as we shall see, from the popular belief in the hidden agency of "infection" so deeply associated in nineteenth-century minds with the miasma believed to originate from swampy terrain and used again and again by American romancers to embody the infernal tendencies of the imagination. Here the identification of self with environment that normally enlarged one's perspective and invigorated one's faculties overextended itself and gave way to the prospect of a loss of control signified by unlimited growth. The fear that reason might be supplanted by intuitive and unconscious responses lies behind the most sophisticated Romantic distrust of the swamp, just as it does behind popular prejudice.

In considering this atmospheric dimension of the swamp, our metaphor leads us to the point that linguistic concerns become primary. As the imagery of infectious atmosphere implies (being neither matter nor spirit but somewhere in between), the dematerialization of cultural forms that points the way to Modernism takes place, ironically, through an increasing appreciation for the materiality first of images and then of words.

Although my analysis will focus on Melville's *The Confidence-Man,* it should be noted that atmospheric imagery (only loosely connected to landscape and that only vaguely swamplike) plays a more prominent role in *Pierre,* in which it is associated with the hero's dark anima, his half-sister Isabel. Largely through her connection with an atmospheric agency, with the "haze" of ambiguities that Pierre confronts when he turns toward her and away from traditional sources of authority (as in "He strove to condense her mysterious haze into some definite and comprehensible shape"[23]), Isabel becomes a figure for the undoing of all cultural mediations, even language itself. For instance, given her illegitimate origins and isolated upbringing, the word *father* (the locus of patriarchal and logocentric authority) has only an oblique meaning for her. But although she causes everything to lose material grounding, it is paradoxically her striking physicality (and the image of mortality that her appearance evokes) that makes Isabel so much more compelling to Pierre than the ethereal Lucy is.

As a representation of the physical side of existence that has been disenfranchised by the sublimations of idealism, Isabel threatens a "return of the repressed." We shall later explore the dialectic of this return of the repressed in the metaphor of infection. Suffice it to say here that by entering into a

Figure I.3. Martin Johnson Heade, *The Great Florida Marsh* (1886). The Collection of Flagler System, Inc., Palm Beach. Courtesy of Washburn Gallery, New York.

struggle with the physical aspect of his being awakened by Isabel's animal magnetism, Pierre leads us to question his motivation: Is he driven by idealism or libido? The desire to commit incest with Isabel and the barrier of the incest taboo demarcate the wavering line between nature and culture, between the appeal of the image (unstructured by language or other forms of cultural mediation) and the need to transcend it through idealism, which draws attention to the artificial distinction that separates spirit and matter. Melville's discovery in *Pierre* that the basic antinomies of thought are human constructs rather than ontological truths led him into the orgy of self-referentiality that usurps the authority of the book's narrative and that Melville honed into the radically symbolistic technique of later works like "The Piazza" and *The Confidence-Man*.

But to suggest the trend toward Modernist thought is not merely to point to the deflation of nature's spiritual and transpersonal content – a preview of the wastelands of twentieth-century literature. Although literary and cultural historians have interpreted the empiricism with which Americans approached nature in the 1850s as testifying to a loss of transcendental vision, greater fidelity to the natural image (especially in the case of the swamp) could also lead to alternative sources of relationship, conviction, and power in the face of declining religious dogma and traditional social structures. This is especially true of isolated figures like Thoreau, the painter Heade, and the poet Frederick Goddard Tuckerman. But it is also applicable to some who enjoyed a more popular audience. Among others, Harriet Beecher Stowe (in her novel *Dred*) and the famous journalist "Porte Crayon" both discovered in the swamp a means of repossessing primitivistic modes of being that, though they might approach them with real ambivalence, offered a symbolic resolution of threatening cultural contradiction and its psychosocial tensions.

Close observation and a less socially monitored intercourse with the landscape helped mobilize the psychic projections that give the image an animistic intensity. In tracing the configuration of these projections, I have drawn on the work of depth psychologists, in particular that of C. G. Jung and his disciple Erich Neumann. It is probably no coincidence that these writers and their nineteenth-century predecessors in the study of primitive mythology – above all Friedrich Nietzsche and J. J. Bachofen – used swamp and jungle imagery to illustrate certain primitive or deeply repressed psychological complexes. I make no claim for the validity of these analogues, however, other than to suggest that they help distinguish the archetypal patterns (and here one need not accept Jung's premise of a collective unconscious to concede the point) of human interaction with nature. As such, the psychological aspect of the swamp metaphor represents simply an extension of our phenomenological treatment of the image, a deeper stratum of its meaning.

It is this dimension of the Romantic struggle with the image – too often ignored in literary and cultural studies – that I wish to discuss: The imaginative "inhabiting" to which the work of Bachelard sensitizes us helps bring Modernist sensibility out of the Romantic failure.

This is what I hope to show in the conclusion of this study, in going beyond a concern with the specificities of the swamp or jungle landscape to consider the "Mount of the Titans" passage in Melville's *Pierre* and Emily Dickinson's

"Further in Summer than the Birds." These two texts (as I shall show in a discussion of Katherine Anne Porter's "Pale Horse, Pale Rider") occupy opposite sides of a fault line in nineteenth-century culture that divides the failed "male" quest for absolute meaning from a "feminist" self-consciousness and sensitivity to the ability of the image to transcend its material origins. Likewise, the image transcends its social construction by displaying the paradoxical tension between matter and spirit. Pierre is unable to inhabit the body of the world in his imagination, losing, in his impatience, his sense of humor along with his aesthetic awareness (and proving himself to be more like Ahab than like the empathetic Ishmael). But Dickinson, in perhaps her greatest poem, holds the image in a tense and revelatory relationship to its fabrication. We see at once both the product and the process of semantic production behind it. This is, after all, the principal lesson of the swamp, in which an animism that is both spiritual and material and yet neither – the product of ourselves and yet an otherness all but inaccessible to us – apprises us of the conditions for keeping the world alive.

An explanation if not an apology needs to be made with regard to the conception of my book. A subject as slippery as a particular landscape or a category of landscape will lead to philosophical inconsistencies unless it is also defined according to a broader set of criteria. I am dealing with a period in which natural phenomena still retained a high degree of objectivity. Nonetheless, much of my book is a commentary on the development of the natural image from a discrete entity to one related to a potentially unlimited number of objects and experiences.

As I will argue in my conclusion, the swamp as a particular landscape with established iconographic features is eventually subsumed by more abstract and general categories such as "the material," "the primitive," or "the feminist." It is as if having undermined its inherited cultural norms, it is ready to be discarded (though the power of swamp imagery, for some, continues even today). Note that I have extended the meaning of the word *swamp* in the early nineteenth century to include the figurative sense of "to overwhelm." The Oxford English Dictionary quotes Todd (1818): "To *Swamp*, to whelm or sink as in a swamp. A modern word." Such a development represents a significant step toward the linguistic multivalence that prefigures the dematerialization of culture.

The transformation with which I am concerned can be seen in other terms as a shift away from the commonsense subject–object relation to the world fostered by "seeing" it, through the less stable aural and tactile relations created when it is experienced as an environment, and eventually beyond the sensorium altogether as "reality" becomes primarily linguistic. The persistence of the tradition of *ut pictura poesis* (the perception of painting and poetry as sister arts) well into the nineteenth century in America justifies my comparison of texts and images and emphasizes the descriptive over the expressive function of language in this period. Language still serves an objective reality. This tradition gradually lost ground, however, to more modern ways of thinking about the arts that were essentially nonrepresentational, specifically, the comparison of both painting and literature with music.

In order to span this momentous transformation of outlook, I have chosen the experience of immersion in the unknown as the lowest common denominator of the images and narratives to be examined. Immersion in the unknown involves descent into the body of nature, as opposed to the activity of ascent associated with traditional religious and moral instruction; hence it represents the subversive forces at work in culture. Although it begins with an encounter with the image as concurrently constituted, immersion in the unknown quickly moves consciousness beyond the parameters of the image, where cultural values are most deeply invested, and thereby sets the stage for its reconfiguration through a new group of constructs. Within the matrix of immersion in the unknown, that is, all aspects of the swamp or jungle experience (whether physical or psychological) take on the function of synecdoche: They are parts of a whole, each of which not only symbolically equals the whole but also stands for an even larger, almost all-encompassing, reality. Thus such diverse attributes of the swamp as dense vegetation, stagnation, mephitic atmosphere, or nameless terror all can be seen from a broader perspective in order to condense the sum of interlocking metaphors that masks a fundamental aspect of human experience. As their equivalence and interchangeability comes to the fore, the swamp's specific attributes betray their essential arbitrariness.

The vegetation of the swamp may be entangling, its morass treacherous, its atmosphere poisonous, its denizens devouring. Whatever the case, the experience that is common to these metaphors and to which our criterion of immersion in the unknown refers is the simultaneous fear of and desire for annihilation. Yet as Thoreau realized, "Generally speaking, a howling wilderness does not howl: it is the imagination of a traveller that does the howling."[24] Just as it turns experience inside out, this insight (though it slights the necessary element of physical danger) makes possible a transference from human destructiveness to a nearly opposite order of human motives.

From Thoreau's perspective, the dangers of the swamp recede and a new set of attributes emerges. The naive projections of folklore surrender to more complex and subtle projections – containing the seeds of regeneration – as the process of projection itself gains self-consciousness. In the subordination of destructiveness to creativity, a dynamic of creativity is rehabilitated (what I mean, finally, by the transition from a primarily moral relationship to nature to one that is largely psychological). Likewise, an awareness comes into being that allows the swamp, or any landscape for that matter, to flow into more generalized categories of meaning. All the while, the experience of immersion in the unknown remains intact as the basic point of reference. It has simply assumed a new orientation in consciousness.

Because my argument is so multidimensional, a brief explanation of its sequence is in order. Far from being chronological, this sequence is meant to illustrate the process of metaphorization which begins with immersion in the unknown.

Part I sketches the cultural matrix of transformation through its somewhat oblique manifestation in the changing perception of the swamp among writers and artists. My focus is on the interrelationship of iconology and iconography. The first chapter is an overture to the entire essay, rehearsing many of its basic themes through a discussion of the literature surrounding the Great Dismal Swamp of Virginia, the most famous of all American swamps. Here I deal with issues pertaining to the movement out of the sentimental ethos into one that is more realistic and exploratory. Chapter 2 is a more comprehensive overview, establishing the terms with which I define the transformation, during the nineteenth century, of the swamp as both image and symbol. The change is from moral emblem to object of aesthetic delight. The experience of Thomas Wentworth Higginson examined here serves as a paradigm for the discovery of the return to origins that follows from this transition. It also looks forward to twentieth-century vision, in both its assertion of the power of psychic renewal immanent in nature and the enervation of traditional moral force that such power ironically implies. Higginson's lack of concern with the traditional iconography of the swamp turns the experience of immersion in the unknown into a transcendence of the image in its specificity. This approach sets the stage for the dematerialization of culture, which is my concern later in the book. Chapter 3 outlines my general theory concerning the relationship between images and the development of cultural values in a discussion of the meaning of swamp imagery in the work of William Gilmore Simms and Harriet Beecher Stowe. The contrasting perspectives of these two writers reflect basic gender distinctions as well as differences in the larger mythic patterns of the North and South in the antebellum period.

Whereas Part I is concerned with the various cultural matrices – codes, paradigms, and structures determined by cultural issues and interests – that influenced the changing profile of the swamp, Part II examines the images themselves and how they challenged, through their distinctive phenomenology, the prevailing assumptions about reality. This examination culminates, in Chapter 9, in the implications of the poisonous atmosphere often associated with swamps. We shall explore the tendency of swamp imagery to undermine inherited ways of perceiving, thinking, and feeling, as well as the alternative values it produces. We shall also trace the progressive loss of vision based on cultural consensus and the parallel transition from the more articulate levels of culture to the expression of largely unconscious modes of being.

Part III probes the roots of the regenerative impulse in American literature dealing with the swamp and other desert places, an impulse that is centered in the thought of Ralph Waldo Emerson and Thoreau. I do not mean to suggest any necessary logical or chronological relationship here to the pursuit of the swamp's disintegrative aspect, only an alternative tradition. The discussions of William Byrd of Westover and the contemporary poet David Wagoner's "Wading in a Marsh" comprise prologue and epilogue to the moment when the swamp gained a regenerative symbolic import. Martin Johnson Heade and Frederick Goddard Tuckerman, in their respective media, expressed an innovative orientation toward nature that developed out of their interest in immersion in the unknown. The new sensibility they represent is further reflected, and to different degrees, in the later work of Sidney Lanier and in the lifelong quest of Lafcadio Hearn. Both Lanier and Hearn were Romantics in a post-Romantic age faced with the problem of reconciling spiritual aspiration with a commitment to Darwinian science. With these two figures, the growth of sensibility I have been charting bears the final blossoms of a full-fledged American Romanticism.

The conclusion looks at texts by Dickinson, Melville, and Katherine Anne Porter that may have little specifically to do with the iconography of the swamp but that have much to do with the way in which my concern with immersion in the unknown bridges this traditional iconography and more general and metaphoric categories of meaning and literary practice. It is at this point that the dynamic methodology I have detailed in this introduction reveals its underlying pressures and converges with the sequence of the book as a whole.

PART ONE

The Matrix of Transformation

Ceylon captivated me even before I set foot on it. While we were still some distance from shore, the strong odors and aromas of the jungle intoxicated me. But only after seeing Kandy and Anuradhapura did I have a true revelation of the jungle: trembling in awe and exultation before cataracts of fresh sap and unrestrained vegetal cruelty. Millions of plants crushed and buried from sight under half-decayed tree trunks, gigantic ferns and lichens struggling to make room for themselves among spider webs, fungi, and mosses of all colors. Memories of that week in Ceylon and of my first days in South India have continued to haunt me.

Mircea Eliade, *Autobiography* (1981)

Surrounded as they were, too, by the luxuriant vegetation of a tropical climate – swift in its growth and more swift in its decay – the Hindus meditated much on the mysterious force productive of life; and out of the conception which they formed of this force, combined with the reciprocal one of the destruction or death of all objects possessing life in nature, grew at length the conception of the god Siva, as at once both the destroyer and also the renewer of life.

William M. Bryant, Introduction to Hegel's
"The Philosophy of Art" (1879)

1

To the Lake of the Dismal Swamp: Porte Crayon's Inward Journey

Recounting his visit to Virginia's Great Dismal Swamp in early spring of 1856, David Hunter Strother – better known to Americans as the peripatetic raconteur and illustrator Porte Crayon – presented readers of *Harper's Monthly* with the narrative of a magic inward quest.[1] Porte approached the sojourn to Lake Drummond, at the center of the swamp, as a journey back to origins, to a repossession of childhood idealism. As he notes at the outset, "the lake of the Dismal Swamp has haunted my imagination from my earliest recollection . . ." (p. 441). His regression follows the archetypal pattern of a return from civilization through a dangerous realm where all distinctions blur. In a symbolic transformation of awareness, Porte reaches a source of self-renewal, an idyllic world, after passing through this region of death.

"Before I was aware of it I was in the Swamp." As he travels through the alien landscape by canal barge, Porte undergoes a frightening immersion. His senses are relentlessly assaulted as the barge makes its way through a tunnel of vegetation: "Lofty trees threw their arching limbs over the canal, clothed to their tops with a gauze-like drapery of tangled vines; walls of matted reeds closed up the view on either side, while thickets of myrtle, green briar, bay and juniper, hung over the black, narrow canal, until the boat could scarcely find a passage between" (pp. 441–2) (Figure 1.1). Confronting this spectacle of unconscious life, Porte quickly succumbs to a sense of oppressive dreariness: "The sky was obscured with leaden colored clouds, and all nature was silent, monotonous, death-like." His surroundings force him inward (as we follow the text from line to line):

> The surface of the canal was glassy smooth, and reflected the towering trees, the festooned vines, and pendant moss, with the clearness of a mirror. Before and behind the perspective lines ran to a point. The low whispering ripple of the water, and the sullen tramp, tramp, tramp, of the bargemen, did not disturb the stillness, but made it seem all the more dreary, like the ticking of an old clock in a deserted house at midnight. I was alone, utterly alone. (p. 443)

23

THE BARGE.

Figure 1.1. David Hunter Strother, *The Barge*. *Harper's New Monthly Magazine*, September 1856.

The description recalls the opening passage of Poe's "The Fall of the House of Usher": the narrator's mysterious journey on horseback to the abode of his boyhood friend, Roderick Usher, on a "dull, dark, and soundless day . . . through a singularly dreary tract to country"; the "sense of insufferable gloom" that pervades his soul; and the mirrorlike reflection of the "black and lurid tarn" that affronts him at the foot of Usher's forbidding edifice. Porte's experience too is modulated by the portentous accents of the voyage into the depths of the self: the claustrophobic proximity of sprawling vegetable life, the pressure of the canal's mirror image, the ever-receding vanishing point. As in Poe's tale, all contours converge in the absolute of cosmic narcissism.

What is striking about Porte's account is its atmosphere of the uncanny. In the unfamiliar, smothering environment of the swamp, the ego is forced to face its long-repressed primitive urges.[2] The creatureliness of the self threatens to overwhelm it. Porte imagines himself ushered into a land of the dead (again we think of Poe, of his obsessive fantasy of living inhumation): "My men were voiceless as the mutes of an Eastern despot. With the eternal tramp, tramp, tramp, they might have been ghouls, or cunningly-devised machines, set in motion by some malignant sorcerer, to bear me away living into a region of stagnation and death" (pp. 443–4). There the ego both experiences a loss of autonomy and attempts to assert its independence by marshaling the power of association.

Porte resists the compulsion of his surroundings by invoking the thought of death. Yet the swamp will not bear this association with death so at odds with its energy, its superabundance of life. The landscape, through Porte's language, projects an animistic vitality. Hovering unconcealed beneath its allusions, the landscape repeatedly rends the gossamer veil of meaning to flaunt its nakedness. We are reminded of the reflection with which Strother opened the piece: "Man, like the inferior animals, has his instincts, less imperious and less reliable, but oftener controlling his godlike reason than most are willing to admit" (p. 441).

The implicit tension between impulse-laden image and defensive association undermines the intended opposition between life and death which is the purport of the associations Porte brings to his experience; somehow the swamp suggests both at once. Similarly, the monotonous, rhythmic tramp of the repressive, machinelike boatmen contrasts with the spasmodic apparitions bursting all around: "Occasional glimpses through the thick undergrowth showed on either side extensive pools of black, slimy water, from which rose the broad-based cypress, and grouped around those strange contorted roots, called knees, gnarled and knotted like stalagmites in a cave" (p. 444). From time to time, a momentary view of some grotesque creature is revealed: "There, upon a decayed log, lay coiled a dead snake, dragged untimely from his winter retreat by a hungry otter. As we passed, I heard a rushing of wings above us, and saw a lazy, loathsome buzzard, scared from his perch and sailing away above the tree tops" (p. 444). Such preternatural images elicit a sense of déjà vu as the self regains contact with alienated aspects of its primal being.

The coincidence of monotonous tempo and variegated imagery evokes the hypnagogic state, that half-world between wakefulness and sleep (so fascinating to the Romantics) in which a procession of vivid pictures parades beneath closed eyelids. The intensity of these images derives from the heightened concentration of the mind's eye. The subject, drawn into himself, is held captive in a realm at once enchanting and dangerous. While compelled onward, he is simultaneously threatened with oblivion. Yet his fear is only a reflex of the waking mind, for it is specifically the will (conscious volition) that is jeopardized.

Gèza Roheim, who has written extensively about the hypnagogic experience, sees sleep as "uterine regression" (we can liken the canal through the swamp to the passageway to the womb), and the dream image as a "phallic countermove" against this regression, an effort to get back into the object world.[3] The sardonic character of Porte's images of the swamp might thus be explained by the strength of his attachment to the waking reality being threatened.

By contrast, Poe, certainly less devoted to the object world, referred to "a class of fancies, of exquisite delicacy" that arise "where the confines of the waking world blend with those of the world of dreams" and that have in them "a pleasurable ecstasy . . . of a character supernal to Human Nature. . . ."[4] The tension in Porte's mind between primary- and secondary-process thinking (to invoke Freud's distinction) is emphasized by the fact that while borne passively along on the canal barge, he can also be seen as actively penetrating a sexualized landscape, and the dramatic sense imparted by penetration brings with it the burden of male assertion and the patriarchal domination of nature. Moreover, Porte's immersion is controlled by the sides of the canal, suggesting not only his powerful ego orientation but also the role of technology in transforming the human relationship to nature through its suppression.

Paradoxically, it is the strength of the ego's identification with the object world and with tradition (the superego) that in the long run ensures its demise. As Porte moves deeper into the swamp, the resistance between image and association seems to subside. There is indeed a momentary convergence of the mind's preconceptions with reality when our hero finds himself in a wasteland symbolic of his subjugation to the object world: "The overarching gums had given place to a thick grove of pointed juniper trunks, deadened by a recent fire" (p. 444). Interestingly, he here links the landscape to a vision of bustling commercial activity: "This region bore some resemblance to the crowded docks of a maritime town. The horizontally projecting limbs were the booms and yards, while the hanging vines served as cordage" (p. 444).

This hallucination might well be understood, however, as the final defensive posture of a mind about to give up all resistance to the forces of disintegration. Repression of the swamp's aliveness through the cultural association with death becomes, in other words, the actual means by which the ego is overcome by the hidden conspiracy between superego and id.[5] In psychoanalytic terms, Porte's situation dramatizes the consequences of the narcissistic project in which failure to resolve the Oedipal conflict results in the desire for death – a loss of self – simultaneously through regression (figuratively, seduction by the mother, the "female" swamp) and repression (punishment by the father, the aggressive superego embodied in the bargemen, ministers of an Eastern despot whose ghoulish aura conveys the will to complete control and possession). As Freud put it, "Helpless in both directions, the ego defends itself vainly, alike against the instigations of the murderous id and against the reproaches of the punishing conscience."[6]

Now everyday awareness succumbs to the monotonous undertow of experience. Even the friction of the hypnagogic is numbed by oblivion: "Then the gums and cypresses reappeared, the same bed of reeds, evergreens, and briars, in endless perspective. We were entering on the fourth hour" (p. 444). The monotony of the landscape becomes one with the deadening effect of the tramping bargemen as the death march continues, leading Porte deeper and deeper into himself: "Monotony is wearisome, dreary, solemn, terrible. Tramp, tramp, tramp. It sounded like the dread footstep of the Commander in Don Giovanni. Tramp, tramp, tramp, like the beating pinions of Sleep and Death, as they bore away the body of Sarpedon" (p. 444).

But for Porte this situation results not merely in obliteration of the ego but also in a consequent self-renewal. As the moral connotations of death – reducing it to the opposite of life – have been transmuted by psychological nuances, a parallel transformation nears culmination. Once adult self-consciousness has been deposed, transcendence can occur through a childlike grasp of reality (what Freud called "the omnipotence of thought") that rises in its place. As Porte explained at the outset, the source of the romance of the "Great Dismal,"[7] indeed, the occasion for his regressive fantasy, is the familiar

Figure 1.2 David Hunter Strother, *Lake Drummond. Harper's New Monthly Magazine,* September, 1856.

ballad "The Lake of the Dismal Swamp," composed by the Irish bard Thomas Moore upon visiting the region in 1803. Porte is reminded of this ballad as it was sung over his cradle, "soothing the real with the wilder sorrow of the poet's fancy" (p. 443). Now, in an effort to relieve the mood that engulfs him, Porte sings it and enjoys a catharsis not afforded by his previous ineffectual associations: As the song rises to his lips unbidden, his voice wakes "the hollow, sullen echoes for the first time" (p. 444).

The song is an incantation. Porte inhabits its imaginative world, forgetting his isolation in the stillness of the swamp. The controlling impulse of association yields to an expansive resonance; the imminence of death merges with a harking back to childhood. Suddenly, the narrow perspective of the canal opens out to the grand vista of the lake, as if in answer to the query of the song, "Oh! when shall I see the dusky lake?" As the barge lands, Porte clambers off by himself to sit on a cypress root and contemplate the vision while sketching it (Figure 1.2). Emerging from the hypnagogic crucible into the relaxation of dream, he awakens to a wonderfully familiar awareness: "There it was, the dream of my childhood fulfilled. It was neither new nor strange. I had seen it a thousand times in my waking and sleeping dreams, as I saw it then; the broad expanse of the dusky water with its dim circling shores, the same dark leaden waves rolling over its surface and losing themselves silently among the reeds and rushes" (p. 446). Like the questing hero of mythology who survives the perilous passage through the Symplegades or clashing rocks to reach the legendary Fountain of Youth beyond,[8] Porte's immersion in an alien, formless realm has led to his spiritual rebirth.

But as he surveys the lake, Porte's reflections assume a somber cast appropriate to the melancholy mood of Moore's poem: "Then those gigantic skeletons of cypress that rose so grandly in the foreground, their wild contorted limbs waving with weepers of funereal moss, that hung down even to the water. It was at all points, a picture of desolation – Desolation" (p. 446). Curiously, this vision of the lake, like the sacred it embodies, is ambivalent. Only the man who is happy, "whose love is true, whose debts are paid, whose children blooming," muses Porte, "may find strange pleasure in thus fancifully wooing this awful phantom; but when inexorable fate has laid its icy grasp upon the heartstrings, then a man puts this by impatiently, and beckons joy to come – even folly and frivolity are welcomer guests to him" (p. 446). The lake too, then, is a test of the self's inner resources. The pleasurable sensations Porte feels in its presence are tokens of personal mastery.

Porte Crayon's account of his Dismal Swamp journey represents an adaptation of the formulas of sentimentalism to the purposes of an emerging ethos at once more realistic, dynamic, and psychologically oriented. His recognition of the lake stands for a personal reintegration poised between sentimentalist aspiration and symbolistic exploration. Although sentimentalism (a purely emotional relationship to the world) is personalized and charged with new energy in response to the physical environment of the swamp, the symbolistic impulse (an effort to probe the deepest recesses of thought and emotion) gains a means of controlling its potential excesses. Porte overcomes a possibly "fatal" empathy with the landscape (implied by the affinities of his account with the fantasies of Poe) through the emotive power of the nostalgia that wrenches him back to the traditional terms of human experience. Conversely, unlike mere sentimentalism, which involves escape to an idealized or imaginary past, Porte's experience refers to an actual personal past – not the world of the ballad but his own youthful response to it – and is thus a step toward a rudimentary historical consciousness of and responsibility to time.

That Porte's account incorporates such tension is more significant in view of the great popularity that his creator, David Hunter Strother, enjoyed in his day and the representative character of his work. From the 1850s through the 1870s the journalist was among the best-known and most highly paid writers in the country. His feature articles for *Harper's Monthly* answered the public's eagerness for descriptions of exotic places with humorous sketches accompanied by the author's own illustrations. The annals of Porte Crayon were keenly attuned to a shifting popular taste. As his biographer notes, Strother's work combined "the genteel romanticism of the sentimental novelists" and the "earthy realism of the frontier humorists."[9]

Porte functioned as a cultural symbol that, like a latter-day Quixote, was dedicated to a system of values out of touch with the present. Like his namesake, Washington Irving's Geoffrey Crayon, Porte evoked the genial, innocently homosexual world of the spectator and tourist whose responses to things were still redolent with an eighteenth-century fragrance. Especially appealing to readers was the indulgent satire with which Strother cut Porte's sentimental effusions down to size. It is interesting, therefore, that confronted with the Dismal Swamp, Strother for once relinquished his customary anecdotal style and jocular tone and allowed Porte to speak for himself in all his unabashed lyricism. The conflict of rhetoric and image at the heart of the narrative becomes even more suggestive in light of this tactic. Through his alter ego, Strother – otherwise the opportunistic reporter and social satirist – could himself indulge in sentiment. And his catharsis was twofold, as the ironic perspective was surely not forgotten. Strother undermined Porte even while identifying with him.

Yet in the end, Porte is not so much undermined as he is made to undergo a basic reorientation to experience. Strother's strategy (not altogether intentional, of course) not only reveals the tensions of a culture in transition; it also provides an effective symbolic resolution to the countervailing forces behind those tensions. Symbolically, Porte's attitude is purged of the detritus of a cultural outlook that has lost much of its relevance but whose sources are still fertile. His journey acts as a ritual purification wherein Thomas Moore's ballad – a communal property – becomes identified with the deepest aspirations of the self.

By singing the ballad in the midst of the swamp, Porte comes to terms with the irreconcilable aspects of experience through a return to the roots of culture where utterance, representing a magical relationship to the universe, unifies art and ritual. At the same time, he regains touch with his childhood self, not as an inert image, but as an active psychic force. At this level, the two functions of art – as a mode of making meaning and as a compensatory activity – are joined against all the factors that threaten disintegration. In this context, the swamp stands for the divergence of Strother's two selves, the disjunction between affections and critical faculties, heart and mind, reality and ego ideals. Porte's journey through the swamp is a way of reuniting these two selves, a testament to the power of culture to give coherence to life.

It is difficult to comprehend fully the significance of Porte Crayon's narrative of the Dismal Swamp without an awareness of the popular tradition in which it occupies a pivotal position. The vision of Lake Drummond was an image well known to the American reading public throughout the nineteenth century. This specter haunted not only Porte but also the collective mind of the genteel America to which he appealed, playing in particular on its affinities with Anglo-Irish culture. In invoking Moore's ballad, Strother joined a long line of travelers whose encounters with the gloomy lake fell under the spell of the Irishman's sentiment. The sense of redemption experienced upon emerging from the dense jungle is clearly at the source of the local legend (probably of Indian origin) that inspired Moore. The poet heard the story while visiting the town of Norfolk at the edge of the swamp and summarized it in the preface to his verses:

> They speak of a young man who lost his mind upon the death of a
> girl he loved, and who, suddenly disappearing from his friends, was
> never afterward heard of. As he had frequently said, in his ravings,
> that the girl was not dead, but gone to the Dismal Swamp, it is sup-

posed that he had wandered into that dreary wilderness, and died of hunger, or been lost in some of its dreadful morasses.[10]

In the poem the lover and his maiden are mysteriously reunited on the waters of the lake. The young man has beaten a grief-stricken path through the swamp,

> Through tangled juniper, beds of reeds,
> And many a fen, where the serpent feeds,
> And man never trod before.

Having fallen asleep exhausted, he is awakened by the stir of the she-wolf and the breath of the copper snake to cry:

> "Oh when shall I see the dusky lake,
> And the white canoe of my dear?"

Pursuing a "meteor-bright," he finds the lake at last: "And the dim shores echoed for many a night/The name of the death-cold maid" (p. 37). Finally, after constructing a canoe, he sets out on the lake, and forever after, the lovers appear by "fire-fly/lamp," paddling across its waters. So engaging was Moore's interweaving of image and fancy that toward the end of the century, another Irish poet, John Boyle O'Reilly, in reference to his own pilgrimage to the Dismal Swamp, could claim that "its name is almost as familiar as Niagara or the Rocky Mountains."[11]

The view that attracted so many devotees was the epitome of the sentimental version of nature. Full of wildness and melancholy, it offered a symbolic antidote to civilization's discontents. Even a cursory review of sentimental themes reveals a pattern of values and concerns clustered about an obsession with the depredations of time and the onslaught of civilization. Sentimentalists were given to morbid rumination on the loss of childhood and the inevitability of death. They voiced endless paeans to motherhood, the family, and home, and meditated on the destruction of the Indian or the disappearance of a once great civilization, the Mound Builders, from the face of North America. Above all, they exalted feeling for its own sake.

According to one critical commentary of the 1850s, whereas feeling flies to the relief of distress, sentiment selects only those forms of distress "the contemplation of which may throw [one] into that luxurious and dream-like melancholy which unnerves the soul and makes it unfit for efficient action. . . ."[12] By this token, the associations called to mind by the landscape prevailed over what was physically present; actuality was submerged by aspiration, usually backward in time.

The mystic aura of Lake Drummond pandered to the sentimentalist's nostalgia by calling to mind both the exotic and the dead. An engraving that appeared in *The Magnolia,* a gift book of 1837, after a work (now lost) by the Virginia artist John Gadsby Chapman, embodies these qualities (Figure 1.3). In "The Philosophy of Furniture," Poe mentioned Chapman's work as an example of the sort of painting that would adorn his ideal room, wherein *"repose* speaks in all."[13] The great value placed on repose by Poe as well as sentimentalists of every hue bespeaks a compelling desire for return to a former state of stability and contentment that could take on overtones of death.

Figure 1.3. John Gadsby Chapman, engraving after *View of the Dismal Swamp*. *The Magnolia*, 1837.

Pervaded by gloom, the image of Lake Drummond prodded the sentimentalist's pleasure in its charms with the gentle reminder of pain. It had *chiaroscuro*, a delicate veil of shadow that softened the harshness of life by imparting a sense of the illusory. The almost palpable silence and repose gave rise to a brooding suggestiveness. As one writer noted: "A solemn stillness pervades the shores – a silence broken only by the melancholy dirges of the breeze in the thick foliage above, the notes of the feathered songsters, the splash of the leaping, fluttering perch."[14] The lake's appearance met the demand for indistinctness levied by the vogue for the sublime and the picturesque, those aesthetic categories that spurned the unveiled.

The lake was above all picturesque; the scenery along its shores manifested the requisite degree of variety and irregularity and harmonized with the smooth surface of water. But there was also an undeniable note of the sublime in the expansiveness of the vision and in the pallor of the cypresses, evoking grandeur and death. Much of the power of this cultural icon lay in the way its integrated composition complemented an imagery of disintegration. The contour of the lake imparted structure as well as spaciousness to the image, compensating for the wild and threatening character of the dense jungle that bordered the lake.[15] Whatever escape from civilization might be proposed was strictly limited, which demonstrates that sentimentalism was ultimately an apology for those forces of contemporary society – urbanization, capitalism, materialism – that it ostensibly opposed.

Similar images appeared in the gift books and periodicals of the 1830s and 1840s: the never-never land of the soul's spiritual yearnings, as in Robert C. Sands's "Song" from the popular narrative poem "Yamoyden" (1820), which tells of a "fair lake, unruffled and sparkling" in the midst of "fens where the hunter ne'er ventured to tread." Over its waters lies "the green isle of lovers." But isle and lake exist (alas!) only in imagination: ". . . he who has sought to set foot on its shore, / In mazes perplexed, has beheld it no more."[16] A kindred pathos – a longing for something lost before it was ever fully known or possessed – was brought to life in the common sentimental theme of the departed or phantom lover.

The mood of lugubrious harmony between self and universe that fed on this theme characteristically found its natural correlative in the swamp, as in, for example, Henry Wadsworth Longfellow's *Evangeline*:

> Over their heads the towering and tenebrous boughs of the cypress
> Met in a dusky arch, and trailing mosses in mid-air
> Waved like banners that hang on the walls of ancient cathedrals.
> Deathlike the silence seemed, and unbroken, save by the herons
> Home to their roosts in the cedar-trees returning at sunset,
> Or by the owl, as he greeted the moon with demoniac laughter.
> Lovely the moonlight was as it glanced and gleamed on the water,
> Gleamed on the columns of cypress and cedar sustaining the arches,
> Down through those broken vaults it fell as through chinks in
>
> a ruin.[17]

The lovely watercolor by James Hamilton, *Bayou in Moonlight* (Figure 1.4), though ironically depicting an escaped slave, is a perfect analogue for these lines.

Such imagery represents, at the deepest level, the simultaneous attraction to and flight from death that typified Victorian culture in America. If, on the one hand, sentimentalists sought relief from capitalistic individualism by means of regression, in an even more basic way they tried to escape death by means of repression. Whereas regression meant the relaxation of ego rigidity through preoccupation with a symbolic world in which time and culture had been abolished and mother worship sometimes verged on incest fantasies (usually with a sister substitute), repression allowed for the dedication of energies to immortalizing the ego for the sake of the new capitalistic and individualistic order.

Romantic attitudes toward death, which took shape in the rural cemetery movement of the 1830s, stressed the significance of death as a release from the aggressive, acquisitive stress of life in the public world. Nature stood with death and the mother-dominated world of the family against the new social forces.[18] By the 1850s, however, repressive formulations of death had gained the upper hand over these regressive propensities as American culture came to accept laissez-faire bourgeois civilization.[19] The materialization of spirit that coincided with this acceptance of capitalism was manifested in the popular view of heaven as the idealization of society rather than as a world totally apart.

In discussing what he named the "Sentimental Love Religion" that pervaded

Figure 1.4. James Hamilton (American, 1819–1878), *Bayou in Moonlight* (watercolor). Courtesy, Museum of Fine Arts, Boston.

Figure 1.5. Henry Inman, engraving after *The Great Dismal Swamp*. *The Talisman*, 1829.

the world of Emily Dickinson, Barton L. St. Armand called attention to the gospel of consolation – the idea of eventual reunion in heaven with dead family members or unrequited lovers – that lay behind Dickinson's own progressive version of heaven. Such confusions of spiritual and material realms are present in the paradox that St. Armand sees between the corporeal and the marmoreal.[20] The Victorian flight from death culminated in the Victorian funeral which sought to avoid the disintegration of the body, by means of embalming, and created the illusion that death was really sleep.

Similarly, the vogue for spiritualism at this time colonized the spirit world along the lines of the here and now.[21] With the loss of faith in a reality wholly other than this one, concern shifted focus from the departed loved one to the mourning survivors. The cult of mourning became, in the words of Karen Halttunen, "an important ritualistic expression of bourgeois pride and self-confidence"[22] that replaced the earlier Romantic concentration on the dead as symbolic of the dispossessed members of society.

Along with the domestication of death and of heaven, all the talk about motherhood and family life simply concealed or compensated for the liabilities of masculine economic enterprise and the attacks of a superego made overly aggressive by the guilt incurred in the narcissistic project of becoming one's own father as capitalistic competition and increasing egalitarianism vaunted the individual and led to the atomization of society.[23] As a salve for such guilt, attraction to death – the compensatory fantasy of self-dissolution – merged with the view that death was the crowning tragedy of life. Narcissism and sublimation lay behind the sentimental eroticization of death, and there is surely a subterranean correspondence between the popular image of the dead, beautiful lady, say, and the aesthetic of "dead" nature exemplified by the image of Lake Drummond.

Because death was seen as separate from and even antagonistic to life, sex – a kind of death within the context of nineteenth-century moral and economic striving (reflecting a confusion of biological and cultural realms)[24] – was viewed in the same way. The divorce of both death and sex from life in the cause of the civilizing process was almost didactically reinforced by the unattainable nature of their symbolic embodiments. Both the dead, beautiful lady and the idyllic lake were "safe" repositories of unchanneled libidinal energies – and this is the important point – precisely because they permitted no chance for actual fulfillment. Energies could thereby be diverted into the ongoing aggrandizement of life, contributing to its indefinite perpetuation through artificial or symbolic means. Morbidity was a way of not facing up to biological death, a reversal of earlier attitudes that saw death as essentially different from life.[25] At the same time, the gloomy appearance of the lake stood for the sense of loss felt by Americans, the inevitable consequence of a civilization that pulled at the bonds of family and community life, thus giving a particular poignancy to death.

Porte Crayon's encounter with Lake Drummond reflects this sentimental tradition in its expression of nostalgia, aspiration, and ambivalence. But despite the hint of complacency in Porte's tone, these qualities emit new psychological repercussions. Ironically, this enrichment is achieved largely through the apparatus of the sentimental mind – overdefensiveness, ego rigidity – that is being dismantled. Beneath the sentimental denial of death lies a failure to resolve satisfactorily the Oedipal conflict in order to establish not only individual autonomy but also the integration of conscious and unconscious selves. Porte's encounter with the lake is, however, a step toward self-realization; his recognition of the lake is an insight nearly free of its sentimental husk.

In the final analysis, his regressive journey cannot be dismissed as sentimental escapism, for he has struck on a powerful psychological truth, namely, that the soul recovers its sonority by revitalizing the life force deep within and by coming to terms with death and the unconsciousness it implies. Indeed, Porte's account of the journey to Lake Drummond shows that revitalization depends on death.[26] His experience is a dying to his old self that is the psychological prelude to spiritual rebirth. Accordingly, the lake both stands as a symbol of psychic integration – as Porte's musings on its ambivalent appearance suggest – and assumes the occult power of a sacred place.

Moreover, Porte's insight gains conviction and psychological efficacy because his vision of the lake is part of an enactment: His rediscovery relates intrinsically and dynamically to the journey that precedes it. In contrast with its sentimental progenitor, Porte's lake exists in the real world; he does indeed reach it. And by mobilizing the sexual analogy implicit in the situation (the sense of penetrating a female landscape by way of the narrow channel; the rhythm of mounting tension and orgasmic release in the narrative) and by realistically portraying the landscape (despite the sentimental allusions), Porte brings death at the symbolic level into a dialectical relationship with life. He thereby ensures vitality where sentimentalism provided an emotionally feeble chastity and where Poe's introversion led to self-destruction. Finally, the sexual resonance itself suggests the undoing of boundaries that marks the narrative and that acts as the catalyst in the interiorization of the lake: a transformation in which the symbol is turned from a static ideal into the culminating moment in a process of self-discovery.

The key to Strother's innovation in the tradition of visitors to the Dismal Swamp is in his treatment of the journey to Lake Drummond, especially in his translation of certain conventional terms for conceiving this journey into those of a psychological encounter with the landscape. There was a religious motive entangled in the customary conception of the journey that veiled a compensatory fantasy. Reunion with the departed lover in some supernatural realm is the reassuring theme of Moore's ballad, and it was naturally associated with the traveler's sudden emergence onto the lake after toiling through the fastnesses of the swamp. Characteristically, as in Porte's case, the lake's dramatic appearance produced an enlargement of the soul akin to the sense of redemption. The journey to the lake thus paralleled the pilgrimage to faith. After all, according to the hymn by Isaac Watts, "Through Dismal deeps and dangerous Snares/We make our way to God."[27] The association points to the reconstitution of the Protestant drama of salvation in the topography of the sentimentalist's inner being: The swamp was a convincing valley of the shadow of death.

This religious motive is still salient in a story that appeared in *The Talisman* of 1829. In a "state of doubt and incipient anxiety" after losing himself in the swamp, the protagonist reaches the lake:

> As his light canoe shot forward from the doubtful glimmering light of the narrow watery forest labyrinth, filled with dead trees and half-sunken logs, into the deep water and open air, and the broad light, our intrepid adventurer rested for a moment and gazed with delight on the beautiful scene.... Before him lay the wide lake of juniper-tinged water, reflecting from its smooth bright brown surface the glorious rays of the descending sun.[28]

The redemptive moment, as an archetypal experience, is clearly at the source of the legend that inspired Moore who, though not the first to write about the Dismal Swamp, was the first to see it as more than simply a desert place. Rather it is an excrescence on the surface of the earth, an ancient notion reflected in William Wirt's description (1803) of the effort involving William Byrd of Westover to establish the dividing line through the Dismal Swamp some three-quarters of a century earlier:

> Imagine to yourself an immense morass ... its soil a black, deep mire, covered with a stupendous forest of juniper and cypress trees, whose luxuriant branches, interwoven throughout, intercept the beams of the sun and teach day to counterfeit the night. This forest, which until that time, no human foot had ever violated, had become the secure retreat of ten thousand beasts of prey. Below is a thick, entangled undergrowth of reeds, woodbine, grape vines, mosses, and creepers, shooting and twisting spirally around, interlaced and complicated.... The adventurers ..., beside the almost endless labour of felling trees ... moved amid perpetual terrors, and each night had to sleep *en militaire,* upon their arms, surrounded with the deafening, soul-chilling yell of those hunger-smitten lords of the desert.[29]

Moore shifted his focus from this "horror" of the jungle – that, in the terminology of the Gothicist Ann Radcliffe, "contracts, freezes, and nearly annihilates"[30] the faculties – to the soul-expanding power of the lake. In doing so, he restored the archetypal pattern of the folktale that inspired him and that presumably was suggested by the landscape itself.

As with the polarized worlds of romance,[31] jungle and lake comprise a gestalt, with the rise of tension and its sudden release being the basis of emotional (and sexual) life. Because of the universality of this rhythm, the two elements vibrate to an unlimited number of impulses, though in sentimental minds such impulses were rigorously limited. The lake represented an idyllic world, a refuge of innocence. That it invited melancholy contemplation, leading the beholder to vaguely religious emotions, confirms the sense of loss with which sentimental Americans regarded this innocence.

The jungle, on the other hand, as Wirt's description makes clear, stood for a world of adventure, of the violence and self-sacrifice that call to mind the rite of initiation. Conceived thus, it is demonic, the image of human alienation, but also daemonic, a potential source of creativity. Adopting this structure, Moore's narrative ascends to the wish fulfillment essential to it (though romance does not distinguish between the reality and illusion implied by this term). The tale of the separated lovers recapitulates the archetypal progress from chaos to cosmos. Yet, and this is the point I want to emphasize, in failing to exploit the horror of the jungle in his poem, Moore lost much of the emotional power evident, for instance, in Wirt's description (a point to be discussed at greater length later in this chapter). Subsequent visitors to the swamp followed Moore in ignoring the psychological efficacy of the encounter with the jungle that preceded the apparition of the lake.

The impact of this encounter with the jungle echoes near the end of the century in Robert Frost's tale of his own youthful journey one night through the Dismal Swamp, after traveling all the way from Massachusetts just to find it! His visit coming just after an unrequited love affair, Frost probably wanted to reenact the gesture of the young lover of Moore's ballad (though he never revealed the source of his actions).[32] Unlike Moore's lover, Frost did not reach the lake. As Lawrence Thompson retells the story,[33] the poet entered the swamp by moonlight – notions of suicide on his mind – to endure exposure and danger ending only near midnight when he discerned lights in the distance. They proved to be those of a canal boat which rescued him from the swamp.

Frost's descent into the swamp in darkness apparently functioned as a self-surrender or symbolic death. In one variant of the tale, he is stalked for several miles by a huge black man shouldering an axe and is convinced the man could kill him at any moment and shove his body into the slime.[34] This flirtation with oblivion has a largely unconscious significance. Frost has no vision of the lake, with its stabilizing influence and sentimental associations. Lacking the possibility of redemption, he confronts the ambiguity of nature to the fullest. The veil has been lifted; immersion is total and potentially disastrous. By the same token, his act is entirely personal, a ritual fragmented and buried, though not without efficacy. Shortly after his return home, the young man referred to this and ensuing experiences in which he turned hobo as "so desperately absorbing that I am nothing morbid now."[35]

The contrast between Moore's fantasy and Frost's enactment is a measure of the shift in emotional climate that occurred between one end of the nineteenth century and the other. By Frost's day, the idealism of the eighteenth century, though still enjoying a certain vogue in its capacity to stir young hearts, had been submerged almost totally in the depths of the unconscious. Its self-transforming power eventually failed altogether. But up to a point it continued to adapt to the demands of evolving sensibility. Porte Crayon's narrative is one such adaptation.

By examining the influence of Moore's ballad on some of the later literature of the Dismal Swamp, we glimpse a change in the motives with which pilgrims approached it. We may also gauge the impact of the image itself on awareness. In an 1850 issue of *Chamber's Edinburgh Journal,* a correspondent complained that the expectations bred in him by familiarity with the famous ballad had not been fulfilled by his visit to the site. As his party rowed up the canal to Lake Drummond, "no venomous reptile fell from the boughs into our boat, no 'she-wolf stirred in the brake.' " Although the first sight of the lake seemed "almost like enchantment . . . soon the feeling creeps over you that this is not the spot which the airy elves would choose for their revels." Instead, the lake is "a strangely solemn scene, and our spirits fell lower and lower as we surveyed it: even the sunny sky failed to cheer. . . ." Such deromanticization of the place has at least partly to do with the writer's conviction that the Dismal Swamp offers refuge to as many as a thousand runaway slaves. "Alas for a slave ridden land!" he exclaims.[36]

The foreigner seemed to be setting the stage for Porte Crayon's subsequent dramatization of the Dismal Swamp journey, an account that became as tenacious as its predecessor. In fact, more than a half-century after its publication, Walter Prichard Eaton, in an article for *Harper's Monthly* entitled "The Real Dismal Swamp," declared that Crayon's description still rang true: "The same great turkey-buzzard sailed languidly on ahead. The same tall, slender reeds made a feathery hedge along the bank. The same wild profusion of 'myrtle, green-briar, bay, and juniper hung over the black, narrow canal.' " While endorsing Porte's accurate observation, Eaton argued that the swamp had "suffered in popular estimation from its associations. Intrinsically, it is the opposite of dismal; it is a virgin paradise."[37]

From time to time, nineteenth-century visitors to the Dismal Swamp portrayed the landscape realistically – whatever that might mean – in defiance of prevailing convention. This move toward close observation is in fact evident in comparing the engraving after a lost work of the late 1820s by the fashionable artist Henry Inman (Figure 1.5) with the engraving after Chapman's view of the swamp, with a painting of the Dismal Swamp by Flavius Fischer (1850s?) (Figure 1.6), again with Porte Crayon's version of the scene, or, finally, with an engraving that appeared in *Harper's Weekly* in 1873 (Figure 1.7).

In depicting Moore's lovers in their canoe, Inman showed little interest in the landscape itself. The picture was criticized by Gulian Verplanck in a piece accompanying it in *The Talisman*. Verplanck doubted whether either Moore or the artist himself had actually seen the region. He then attempted to reconstruct attitudes toward the landscape by viewing the jungle itself as sacred space. Stepping into the deeper recesses of the swamp, Verplanck encountered a "religious twilight gloom" covering every object, as if he were in a Gothic cathedral: "There the cypress and the juniper, rising without a branch to interrupt the regularity of their tall trunks for eighty or a hundred feet, stood thick and close together, like so many tall columns supporting fantastic capitals and thickly interlaced arches of small-leaved foliage." Undergoing the now-stock reaction to sublime landscape, his soul is "thrilled with awe and astonishment." But for all this sweeping away of ageless prejudice, Verplanck's description reveals little real interaction between himself and the swamp. The landscape, under his treatment, ossifies into the predictable *memento mori*. We soon are on familiar ground again (reminding us of Moore's rendering) when the author explores the many lakes and openings, "little islets" of the swamp, "which might well have been scenes of the magic and mystery of times long past. . . ." The sketch ends with the lament that "it is singular that we have no real story or tradition respecting that remarkable tract of country" – by an American, that is. The tale that follows, about a man named Drummond (not the historical figure credited with discovering the lake), is a tedious attempt to provide such a narrative.[38]

Closely intertwined in Verplanck's approach to the swamp were two mo-

Figure 1.6. Flavius Fischer, *The Dismal Swamp* (oil on canvas, 30 × 50 in., 1857?). Maier Museum of Art, Randolph-Macon Woman's College, Lynchburg, Va.

Figure 1.7. Anonymous, *Lake Drummond, Harper's Weekly Magazine* (1873).

tives activated by the landscape that could be reconciled only with difficulty: one concerning the religious and communal aspirations of nationalism and the other reflecting the complicated and even subversive feelings brought to the surface by actual contact with the swamp. Verplanck tried to be true to his experience of the swamp, to create a feeling for its "singularity"[39] while concentrating on the jungle rather than the lake, or so he claimed. At the same time, he tried to provide a historical or literary context for the place that could give it a mythic status. He thus betrayed a latent problem that would trouble Americans responding to a natural phenomenon both impressive yet elusive.[40] A person with Federalist spirit like Verplanck's could certainly withstand the influence of the swamp's disturbing implications; his Gothic metaphor was an effective means of control. But what about a mind that was less sure of its convictions and more impressionable?

This was possible for the most part only with the weakening of the theological worldview to which most American writers ascribed in the period. Yet there is at least the lonely example of Poe. And it might indeed be useful to consider the alternative he presents, especially because we have already noticed certain affinities between his work and Porte Crayon's Dismal Swamp journey. That the Dismal Swamp fascinated Poe is little to be doubted, though the lineaments of the actual landscape in his writings tend to disappear, as do Roderick Usher's paintings which grow "touch by touch into vagueness."

In Poe's poems and tales, the landscape alternates between images of stagnation and disintegration (as in the tarn of "The Fall of the House of Usher") or an iconography of fantasy. The visitor to "The Domain of Arnheim," for instance, enters this visionary world by way of a labyrinthine channel that gradually narrows. Its precipitous banks are clothed in progressively "richer, more profuse, and more sombre foliage." The narrator feels "imprisoned within an enchanted circle." As the channel becomes a ravine, "long plumelike moss which depended densely from the intertwining shrubberies overhead" gives the chasm a "funeral gloom." Finally, "a sharp and unexpected turn" brings the vessel, "as if dropped from heaven, into a circular basin of very considerable extent when compared with the width of the gorge." Poe transfigures the natural landscape. Its ideality allows nothing arbitrary; everything falls into "a weird symmetry, a thrilling uniformity, a wizard propriety."[41] Gone from this wonderland of solitude and repose is the danger and sensuous immediacy of the swamp.

It has been noted elsewhere that the early poem "The Lake: To ——— " (1827) has its source in Moore's ballad.[42] That Poe's lake is not Lake Drummond is obvious because it is "with black rocks bound," and tall pines encircle it. Nevertheless, his lake conveys an almost identical mood, especially in the line "So lovely was the loneliness" and the terror that "was not fright, / But a tremulous delight." It is "A feeling not the jewelled mine / Could teach or bribe me to define."[43]

As he moved away from the actual, Poe developed a montage of images and associations. The ghost of the Dismal Swamp seems to float on the landscape of "Ulalume" (1847). This is in fact a recognizable place, between Fordham and Mamaroneck, New York, where Poe buried his wife Virginia not long before writing the poem. Yet it conjures up an uncanny association with that other landscape. Here is the "dim lake" or "dank tarn" and the "alley Titanic/Of cypress" through which the speaker of the poem passes, accompanied by his Psyche. The action occurs in the midst of the "misty mid region of Weir" which is "ghoul-haunted." There is no reason to reject the standard attribution of the proper name here to the painter Robert Walter Weir, who portrayed the Hudson River area in "wild, misty, weird, and tortured shapes."[44] There is also a point of cleared land in the Dismal Swamp known as the "Waste Weir."

In any case, to see these figurative connections between the two landscapes is perhaps only to exploit the rather generalized affinities between Poe's subjective imagery and the panoply of sentimental images in the cultural milieu in which he worked. The particular relationship between the mind of the speaker in "Ulalume" and the landscape he inhabits nonetheless mirrors a deeper problem, suggesting an interesting parallel with the tradition of response to the Dismal Swamp. The speaker's moment of recognition in the poem's final stanza corresponds to his identification with his environment. His earlier visit to the region had been marked by antagonism to it, as he implies in the second stanza when referring to the "alley Titanic / Of cypress" through which he formerly roamed:

> These were days when my heart was volcanic
> As the scoriac rivers that roll –
> As the lavas that restlessly roll
> Their sulphurous currents down Yaanek
> In the ultimate climes of the pole –

Such imagery connotes youthful rebelliousness, ambition, and, above all, alienation from the environment. The polar volcano (itself a sort of oxymoronic image) intrudes on the somber setting.

In the final stanza, however, the speaker abruptly identifies with the landscape just as the mystery of the situation is solved. His tentative progress toward the star he sees beyond the valley of cypresses is halted by the tomb of his lost lover:

> Then my heart it grew ashen and sober
> As the leaves that were crisped and sere –
> As the leaves that were withering and sere . . .

In the very last lines, the speaker's recognition of the place, his identification with it, and a new knowledge of his mortal limitations all converge:[45]

> Well I know now this dim lake of Auber –
> This misty mid region of Weir
> Well I know now this dank tarn of Auber,
> This ghoul-haunted woodland of Weir.

Time and space, which the speaker had somehow forgotten, have reasserted themselves. The poem presents, as Edward H. Davidson observed, the inviolability of external reality,[46] the ego's realization, in other words, that death is inescapable (Psyche knew better from the start), that it is caught in an endless drama of repetition. The limits of symbolism are signified by the encounter with the tomb and by the deathly appearance of the landscape. The inviting apparition of a fairyland beyond the zone of death has led the speaker only to a rude awakening to doom.

The conclusion of "Ulalume" represents a dissent from the dominant sentimental myth so lyrically articulated by Moore and from the communal enterprise his ballad served. We confront a similar dissent in Melville's "The Piazza" (1856): "Through blackberry brakes that tried to pluck me back, though I but strained toward fruitless growths of mountain-laurel; up slippery steeps to barren heights, where stood none to welcome. Fairy land not yet, thought I, though the morning is here before me."[47] Despite the hopefulness expressed here, the narrator is bound to find fairyland endlessly deferred. It is the fact of the journey, the transformation from the stable picturesque view (preserving the duality of subject and object) to the process of penetrating the veil that makes the difference.

The issue is clarified by a second look at the symbolism of Moore's ballad. In this recasting of the Orpheus and Eurydice story, the youth in quest of his dead lover stands for poetic genius or imagination seeking union with the spirit of place. The maiden, in her ethereal femininity, personifies the lake that is her sanctuary; she is its *genius loci*. The youth in his madness symbolizes the poet impelled toward this ideal. The two consummate a sacred marriage, and imagination and nature become one in a realm beyond time and space. The ballad is an allegory of that preeminent theme of Romantic poetry, the meditation on the landscape. Yet Moore stays well within the allegorical mode, never approaching the Wordsworthian manner because the landscape remains an inert and conventionalized stage prop:

> He lay where the deadly vine doth weep
> Its venomous tear, and nightly steep
> The flesh with blistering dew.

As symbols, hero and maiden as well as swamp are realized in a highly abstract manner so that they equate respectively with the discrete psychological archetypes of libido, anima, and shadow. As shadow, the swamp is merely the emblem of death (the villain of the piece) which the libido overcomes by reuniting with the anima, an integration that is the psychic equivalent of eternal life. According to the legend summarized by Moore, the source of the youth's daemonic power is not simply the undifferentiated energy of libido but, rather, is its transformation into the semidivine phenomenon of madness, exactly what leads him to deny (and, by the logic of wish fulfillment, to overcome) the distinction between life and death.

But what is implied by the legend and what the ballad actually exploits are two different things. The ballad fails to tap the symbolistic potential of madness because of its moral preoccupation with dramatizing the antagonism between libido and shadow, life and death. (Such allegory differs from the ritual behind it, for ritual does recognize a crucial moment when life and death merge). Because of the polarization of libido and shadow, there can be no dialectic of projection and introjection. The swamp is not energized nor is the youth's inner world – his madness – given shape by the landscape. Until libido and

43

shadow interfuse, the swamp fails to assume the animistic vitality it possesses in Porte Crayon's account or in Poe's landscapes. By the same token, however, it never threatens the self, as it would were it to take on such animistic power.

The real genius of Moore's ballad resides not in its imagistic qualities but in its power as an utterance, as an irreducible expression of pathos and longing issuing from the depths of the soul. The youth's urgent question ("Oh! when shall I see the dusky lake . . . ?") is the dynamic center of the song and exactly what lifts Porte out of his oppressive circumstances. As Porte himself seems to realize, the ballad thus works rhetorically rather than symbolistically. It is a holdover from an oral culture that by the early nineteenth century had receded enough to glow with a penumbra of nostalgia. We understand why it was so irresistible to sentimental minds, for although its expressiveness is affecting, it offers only catharsis, not engagement or discovery. So it was easily adapted to bolster communal identity.

Fundamental to this mythic orientation is the dualism of natural and supernatural that Moore maintains in the poem. Spirit floats above the landscape but does not enter into it. As Geoffrey Hartman pointed out in regard to the problem of the *genius loci,* it was Wordsworth who first made the transition to an "unghostly" poetry, in which the poet appears as a quester in search of his own identity and in which the ghost becomes "an intensely local and numinous self-awareness," a presence immanent in the landscape.[48] Moore's supernaturalism, by contrast, keeps the implications pointing away from the personal and immediate and toward the ideal. The youth's yearning accordingly contributes to the collective nostalgia. As a yearning for what is manifestly unattainable, it is a sublimation of the instinctual urge. Similarly, the ornamental quality of Moore's swamp imagery derives from a self-conscious exoticism, not a spontaneous primitivism. Exoticism too lends to the sense that the vision from the shores of Lake Drummond is not a self-recognition at all but a specter from the distant, irretrievable "past" of the race.

That is just what it remained in the popular imagination during the turbulent years of the first half of the nineteenth century. If Americans have periodically turned from history to the evocation of a mythic past in order to reassure themselves in the wake of history's depredations, so those of the "sentimental years" took solace in "fairyland." The lake, along with other sentimental icons, was a collective enterprise, and its assumption to the symbolic realm proceeded accordingly.

The eighteenth-century solution to the horrors of the desert is epitomized by George Washington's efforts, following the Revolution, to drain the Dismal Swamp and convert it into farmland. This mission, later pursued by others to the extent of building a canal to Lake Drummond (completed in 1828),[49] was undertaken in the realm of imagination, naturally enough, by sentimental Americans who evinced a peculiar blend of "the very melancholy and the very sanguine, the very contemplative and the very active"[50] that Hoxie Fairchild detected at the heart of the sentimental ethos. The paradox of primitivism and progress innate in the symbolism of the Dismal Swamp goes to the core of the matter. The sentimental version of nature involved nothing if not the image (despite superficial appearances) of a terrifying wildness bound and subdued. Though the appeal to untamed nature was, at one level, "protective adaptation"[51] to the rigors of civilization, at a more profound level, nature continued to serve the cause of civilization.

Yet if the sentimental ethos shackled the anarchic, "female" powers of nature and of the unconscious, certain elements of American culture were, by the 1850s, involved in a hesitant but fecund intercourse with those powers, though still very much from a "male" perspective. In engaging the experience of the jungle within the quest's overall narrative pattern, David Hunter Strother symbolically recapitulated an initiatory rite that addressed the anxiety of a culture undergoing transition to a new understanding of the world. Until this altered worldview was established, the lake could serve as a source of stability, a safety valve, for the inner pressures of the quest. It served this function even more effectively after taking on a personal resonance. In uniting the experience of jungle and lake, Strother resolved the dilemma of how to transform a desert place into a communal symbol while sustaining its psychological power as a desert place. His narrative, completing a circuit between the ideal and the actual, between communal allegiance and self-fulfillment, cooperative and aggressive impulses (all at the symbolic level, of course) is relevant to the psychological sources of the crusading spirit that gripped the North on the eve of the Civil War.

A culture dominated by the models of domesticity and by sentimental regression was one dedicated to a spirit of compromise, satisfied by merely rhetorical assertions of unity. A culture in which, as George Forgie contended, regressive tendencies were reconciled with the aggressive impulses of the unconscious, in which rhetoric could galvanize the deepest sources of motivation, was a culture capable of the most concerted imperial aggrandizement.[52] It is revealing in this respect that Strother, a Southerner, chose to fight on the Union side. If the Southerner Poe's subjective apprehension of the swamp can be traced to the wellspring of the unconscious, Strother's subjective yet relatively realistic approach to the landscape helped chart the highway to this source, one that helped bourgeois Northern civilization implement its aggression on the wayward South.

It is testimony to the continuing imaginative impact of the Dismal Swamp journey on Americans that we find it parodied in Kate Chopin's early novel *At Fault* (1890). Though it concerns two subordinate characters, the passage in question is crucial to the thematic development of the novel in which a creole woman, the widowed mistress of a Louisiana plantation, learns to take a larger view of the moral world of love and marriage. The scene depicts two subordinate characters, Millicent and Grégoire, in a pirogue, rowing through the bayou. Millicent is visiting for the summer from the North. An attractive girl, her face is "awake with an eagerness to know and test the novelty and depth of unaccustomed sensation."[53] Owing to this taste for the exotic, she encourages Grégoire's advances, only to reject him coldheartedly later on (once he has fallen hopelessly in love) because she is repelled by a murder he commits, the circumstances of which are morally ambiguous.

Grégoire, for his part, is sullen and feral, speaks in a soft, effeminate manner, and, despite his apparent gentleness, possesses a smoldering violence. As he feels the first stirrings of passion for Millicent while sitting with her in the pirogue, we are made to sense that the setting portends the unprecedented moral situation these two are about to enter. Indeed, the passage in great degree conforms to the outlines established by Porte Crayon:

> He pulled rapidly and in silence down the bayou, that was not so entirely sheltered from the open light of the sky by the meeting branches above, as to seem a dim leafy tunnel fashioned by man's ingenuity. There were no perceptible banks, for the water spread out on either side of them, further than they could follow its flashings through the rank underbrush. The dull plash of some object falling into the water, or the wild call of a lonely bird were the only sounds that broke the stillness, besides the monotonous dipping of the oars and the occasional low undertones of their own voices. When Grégoire called the girl's attention to an object near by, she fancied it was the protruding stump of a decaying tree; but reaching for his revolver and taking quiet aim, he drove a ball into the black upturned nozzle that sent it below the surface with an angry splash.[54]

Unlike the novel's main character, Thérèse Lafirme, who overcomes her rigid moral scruples in order to find fulfillment with the man she loves, Millicent never seems to learn anything from the tumultuous and poignant events she lives through. In the final chapter she appears to be the same thoughtless, romantic person she has always been. Like her prototypes in earlier sentimental fiction, she is doomed to a life of repetition and emotional celibacy as a result of her inability to come to terms with ambiguity and ambivalence, directly encountered in Grégoire and figured in the chaos and barely suppressed violence of the swamp. Instead, she responds predictably to the appeal of sudden imaginative escape from her oppressive surroundings; the passage contains all the appropriate romantic allusions:

> "Oh," cried Millicent in surprise. Her exclamation was like a sigh of relief which comes at the removal of some pressure from the body or brain.
>   The wildness of the scene caught upon her erratic fancy, speeding it for a quick moment into the realms of romance. She was an Indian maiden of the far past, fleeing and seeking with her dusky lover some wild and solitary retreat on the borders of the lake, which offered them no seeming foot-hold save such as they would hew themselves with axe or tomahawk.[55]

Millicent's escape to a romantic past is an effort to avoid the responsibility to time that constitutes maturity and is the basis for Chopin's critique of Victorianism's sentimental moralism. In this context, the description of the lake that ends the passage sounds a note of warning: "Here and there, a grim cypress lifted its head above water, and spread wide its moss-covered arms inviting refuge to the great black-winged buzzards that circled over and above it in mid-air. Nameless voices – weird sounds that awake in a Southern forest at twilight's approach – were crying a sinister welcome to the settling gloom."[56]

2

The Elusive Eden:
The Mid-Victorian
Response to the Swamp

From a time beyond memory the swamp repulsed Western civilization as a place of evil, a land of the dead.[1] Like an incubus, it pressed upon worldly hopes the burden of human fate. In biblical times, the prophet Ezekiel learned from an emissary of God that certain portions of the wilderness of Judah, once transformed into a paradise by the waters of life, would nonetheless remain swamps and marshes – brackish, stagnant, and dead (Ezek. 47:7–12). In the fantasy of medieval northern Europe, superstition mingled with this theological conviction. The Meer of the hideous Grendel in *Beowulf* is situated amid the swamp's lowering precincts:

> In doubtful land
> Dwell they, wolf-shapes, windy nesses,
> Fearsome fen-paths, where the force from the mountains
> Under misty nesses netherwards floweth,
> A flood under the fields. 'Tis not far from hence
> As miles are marked that the mere standeth,
> Above which hang rimy bowers;
> A wood fast-rooted the water o'er-shadows.
> There will, every night, a wonder be seen,
> Fire in the flood. There is none found so wise
> Of the sons of Men, who has sounded those depths...

The association of swamps with monsters and other anomalies was tenacious, designating a nature intractable if not destructive. Indeed, Caliban curses his masters, Prospero and Ariel, only to betray his own first affinities:

> "As wicked dew as e'er my mother brushed
> With raven's feather from unwholesome fen
> Drop on you both!"
>
> (Act 1, sc. 2, lines. 321–3)

To Christians from the Middle Ages on, the swamp provided the imagery of hell. In medieval vision literature, the netherworld is characteristically a frozen swamp; the beast of hell in the Vision of Tundalus sits "*super stagnum*

47

glacie condensum."² We think most readily perhaps of the Serbonian Bog in *Paradise Lost*. Milton brought to culmination the ancient idea of the curse on nature wrought by the Fall and conflated it with his vision of Satan's realm. After their release from the burning lake, roving bands of fallen angels pass through

> . . . many a Region dolorous,
> O'er many a Frozen, many a Fiery Alp,
> Rocks, Caves, Lakes, Fens, Bogs, Dens, and shades of death,
> A Universe of death, which God by curse
> Created evil, for evil only good,
> Where all life dies, death lives, and Nature breeds,
> Perverse, all monstrous, all prodigious things,
> Abominable, inutterable, and worse . . .
>
> (Bk. 2, lines 619–26)

The swamp here takes its place in the category of desert places. By the early eighteenth century, attitudes toward desert places, first in England and then in Europe as a whole, were undergoing a momentous transition. C. S. Lewis called attention to "the change from an age when men frankly hated and feared all those things in Nature which are neither sensuously pleasing, useful, safe, symmetrical, or gaily coloured, to an age when men love and actually seek out mountains, waste places, dark forests, cataracts, and storm beaten coasts."³ Marjorie Hope Nicolson traced the sources of this shift in taste toward the infinite and fearful and located its chief dynamic in the tensions that developed during the "century of genius" between religion and the new science.⁴

Obviously, the swamp as a distinct image had something to gain from the new aesthetics of the infinite, especially from the concomitant demand for irregularity. In the enthusiastic view of the third earl of Shaftesbury, speaking generally of deserts, the swamp might take its place in the benevolent scheme of nature:

> All ghastly and hideous as they are, they want not their peculiar Beau-
> tys. The Wilderness pleases. We seem to live alone with Nature. We
> view her in her inmost Recesses, and contemplate her with more De-
> light in these original Wilds, than in the artificial Labyrinths and
> feigned Wildernesses of the Palace. The Objects of the Place, the scaly
> Serpents, the savage Beasts, and poisonous Insects, how terrible
> soever, or how contrary to human Nature, are beauteous in them-
> selves . . .

With Shaftesbury, this novel aesthetic apprehension of nature's dark side becomes the way to a more profound communion with divinity than had been offered by the traditional earthly beauties. In the sublime landscape, "Space astonishes; silence itself seems pregnant, whilst an unknown force works on the mind, and dubious objects move the wakeful sense." Such experience points to the conclusion that those "who in plain characters may read divinity from so many bright parts of the earth, choose rather these obscurer places to spell out that mysterious being, which to our eyes appears at best under a veil of cloud. . . ."⁵

Yet the swamp retained its negative associations in the face of the rising Mountain Glory. This was partly due to the landscape's unique character, which Shaftesbury slights in referring to a much more general category. Moreover, for all his talk of "inmost Recesses" or "scaly Serpents," Shaftesbury's appreciation of deserts rests securely on the new equation between spirituality and space.[6] Though "grandeur" might on occasion be attributed to it, the swamp's association with physical immersion continued to dominate its range of meaning. The implications of the tactile experience for the new sensibility that Shaftesbury charted probably never crossed his mind. The early aesthetics of the infinite determined an imagination that favored the visual and, to a lesser extent, the aural aspects of experience.

As long as the characteristic image of the swamp eluded the transfiguring light of the new canon of beauty, the status of the landscape remained under the control of its powerful primitive and theological associations. These associations were reinvigorated in the context of the Puritan quest for salvation. As an image of physical immersion, the swamp served as a perfect symbol for the toils of the would-be spiritual person in the life here and now. Bunyan's Slough of Despond is not simply an emblem; it is an intensely imagined interior landscape: "As the sinner is awakened about his lost condition, there ariseth in his soul many fears, and doubts, and discouraging apprehensions, which all of them get together, and settle in this place. And this is the reason for the badness of this ground."[7]

There is an exceptional congruity here between image and meaning that confined the range of the swamp's symbolism for decades. Even among the English Romantics the landscape continued to signify moral and spiritual waywardness. John Keats and Percy Bysshe Shelley used it in their quest poems as a correlative of psychic disintegration,[8] and Coleridge spoke of the "mists and clouds from uncultivated swamps . . . few have courage to penetrate" that hide the first range of hills that constitutes the horizon of most men.[9]

English Romanticism did nonetheless provide the basis for a departure from the traditional conception of swamp and jungle images. The organic metaphor for human artistic invention, originated by the Germans and adopted and further developed by Coleridge and Thomas Carlyle, called on swamplike imagery and associations. Arguing that all creative expression issues from unconscious mental processes, Carlyle pointed to "a basis of Darkness," concealed by nature yet underlying all its works. He spoke of "roots and inward circulations which stretch down fearfully to the regions of Death and Night. . . ." Only "the fair stem with its leaves and flowers, shone on by the fair sun, shall disclose itself, and joyfully grow."[10]

Similarly, Coleridge evokes the dense interpenetration of jungle growth in his description of William Wordsworth's poetry. He speaks of

> words and images all aglow which might recall those products of the vegetable world, where gorgeous blossoms rise out of the hard and thorny rind and shell within which the rich fruit was elaborating. The language was not only peculiar and strong, but at times knotty and contorted, as by its own impatient strength; while the novelty and struggling crowd of images acting in conjunction with the difficulties

49

of the style demanded always a greater closeness of attention than poetry (at all events than descriptive poetry) has a right to claim."

Although there is, of course, no literal swamp here, such analogies indicate
how a fully developed swamp or jungle image might later be invoked to
illustrate the workings of the unconscious and the language it generated.

In any case, the English Romantics had a highly suggestive sourcebook for
swamp imagery in William Bartram's *Travels,* first published in 1792.[12] Bartram described in detail an array of natural curiosities relating to the swamps,
pine barrens, and savannas of Georgia and Florida. His images and even his
language were echoed by Wordsworth, Coleridge, and others but were normally taken out of their specific geographical context. The swamp remained
almost entirely abstract and allegorical in England.[13] The dramatic focus eventually granted to it in America as a result of the development of Romantic
sensibility simply could not occur where there was none of the excitement of
discovery nor the immediacy afforded by the collision of changing social factors
with the novel and demanding New World environment.

With little interest in the most sophisticated English Romantic thought, Americans of the first half of the nineteenth century followed tradition and continued
to look superstitiously upon the swamp or to see it in theological terms as an
emblem of evil and death. In the *National Magazine* of 1853, a Methodist
minister offered an account of "Crossing the Mississippi Swamp" in which
he called it "the most dreary and desolate place in the world." In the tradition
of Bunyan, he told of falling into a deep depression after entering the swamp,
of becoming lost, and of finally submitting himself to die for the glory of
God. Predictably, however, this condition is precisely what prepares him to
be saved. After his release from the bondage of the swamp, he reflects:
"Through the day the Lord had brought me low; he had tested me in regard
to my call to the ministry. Grace had been given me to stand fast, and now
I was brought into a large place. My fever subsided, and all without was
lovely, and all within was buoyant and joyous."[14]

Similarly, the Reverend Timothy Flint, a novelist and geographer who
around 1820 traveled extensively as a missionary in the Mississippi valley,
confronted the swamp by calling to mind the well-worn allusions:

> No prospect on earth can be more gloomy. The poetic Styx or Ach-
> eron had not a greater union of dismal circumstances. Well may the
> cypress have been esteemed a funereal and lugubrious tree. When the
> tree has shed its leaves . . . a cypress swamp, with its countless inter-
> laced branches, of a hoary grey, has an aspect of desolation and death,
> that often as I have been impressed with it, I cannot describe.

Like so many others, Flint stressed the experience of immersion: "I travelled
forty miles along this river swamp, and a considerable part of the way in the
edge of it; in which the horse sunk at every step half up to his knees. I was
enveloped for the whole distance with a cloud of mosquitoes." And he concluded with a further comment on the hostile nature of the place: "If you
would inspire an inhabitant of New England, possessed of the customary

portion of feeling, with the degree of home-sickness which would strike to the heart, transfer him instantly from the hill and dale, the bracing air and varied scenery of the North, to the cypress swamps of the South, that are covered with the long moss."[15]

At a somewhat higher literary level, we encounter Washington Irving's vision of the landscape in "The Devil and Tom Walker" (see also the painting by John Quidor of the same name in the Cleveland Museum of Art). Irving exploited the imagery of the morass as an emblem of the miser's peculiar lust: "It was full of pits and quagmires, partly covered with weeds and mosses, where the green surface often betrayed the traveller into a gulf of black, smothering mud: there were also dark and stagnant pools, the abodes of tadpoles, the bullfrog, and the water-snake; where the trunks of pines and hemlocks lay half-drowned, half-rotting, looking like alligators sleeping in the mire."[16] It is here that Tom Walker strikes his bargain with the Devil and where his troubled spirit is condemned to wander after his death.

The connection between the swamp and nefarious consorts had a long tradition in New England, from which Irving doubtlessly drew. William Bradford, for instance, spoke of how the Native Americans, before coming to make friends with the English, "got all the Powachs [Powows, medicine men], of the country, for three days together in a horrid and devilish manner, to curse and execrate them with their conjurations, which assembly and service they held in a dark and dismal swamp."[17]

The characterization of the swamp as dark, dismal, and deceitful was continued into the Mid-Victorian period by the Boston historian Francis Parkman, in some memorable passages. Parkman's histories of the exploration and colonization of North America pictured tough, antiromantic heroes locked in mortal combat with the wilderness. Parkman conceived of Robert La Salle as the perfect example of the determined and ruthless adventurer led to annihilation, by the treachery of his own men, in the tangled wilds of the lower Mississippi. The opening chapters of *The Pioneers of the New World*, serialized in *The Atlantic* during the Civil War, dramatize the vulnerability of the gold-greedy French Huguenot settlers in the seething wastes of Florida. Though outwardly inviting, the wilderness that the Europeans explore reveals a rather less congenial interior:

> Then the deep cypress swamp, where dark trunks rise like the columns of some vast sepulchre. Above, the impervious canopy of leaves; beneath, a black and root-encumbered slough. Perpetual moisture trickles down the clammy bark, while trunk and limb, distorted with strange shapes of vegetable disease, wear in the gloom a semblance grotesque and startling. Lifeless forms lean propped in wild disorder against the living, and from every rugged stem and lank limb outstretched hangs the drapery of the Spanish moss. The swamp is veiled in mourning. No breath, no voice. A deathly stillness, till the plunge of the alligator, lashing the waters of the black lagoon, resounds with hollow echo through the tomb-like solitude.[18]

Parkman's conservative social organicism is linked to his Puritan distrust of the natural world, so effectively revealed here. Yet we can also see how a traditional iconography, when handled sensitively, could give rise to the intimations of the unconscious and the undertones of the sexuality against which it was meant to stand as a warning.

By the time he was writing his histories, Parkman's image of the swamp was no longer so representative. Traditional attitudes toward the swamp began to subside (though they continue even today in the folk and popular imagination) in the years immediately before the Civil War. There is indeed a reversal of the ancient imagery and prejudice in Thomas Wentworth Higginson's discovery one spring morning while walking through a copse of birches:

> Suddenly, as if entering a cavern, I stepped through... into a dark little amphitheater beneath a hemlock grove, where the afternoon sunlight struck broadly through the trees upon a tiny stream and a miniature swamp, – this last being intensely and luridly green, yet overlaid with the pale gray of last year's reeds, and absolutely flaming with the gayest yellow light from great clumps of cowslips. The illumination seemed perfectly weird and dazzling; the spirit of the place appeared live, wild, fantastic, almost human.[19]

Unitarian minister and man of letters, servant of a far more liberal-minded deity than the Almighty served by the likes of Timothy Flint, Higginson is surprised by the swamp as a newfound image of the natural world, minutely perceived. Higginson's moment of discovery has all the energy of a new beginning, and it is significant that he mentions it in relation to Alfred, Lord Tennyson's poetry. Having just referred to Tennyson's "word pictures" which "bear almost as much study as the landscape," he is reminded of the poet's lines, "And the wild marsh-marigold shines like fire/in swamps and hollows gray."[20]

Critics since Arthur Hallam have emphasized Tennyson's sensitivity to the imagistic qualities of language. As early as 1831 Hallam wrote of Tennyson's "power of embodying himself in... moods of character, with such extreme accuracy of adjustment, that the circumstances of the narration seem to have a natural correspondence with the predominant feeling" as well as his "vivid picturesque delineation of objects; and the peculiar skill with which he holds all of them *fused*... in a medium of strong emotion."[21] In an article entitled "My Out-Door Study" – one of the remarkable series of pieces on nature he wrote for *The Atlantic* around 1860 – Higginson invoked both Tennyson and the swamp to argue for the direct dependence on nature that "leads to deeper thought and affords the promise of fresher results." Dazzled by the refulgence of nature's "imperishable beauty," the soul casts aside the "perishable memories of man."[22] Ageless association must give way to intimate, and consequently novel, awareness.

It is revealing that Higginson's swamp is in miniature. As Gaston Bachelard pointed out, "Miniature is an exercise that has metaphysical freshness; it allows us to be world conscious at slight risk." Higginson's swamp is more like a painting than an actual environment. He is not immersed in it; instead he receives a vision that leaves him delighted, if a trifle wistful. It offers him an opportunity to confront his primitive self in a purely aesthetic way, and furthermore, it is an illustration of the sanative influence of nature, a force for equilibrium amidst the vicissitudes of the active life. Bachelard stressed the possibilities for renewal afforded by miniature: It "rests us without ever putting us to sleep . . . the imagination is both vigilant and content." Renewal is attained through the very act of close observation; the miniaturist is opposed to the intuitionist who "always sees big."[23] Only the former has the patience to take in gradually all the details of the object under scrutiny.

Higginson likewise took delight in the mysterious insular world of the lily pond, the domestic younger sibling of the swamp. In "Water-Lilies," he celebrated this "realm of dark Lethean water, utterly unlike the sunny depths of the main lake" and so dear to boys and maidens. The lily pond is a tiny primordial world subject to the same ongoing process of growth, destruction, and renewal as the great swamp world that once covered the face of the earth. It has a rebellious and grotesque nature that struggles against the encroachment of civilization:

> Hither the water-lilies have retreated, to a domain of their own.
> Darker than these waves, there stand in their bosoms hundreds of sub-
> merged trees, and dismasted roots still upright, spreading their vast,
> uncouth limbs like enormous spiders beneath the surface. They are
> remnants of border wars with the axe . . . still fighting on their
> stumps, but gradually sinking into the soft ooze, and ready, perhaps,
> when a score of centuries has piled two more strata of similar remains
> above them, to furnish foundation for a new New Orleans. . . .

In the pullulating recesses of the pond, the eye seeks a glimpse of fairies, losing vision in the murkiness. "Do not start," the author warns, "when, in such an effort, only your own dreamy face looks back upon you, beyond the gunwale of the reflected boat, and you find that you float double, self and shadow."[24]

Higginson could well afford to luxuriate in such benign manifestations of nature's underside. His images of miniature swamp and lily pond project a quietly ecstatic sense of being at home in the world. They provoke encounters with the inner self that exact little if any active exploration. The self is at its ease, receptive to the gentlest impulses of reverie. Yet one cannot help wondering how such a blithe sensibility as this would react were nature to turn dangerous, overwhelming. Would Higginson's delicate awareness be strong enough to accommodate immersion in a real swamp? There is at least a partial answer to the question in the naturalist's account of his Civil War experience, *Army Life in a Black Regiment* (1869).

During the war Higginson commanded the first regiment of freedmen to fight on the side of the Union. His narrative of army life along the tropical coasts of Georgia and Florida and of the various strategic maneuvers and battles in which he and his troops engaged is filled with enraptured descriptions of magical moonlit evenings, warm sympathies among comrades in arms, and the "childlike" antics and amusements of the black soldiers. Higginson acquiesced in "the general impression of heat and lassitude, existence appearing to pulsate only with the sea breeze."[25] He accepted the tangled vegetation along with whatever impression – even the violence of the life and death struggle – might be proffered by this sensuous, exotic world. He reveals a disconcerting ability to veil the horrors of war behind an oneiric haze: "Again there was the dreamy delight of ascending an unknown stream, beneath a sinking moon, into a region where peril made fascination. Since the time of the first explorers, I suppose that those Southern waters have known no sensation so dreamy and so bewitching as those which this war has brought forth" (pp. 110–11).

Letting himself go in this tumescent world, Higginson skirted mental disintegration. He devotes an entire chapter, "A Night in the Water," to the sensuality and thrill of swimming naked at night underneath the watchful eyes of rebel sentinels. His practical objective of scouting the enemy's position from the islands along the South Carolina shore is forgotten amid the raptures of novel sensation; the mainland toward which he swims "has all the fascination of forbidden fruit" (p. 151). Higginson is transported:

> I do not remember ever to have experienced a greater sense of exhilaration than when I slipped noiselessly into the placid water, and struck out into the smooth, eddying current for the opposite shore. The night was so still and lovely, my black statues looked so dreamlike at their posts behind the low earthwork, the opposite arm of the causeway stretched so invitingly from the Rebel main, the horizon glimmered so low around me . . . that I seemed floating in some concave globe, some magic crystal, of which I was the enchanted centre. With each little ripple of my steady progress all things hovered and changed; the stars danced and nodded above; where the stars ended the great Southern fireflies began; and closer than the fireflies, there clung around me a halo of phosphorescent sparkles from the soft salt water. (p. 154)

So far Higginson remains in control, hovering about this portal of mystery. Still, he is alive to the dangers of the unknown: "It appeared impossible that anything uncanny should hide beneath that lovely mirror: and yet when some floating wisp of reeds suddenly coiled itself around my neck, or some unknown thing, drifting deeper, coldly touched my foot, it caused that undefinable shudder which every swimmer knows, and which especially comes over one by night" (p. 155).

Fully immersed, Higginson soon undergoes a dissolution of the normative structures of the world. While he completely loses track of time, objects succumb to an alteration scarcely conceivable, as the eye's perspective is collapsed to the angle of the low horizon: "Foreshortening is impossible, and every low near object is equivalent to one higher and more remote" (p. 158). With this loss of perspectival hierarchy, the mind quickly becomes not only useless but a hindrance. Fearful that he might be seen by the enemy. Higginson has the impression that his head has grown to enormous size: "Plotinus was less ashamed of his whole body than I of this inconsiderate and stupid appendage" (p. 156).

His real disorientation, however, begins on his way back across the river, his mission accomplished. The tide has evidently changed, leaving him unsure of where he is. He likens his growing bafflement and panic to the faltering of the Christian in the labyrinth of life, but the context is charged with psychological overtones: "I found it difficult to keep my faith steady and my progress true; everything appeared to shift and waver, in the uncertain light" (p. 158). Moments later he reaches a critical juncture: "For about one half-minute the whole vast universe appeared to swim in the same watery uncertainty in which I floated." He begins "to distrust the stars, the line of low bushes for which I was wearily striving, the very land on which one might become insane in an instant. It was as if a fissure opened somewhere, and I saw my way into a mad-house; then it closed, and everything went as before." He feels no well-defined anxiety, no fear; yet he is saved at the brink of disaster only by the recollection that if he is ever to return to his camp, he must keep his wits about him: "Imagination had no business here. That way madness lay" (pp. 159–60).

One could hardly imagine a more drastic departure from the traditional image of the swamp to which earlier generations of Americans ascribed. Although from a literal standpoint it is scarcely fair to compare Higginson's sensual nocturnal swim with encounters with a landscape full of mud and mosquitoes – if not alligators – the point is that, metaphorically, Higginson's experience represents an exploration of just that realm of subjective response precluded or at least masked by the conventional symbols, with all their negative features. Indeed, the significance of the swamp's traditional iconography is minimized by the fact that it is a highly conditioned reaction, a defense mechanism, against the prospect of immersion. Higginson's response, on the other hand, submerges the local and judgmental characteristics of this iconography in the sensation itself. Up to a point, the effect is liberating, but Higginson is eventually forced to acknowledge the limits of imagination beyond which lies only hopeless disorientation.

Higginson's imagistic sensibility held him, then, in good stead when he confronted the domineering environment of the South. Of his night in the water he remarked, "I have been on other scouts since then . . . but never with a zest so novel as was afforded by that night's experience" (p. 162). His general regard for the landscape of the South contrasts with the view expressed by Timothy Flint and other Americans earlier in the century. Sensual delight has replaced moral censure. But even more fundamentally, Higginson's awareness of the way in which the unconscious dictates his relation to the unknown operates here to transmute into insight and aesthetic pleasure what would otherwise have been merely fear and revulsion. In earlier versions of the swamp, this motive had at best been channeled into well-established patterns such as the scheme of salvation or sublimated into the *frisson* of the ghost story. Higginson pushes beyond the threshold of fear to enter the very body of mystery.

Accordingly, his experience begins with the sensation of inward stirrings and magical reverberations (signified by the tremulous vision of stars, fireflies, and phosphorescent sparkles of water) that come alive as his conceptual schema loses its hold. The image relinquishes nearly all of its defining characteristics, turning it into a turmoil of sensation. Such awareness is paced by a progressive suspension of the will. Higginson's openness to the drift of the unconscious (a renewed realization of the power of faith to achieve harmony with the world) leads him, however, into real danger when that drift imperceptibly shifts and becomes a surge. Only his vigilant rationality (restoring the force of will) saves him from annihilation. This rationality is thrown into relief at the beginning of Higginson's account, when he remarks:

> Had I told any one of my purpose, I should have had warnings and remonstrances enough. The few Negroes who did not believe in alligators believed in sharks; the skeptics as to sharks were orthodox in respect to alligators; while those who rejected both had private prejudices as to snapping turtles. . . . But I knew the folly of most alarms about reptiles and fishes; man's imagination peoples the water with many things which do not belong there, or prefer to keep out of his way, if they do. . . . (pp. 154–5)

In its fullest context, this passage indicates more than simply the opposition between superstition and rationality. Higginson's imagination is dedicated, after all, to a spirit of regeneration and rehabilitation. Just as he wants to "bring up" or civilize his black troops, for all his amusement at their "childish" ways, Higginson is fascinated by the project of bringing the unruly, primitive impulses and prejudices of his own inner being under the sympathetic command of consciousness. This trajectory of his personality is spelled out in the military leader's love of discipline and in his esteem for courage and cool thinking under fire. If it results in paternalism, it is also the basis for an inherent trust in the world.

Yet we might ponder the ultimate loss of moral force, the intellectual enervation, implied in Higginson's psychogenic journey in "A Night in the Water." The curious self-control and self-consciousness that moderate Higginson's experience look forward to a similar blend of instinctual liberation and prudential considerations that marked what T. J. Jackson Lears called the "therapeutic culture of consumption" that emerged in the early twentieth century as a response to the rationalization of society.[26] The sometimes almost precious aestheticism with which Higginson invests his experience, his failure to retain a sense of the horror with which it confronts him, deprives his unconscious energies of any convincing connection with evil and taints the whole adventure with banality. There is something a little too self-congratulatory about it all. The restless and merely therapeutic quest for "authentic" experience propelled by American advertising in the twentieth century is not all that far away.

Higginson's response to the swamp illuminates important aspects of the general transition in attitudes toward nature during the Mid-Victorian period. Public acceptance of the swamp – and here we are largely concerned with Northern regard for the landscape of the South – did not come until after the Civil War, for obvious reasons. But Higginson's reflections indicate the submerged tendency of thought in the North that was allowed to surface after the war. The sardonic images of gloomy and alligator-infested swamps that had taken hold in Northern conceptions about the South's social condition lost much of their hold on the imagination once the war was over. During the war, Northerners had been apt to see the swamp as a symbol for the depredations of slavery on Southern life.

In her novel *Dred, A Tale of the Dismal Swamp* (1856), Harriet Beecher

Stowe used the swamp image both as the objective correlative of the inner world of her antihero Dred, an escaped slave who has assumed the mantle of biblical prophet in the wilderness, and as the metaphor for a "grotesque" social condition festering with revolutionary potential. She wrote: "The wild, dreary belt of swamp-land which girds in those states scathed by the fires of despotism is an apt emblem, in its rampant and we might say delirious exuberance of vegetation, of that darkly struggling, wildly vegetating swamp of human souls, cut off, like it, from the usages and improvements of cultivated life."[27]

Even Higginson himself shared this view. In an essay entitled "Barbarism and Civilization," published in his *Out-Door Papers* (1863), he made his own indictment of the South and its peculiar institution: "But there lingers upon this continent a *forest* of moral evil more formidable, a barrier denser and darker, a *Dismal Swamp* of inhumanity, a barbarism upon the *soil*, before which civilization has thus far been compelled to pause, – happy, if it could even check its spread."[28]

During the war the influential articles of A. R. Waud for *Harper's Weekly* contributed to the South's association in Northern minds with the conventional image of the swamp. Waud's reports from Louisiana included detailed descriptions of swamps and canebrakes accompanied by vivid engravings from his own drawings (Figure 2.1). Referring to the illustration *On Picket Duty in the Swamps of Louisiana* (Figure 2.2), which appeared as the frontispiece of the May 9, 1863, issue of *Harper's,* Waud commented that it showed "what our brave soldiers have to encounter in their campaign under General Banks. Alligators and rattlesnakes abound in the bayous and in the swamps, and all manner of unpleasant creeping, flying, and walking creatures swarm under the luxuriant tropical vegetation."[29] Waud admitted that such landscapes had their charms, but his emphasis was mostly on their inhospitable qualities, as in another piece entitled "Cypress Swamp in Louisiana": "The trees closing together at the top shut out the light so that the weird and funereal aspect of the place is perfect, presenting a forbidding appearance sufficient to appall a stranger."[30]

After the war, however, Waud suddenly began to cultivate a new reverence for the swamp and a sensitivity to its aesthetic qualities, as he revealed in an article for *Every Saturday Magazine* written in 1871:

> As we drew nearer the thick solitude of the magnificent old cypresses, we could occasionally disturb the snake or an alligator, but our unwonted presence in the heart of the swamp soon hushed all its usual voices. . . . There was a strange stillness in the air. The Spanish moss drooping a hundred feet above our heads from the tallest trees had not the slightest motion. Gothic aisles dim with the incense of a thousand creepers and mosses led off into deep recesses which we could not explore. . . . Some creature unrecognizable would suddenly dart along a vine-clad limb and vanish beneath a wilderness of moss. Woodpeckers resumed their hammering upon the echoing boles of the cypresses. A white crane rose like a spectre out of the mysterious undergrowth close at hand and flew diligently away. Herons and sheldrakes and all the feathered and reptile brethren in their vast cathedral went on with

Figure 2.1. A. R. Waud, *Cypress Swamp on the Opelousas Railroad, Louisiana. Harper's Weekly*, December 8, 1866.

Figure 2.2. A. R. Waud, *On Picket Duty in the Swamps of Louisiana. Harper's Weekly*, May 9, 1863.

their beads and paternosters reckless of the intrusion or possible heresy in their midst. And then those rank iconoclasts, the mosquitoes. . . .[31]

Waud went on to speak of the "green solitude . . . this lush mystery of vegetation," the "magnificent effects" of a passing thunderstorm, and the "slanting gleams of the sun . . . gilding with startling distinctness some solitary spray of vine . . . against gray mossy depths" (p. 141). His earlier focus on the fearful and repugnant had yielded to an effort – not without humor – to recreate the delicate impressions conveyed by a world very much alive, sacred, and self-absorbed. The swamp no longer invades humanity; humanity has become the invader. Even the mosquitoes have acquired a certain license.

The publication in 1872 of *Picturesque America,* edited by William Cullen Bryant, marked the induction of the swamp into the canon of the predominant American landscape tradition. Earlier hallmarks of popular American scenery like N. P. Willis's *American Scenery* (1840) or *The Home Book of the Picturesque* (1852), confined in scope to the northeastern part of the country, had ignored the swamp. In 1853 the southern artist T. Addison Richards noted in *Harper's Monthly*: "But little has yet been said, either in picture or story of the natural scenery of the Southern states . . . ." He wrote glowingly of the South's "broad savannas, calm in the shadow of the palmetto and the magnolia" and of its "mystic lagunes, in whose stately arcades of cypress, fancy floats at will through all the wilds of past and future."[32] Walt Whitman, perhaps the most original mind in all of America, was indeed a lonely example of favorable response to the charms of the southern swamp before the war. In his poem "O Magnet-South" (1860), he wrote:

> O the strange fascination of these half-known half-
>   impassable swamps, infested by reptiles, resounding
>   with the bellow of the alligator, the sad noise of the
>   rattlesnake. . . .

Picturesque America helped rectify the traditional neglect, by featuring, among the more typical sights, the landscape of the lower Mississippi and the St. John's and Ocklawaha rivers in Florida (Figures 2.3, 2.4, 2.5, and 2.6). The Ocklawaha River was becoming a national tourist attraction. Shortly after the war, northern sightseers – including a host of consumptive invalids seeking a healthy climate – began pouring into Florida. The "New Eden" of the South prompted a spate of guidebooks and travelogues.[33]

Numerous accounts pictured the state's swamp-laden rivers as natural won-derlands, offering among other charms the novel recreation of taking potshots at alligators while safely ensconced behind the railings of steamboats. In 1865 the epicurean Fitzhugh Ludlow proclaimed the St. John's "one of the most picturesque and beautiful streams in the world" and described it as

> an infinitely tortuous avenue, peopled with myriads of beautiful wild-
> birds, roofed by overhanging branches of oak, magnolia, and cypress,
> draped with the moss that tones down those solitudes into a sort of
> day-moonlight, and, in the greatest contrast with this, festooned by
> the lavish clusters of odorous yellow jasmine and many-hued morn-
> ing-glory, – the latter making a pillar heavy with triumphal wreaths
> of every old stump along the plashy brink, – the former springing
> from tree-top to tree-top to knit the whole tropic wilderness into a
> tangle of emerald chains, drooping lamps of golden fire, and censers
> of bewildering fragrance.[34]

The semitropical phantasmagoria along the riverbanks made an even more unusual impression after dark when illuminated by torchlight, as reported in *Picturesque America:* "From the most intense blackness we have a fierce, lurid glare, presenting the most extravagantly-picturesque groups of overhanging palmettos, draped with parasites of vines of all descriptions. . . ."[35]

Sidney Lanier, whose guidebook of Florida (1875) only occasionally reached beyond the current clichés, submitted his own prescription for a unique sen-sation to be enjoyed on the pleasure cruises of the Ocklawaha. Having placed your chair at a particular point on the boat next to the railing, tipped it back to a certain angle so that you rest your head in a particular way (the directions are meticulous), repulsed all interruptions, and opened wide the eyes of body and soul, you will then be in the proper position to "sail, sail, sail, through the cypresses through the vines, through the May day, through the floating

A Sudden Turn in the Ocklawaha.

Figure 2.3. Harry Fenn, *A Sudden Turn in the Ocklawaha. Picturesque America*, vol. 1.

Ascending the Ocklawaha River at Night.

Figure 2.4. Harry Fenn, *Ascending the Ocklawaha River at Night. Picturesque America,* vol. 1.

suggestions of the unutterable that come up, that sink down, that waver and sway hither and thither; and so shall you have revelations of rest, and so shall your heart forever afterwards interpret Ocklawaha to mean repose."[36]

Visitors to southern swamps acknowledged responses that were quite different from those linked to the type of landscape long revered by the American public. To the swampy country along the lower Mississippi, a writer in *Picturesque America* attributed "mysterious interest":

Destitute though it be of the charm of mountains and water-falls, with no distant views, no great comprehensive exhibitions, it nevertheless inspires a sort of awe which it is difficult to define or account for. All objects are upon a water level; and when you look aloft through the gloom of the towering trees, you feel as if you were in a well, and below the usual surface of the earth, and that the place is born of the overflowing waters.[37]

Edward King, in *The Great South* (1875), was so moved by the scenery along the St. John's River that he claimed that "one ceases to regret hills and mountains and can hardly imagine ever having thought them necessary, so much do these visions surpass them. It is not grandeur which one finds on the banks of the great stream, it is nature run riot. The very irregularity is delightful, the decay is charming, the solitude is picturesque." After characterizing the swamp as a "tract of hopelessly irreclaimable, grotesque water wilderness, where abound all kinds of noisome reptiles, birds and insects,"

Waiting for Decomposition.

Figure 2.5. Harry Fenn, *Waiting for Decomposition. Picturesque America*, vol. 1.

King quickly went on to the almost hallucinatory quality that gave such a place its mystique: "One should see such a swamp in October, when the Indian summer haze floats and shimmers lazily above the brownish-gray of the water; when a delicious magic in the atmosphere transforms the masses of trees and the tangled vines and creepers into semblances of ruined walls and tapestries."[38]

The novelty of the swamp image, as it received such semiofficial sanction, encouraged several painters to experiment with its possibilities. A new iconography – distinct from the dramatic and pastoral concerns that had dominated American landscape painting from its inception – came into fashion. During the 1870s and 1880s New Orleans became the home of a group of northern and foreign-born artists who, together with a few native sons, turned to the swamps and bayous around the city for much of their subject matter – with interesting results (Figures 2.7 and 2.8).

A Florida Swamp.

Figure 2.6. Harry Fenn, *A Florida Swamp*, *Picturesque America*, vol. 1.

Anyone with actual experience of the innermost recesses of the Atchafalaya basin knew how insufferable and treacherous travel in search of the hidden beauties of this country could be. Toward the end of the century George A. Coulon, a photographer whose father had made a career of painting swamps, recorded the ordeal he underwent for "350 Miles in a Skiff Through the Louisiana Swamps." Coulon sought out interesting sights to photograph. What is significant is that he could justify such an ordeal. Before departing, he had to face the skepticism of several street-corner pundits: "For beyond the endurance of hardships and privations, the sight of reptiles and even wild animals, they foresaw nothing to be derived from such an outing; whilst I on the other hand held these discomforts as secondary to the novel and beautiful sights which awaited me."[39]

Mystery and repose were the two qualities most prized in swamp landscapes,

Figure 2.7. Harold Rudolph, *Bayou Sunset* (1872). Owners are Karolyn Kuntz Westervelt and Rosemonde Kuntz Capomazza. Felix Kuntz Collection, New Orleans.

though they often were at odds with the boisterous, elemental energies of tropical growth. Sometimes, however, a reconciliation was managed. Julia E. Dodge's description of tangled vegetation, in an article for *Scribner's* about Fort George Island (at the mouth of the St. John's) which was illustrated by Thomas Moran, is a still life seething with suppressed movement:

> As you turn to go down several steep steps formed upon projecting
> roots, a little tropical picture meets your eye which might be placed in
> South America with scarcely a change. The low hill-side . . . is covered
> with scrub palmetto, whose huge leaves stand and hang and sprawl in
> wildest confusion, while its brown, hairy roots seem to writhe and
> twist around and through them. Among them small palms uphold
> their spreading fans, and larger ones raise their scaly stems. Wild vines
> wreathe and loop among the foliage and upon the ground, and over
> all an old live-oak gnarled and contorted like one of Doré's trees in
> the "Inferno," stretches out and droops to the earth a long, enormous
> branch, fringed with feathery fern and dashed with spots of blood-red
> lichen, and hung with rags and tatters of long gray moss.[40]

Dodge's verbal description, with its intricate visual detail, has numerous analogues in contemporary painting (Figure 2.9) and indicates the growing iden-

Figure 2.8. Meyer Strauss, *Bayou Têche*. Private collection, New Orleans.

Figure 2.9. Granville Perkins, *Florida Landscape* (1888). George Arden Collection, New York.

tification of the southern swamp with the tropical jungle that was transforming the conception of both landscapes.

Mystery and repose of a more romantic sort, and devoid of any such tension, suffuse the works of the St. Louis-based artist Joseph Rusling Meeker, who deserves mention here as an accomplished painter and constant chronicler of the swamps along the Mississippi River. Influenced by J. M. W. Turner, Meeker relied on the mists that arose from these swamps and on nimbus clouds to lend "obscurity to portions of the picture suggestive of something more than can be seen, making us wish to explore the half-hidden vistas." The drapery of moss, with its connotations of mournfulness, added to this effect (Figures 2.10 and 2.11). With regard to composition, Meeker believed that the point of repose, "where the eye finally rests, quietly and peacefully, in refreshing indolence, after scanning the multitudinous detail," was the most important element.[41]

The revision of Northern attitudes toward the semitropical landscape of the South following the Civil War is certainly one symptom of the general transition signaled by Edward King's *The Great South* (1875). As a correspondent for *Scribner's,* King traveled more than 25,000 miles through the southern states, reporting on material resources and social and political conditions. His narrative integrates such information with detailed descriptions of cityscape and landscape as well as local color. The excellent illustrations were provided by J. Wells Champney, who accompanied King. *The Great South,* which brought together in one volume King's numerous articles, gave Northerners their first view of the South which was at once comprehensive and intimate.

Even more significantly, King's sympathy for the social problems of Southerners and his enthusiasm for the attractions of the southern landscape answered a new willingness on the part of the North not only to forgive and forget but also to embrace the full potential of reconciliation. As Anne Rowe observed about the period inaugurated by the end of Reconstruction, "Now that deviation from the national norm was no longer a threat to the Union, depiction in literature of life-styles free from the taint of northeastern big business and urbanization could be enjoyed for their very differences."[42] Northern writers, according to Rowe, forsook the "thesis-laden" criticism of Southern life that was related to the war and succumbed to "unconscious idealization" of both the Southern environment and the Southern social types.

The contrast between Harriet Beecher Stowe's swamp images in *Dred* (descriptions of a landscape she had never actually seen) and the sensual luxuriance depicted in *Palmetto Leaves* (1875) (after she had established residence in Florida) offers a case in point. Referring to the land around her house, Stowe gushed: "Verily it is the most gorgeous of improprieties, this swamp. . . ."[43] And she evoked her swamp environs in a letter to George Eliot as "this wild, wonderful, bright and vivid growth that is all new, strange, and unknown by name to me...the place to forget the outside world and live in one's self."[44] The swamp had become genteel!

Yet more was implied by this dramatic change of perspective than merely the abatement of sectional conflict. This development allowed for a resuscitation in the Victorian period of the long-submerged tropical ideal of instinctual license. To embrace the southern swamp was a declaration of freedom from

Figure 2.10. Joseph Rusling Meeker (American, 1827–1887), *Bayou Têche* (oil on canvas, 1879). Anonymous gift in memory of Judge and Mrs. Samuel Treat, St. Louis Art Museum.

Puritan restraint. In her novel *East Angels* (1886), about life in Florida, Constance Fenimore Woolson begins by having the hero, Evert Winthrop – descendant of the illustrious Puritan – enunciate the delicious heresy of the day:

> I confess to a liking for an existence which is not, for six months of the year, a combat. I am mortally tired of our long northern winters ... of our springs – hypocritical sunshine pierced through and through by east winds; and I have at last, I think, succeeded in breaking loose from the belief that there is something virtuous and heroic in encountering these things – encountering them, I mean, merely from habit, and when not called to it by any necessity. But this emancipation has

Figure 2.11. Joseph Rusling Meeker (American, 1827–1899), *Swamp on the Mississippi* (oil on canvas, 32⅛ × 42³⁄₁₆ in. [81.5 × 107.2 cm.], 1871). A. Augustus Healy Fund, The Brooklyn Museum, New York.

Figure 2.12. Anonymous, *My Saurian's House*. Sidney Lanier, *Florida: Its Scenery, Climate, and History* (Philadelphia: Lippincott, 1876).

taken time – plenty of it. It is directly at variance with all the principles of the country and creed in which I was brought up.[45]

Dalliance with tropical felicity also relieved a variety of outward tensions. Relative to both tradition and the contemporary social environment, swamp scenery emerged as the landscape equivalent of the Cavalier myth that had long attracted Northerners apprehensive of the rise of an acquisitive, atomistic Yankee civilization.[46] No one better understood the appeal of the southern landscape as an antidote to civilization's discontents as it was materializing in the North than the Georgia-born poet Sidney Lanier, who pitched his "spiritualized guidebook" of Florida in the following key (Figure 2.12):

> The question of Florida is a question of an indefinite enlargement of
> many people's pleasures and of many people's existences as against
> that universal killing ague of modern life – the fever of the unrest of
> trade throbbing through a long chill of a seven months' winter. . . .
> Here, walking under trees which are as powerful as they are still,
> amidst vines which forever aspire but never bustle, by large waters
> that bear their burdens without flippant noise, one finds innumerable
> strange and instructive contrasts exhaling from one's contemplations;
> one glides insensibly out of the notion that these multiform beauties
> are familiar appearances of vegetable growths and of water expanses;
> no, it is Silence, which, denied access to man's ear, has caught these
> forms and set forth in them a new passionate appeal to man's eye; it is
> Music in a siesta; it is Conflict, dead, and reappearing as Beauty; it is
> amiable Mystery, grown communicative.[47]

Lanier's imagery clearly shows the adaptation of the South's traditional imagery to a nascent aestheticism that valued repose and cultivation of the gentler side of life over bustling commercial activity.

If the suspension of its critical stance toward the South gave the civilization of the North an important safety valve for the pressures of capitalism and urban life, as well as an escape from rigid religious and moral beliefs, Northern indulgence in the sensual extravagance of Southern life simply flowed into the larger current of cosmopolitanism that had begun before the Civil War.

According to Howard Mumford Jones, an important question facing Americans in the "Brown Decades" was: "How infuse into this drab culture, this uniformity of existence, which everyday threatened to become more unendurable, the color, the tang, the variety it lacked?" By traveling, if only in one's imagination, to "remote, tropic, primitive, or 'different' lands"[48] came the ready answer. So Americans flocked to the pleasure grounds of the South, or they absorbed accounts of exotic lands and life-styles all over the world. The vogue for painting the swampy country of Mexico, the isthmus of Panama or farther south, and even India during the 1880s, among artists in San Francisco who followed the lead of Frederic Church (at least two of whom, Norton Bush and Fortunato Arriola, devoted themselves primarily to this subject), is one example of a wider trend (Figures 2.13 and 2.14). The Pacific and Asian exoticism that attracted such late nineteenth-century figures as Percival Lowell, John LaFarge, Henry Adams, and Lafcadio Hearn is another.

But regardless of its object, the flourishing of genteel exoticism after the Civil War betrayed – with a few exceptions to be sure – a certain shallowness. There is, for instance, more than a trace of consumerism in nearly all the post-bellum literature celebrating the witchery of the southern landscape. It was not uncommon for writers to flit from effusions of aesthetic pleasure to observations on the commercial opportunities connected with such beauty. Even the tone of Lanier's guidebook of Florida – at one level closely tied to the themes of his best poetry, in which he sought transcendence through communion with nature – suggests something of the "potboiler," as critics have been quick to charge. Its attenuated fancies are woven together into what amounts to an advertisement for pleasure. For all its new imagistic vividness, nature had lost much of its moral and symbolic dimension, along with its ability to threaten; instead, it was coming to represent a means of escape without paying the consequences. Exploration was giving way to tourism.

This shift was symptomatic of a larger change in outlook. As Bayard Taylor summarized the effects of the war on the national spirit: "The people have become materialized, their culture is temporarily disturbed because not well grounded, the very best of the younger generation lost, the rage for mere diversion and intellectual excitement taints the public taste, – and so nothing is left to us artists but to possess our souls in patience until the better time comes."[49]

The modification of nature apparent by the 1870s rewards further thought from a Marxist perspective. It attests to the reification of self and environment being effected through the growth of capitalism. Carolyn Porter discussed the gap between seeing and being in the writings of Emerson and other American literary figures as an aspect of this process of reification that had the conse-

Figure 2.13. Norton Bush, *Misty Day in the Tropics* (oil on canvas, 30 × 60 in., 1884). Collection of D. C. and Marion Miller, Palo Alto, Calif.

Figure 2.14. Fortunato Arriola (1827–1872), *Tropical Landscape* (oil on canvas, 48 × 76¾ in., 1870). Kahn Collection, Oakland Museum, Oakland, Calif.

quence of sapping the purposiveness of "sensuous human activity."[50] It is illuminating to keep this perspective in mind as we continue to examine the conflict between idealism and materialism that was so much a part of the way the swamp was encountered in nineteenth-century America. If this split was the consequence of an emerging capitalist economy, it continued to trouble thinkers who struggled to bring body and soul together against the backdrop of a society whose foundations in the American liberal tradition were based on thinking that promoted the division while ignoring or denying its existence.

In any case, the evisceration of the swamp's cultural meaning during the 1870s occurred indirectly as a result of factors originating two decades earlier. It is not enough to say that the sensualist and escapist inclinations that in Northern minds became associated with the swamp resulted from the termination of moral censure of the Southern way of life. Such inclinations were already present, at least in embryo, in much of the swamp and jungle imagery that had appeared before the war. Indeed, the real source of the swamp's imagistic awareness openly expressed after the war can be found in a convergence of determinants during the 1850s of which sectional antagonism was itself a symptom.

Before the war, many of the motives for Northern condemnation of the South correlated with anxieties that Northerners felt in the presence of the swamp and that had led them to suppress its implications. What made the swamp appear so dangerous was its opposition to social instincts and moral judgments that had preserved an inherited structure of values. Just as the Southern way of life was seen as threatening republican institutions and mores – above all the prevailing habits of industriousness and standards of moral conduct – the swamp was likely to appear as the natural embodiment of this threat, promising indolence and moral waywardness if not regression and reversion to savagery. But with the gradual breakdown of the inherited structure of values that accompanied the formation of a middle-class identity; with the weakening of internal controls of the self; and with the increase of personal anxiety, moral uncertainty, and the general feeling of being cut off from the sources of creativity, of being "overcivilized," what had seemed dangerous became exhilarating.[51] Let us not forget, too, that advancing technology was making environments like the swamp more accessible to the public and less physically threatening.

In the largest context, the popular desire for escape and nonthreatening immersion in the lavish tropical environment was an early expression of resistance to the growing sterility and spiritual decomposition of American middle-class life. Yet as Jackson Lears contended, this resistance in the long run merely allowed for acquiescence to a secular and bureaucratic civilization by sugar coating the pill. Tourism was the surrogate for any real alternative to progress. In the latter part of the century, Americans reacted in a variety of ways to the sense that authentic experience was no longer in their grasp. As Lears showed, such *fin-de-siècle* cultural phenomena as medievalism, the martial ideal, the Arts and Crafts movement, and Asian and Pacific exoticism can be seen as manifestations of the search for sources of primitive experience to counteract what he termed the "crisis of bourgeois values" that beset those

Americans most sensitive to the loss of religious certitude and personal autonomy.[52] It is important to remember that the first tremors of this cultural earthquake were sensed long before the final decades of the century and, indeed, jolted the complacency of more than a few Americans.

Mid-Victorian Cultural Values and the Amoral Landscape: The Swamp Image in the Work of William Gilmore Simms and Harriet Beecher Stowe

Before considering the phenomenology of the swamp image more closely in the next several chapters, I want to address the question of "intrinsic" meaning – of the cultural context itself – that underlay the new assessment of the swamp and other desert places in the 1850s and 1860s. Clearly, "intrinsic" and "expressional" meaning can never be separated completely (as implied by Bachelard's notion of the integral relationship between images and moral thought).[1] My intention here is simply to focus on one aspect at a time of a complicated dialectical interaction that reflected a period of increasing sectional conflict and cultural strain. In stressing the pole of moral thought as a salient aspect of the iconology of the swamp, I will be concerned with attempts by two writers, one Northern and the other Southern, one female and the other male (the gender distinction both compounds and complements the difference in region), to adjust the contours of the self by symbolic means in response to a cultural ethos conceived of as either too rigid and restrictive or as too amorphous and irresponsible.

In the cases of William Gilmore Simms and Harriet Beecher Stowe, it is the compensatory role played by the two poles – imagistic and moralistic – in relation to each other that was instrumental in formulating a model of integrated selfhood that might satisfy the demands of the dominant ideology in Mid-Victorian America. Yet the interesting and unforeseen consequence of such a project was in neither case the realization of any simple sense of wholeness. Instead, what resulted in the long run was, in the instance of Simms, a defensive repression pointing toward anomie and, in that of Stowe, the dim apprehension of a far more complex and dynamic selfhood that could emerge only in creative interaction with an unstable yet productive symbolic mode, one that responded to Stowe's need for a more profound religious experience than was offered by her cultural and familial heritage.

The coexistence of imagistic and emblematic (or moralistic) modes of representation and signification in works relating to the swamp by these two writers is what generated the contradictions that give them their symbolic power. By the 1870s, as I have suggested, much of this dynamic in the cultural context had relaxed, leaving the swamp all the richer as an image but flaccid and unproductive as a symbol. At its peak, however, the tension between imagistic and moralistic modes can be termed *symbolistic* (to invoke a term applied to American Renaissance literature by Charles Feidelson): It distills ambiguities out of the opposition between inherited or intentional meanings and the intrinsic formlessness and meaninglessness (or all-meaning) of existence.[2] Under the pressure of these ambiguities, conventional meaning gradually gives way. An image so inherently ambiguous as the swamp seems all the more subversive when seen under such culturally constituted meaning, for it is primarily through its place in the dialectic with traditional modes of seeing and understanding that it comes alive in all its menace but also in all its latent creativity.

As an ambiguous realm (neither land nor water), the swamp defies the pervasive logical distinctions at the basis of culture: the demarcation between life and death and polarities such as good and evil, light and dark, male and female. That is largely why it has always seemed so threatening, the antithesis of civilization. The anthropologist Mary Douglas observed that in cultures throughout the world, such ambiguity is associated with ideas of pollution and their attendant sense of danger. Douglas demonstrated how cultures sometimes use pollution creatively to overcome the constricting influence of established moral rules and boundaries of behavior. She wrote:

> Dirt was created by the differentiating activity of mind, it was a by-product of the creation of order. So it started from a state of non-differentiation; all through the process of differentiation its role was to threaten the distinctions made; finally it returns to its true indiscriminate character. Formlessness is therefore an apt symbol of beginning and of growth as it is of decay.[3]

Much of her book, however, is concerned with showing how pollution beliefs clarify and bolster moral rules and boundaries that have become obscure or incongruous. As Douglas asserted, pollution flourishes where there is cultural contradiction.[4]

Douglas's generalizations about primitive cultures are to some degree applicable to modernized cultures as well. An example of the way in which the swamp was enlisted in Mid-Victorian America to anchor values that were losing contact with reality occurs in a story entitled "The Patriarch" by Lydia Sigourney, the doyenne of sentimental culture. In this, the opening tale of the 1848 edition of *A Young Lady's Offering*, Sigourney portrays an ideal society established in "the heart of one of the deepest Carolinian solitudes"[5] and restoring the sacred ways of the past. The little colony of New Englanders, which is religious to the core and finds spiritual leadership in its patriarch, is "swamp-encircled" (p. 247). The narrator, a minister who visits this remote outpost, must first pass through a morass, "the bulwark thrown by Nature around this little city of the desert" (p. 249). The cultivated fields of the prosperous colony contrast sharply with this wasteland: "Alighting, I led my horse over the rude bridge of logs, which surmounted the pools and ravines, until our footing rested upon firm earth. Soon, an expanse of arable land became visible, and wreaths of smoke came lightly curling through the trees, as if to welcome the stranger. Then a cluster of cottages cheered the eye" (p. 249).

The obvious allusion is to the Israelites in the wilderness. The encircling swamp is in one sense a relic of the adversity suffered by those who aspired to the righteous life. The colony occupies a circle of purity; it is a refuge from the ambiguity (both moral and physical) of the swamp. At the center of the colony the narrator comes upon a sanctuary devoted to the dead: "It was surmounted by a neat enclosure, and planted with trees. The drooping branches of the willows swept the grave of the mother of the colony . . . " (pp. 262–3). In this symbolic center (associated with the mother principle) life and death are one. Pollution has been identified and shunted to the outside, thus allowing for a reconciliation of instincts and social mores.

The swamp in this story assumes the form of a hedge (we recall the hedge separating the Puritan community from the surrounding wilderness), closing off the corruption and compromise of contemporary American society, which in Sigourney's mind was becoming disarmingly atomistic and acquisitive. Under these conditions, death, which earlier had been simply a fact of life, appeared alien and disturbing. Death focused symbolically on a range of anxieties resulting from the pressures on traditional family and community life.

In contrast with the male-centered, expansive culture of mid-nineteenth-century America, the colony of "The Patriarch," as Ann Douglas maintains,[6] is female dominated and structured according to the principles of deference and cooperation. As one of its members asks, "For what should we contend? We have no prospect of wealth, nor motive of ambition" (p. 256). The value system espoused here is a retreat from the kind of situation dramatized by Sigourney in another tale in the collection, "The Father." The father is "in the full tide of a laborious and absorbing profession, – one of which imposes on intellect an unsparing discipline but ultimately opens the avenues of wealth and fame" (p. 5). In the end, he is led by his all-consuming ambition to sacrifice, unintentionally, the one genuine human tie left him: His demands on his daughter rob her of her health and eventually her life.

The symbolic exorcism of pollution from the community of "The Patriarch" to the surrounding area restores harmony and reinforces social cohesion.[7] Pollution is converted into a positive force. The swamp that might have invaded the boundaries of purity instead fortifies those boundaries. This altered role depends on the aura of prohibition (taboo) that inheres in pollution. Accordingly, Sigourney does not permit herself to explore the swamp. Barely visualized, it is present merely as a symbolic counter, an emblem. To this degree, she stops well short of the feminist implications of her story, remaining within the confines of a moderate domesticity, still constricted by essentially patriarchal standards.

A more problematic instance of the use of the swamp to assert and clarify moral rules is found in William Gilmore Simms's poem, "The Edge of the Swamp," a virtual compendium of traditional swamp imagery and symbolism.[8] Significantly, Simms's description of the swamp penetrates no further than its outskirts. Here the eye encounters a scene full of blight and filth where

> Fantastic vines,
> That swing like monstrous serpents in the sun,
> Bind top to top, until the encircling trees
> Group all in close embrace...

The swamp swarms with dangerous and repulsive animals but Simms notices that the place,

> ...so like the gloomiest realm of death,
> Is yet the abode of thousand forms of life, –
> The terrible, the beautiful, the strange, –

Part of the hideous picture Simms creates is an exploitation of the swamp's ambiguous ecology and deceptive appearance. Gigantic cypresses are surrounded by buttresses,

> ...not seeming to sustain,
> Yet link'd by secret twines, that underneath,
> Blend with each arching trunk.

The poem concludes with a vignette in which a butterfly accidentally lands on the brow of a "steel-jaw'd Cayman," rising from the muck like a half-submerged log. When the monster suddenly lowers his head,

> The dandy of the summer flowers and woods,
> Dips his light wings, and soils his golden coat,
> With the rank waters of the turbid lake.

Simms ruminates for several lines on the striking contrast between the butterfly (a traditional symbol of the psyche and spirit) and the dark region into which it has wandered; the meaning of the poem congeals into a moralistic mold. The poem ends with a turgid pronouncement, urging the reader to follow the example of the butterfly as it spreads its wings and flies to "a more genial home" than "these drear borders offer us to-night."

Simms's admonition to avoid contamination by the swamp is, however, subtly undermined by his fascination with the landscape. Unlike Sigourney, Simms was intimately acquainted with the swamp, and his relative fidelity to the complex implications of the image uneasily fits his didactic purpose. The message is animated by glimpses of a barely suppressed psychological reality pertaining to the swamp's paradoxical processes. It is a realm of both life and death, at once terrible, beautiful, and strange; it is hallucinatory. By contrast, the realm of purity marked off by the discriminating mind represents only one side of a fundamentally dialectical process: Life is affirmed and death denied.

The intermingling of life and death in the swamp's ecology affronted this way of thinking. No less luminous a beacon of mid-nineteenth-century Anglo-American values than John Ruskin is a case in point. According to Ruskin, "there is a peculiar painfulness attached to any association of inorganic with organic matter." He attributed the idea of purity to a "vital and energetic connection" among the particles of matter, impurity to its negation, "as in corruption and decay of all kinds."[9] The universe falls into proper moral perspective along this axis: light, life, and the Deity are embodied in flowing water; darkness, death, and the withdrawal of the divine presence are exemplified in stagnant water. Because of this one-sidedness, Ruskin failed (his evangelicism is reflected here) to acknowledge that purity can lead to sterility, that it can become antagonistic to flux and development. Contact with pollution, on the other hand, provides a way of relativizing assumptions and thus opens the way for creativity.

As the essentially anomalous character of the swamp came into view, the image provided a conduit into that area of problematic reality that increasingly impinged on Americans in the years before the Civil War. This disturbing reality, which of course had political and social as well as epistemological and ontological aspects, could be imaginatively resolved in a number of ways. The conservative efforts of Simms and Sigourney, nearly complementary to each other in approach, are to some extent geographically based. Northern swamps were, on the whole, neither spectacular nor dangerous. Unless they had traveled to the South, Northerners knew only vaguely what many Southerners knew well. Yet the geographical factor is interlaced with questions of cultural identity, which we must consider in order to understand the special power the swamp was to wield as a symbol in the antebellum period.

In view of this relationship between geography and culture, we should explore at greater length Simms's ambivalence toward the swamp as it emerged during his career. By the time he wrote "The Edge of the Swamp" in the early 1850s, he was taking an aggressive stance toward what he recognized as the amoral implications of the landscape. His solution contrasts with Sigourney's. Sigourney's narrator moves through the borderland of the swamp to reach an enclosed area offering sanctuary.

The same spatial configuration, using jungle imagery, was visualized by the nineteenth-century French graphic artist Rodolphe Bresdin (Figure 3.1). For Bresdin such a configuration is charged with obvious psychological resonance; it presents a unity of light and dark elements, roughly a circular center and an amorphous surrounding area. The eye is invited to move through this encompassing area in order to reach the center in which the complex visual pattern is relieved by blank ground.

In adopting the contours of her ideal community to this archetypal design, Sigourney unconsciously sought to broaden this experience beyond the limits imposed by the willful mind (exemplified by the ambition of "The Father") and to give it psychological completion by reconciling opposites. Reflecting the values of domesticity, she strove to restore personal stability against the disruptive incursion of outside social forces. For Simms, on the other hand, the goal is maintaining stability in the face of natural excess. His moral didacticism reflects the spirit of masculine confrontation with nature.[10] Both writers compensated for an imbalance between nature and civilization, but from inverse points of view.

Figure 3.1. Rodolphe Bresdin, *Eclaircie dans la Forêt*. Bibliothèque Nationale, Paris.

The social and psychological propensities that Simms associated with the swamp were personified by his long-time friend James Hammond, the South Carolina planter-politician. Hammond himself made the connection explicit when he complained of ill health in his diary of 1846, striking an uncharacteristically lyrical note. "There is something in the solemn gloom of these swamps," he wrote, "which suits me more than any other kind of landscape. Even this stale, dead, black water seems to concert with the sluggishness of my spirit."[1] Hammond here succumbs to the downward tug of a fate that has long gripped him, which has even become pleasing by virtue of its familiarity. In the sense of stagnation he links with the swamp, he recognizes not something hitherto lost but a feeling he has somehow always known. For all the freight of his language, his meaning is thus inherently preconceptual. A sense of discovery cannot arise where self-consciousness has never existed. There is thus no chance for insight, the moment of reorientation to experience that enables artistic awareness.

W. J. Cash's description of the Southern landscape and his formulation of its relationship to the character of Southerners in *The Mind of the South* (1941) helps us generalize from Hammond's experience and indicates the extraordinary tenaciousness of this mythic conception of the South:

There was the influence of the Southern physical world – itself a sort of cosmic conspiracy against reality in favor of romance. The country is one of extravagant colors, of proliferating foliage and bloom, of flooding yellow sunlight, and, above all perhaps, of haze. . . . The dominant mood, the mood that lingers in the memory, is one of well-nigh drunken reverie – of a hush that seems all the deeper for the far-away mourning of the hounds and the far-away crying of the doves – of such sweet and inexorable opiates as the rich odors of hot earth and pinewood and the perfume of the magnolia in bloom – of soft languor creeping through the blood and mounting surely to the brain. . . . It is a mood, in sum, in which directed thinking is all but impossible, a mood in which the mind yields almost perforce to drift and in which nothing any more seems improbable save the puny inadequateness of fact, nothing incredible save the bareness of truth.[12]

Hammond occupies an environment that invades him and could overwhelm and destroy him. His spiritual fatigue shades into a morbid premonition of death. The landscape is indeed a fitting image with which to symbolize his entire life. This "fire-eater" and persuasive advocate of slavery as a positive good was characterized by Clement Eaton as "a Hamlet-like statesman with a brilliant encompassing intellect, very practical but also fatally weakened for action by his capacity to see the complexities of life and by an overweening pride and a wavering will."[13]

After Hammond's marriage to a Charleston heiress gave him the fortune to lead a life of indolence (he had been born a commoner in the up-country), his political ambitions were continually undercut by his habitual torpor and hypochondriacal temperament. The luxuriance of his self-pity stifled concerted action. A mysterious personal scandal involving his alleged seduction of the daughters of his wife's brother-in-law, Wade Hampton, dealt a serious blow to his political career, which was damaged even more by his failure to answer to the public for his actions. Following a two-year tenure as governor of South Carolina, Hammond's retirement to Silver Bluff (his wife's plantation) in the mid-1840s lasted for thirteen years. Though he reentered political life in the 1850s, Hammond's prestige again suffered from his continuing reticence over the issue of secession. He feared the consequences – for his personal fortune, as Eaton surmises, as well as for South Carolina – should his state act alone.[14]

Hammond's correspondence with Simms, his one close friend, reveals the depths of his depression. Aside from common political interests, he found in the novelist a kindred spirit.[15] As he commiserated with Simms in 1853:

Ours is [sic] in great measure mental maladies. The sad truth is we have both reached & almost turned the summit of the hill of life & neither of us are satisfied with the positions we have achieved for ourselves. Satisfied! Mine is about as comfortable as the shirt of Nessus & as fatally wedded to me. . . . Our races have been run. Let us realize this truth, & contemplate it philosophically. Let us make up our minds to bear our lots such as they are, & casting off, if not all toil & care, at least all violent exertions & all heart oppressing anxieties, take what good the gods have given & glide as quickly and smoothly as we can down the hill which we ascended with such exhaustive ardor & – in my case so little purpose. . . .[16]

Simms, who had only the highest regard for his friend's native intelligence and abilities, advised Hammond to cope with his proclivity for melancholy introspection, urging him to return to political life or at least to devote himself to writing: "Let me entreat you to give such exercise to your mind daily, as will keep it from recoiling upon itself."[17] The novelist realized as he wrote his friend that

> reverie itself, though, perhaps, the most grateful mental exercise, is for this very reason dangerous since it induces a corresponding inertness of the animal, and beguiles perpetually into provinces which make it daily more & more ungrateful to return to the earth. We must touch earth perpetually, to renew our wholesome strength & energies, and the fable of Anteus was figurative of the first of human necessities.[18]

Simms no doubt spoke from a personal commitment that drove him, when not sick, to work frantically (his total literary corpus, not including an immense correspondence, runs to eighty-two volumes). He observed to Beverly Tucker that Hammond's wealth kept him from "stripping to the buff and fighting through the thick of enemies."[19] Yet Simms's own industriousness, compulsive as it was, must have been based on more than mere financial need. His letters to Hammond consistently reveal a decadent undercurrent, evincing a similar morbid propensity to infirmity, self-pity, and lassitude.

The key to Simms's affinity with Hammond, despite his awareness of the latter's weaknesses, was the dedication of both men to those characteristics given shape in the Cavalier legend. If we accept the argument of William R. Taylor, Simms's fall into political apathy in the 1850s – following his disenchantment with the North and with the promise of democracy – was part of his identification of this Cavalier character with the problem of Hamlet.[20]

The indecisiveness of certain Southerners preyed increasingly on Simms's mind. As Taylor found, Simms felt that Hamlets "were most apt to appear in societies where there was no progress and where life is accordingly consumed in trying to meet the requirements of an elaborate social code."[21] Simms clearly saw Hammond as a fulfillment of the Hamlet type, and he had admonished his friend in 1849 to "Remember Hamlet – 'Whose native hue of resolution / Was sicklied o'er by the pale cast of thought.' " Late in 1853 he told a Northern audience – in a lecture based on four earlier articles on "The Moral Character of Hamlet" (1844) – that he had known "several Hamlets" in Charleston.[22] Simms connected the Hamlet type to the Southern hothead (Hotspur), showing that one type followed from the other, "that impetuous, precipitant activism grew out of irresolution and indecision."[23]

Well before the tensions of the 1850s, however, Simms had often dwelt on the lack of resolution and energy characteristic, he thought, of the South. As early as 1841, in an article on Southern literature for his magazine *The Magnolia*, Simms related this weakness to the low regard for literary pursuits held by most Southerners. Identifying literature with the Ideal ("a corrective against the dangers of the *Real*"), Simms stated that "the painful conviction which is forced upon us by surveying these characteristics of our people, is that they want fixed principles and leading and high purposes. There is no stern morality at the bottom of their labors, urging on their industry and making them sleepless in the prosecution of their designs." The South had not profited from "that old genius of Puritanism" that had been transmitted instead to New England's "sterile soil" and had produced there, in comparison with the other states, a "wondrous moral and social strength."[24]

Simms's analysis of New Englanders closely fit the myth of the Yankee. Their "pride of character" and "just consciousness of strength" were shown in their intolerance and bigotry. They were "diseased in consequence of too much homogeneousness." In this equivocation, it is impossible to miss the envy of a writer well aware that most of his audience was Northern:

> The people were more slow, but more stable, in their movements
> than the other races of mankind. Less bright, less sparkling, more
> coarse and more disdainful of courtesies, but, proportionably, far
> more resolute, more manly, and governed by principles of more uner-
> ring integrity. With little imagination, they had far more solidity; and
> where they seemed to lack enthusiasm, they supplied the want, with a
> sharp and subtle and searching perseverance. The habit of acting *en
> masse* from the beginning, prepared them for nationality much sooner
> than the Southern Colonies, which were settled chiefly by individuals
> . . . and influenced by laws which were unhappily all furnished from
> abroad. The New England pilgrim was a law unto himself. . . .[25]

Still, Simms chose to cast his lot with the Cavaliers of his beloved native state, and the nature imagery of his writings, no less than their reiterated themes, is testimony to his emotional stake in this association. The younger South Carolina poet, Henry Timrod, offered Simms a tribute that hints at the extent of the novelist's devotion to the local cause:

> His be the meed whose pencil's trace
> Hath touched our very swamps with grace,
>   And round whose tuneful way
>   All Southern laurels bloom;
> The poet of 'The Woodlands' . . .[26]

In Simms's romances of the Revolutionary War in South Carolina, this spirit of localism is suggested in the guerrilla warfare of the rebel partisans in the swamps of the Carolina low country. Against the tendencies toward homogeneity, acquisitiveness, and bigotry that Simms found in Northern society, the guerrillas' situation underscored their independence, their willingness to put up with deprivation for the cause of liberty, and the enlargement of their perspective brought about by the habitual intercourse of cultivated faculties with the wilderness.[27]

Largely through the use of swamp imagery, Simms managed to suggest a kind of *participation mystique* between the patriots and the landscape of the homeland they were defending. Annette Kolodny, quoting from *The Forayers* (1855), emphasized the regressive aspects of the relationship between partisan and environment in Simms's romances: "If we follow any of Simms's many partisan 'wayfarers' through 'the dark and silent recesses of those thickets that seemed impenetrable from without' . . . , we consistently enter a region whose landscape, both symbolically and geographically, images a return to a passive, infantile orientation."[28] The movement, in other words, is away from the normal social self symbolized by the autonomous male ego. In this pattern of reverse initiation, the swamp, a sanctuary from the threat of invading British troops, is transformed into a nurturing mother symbol.[29]

Following the detailed description of a gloomy and impenetrable swamp that opens *The Scout* (first published as *The Kinsman*, 1841), Simms observes:

> But, in the perilous times of our history, these seeming discourage-
> ments served the kindly purposes of security and shelter. The swamps
> of Carolina furnished a place of refuge to the patriot and fugitive,
> when the dwelling and the temple yielded none. The more dense the
> wall of briers upon the edge of the swamp, the more dismal the ave-
> nues within, the more acceptable to those who, preferring Liberty
> over all things, could there build her altars and tend her sacred fires,
> without being betrayed by their smoke.[30]

As he forces his way through the swamp, clusters of wild grapes "hang around the brows of the fainting and feeble partisan." He forgets the cruelties of his fellows "in solacing himself with the grateful tributes which are yielded him by the bounteous nature."[31]

In *The Forayers,* which also begins with an elaborate swamp description, penetration to the interior of the landscape is a sign of membership in a select brotherhood:

> The path grows sinuous and would be lost, but for certain marks
> upon the branches of the trees under which we are required to move.
> *You* would not see these marks. No one could see them, were they not
> shown, or decipher their mystic uses, were they not explored. They
> have been carefully made, not only to escape the casual glance, but to
> shape, step by step, the course of him who has been taught the cipher.

Following a faint gleam of light appearing occasionally through the tangle of vegetation, we eventually reach a clearing that Simms fancies is a retreat for the *genius loci*, "the High Priest of a perished people."[32]

After a period of embitterment toward the South, during which he con-templated moving to the North, Simms returned in the 1850s to his favorite subject, the romance of the Revolution. According to Joseph V. Ridgeley, Simms made a deepening emotional connection between the Revolutionary period and the present when "the South increasingly felt beleaguered . . . and was subject to attacks by hostile outside forces as it had been in the late eighteenth century."[33] In this context, Simms's Revolutionary War romances were, as Ridgeley asserted, a blueprint for the ideal Southern society.[34] The structure of this ideal followed the lines of partisan resistance. Simms was thus faced with applying the lessons learned from an ephemeral social situation to the practical needs of rebuilding a shattered society in peacetime.

The issue is especially relevant to Simms's motive in writing *Woodcraft* (first published as *The Sword and the Distaff*, 1852), in which he attempted to correct Northern misconceptions about Southern society and specifically to counter the image of slave owners presented in *Uncle Tom's Cabin*.[35] In *Woodcraft* Simms brings the memorable Cavalier partisan, Captain Porgy (likened by Simms himself to Falstaff), home from the war to face the restoration of his miserably wrecked plantation while being hounded by the ruthless Tory creditor, M'Kewn. At the same time, Porgy tries to make the parallel transition from a social life based on the exclusively male camaraderie he enjoyed in the swamps to that of a married man. Although he succeeds in resurrecting his plantation, his efforts at marriage fail.

Porgy's story has been retold and analyzed too often to warrant close consideration here. Suffice it to say that Simms felt the need to provide ballast, in the figure of Sergeant Millhouse, for Porgy's extravagant yet refined sensibilities and lack of practicality and money sense.[36] Millhouse, a kind of transplanted Yankee whose philosophy is utilitarian, agrees to be Porgy's overseer and has difficulty restraining himself from extending his dominion to Porgy's personal life as well, much to the latter's discomfiture. Obviously, Simms regards Millhouse as something of a necessary evil. But Porgy's setbacks in courtship are evidence that Simms had no solution to the problem of converting the energies of warfare into those of domesticity. Simms's romantic attachment to the Cavalier legend was preserved only in the idyll of Porgy's virginity.[37]

Simms's apprehensions regarding the South and its prospects outside the context of resistance (South Carolina's anticipated opposition to the Union is obviously the issue here) explain his contradictory associations with the swamp. Although the landscape under the conditions of war posed as a symbol of regional allegiance – especially in *The Partisan* (1835) – when the scene shifted to peacetime, it changed to something different. In *Woodcraft,* which is exclusively concerned with peacetime, the swamp is figuratively connected with the squatter Bostwick, a despicable individual who has formed an uneasy alliance with Porgy's creditor, M'Kewn. Bostwick leads a squadron of ne'er-do-wells in an attempt to recapture some slaves pilfered by M'Kewn from Porgy and his loyal neighbor, the Widow Eveleigh, while Porgy was away at war. When his ambush of the widow's entourage is foiled by Porgy and his men, happening on the scene at a timely moment, Bostwick escapes to the swamp, where he hides with a box of guineas and valuable papers he has taken from the widow which later enable him to blackmail M'Kewn.

In the course of his various machinations, Bostwick repeatedly finds refuge in the swamp, a habitat he seems to feel is more congenial than the home kept by his wife and children. His immersion in the swamp stresses its function as the natural equivalent of the squatter's moral destitution and estrangement from all human ties save that with his daughter Dory. By the end of the novel, when Bostwick dies horribly of smallpox, the swamp has emerged as an emblem of his isolation, physical exhaustion, and hopelessness. Returning the reader to the scene where Bostwick had been left up to his neck in swamp water, Simms sermonizes:

> No condition could have appeared more hopeless – no situation more humbling or perplexing. It is, perhaps, the case commonly, that the habitual criminal is habitually an unthinking person, else how should the utter profitlessness, and certain perils of crime, fail to impress themselves upon the mind of him who toils in his vocation of sin, and

is taught by the bitter experiences of each day the terrible truth that
the only wages he can earn, in this employment, is [*sic*] shame and
scorn, and foes, and ignominy and death.[38]

The link between the swamp and the nihilism represented by Bostwick's life
is also made in *The Forayers*, in which the swamp is the setting for the adventures of a gang of incorrigibles led by the uproarious "Hell-Fire Dick."[39]

The moral status of the swamp in Simms's romances thus changed in ac-
cordance with the author's predominant rhetorical concern. When he sought
to create a mythic identity for Southerners by recalling the heroic exploits of
South Carolina's past patriots, the swamp acted as a positive symbol. When
he turned to address the demands of the ordinary social sphere, the landscape
became threatening in its amoral indifference. The lowest common denominator of this range of meaning involves those elements opposed to the Ideal,
by which Simms meant the fixed principles and industriousness that he found
lacking in the Southern character, whether personified by the Cavalier James
Hammond or the derelict Bostwick. Even Porgy's sense of honor could not
fully substitute for "stern morality" when it came to building a civilization of
nationalistic pretensions. Such qualities had to be alloyed with the mercenary
and utilitarian influence of a Millhouse.

Within this context, the swamp represented everything subversive of the
Ideal. It was the essence of what Simms designated as the Real, and we might
better understand what he meant by exchanging his terms for the anthropological distinction between purity and pollution. Because by its very nature it
eluded any clear-cut distinction between good and evil, the swamp assumed
for Simms a function analogous to that of pollution in the definition of cultural
values and mores. Simms could not escape the fact that for all its associative
value, the swamp sheltered everyone equally well, regardless of temperament
or persuasion.

Moreover, by playing off the environment's desolate and horrific aspects
against its nurturing role, Simms generated a dynamic and ambiguous symbolic backdrop that expressed the complexity of the moral situation in his
novels but did not resolve the dichotomy in his own mind between Cavalier
and Yankee. The advent of Simms's deepening Southern parochialism in the
1850s led him, it seems, toward his repudiation of the swamp in "The Edge
of the Swamp," as a way of compensating for the inadequacies of what he
took to be the Southern character.

If the peculiarly Southern dilemma of William Gilmore Simms moved him to
turn his back on the richer implications of the swamp experience, by constricting it within a moralistic frame, certain Northerners were at the same
time discovering the swamp as a means of liberation from restrictive traditional
religious and behavioral patterns. When considering the upsurge of interest
among artists and writers in swamp, jungle, or other desert landscapes, we
must deal with those Americans close enough to their cultural boundaries to
participate in expanding them. The landscape is not only a free field for the
projection of unconscious content – not just symptomatic of the culture's inner
life – but, because of its ambiguous features, it actually provokes projections

and even helps determine their form. It can therefore be viewed as an active force in the unfolding of cultural sensibility during a period when Americans still looked primarily to nature for their understanding of the world. It figures among the instruments for mapping the way through regions of difficult social reality. Here the creative rather than the preservative aspect of pollution stands out.

The impact of cultural transition on the relatively stable popular domain – at least that aspect of it generally designated as middle class – is reflected in the widespread assault on rational structures and on the moral rigidity and patriarchalism that were the legacy of New England's Puritan heritage.

The liberal Protestantism arrived at in the late 1860s by Henry Ward Beecher, the leading spokesman of American religious values, is an example. As William G. McLoughlin showed, Beecher signaled the effective demise of American Calvinism in its last bastion, the Northeast, by adopting the experimental method of Emersonian idealism as the means of coming to God.[40] Beecher has Dr. Wentworth, the proponent of his views in his novel *Norwood* (1867), proclaim that "the alphabetic forms of moral truth found at large in the world will serve to teach one at length how to read those clearer manifestations of the divine nature and of moral government, which are perfectly disclosed only in the life and teachings of our Saviour."[41] As Beecher summarized the plot, "the man of philosophy and theology and the woman of nature and simple truth, are to act upon each other and she is to triumph."[42]

At all levels of New England culture in this period there is a turn toward what might be designated as a kind of primitivism, an attitude generally too superficial and self-conscious to be dignified as "primitivistic sensibility" but still significant in its attraction to unconscious, premodern modes of being. In many ways, the "feminization of American culture" that Ann Douglas charted underlies the new receptivity to the unconscious mental processes that transformed the meaning of the swamp. Invoking the title of one of Harriet Beecher Stowe's novels, *Pink and White Tyranny*, Douglas documented "the drive of nineteenth-century American women to gain power through the exploitation of their feminine identity as their society defined it."[43] This exploitation of identity was known as "influence," which Douglas defined as "suasion of moral and psychic nurture . . . unobtrusive and everywhere at the same time."[44] Feminine "influence" was a prototype for the communication of culture that replaced older versions of knowledge and well-defined beliefs that could be passed on from generation to generation through reasoned discourse and patriarchal authority.[45]

The phenomenon that George W. Frederickson called "romantic racialism" is another manifestation of primitivism among New Englanders of a certain social status.[46] Romantic racialists held that blacks were natural Christians because of their "childlike" qualities, their innocence and docility. In effect, these racialists often exalted the black race above the white for this very reason (though on the whole they rejected the notion of racial hierarchy). The stereotype was attractive, Frederickson pointed out, as a symbol of discontent over the materialism and acquisitiveness of white American civilization. He called attention in this respect to the common tendency to associate blacks and women and quoted a leading male feminist of the day, Theodore Tilton:

In all the intellectual activities which take their strange quickening from the moral faculties – which we call instincts, intuitions – the negro is superior to the white man – equal to the white woman. It is sometimes said . . . that the negro race is the feminine race of the world. This is not only because of his social and affectionate nature, but because he possesses that strange, moral instinctive insight that belongs more to women than to men.[47]

As we shall see, however, there is evidence that the appeal of blacks – especially when brought into relationship with the swamp – could touch reservoirs in the Northern white self that lay considerably deeper than this sentimental stereotyping indicates.

A prime example of the use of the swamp image to undermine religious strictures and shibboleths that had become ennervated or contradictory occurs in Harriet Beecher Stowe's second novel, *Dred, A Tale of the Dismal Swamp* (1856). The novel represented an important step in Stowe's gradual modification of the New England theology passed on by her father, Lyman Beecher. Curiously, when she wrote the novel, she had never seen a southern swamp. Her lengthy descriptions of the swamp exude conventionalism, continually casting forth the sentimental flotsam and jetsam readily available to her. Yet for all its secondhand quality, Stowe managed to give her swamp a psychological vitality and an innovative symbolic context.

Setting forth her plans for *Uncle Tom's Cabin* to Gamaliel Bailey, editor of the *National Era*, Stowe claimed that her vocation was "simply that of a *painter*"; her object in writing was "to hold up in the most lifelike and graphic manner possible Slavery, its reverses, changes, and the negro character, which I have had ample opportunity for studying." As she realized, "There is no arguing with *pictures* and everybody is impressed with them, whether they mean to be or not."[48] Stowe intended her second novel as another sally at the antislavery theme. But she managed to offer only rather pallid variations on the pictures that, beneath the banner of novelty, had taken the public by storm in the earlier work: the beating to death of Uncle Tom, the transfiguration of little Eva, and Eliza's escape to freedom over the ice-choked Ohio River. The one major exception to this generalization about *Dred* is Stowe's exploitation of the popular image of the fugitive slave in the swamp, an image perhaps pivotal in focusing and dramatizing Northern attitudes toward the South's peculiar institution.

Although the presence of large numbers of escaped slaves in southern swamps had long been noted,[49] the earliest tendency to link the slaves imaginatively with their strange sanctuary surfaced in the wake of the Nat Turner rebellion, which took place in the vicinity of the Great Dismal Swamp of Virginia and North Carolina. Into the swamp Turner's "banditti" fled after their murderous rampage (Figure 3.2).

Samuel Warner, in the first full-scale publication devoted to the incident (written while Turner was still at large),[50] seemed fascinated with the slaves' ability to survive "within the deep recesses of this gloomy Swamp, 'dismal'

Figure 3.2. John Adam Houston, *The Fugitive Slave* (1853). The collection of Jay P. Altmayer, Mobile, Ala.

indeed, beyond the power of human conception . . . subsisting on frogs, tar-ripins, and even snakes!"[51] In seeking to justify at least partially the rebels, Warner found it almost incredible "that there could be found an individual of the human species, who, rather than wear the goading yoke of bondage, would prefer becoming the voluntary subject of so great a share of want and misery! – but, such indeed is the love of liberty – the gift of God!"[52]

Warner's description of the swamp plagiarized that of William Byrd of a hundred years earlier and stressed the weird and noxious aspects of the place, fixing it as a repulsive if intriguing emblem of evil, a natural hell:

> Neither beast, bird insect or reptile, approach the heart of this horrible desert; perhaps deterred by the everlasting shade, occasioned by the thick shrubs and bushes, which the sun can never penetrate, to warm the earth: nor indeed do any birds care to fly over it, any more than they are said to do over the lake Avernus, for fear of the noisome ex-halations that rise from this vast body of filth and nastiness.[53]

This traditional characterization of the swamp was sentimentalized by Henry Wadsworth Longfellow in "The Slave in the Dismal Swamp" (1855). Long-fellow's slave is a pitiful outcast condemned like Cain to live

> Where hardly a human foot could pass,
> Or a human heart would dare,
> On the quaking turf of the green morass
> . . . crouched in the rank and tangled grass,
> Like a wild beast in his lair.

While the birds and squirrels around him flaunt their freedom, the misbegotten fugitive lives under the "doom of pain."[54]

In contrast with Longfellow's sentimental evocation, Porte Crayon de-scribed an encounter with an escaped slave named Osman who appeared heroic:

> About thirty paces from me I saw a gigantic negro, with a tattered blanket wrapped about his shoulders, and a gun in his hand. . . . His hair and head were tipped with gray, and his purely African features were cast in a mould betokening, in the highest degree, strength and energy. The expression of the face was of mingled fear and ferocity, and every movement betrayed a life of habitual caution and watchfulness.[55]

The accompanying illustration (Figure 3.3) shows Osman immersed in the swamp and encircled by dense roots and vines, and plays on the analogy between human and natural in the moss which echoes the form of the fugitive's enormous hand.

This suggestion of psychological affinity between the swamp and its black denizens is even more pronounced in Thomas Moran's *Slaves Escaping Through a Swamp* (1865) (Figure 3.4), in which the runaways are ensconced in the dense jungle. Here the impenetrability of the swamp recalls the gothic drama of flight and pursuit (notice the slave hunters taking aim amid the entanglement on the right side of the picture and the dogs bounding after their human

Figure 3.3. David Hunter Strother, *Osman*, *Harper's New Monthly Magazine*, September, 1856.

quarry), the sublime aspect of the scenery (echoing the seventeenth-century Italian artist Salvator Rosa's pictures of banditti), and the implied social horror of human bondage. Whether appealing because of its sentimental, its heroic, or its horrific associations, the image of the escaped slave often evoked the normally repressed darker side of the Northern white psyche.

All of this relates to Stowe's use of the same image. Where she actually found her imagery is impossible to tell; there were certainly available many descriptions of Southern swamps. And Simms's possible influence should not be discounted. Simms had written *Woodcraft* in direct response to *Uncle Tom's Cabin* (remember the swamp that surrounds Simon Legree's plantation), and Stowe may have wanted to reply to the Southern writer on his own ground (so to speak), though I have found no definite evidence that she ever read his books. Simms frequently uses the idea of a wilderness clearing, inaccessible to outsiders because of "impervious jungle" but offering sanctuary to the initiated, and Stowe also uses this idea in describing the stronghold of her band of fugitive slaves. Stowe likewise recalls Simms's work in her occasional allusion to the beneficent, maternal side of the swamp. Stowe's Dred may even owe something to the depiction of the "maniac" elder Frampton in *The Partisan*, surely the most suggestive identification of human character with the swamp in all of Simms's work.

Father of the juvenile patriot Lance, the elder Frampton loves the swamp, as his habitual appearance betrays: "His thick, black hair was matted down

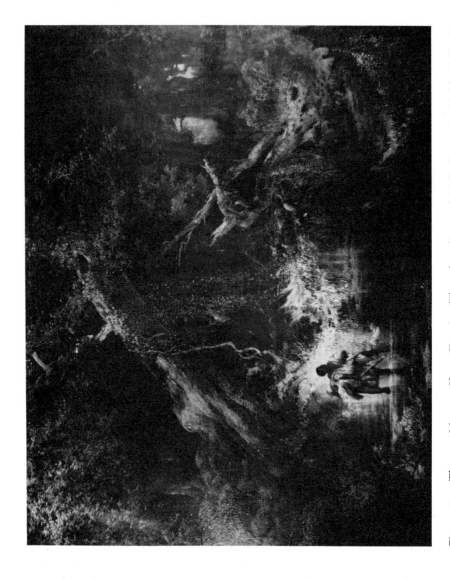

Figure 3.4. Thomas Moran, *Slaves Escaping Through a Swamp* (1865). Laura A. Clubb Collection, Philbrook Museum of Art, Tulsa, Okla.

upon his forehead, and was deeply stained with the clayey ooze of the swamp through which he had crawled. . . ."[56] The old man is loyal to the cause and hates the Tories. But he acts irresponsibly: Without intending evil, he brings about harm and confusion, presaged by his maniacal laughter. As Lance apologizes for his father: "Sometimes, sir, he plays dangerously with you. But it's all in play, for he laughs and doesn't look in earnest; but he is apt to hurt people then."[57] As if he were some perverse prophet, the lunatic's eyes glare "with a baleful, and malignant sort of light . . . full of evil omen. . . ."[58] He is obsessed by the murder of his wife by British troops and calculates a revenge that is carried out when he surreptitiously escorts a British prisoner of war from the partisan encampment to his wife's grave in the inner sanctum of the swamp and suffocates him to death in the mire.[59] Simms means this primitive lust for blood revenge to contrast with the transcendent patriotism and code of honor that dignify the rebel cause. The partisan whose negligence allowed the madman to commit his revenge is severely reprimanded by Major Singleton, the leader of the guerrillas.

The primitive, vengeful fervor motivating the elder Frampton and the anarchy sowed by his madness associates him with Dred, a self-styled biblical prophet in the wilderness of the Dismal Swamp, though Dred is both more complex and more sympathetic than the maniac is. As spokesman for the wrathful Old Testament Jehovah, Dred is forced to concede to the self-sacrificing love of Jesus, personified by the old slave mammy Milly, a female Uncle Tom. Milly's vision emerges victorious at the end of the novel (after Dred's violent death in the swamp), once she has escaped slavery and started a nursery for foundling children. Still, in Stowe's view, there is much to be said for Dred.

Critics have been quick to dismiss Dred as an absurd concoction of the literary imagination,[60] a point easily granted by any standard of realism. Of seemingly superhuman strength and agility, Dred manifests an equally unlikely combination of fanatical devotion to the cause, preternatural empathy with nature, and boundless compassion for all things lowly and helpless. His imagination is apocalyptic, and his conversation is a pastiche of biblical prophecies and jeremiads. But this fictional representation of Nat Turner (whom Stowe fancies to be the son of the Charleston insurrectionist Denmark Vesey) deserves consideration, all the more because of the revealing metaphorization of Dred's inner character through swamp imagery. Stowe projected onto Dred fugitive, unfulfilled impulses that testify to inner conflicts for which the slavery issue was in part only a screen.

Dred's appearance in the swamp in the eighteenth chapter (after more than two hundred pages of narrative) rescues Stowe's novel from almost unrelenting mediocrity. Largely through this startling image, *Dred* does sporadically radiate energy and even achieves a degree of thematic coherence, despite the polemical character of many of the dialogues, frequent interludes of preaching, and a listless plot that follows the courtship of Nina Gordon and Edward Clayton (ending pointlessly in Nina's death two-thirds of the way through the novel). Stowe periodically interrupts the narrative to return her reader to the swamp and its inhabitants. These passages intrude like a haunting leitmotiv, conjuring up a saturnalia of half-realized moods and mental images. It is likely that Stowe was moved to introduce Dred to the story in response to the vicious blud-geoning of Charles Sumner in the chamber of the Senate by Preston Brooks, a congressman from South Carolina.

The attack occurred in May 1856; Stowe had been writing the book, to be called *Nina Gordon*. since about the end of February. Her friend Sumner hung between life and death for several days and remained a partial invalid for the rest of his life. The incident stunned the North; Brooks became a hero in the South. Within a fortnight, the Reverend Henry Ward Beecher had inaugurated his sensational "slave auctions." It would seem that Stowe's feelings toward the South, given a sharp personal edge by this incident, penetrated the novel she was writing. The national scope she had maintained so well in *Uncle Tom's Cabin* was narrowed, and her tone now often bordered on invective. But a more substantial change resulted as well in the emergence of an entirely new dimension to the novel. Her change of title from *Nina Gordon* to *Dred* denotes the shift of Stowe's concern, and she was willing eventually to dispense with her love story altogether.

What is new at this stage of the novel's development is the appearance of a "symbolistic" context. The swamp is not simply an objective environment, one that Dred inhabits; it is suggestively integrated with intimations of his inner self. We have an instance, in other words, of that special quality of the American romance in which as Richard Chase put it, "the field of action is conceived not so much as a place as a state of mind – the borderland of the human mind where the actual and the imaginary intermingle."[61] Dred is so much in spirit with his natural surroundings, so completely a product of their influence, that the description of the swamp moves easily from outer to inner worlds.

This impression of interiority is, of course, augmented by the luminous character of the swamp itself. Thus Stowe writes of Dred:

> It is difficult to fathom the dark recesses of a mind so powerful and active as his, placed under a pressure of ignorance and social disability so tremendous. In those desolate regions which he made his habita-tion, it is said that trees often, from the singularly unnatural and wildly stimulating properties of the slimy depths from which they spring, assume a goblin growth, entirely different from their normal habit. All sorts of vegetable monsters stretch their weird, fantastic forms among its shadows.[62]

This juxtaposition of the "dark recesses of the mind" of Dred and "those desolate regions which he made his habitation" establishes a merging of inner and outer realms more radical than the doctrinal formulation Stowe offered earlier in the narrative: "The mind, looking on the great volume of nature, sees there a reflection of its own internal passions, and seizes on that in it which sympathizes with itself" (vol. 1, p. 256). But what intrigues Stowe about this metaphorical figure, and what transfixes it, is the element of growth connected with the swamp. As she continues, "There is no principle so awful through all nature as the principle of *growth*. It is a mysterious and dread [note the play on Dred's name] condition of existence, which, place it under what impediments or disadvantages you will, is constantly forcing on; and when unnatural pressure hinders it, develops in forms portentous and astonishing" (vol. 2, p. 274).

Uncontrolled growth, allowed no expanse, is the source of the dense and convoluted nature of the swamp, seen now as a metaphor of Dred's imagination. The delicate compromise between innate faculties and the environment called for in Romanticism has been destroyed; there is a disquieting inevitability about this imagination that is subsequently projected onto the social situation that it in turn reflects. Having moved inward from an image of nature to an image of the imagination (or the unconscious, perhaps), Stowe moves out again to the image of a society seething with revolutionary potential: "The wild, dreary belt of swampland which girds in those states scathed by the fires of despotism is an apt emblem, in its rampant and we might say delirious exuberance of vegetation, of that darkly struggling, wildly vegetating swamp of human souls, cut off, like it, from the usages and improvements of cultivated life" (vol. 2, p. 274).

This kind of analogical thinking, exciting a constant exchange between the sphere of imagination and the world of social interaction through the realm of nature, gives Stowe's novel a potential thematic, symbolic, and psychological unity beneath the vagaries of its plot and character development.

In order to achieve the most sympathetic and meaningful reading, our discussion of Dred should therefore shift from a concern with overall surface texture and organization to an examination of theme in relation to imagery. Falling as it does near the end of the second volume, the passage just quoted brings into focus a variety of associations developed during the narrative that have interacted with one another to spark a series of creative insights. The highly suggestive physical world of the swamp has emerged as a multivalent symbol capable of extending its frame of reference indefinitely. Stowe is unfortunately not in control of the "message" that could subsume the diverse referents of the swamp under a coherent vision; she falls considerably short of the artistic integration that would enable her to generate a full-fledged symbolistic narrative. The constituents of such a vision are evident, however, and their inchoate status is indicative of Stowe's ambivalence toward her main character. Although she feared the anarchic implications of Dred's religious belief – his dedication to a kind of blood revenge – Stowe was compelled by the sincerity of that belief. As demonstrated by the many fissures throughout Dred between thematic development and emotional commitment, she failed to reconcile these contradictory motives symbolically.

The theme of Dred relates ultimately to Stowe's own effort to define an authentic selfhood in the face of a heritage that no longer offered fulfillment. In The Minister's Wooing (1858), Stowe crystallized this conflict specifically in terms of the Calvinist worldview, a creed at once embraced and resisted by her idealized self-personification, Mary Scudder. Mary's fervent, womanly religion of the heart subtly triumphs over the patriarchal, rationalistic theology of Samuel Hopkins. Though, as Lawrence Buell pointed out,[63] there was much about Hopkins's religious devotion and the grandeur of his theological system (with its central doctrine of disinterested benevolence) that commanded

Stowe's respect, she needed a more humanitarian and intuitive faith, one that would not require her willingness to be eternally damned for the glory of God.

Dred, whose primary thrust is political (antislavery, that is), offers only several formulations preliminary to this solution. Stowe is above all concerned with discriminating nominal from authentic Christians. The distinction is most evident in the contrast between the "piety" of Nina's Aunt Nesbit – a rigid, hypocritical adherence to social conventions and empty doctrines – and the high-toned but flexible moral fervor and social sympathy of Edward Clayton. A closely related formulation is Nina Gordon's conversion (however unconvincingly portrayed) from irresponsible role playing and consumerism to an ardent participation in the utopian visions of her lover, Clayton.

A crucial enactment of this theme of authenticity unfolds during the camp meeting, attended by most of the characters in the novel, which occurs at the end of the first volume. In depicting this gathering, Stowe emphasizes the varying reactions of her dramatis personae, reflecting their most deeply held values. Stowe's own point of view is essentially sympathetic.[64] She is especially fascinated by the "primitive" features of this form of social interaction, so prevalent in antebellum America. Moreover, she is attracted to the presence of what the anthropologist Victor Turner called "communitas," a social phenomenon in which the bonds are antistructural, that is, "undifferentiated, equalitarian, direct, extant, nonrational, existential, I-Thou . . . relationships."[65]

At one point during the meeting, the entire multitude of worshipers experiences a mystical sense of unity as they join together in a hymn:

> It would seem as if the breath that a crowd breathed out together, in moments of enthusiasm, carried with it a portion of the dread and mystery of their own immortal natures. The whole area before the pulpit, and in the distant aisles of the forest, became one vast, surging sea of sound, as Negroes and whites, slaves and freemen, saints and sinners, slave-holders, slave hunters, slave-traders, ministers, elders, and laymen, alike joined in the pulses of that mighty song. A flood of electrical excitement seemed to rise with it, as, with a voice of many waters, the rude chant went on. . . . (vol. 1, p. 304)

Through the reference to "the dread and mystery of their immortal natures," Stowe subtly links what she regards as the truest aspirations of humanity with the aura of the swamp and her black protagonist.

But although she admires the moment of communal transcendence, Stowe also recognizes the manipulation behind much of what goes on during the camp meeting:

> Those who conduct camp-meetings are generally men who, without much reasoning upon the subject, fall into a sort of tact, in influencing masses of mind, and pressing into the service all the great life forces and influences of nature. A kind of rude poetry pervades their minds, colors their dialect, and influences their arrangements. The solemn and harmonious grandeur of night, with all its mysterious power of exalt-

ing the passions and intensifying the emotions, has ever been appreci-
ated, and used by them with even poetic skill. (vol. 1, p. 314)

Such a manipulation of "means" is directly related to the swamp metaphor
when Stowe uses it to describe the preaching of Father Bonnie after the singing
of the hymn: "His discourse was like the tropical swamp, bursting out with
a lush abundance of every kind of growth – grave, gay, grotesque, solemn,
fanciful, and even coarse caricature, provoking the broadest laughter. The
audience was swayed by him like trees before the wind. There was not wanting
touches of rude pathos, as well as earnest appeals" (vol. 1, p. 306). The diverse
sensations evoked by the swamp reveal Stowe's complex feelings about this
kind of discourse.

Moreover, through Clayton's words, Stowe uses the imagery of the swamp
to concretize the opposition between the staid propriety of conventional society
– exemplified by Aunt Nesbit – and the sense of liberation produced by the
social ferment of the religious revival. Responding to his sister's shocked
reaction to the "wild freedom" of such camp meetings, Clayton expostulates:

> There spoke a true, well-trained conventionalist. . . . But look around
> you. See, in this wood, among these flowers, and festoons of vine,
> and arches of green, how many shocking, unsightly growths! You
> would not have had all this underbrush, these dead limbs, these briers
> running riot over trees, and sometimes choking and killing them. You
> would have well-trimmed trees and velvet turf. But I love briers, dead
> limbs and all, for their very savage freedom. . . . Unite any assembly
> of common men in a great enthusiasm, – work them up into an aban-
> don, and let every one "let go," and speak as nature prompts, – and
> you will have brush, underwood, briers, and all grotesque growths;
> but, now and then, some thought or sentiment will be struck out with
> a freedom or power such as you cannot get in any other way. You
> cultivated people are much mistaken when you despise the enthusi-
> asms of the masses. There is more truth than you think in the old
> "vox populi, vox Dei." (vol. 1, pp. 309–10)

Clayton's enthusiasm here carries him well beyond any sober consideration
of the dangerous effects such antinomian freedom might engender.

Stowe's own ambivalence remains understated throughout the scenes of the
camp meeting. The darker implications of the social phenomenon that Clayton
praises are, of course, implicit in the imagery he uses: "You would not have
had all this underbrush, these dead limbs, these briers running riot over trees,
and sometimes choking or killing them." Once again, uncontrolled growth,
as in Dred's imagination, is the frightening prospect. Also noteworthy is that
the piety expressed at the camp meeting, in keeping with the transitory nature
of this institution, allows men engaged in buying and selling slaves to feel
good about themselves. Father Bonnie himself, finely tuned engine of revival-
istic preaching that he is, easily reconciles religion and slaveholding.

Much is made, too, of the inevitable backsliding that follows a revival. The
problem is brought home dramatically, if implicitly, in the final scenes of the
camp meeting in which Dred's thundering voice is heard addressing the as-

sembly as a biblical prophet of doom. Dred cannot be seen as he leaps from tree to tree with incredible agility. Most of those who hear him are apparently taken in by the ruse, bringing to mind the old question of how Abraham knew that the voice he heard was God's and not the Devil's.[66] The moral dilemma is intrinsic to the phantasmagoria of the entire scene, the overwrought excitement of the multitude, the surrounding wilderness, the lurid night. The question still occupies Stowe in the ensuing narrative and influences her judgment of Dred and his fate and her apprehension of the swamp that metaphorically links the social cauldron of the revival with the rebelliousness simmering among the fugitive slaves who follow Dred.

The exchange between Nina and Aunt Nesbit that follows Clayton's panegyric on the wild freedom of the camp meeting places this issue in the broader context of American religious history. Clayton declares for the religion of nature and embraces its democratic implications: "I reverence the people, as I do the woods, for the wild, grand freedom with which their humanity develops itself." On hearing this, Aunt Nesbit turns to Nina and says in low tones, "I'm afraid he isn't orthodox."

> "What makes you think so, aunt?"
> "O, I don't know; his talk hasn't the real sound."
> "You want something that ends in 'ation,' don't you, aunt? – justification, sanctification, or something of that kind." (vol. 1, p. 310)

But if Stowe's sympathies lie essentially with the religion of nature, Dred's character exemplified for her the excesses to which nature could lead the truly devout self. Dred indeed is "perfectly *en rapport*" with nature:

> So completely had he come into sympathy and communion with nature, and with those forms of it which more particularly surrounded him in the swamp, that he moved about among them with as much ease as a lady treads her Turkey carpet.... To walk knee-deep in the spongy soil of the swamp, to force his way through thickets, to lie all night sinking in the porous soil, or to crouch, like the alligator, among the reeds and rushes, were to him situations of as much comfort as well-curtained beds and pillows are to us. (vol. 2, p. 16)

While his body thus comfortably inhabits the swamp, Dred's mind occupies an "indefinite land" (inaccessible to the "hot and positive light of our modern materialism") that lies between the sane and the insane. He passes most of the time in a "strange and abnormal condition": "It was a state of exaltation and trance, which yet appeared not at all to impede the exercise of his outward and physical faculties, but rather to give them a preternatural keenness and intensity, such as sometimes attends the more completely-developed phenomenon of somnambulism" (vol. 2, pp. 5–6).

If Dred is at one with nature, it is a nature exaggerated and distorted, nature as manifested in the swamp. Stowe's vacillation on this point is a measure of her ambivalence. Obviously, there is something exciting, even erotic, in such excessiveness. The prophetic passages in the Bible through which Dred has been "seized and possessed by the wrath of an avenging God" (vol. 2, p. 278) impress Stowe with their "wild, inspiring power, like a wordless yet impassioned symphony played by a sublime orchestra, in which deep and awful sub-bass instruments mingle with those of ethereal softness, and wild minors twine and interlace with marches of battles and bursts of victorious harmony" (vol. 2, p. 215). We are not allowed to forget, moreover, that the essence of Dred's criminality, especially in relation to Southern society, is his ability to take the Bible at its word; the Bible is indeed a revolutionary document.

If we are to grasp the intensity of the conflict in Stowe's mind, we must realize the extent to which she felt drawn, even compelled by, Dred. More than ten years before she created her slave insurrectionist, Stowe set forth the germinal concept he would embody in a letter to her brother Thomas describing her conversion experience:

> The most hopeless class of minds to me are those self-satisfied ones whom a few favorite ideas and theories of their own seem capable of contenting, and who have no conception of the deep, immortal longing which pursues spirits of another order – a longing which, whether developed in diseased action, as in superstition and fanaticism, or in intense, never-satisfied worldly fore-reaching, or haunting the mind amid floods of accomplished wish and successful effort like an unlaid ghost, is yet, in all these forms, a high and sacred relic of a better nature.

Describing how this "more earnest and craving desire" is suppressed by "what is called common sense," Stowe revealed her attraction to the drama of slavery: It was basically a simulacrum of the pent-up condition of her own religious longing. Worldly wisdom crushes desire, lays

> its stern hand upon it, hushes its mouth, as some vagrant gipsy who would degrade a high-born child to unwonted and disgusting servitude, repressing its cries for father and mother, and grinding it down to outward service by stern assurances that such, and such only, are its portion; and yet, though the child learns to be still, and to labor in uncomplaining despair in its bondage – nay, though it becomes so habituated to it that it can scarce conceive of living any other way, and though all its physical habits may have become so reversed and unadapted that a return to that home and father may neither be desired nor attempted, still, deep within, the perverse longing groans, and sighs, and bleeds, and murmurs – all in vain.[67]

Here was the root of slavery's shocking denial: its disruption of paternal love and domestic order in the destruction of the slave family. For Stowe, the emotional bondage of the family was not simply the basis for a healthy social life (her ideal of a matriarchal social order) but also the heart of a vital and authentic religious faith. Dred preserves only a lopsided version of this familial relationship with the world, for his conception of the family has shrunk to exclude his enemies; he lacks true Christian charity. It is Milly, whose love embraces all of humanity, persecutor as well as friend, in maternal patience and forgiveness, who creates the familial situation virtually *ex nihilo*. But despite his ultimate failure, Dred deserves the eulogy Stowe composed for him more than a decade before the fact: "But that repressed and crushed longing, useless, unreasonable, without end or purpose, is all that remains of the captive of a noble lineage and high inheritance; and even though it become mania or moroseness, or though it unfit him for anything else, 'tis all one, there it is, a mournful fragment of something divine.' "[68]

In Stowe's mind, religious longing became equated with the organicism of the swamp, and the rampant, grotesque growth of its forms was associated with an unjust and distorted Southern society (contrasted with the "communitas" experienced during the singing of the hymn at the camp meeting). Accordingly, Dred and the landscape he inhabits represent not ends in themselves but means of redefining values and moral orientation. Like pollution beliefs in primitive cultures, such symbolic means as the swamp tend to be entertained only provisionally, as sources of power from beyond the threshold of the normative, which help bring about adjustment to changing circumstance.[69] But Stowe went beyond this dichotomy to establish a positive value system based on the imagery of the clearing in the swamp.

In *Dred*, primal felicity characterizes the relationship to the swamp of the children Fanny and Teddy, wards of the devoted slave Old Tiff. Into the swamp they escape from their demented father, who is the product of a misshaped Southern society. Their "flight into Egypt" is portrayed in the description of Fanny's sanctuary in the swamp, a "bed chamber" image that melds natural with domestic motifs:

> The moonlight, as it came sliding down through the checkered, leafy roof, through fragments and gleams of light, which moved capriciously here and there over the ground, revealing now a great silvery fern-leaf, and then a tuft of white flowers, gilding spots on the branches and trunks of the trees; while every moment the deeper shadows were lighted up by the gleaming of fire-flies. . . . Everything was so still, so calm, so pure, no wonder she was prepared to believe that the angels of the Lord were to be found in the wilderness. They who have walked in closest communion with nature have ever found that they have not departed thence. The wilderness and solitary places are still glad for them, and their presence makes the desert to rejoice and blossom as the rose. (vol. 2, p. 167)

The children enjoy a spontaneous friendship with Dred, who shows his softest side to them, teaching them about nature as if he were a reincarnated St. Francis. Here, Stowe's fascination with Dred comes into line with her idealism in a reconciliation that serves as the emotional *omphalos* of the entire novel. The clearing in the swamp, the natural correlative of the children's relation to the world, contains both the rootedness and energy of the swamp and the welcoming inner space of the domestic ideal. In this integration of emotional energy and commitment with a holistic sense of experience imparted by the maternal role, Stowe expressed her essential religious conviction, an effective alternative to the patriarchal faith of the fathers.

Like Simms's Cavalier hidden and sustained in the munificent fastnesses of the swamp, Stowe's Dred embodied a deeply embedded intuition of instinctual wholeness and relation to the world that gave some weight to the loftiest aspirations but nonetheless could never be reconciled with the normal demands of communal life. For inherent in instinct is an erratic genius, subverting stable structures. The duality lies at the source of the mythological figure of the Great Mother, an archetype that represents the unconscious power of nature. To the questing hero, this figure of the "eternal feminine," the passionate chthonic goddess, presented an aspect alternately nurturing and threatening. As long as he submitted to immersion in her voluptuous and fecund body, the hero received sustenance from the "Good" Mother. According to Erich Neumann, in this condition man "is bathed in the abundance of vegetative life in forest and steppe, in mountain and valley."[70] This is the condition of Simms's partisans. But the "Good" Mother who bestows sustenance turns into the "Terrible" Mother who threatens annihilation if the hero tries to establish his independence by, in some way, going beyond the objective reality of nature.

Not surprisingly, depth psychologists have fastened on the swamp as an especially suggestive image for the corresponding stage of psychological development. The painful awareness of immersion and the sense of entanglement experienced in the swamp express the menacing aspect of the incestuous mother jealous of her son's growing independence and self-assertion. To those steeped in patriarchy, there is something frighteningly irresponsible about this figure of man's natural estate. The Great Mother "who feeds man with fruits and tubers and grains . . . also poisons him and lets him hunger and thirst in times of drought, when she withdraws from living things."[71]

This is, of course, a romantic account of human development. But it is appropriate, I feel, because it shares its sources and ideological orientation with the Romantic texts we have been examining here. One might well object, however, to the assumption that the psyche experiences an instinctive affinity with nature (as entailed, for instance, in the swamp), an affinity that is untroubled by any sense of threat. Lacanian psychoanalysis provides another version of sexual differentiation that breaks with the essentialism and symmetry of the Jungian view reflected by Neumann. We shall pursue the implications of this other view later when we address those aspects of American culture ready to move beyond an "objective" nature.[72]

In any case, the unpredictability of nature was anathema to the civilizing mind which sought to transcend the primordial chaos through the sublimation of instinct, the denial of impulse in a program of consistent self-sacrifice. For mid-nineteenth-century Americans, self-sacrifice was the fundamental initiation into society. The convention of the Yankee pointed to the abuse of self-sacrifice in the service of a narrow materialism: Puritan self-discipline and Republican virtue in the long run almost inevitably abetted the desire for self-aggrandizement. These cultural modes involved too radical a denial of nature; they suppressed the Mother principle that gave humans a sense of place, an emotional attachment to origins and the instinctual sources of being. The values embodied by the Cavalier myth countered this extremity: The attitude of noble indifference to personal gain – with its grounding in seigneurial assumptions – combined with the personal refinement, spontaneity, and *joie de vivre* of the natural aristocrat to oppose what appeared to be the growing trend toward acquisitiveness, individual isolation, and cultural barrenness, behind which a middle-class identity was forming. The appeal to Christian charity and the domestic ideal represented alternative channels through which this dominant trend could be directed.

We have seen how the image of the swamp was used as a mode of adjustment, of symbolic compensation, to new social forces. Ultimately, this iconology of reorientation to changing social reality was not satisfactory, for it perpetuated, if in less stringent form, the same traditional moral dichotomies that had contributed to the need for adjustment in the first place. This type of adjustment was both conservative and literal in its definition of society. Just as it continued to cast nature in an objective light, thereby subjecting the mind to its control, it also assumed the reality of society and consequently upheld the duality of civilization and nature – the notion of two forces competing against each other for human allegiance – which could lead in the end only to a fundamental ambivalence. This tendency to take nature and society at face value lay behind Simms's failure to reconcile the Cavalier and Yankee types and Stowe's inability (beyond her artistic failure) to unify all the disparate referents of the swamp in *Dred* under a coherent vision, as Melville did with the "Whiteness of the Whale" or Nathaniel Hawthorne with the letter "A."

It is only when we shift our attention from the predominant ideologies to the possibilities for meaning in the image itself that the constituents begin to emerge for a truly new and radical symbolic mode. This is not one that enabled adjustment to an unsatisfactory ratio between nature and civilization, perpetuating ideas conditioned by patriarchy and an emergent market mentality, but one that transcended the duality between nature and civilization itself. Such transcendence, I believe, was most fully realized by Thoreau. Though only a prelude to further struggles, the realization of this mode opened the way to at least some periodic or furtive escape from the treadmill of human subjugation to the world of appearances, to materialism, to the conventional, that had been constructed by capitalism. In at least a few instances in Mid-Victorian America, the experience of the swamp involved a more intense encounter with the overwhelming body of "mother nature" that could transform the meaning of initiation from a mere readiness for citizenship in normal society to full acceptance in a community of grace.

PART TWO

The Phenomenology of Disintegration

When you first feel the ground under your feet
Going soft and uncertain,
Its best to start running as fast as you can slog
Even though falling
Forward on your knees and lunging like a cripple.
You may escape completely
Being bogged down in those few scampering seconds
But if you're caught standing
In deep mud, unable to walk or stagger,
Its time to reconsider
Your favorite postures, textures, and means of moving
Coming to even terms
With the kind of dirt that won't take no for an answer.
  David Wagoner, "Walking in a Swamp" (1976)

A certain fame! But that's nothing to what he will have. How can he paint gray, faint, half-alive things now? He must abound in color, – be rich, exhaustless: wild sea-sketches, – sunrise, – sunset, mountain mists rolling in turbid crimson masses, breaking in a milky spray of vapor round lofty peaks, and letting out lonely glimpses of a melancholy moon, – South American splendors, – pomps of fruit and blossom, – all this affluence of his future life must flash from his pencils now. Not that he will paint again directly. Do you suppose it possible that I should be given him merely for a phase of wealth and light and color, and then taken, – taken in some dreadful way, to teach him the necessary and inevitable result of such extravagant luxuriance? It makes me shiver.
  Harriet Prescott Spofford, "The Amber Gods" (1865)

Frederic Church in the Tropics

Before the swamp could be reconceived and exert an impact on cultural sensibility in Mid-Victorian America, certain things had to occur to bring the unusual phenomenology of this landscape to the fore. The next three chapters indicate how the swamp came to be cast in a new, more intense and objective light. Endemic to this change in perception was the growing spirit of exploration and adventure that was spurred by the transportation revolution and that accompanied capitalistic expansionism. Furthermore, the continuing refinement of perception, with its aesthetic of close observation, resulted from rapid scientific advances. By the mid-nineteenth century, these trends were affecting both American nature writing and landscape painting. Finally, the perception and meaning of the swamp were in part transformed by the swamp's growing association with the Latin American jungle.

On April 8, 1853, the young painter Frederic E. Church embarked from New York for the coast of Colombia to begin a journey of several months' duration through the wilds of the Andes. Church was to become not only the most popular American painter of his day but also the leading exponent of what Henry T. Tuckerman called "the indomitable explorative enterprise of the New England mind"[1] as it pertained to landscape painting. In 1859, with the unveiling of *The Heart of the Andes* (Figure 4.1), critics heralded a new era in American art. The same year saw the publication of Charles Darwin's *On the Origin of Species,* but for the moment most Americans lived with confidence in the ultimate reconciliation of science and religion.[2] Some time around 1850, Church had read the works of the world-famous German scientist Alexander von Humboldt, the last of the great encyclopedic minds of the Enligtenment.[3] Now he was answering Humboldt's challenge to artists to explore the unprecedented aesthetic possibilities in the landscape of the tropics. His trek through Latin America approximated Humboldt's in 1802. Indeed, in the vicinity of Quito, he lodged in the same house and with the same family Humboldt had visited a half-century earlier.

Humboldt had focused on the imagistic qualities of tropical scenery:

Figure 4.1. Frederic Church, *The Heart of the Andes* (1857). Bequest of Mrs. David Dows, 1909. The Metropolitan Museum of Art, New York.

Are we not justified in hoping that landscape painting will flourish with a new and hitherto unknown brilliancy when artists of merit shall more frequently pass the narrow limits of the Mediterranean, and when they shall be enabled far in the interior of continents, in humid mountain valleys of the tropical world, to seize, with genuine freshness of a pure and youthful spirit, on the true image of the varied forms of nature?[4]

Considering the kind of painting he was already producing, Church must have been especially excited by the German scientist's dictum that landscape painting evolves through the periodic infusion of "a large number of various and direct impressions" fertilized by the artist's mind.[5]

Humboldt had been concerned with "that important stage of our communion with the external world, when the enjoyment arising from the laws, and the mutual connection of Phenomena, associates itself with the charm of a simple contemplation of nature."[6] He concluded, "We may here trace the revelation of a bond of union, linking together the visible world and that higher spiritual world which escapes the grasp of the senses."[7] This "philosophy of nature" called for an aesthetic that relied on specificity, not a "vague intuition." "I can not, therefore, agree with Burke," Humboldt declared, "when he says, 'it is our ignorance of natural things that causes all our admiration, and chiefly excites our passions.' " Nature would more fully serve the cause of revelation as it acquired, through scientific investigation, "the certainty of a positive truth."[8]

In his quest "to make the remote wonders of nature known to all the civilized world,"[9] Church reflected Humboldt's reconciliation of the scientific study of nature with religious faith. Humboldt enabled artists to place their visions of nature, as embodiments of religious and moral truths, on a solid basis of fact. Church would have agreed with Louis Agassiz that the "relations and proportions which exist throughout the animal and vegetable world have an intellectual, and ideal connection in the mind of the Creator"; that the plan of creation was "matured in his thoughts, before it was manifested in tangible forms."[10]

Inspired by Humboldt's insights, Church went to nature "not so much with the tenderness of a lover or the awe of a worshiper, as with the determination, the intelligence, the patient intrepidity of a student."[11] Henry T. Tuckerman's panegyric on Church in the *Book of the Artists* (1867) emphasized the artist's scientific approach and its close relation to his realism.[12] Church's grandiose visions of tropical mountain scenery, beginning with the popular *Heart of the Andes* that followed his second trip to Latin America in 1857, amazed viewers with their size and microscopic detail. They were shown alone as "sensation" pictures. Visitors to Church's quarters in New York City, where *The Heart of the Andes* was first displayed – surrounded by black curtains and actual specimens of tropical foliage and lit by hidden gaslights – brought their opera glasses along in order to "traverse" the landscape as if they were actually in it, inspecting its myriad features firsthand.

Besides the minute detail (especially in the depiction of the jungle vegetation), the painting was energized by dynamic lines of force that related directly to evidence in the actual landscape of the continual cataclysmic processes of creation and recreation.[13] The Reverend Louis Legrand Noble, in his broadside for Church's great painting, chose to concentrate on this aspect of its power as essential to a recharged metaphysical awareness:

> Prodigies of volcanic force are those great Andes. In grand tones these pictured ones roll out that truth upon the beholder's imagination with impressive power. Miracles of elemental labor are the summits, sides, and gorges of those huge ranges. The painted vale, with its attending heights, has the tale of that labor written in the thousand lines, graved in the countless fissures, frescoed in the stains and dyes, cut in the keen edges, sculptured in the rounded masses. Everywhere you see the footprints and marks of the busy, toiling elements.[14]

In this respect, Church's art was an accurate index of the prevailing geological theory. As Robert Hunt, in *The Poetry of Science* (1850), observed: "The mutations of the old earth may be read upon her rocks and mountains, and these records of former changes tell us the infallible truth, that as the present passes into the future, so will the form of Earth undergo an important alteration. The same forces which lifted the Andes and the Himalayas are still at work. . . ."[15]

The exciting idea here is the notion of process. In an article called "Nature in Motion," a writer in *Putnam's* called attention to the fact that "the very heart of the globe is restless. Fused, molten stones are dragged from their hidden resting-places in the depths of the earth, passed through fiery ovens and at last, in fierce fury, thrown out of volcanoes, where, as lava streams they soon become solid, fertile and fruit bearing, or form new mountains on lands, new islands in the ocean."[16] This dynamism was particularly evident in the tropical ecology where natural processes were so precipitous as to be actually visible. Here again, according to Noble, Church had achieved a successful translation: "Trees and verdure are painted with a just perception of those life forces in virtue of which all spring from the germ, and swell to maturity: painted also with an intelligent sense of the presence and active influence of the elements."[17]

The theme of Humboldt's works, culminating in his monumental *Cosmos* (first American edition, 1850), was the link between the physical life of the earth – perceived as a complex of harmoniously interacting forces – and the character of its inhabitants. As David C. Huntington found, this idea had particular appeal for Americans in the age of Manifest Destiny.[18] Church's paintings of the tropics like *Cotopaxi* (1862), *Chimborazo* (1864), and *Rainy Season in the Tropics* (1866), as well as such works as *Niagara* (1857), his first major success, reflected the popular notion that the New World awaited the imminent advent of the millennium.[19] Advocates of this theory tended to assume the natural determinism available to them through contemporary science.[20] Robert Hunt, for instance, proclaimed that "from the particles of matter carried from the present lands by the rivers into the sea where they subside in stratified masses, there will, in the great future, be raised a new world, upon which the work of life will go forward, and over which will be spread a vast intelligence."[21] In this context, the scenery of Latin America, unsurpassed in its grandeur, stood as a reinvigorated image of the New Eden, holding forth the promise of a regenerate world.

Church combined his "stereoscopic" space[22] with his careful selection of elements to create an ideal but attainable universe whose scientific precision supposedly precluded the vagaries and self-indulgence of the artist's subjective impressions. As Louis Noble maintained, commenting on *The Heart of the Andes,* "Some apprehension of the process of landscape-*making* by the instru-mentalities of the Creator, is necessary in order successfully to conduct the process of landscape-*painting* by the feeble instrumentalities of man. . . . "[23] Church accordingly used science to renew the tradition of literal-historical typology derived from his Puritan ancestors. By contrast, Church's teacher, Thomas Cole, had declared: "After all, Beauty is in the mind. A scene is rather an index of feelings and associations. History and poetry make the barren hills of Scotland glorious to Scott. . . . " Cole's associationism led him to gloomy meditations on the prospect of decay, the fear that humans might not transcend nature in the long run which prompted the faith that God's great design would not allow the spirit of nature to sink "into the gloomy gulf of non-existence."[24]

This was the difference between allegory and a more literal understanding of the world – appealing to both scientific and self-evident truth – which was easily adapted to communal or even nationalistic ventures.[25] Church's literal-historical hermeneutic of the natural world obviated a subjective response. Like the Bible, the natural revelation needed only the proper context in order to speak for itself. The artist's idiosyncrasies must not intervene.

Though he would not have agreed with Church's "scientific" approach or understood the application of landscape painting to the purposes of Manifest Destiny, John Ruskin shared a similar view of the artist's relation to nature. It is likely that his *Modern Painters* greatly influenced Church as he developed his synthesis. We know that Church read the newly published third and fourth volumes in 1856 and then reviewed the first two. Ruskin touched responsive chords in Church especially when he pleaded, in *Modern Painters IV,* for "pure, plain, and accurate truth" that described God, "not as revealing Himself in any peculiar way . . . but doing what He is still doing before our eyes day by day."[26]

In this respect, Ruskin's message agreed with Humboldt's. Church's Rus-kinism was, however, submerged by the rhetoric of an essentially oratorical style of painting that was uniquely American. As the Reverend George Wash-ington Bethune asked, "What is Art but another form of poetry and eloquence? When do we feel the power of the bard or of the orator most? Is it not when he brings the idea he would impress, fully, as in a picture, before the eye of the mind?"[27] In seeking out "objects in nature as are exceptional and impres-sive,"[28] Church slighted the Ruskinian notion of "truth to nature." Whereas Ruskin's Turner had relied on what his eye actually saw as the criterion of Truth, Church depended on what he knew to be there, as dictated by the need for inspiring effect. It is perhaps this distinction that lies behind Ruskin's judgment of Church, expressed in a letter to Charles Eliot Norton. Despite being impressed by the artist's gifts, Ruskin was doubtful whether Church would "ever know what painting means."[29]

Church's interest in nature lay in the heroic and the dramatic, for these were the qualities that best symbolized the religious and moral tone of the Old Testament. *The Heart of the Andes* was meant to be seen in these terms: as a drama of moral endeavor that climaxes in a vision of serenity and light. In the narrative development of the painting from the shadowy, jungle-cloaked regions of the lower part of the canvas up to the sublime, sun-drenched heights of the great dome ("an emblem of permanent and infinite peace"), Theodore Winthrop – like Church, a latter-day Puritan – saw "one steady movement upward of this bold, earth-born Hyperion higher toward the masterful heights . . . nearer and nearer the region of final mysterious battle in clouds and darkness, on the verge of final triumph beyond the veil." As Winthrop continued, in his pamphlet explicating the painting, "Peace and light dwell upon the Dome. Here is a contrast of mystery and dim chaos; – yet no grim obscure; no shock of hurtling storms. The sun penetrates the veil, and the heights grow pallid-rosy."[30]

Winthrop noted the battle of light and shadow in the picture, a formalistic element that directly contributed to its meaning. The "tumultuous surface" of the canvas "represents vigor and toil and perplexity" (p. 351). The painting unequivocally glorifies the action that leads to the repose of the heavenly dome. Contemporary viewers were familiar with its visual vocabulary. As Ruskin, the ultimate authority, maintained: "Mountains are, to the rest of the body of the earth, what violent muscular action is to the body of man. The muscles and tendons of its anatomy are, in the mountain, brought out with fierce and convulsive energy, full of expression, passion, and strength. . . ."[31] The dome is nothing less than the sum of natural revelation. According to Winthrop, "What Nature has deemed man fit to receive, is here bestowed in one largess. All earth's riches are compacted into one many-sided crystal" (p. 341).

The Heart of the Andes represents a moral drama that encompasses a psychological drama, placing it in a larger, clearer perspective. The victory, in the contention of forces on the canvas, lies in the upper half of the painting, with altitude, action, and light. "Dim chaos" is overcome, and an atmosphere of joy prevails. Referring to the luminous blue sky that constitutes the backdrop around the dome, breaking through the clouds over the Cordilleras, Winthrop commented, "It is pure, penetrable, lucent in every tremulous atom of its substance, and as the eye pierces its depths, it feels the same vital quiver thrilling through a boundless calm" (p. 344). Winthrop deemphasized the dense rain forest on the right side of the painting, what he referred to as "the gloaming mystery of the Montaña" (p. 369), entered through a glade. This region, he noted, contrasts with the open road on the left, guiding the viewer past the cross and toward the dome. Surely there is a warning implicit here not to enter a region as "doubtful and dim" as the Cordillera higher up but offering no challenge, as these mountains do, to "manly energy."

The darker regions of the jungle, defying the penetration of moral insight, fall into "proper" perspective through the immensity of the vista as well as its upward movement. As in Washington Allston's *Elijah in the Wilderness* (1818), the psychological drama (referring to the state of the artist's soul) in the wasteland of the foreground is overwhelmed by the moral and specifically typological perspective of the luminous background.[32] The panoramic view was repeated in American painting to teach the triumph of faith and moral striving over the natural impulses. In such panoramas, the audience maintained a discursive distance from the subject at hand. In one sense, this was an important aspect of the general relation of illusionistic painting to Romantic sensibility. As in the eighteenth-century landscape paintings that expressed the sublime, viewers never lost the sense that they were only looking at a picture on a wall;[33] that is, the terror of the sublime was limited to an aesthetic experience.

Marshall McLuhan and Harley Parker showed that paintings that use illusionistic techniques, especially scientific perspective – providing viewers with a space to see into rather than a space to be experienced through touch as well as sight – isolate viewers from the subject and allow them to rationalize their experience.[34] Church's canvases also function in this way, advancing ordinary experience by creating a sense of stereoscopic space.

Although he translated his experience into an ideal world on the canvas, Church could not avoid confronting certain implications of this experience. First are the sensuality and allure of the tropical vegetation itself, as it is depicted in the nether regions of *The Heart of the Andes*. Artistic prophets had always immersed themselves in the threatening wilds of nature in order to extract their inspiring visions. According to Henry T. Tuckerman, Church was no exception: "Traversing the woods on mules, the artist and his companion endured all the privations, and enjoyed all the wonders of a tropical journey. They were tormented by insects, and passed hours in making their way through the dense undergrowth."[35]

Just as the spectacular scenery of Latin America was summoned to the cause of moral thought, imparting a new charge to traditional associations, so the dense hinterland standing in the way of this scenery levied its psychic toll, not only with renewed vigor, but also with important variations, leading the self in unforeseen directions. Tuckerman tells us of one of Church's adventures that could not have failed to leave a lasting mark on a less exuberant temperament:

> One dark night an accident separated [Church and his companion].
> The bridle paths were dangerous without a guide; not a sign of human dwellings was visible; the hootings of owls and the howlings of beasts increased the interminable brushwood. Now up to his knees in a morass, and now entangled amid the vine-covered trees, the intrepid limner climbed a tree and long shouted in vain. The mules had slipped away, his companion was ill, and worn out by fatigue, he found temporary repose on an anthill. After many disappointments, he succeeded at length in finding the track of his guides, and resuming his journey under more favorable auspices.[36]

Whatever the case, the bewilderment and exposure to the elements that Church (and no doubt others) experienced in such adventure did not come to fruition until his powerful *Morning in the Tropics* (1876) (Figure 4.2). Church was too ebullient, too responsive to the bright sensual appeal of tropical vegetation (as evidenced in his travel journals and letters home) to acknowledge the morbid underside of the jungle. Yet the sequence of his major tropical

Figure 4.2. Frederic Church, *Morning in the Tropics* (canvas, 54⅜ × 84⅛ in. [1.381 × 2.137 cm.], 1876). Gift of the Avalon Foundation, National Gallery of Art, Washington, D.C.

Plates

1 Martin Johnson Heade, *The Great Florida Sunset*
2 Joseph Rusling Meeker, *The Land of Evangeline*
3 Ransom Gillette Holredge, Untitled
4 Thomas Moran, *Slaves Escaping Through a Swamp*
5 Frederic Church, *Morning in the Tropics*
6 Martin Johnson Heade, *Passion Flowers and Hummingbirds*
7 Winslow Homer, *In the Jungle, Florida*

Plate 1. Martin Johnson Heade, *The Great Florida Sunset*. Courtesy of Sotheby Parke-Bernet.

Plate 2. Joseph Rusling Meeker, *The Land of Evangeline* (1874). The Saint Louis Art Museum. Funds given by Mrs. W. P. Edgerton, by exchange.

Plate 3. Ransom Gillette Holdredge, Untitled. Private collection, D. C. Hildebrand.

Plate 4. Thomas Moran, *Slaves Escaping Through a Swamp* (1865). Laura A. Clubb Collection, Philbrook Museum of Art, Tulsa, Okla.

Plate 5. Frederic Church, *Morning in the Tropics*. National Gallery of Art, Washington, D.C. Gift of the Avalon Foundation.

Plate 6. Martin Johnson Heade, *Passion Flowers and Hummingbirds*. Courtesy of the Museum of Fine Arts, Boston.

Plate 7. Winslow Homer, *In the Jungle, Florida* (1904). Museum Collection Fund and Special Subscription, The Brooklyn Museum, New York.

Figure 4.3. Frederic Church, *Morning in the Tropics* (1856). Walters Art Gallery, Baltimore.

works, from *The Heart of the Andes* to *Chimborazo* (1865) to *The Vale of St. Thomas, Jamaica* (1867) to *Morning in the Tropics* seems to chart a progressive loss of vision. Already in *Chimborazo,* the snow-capped peak appears to float specterlike above the jungle, testifying to a certain draining of conviction. *The Vale of St. Thomas, Jamaica* evokes immersion both in the tempest that hovers over and engulfs the mountains and in the immediacy of the foreground jungle. On the other hand, the piquant, sardonic elements of such early works as *Scene on the Magdalene* (1854) or the dreamy mystery of the small *Morning in the Tropics* (1856) (Figure 4.3) prove that from the very beginning of his encounter with the tropics, Church was exploring a mode alternative to the typological. And then again, there are Church's many sketches of jungle vegetation (Figure 4.4).

Still, all these visual conceptions are essentially optimistic in tone. Not so with *Morning in the Tropics*, which places us within the landscape. The background is unrelieved by the translucent blue of overarching sky; rather, it is cloaked in mist and glows with preternatural light. The precisely delineated foliage in the foreground, almost metallic in appearance, seems to shimmer with flashes of malevolent intent. Although the painting can be seen superficially as yet another religious vision (in the reference to morning and in the crosslike form created by the light), its meaning is at best ambiguous.

It is interesting, in this regard, to find a similar attitude reflected in the description of a landscape by Paul Marçoy, whose *Travels in South America,* translated from the French and published in America in 1875, Church owned.

Nothing more attractive can be imagined than this spot, so still, so freshly cool, so mysterious, above which rise the deeply-indented umbels of the Latanias, the spindly stems of the Acrocomias and of the

Figure 4.4. Frederic Church, *Deep Jungle Foliage* (1856, oil on paperboard), Cooper-Hewitt Museum, New York.

> Calami. . . . Here and there on the little grassy islets, which the river sometimes covers, sometimes leaves bare, glitter, like the sheaves and coronas of a *fen d'artifice,* the yellow and pink particles of the Latanus . . . the magnificent corolla of an *Amaryllis reginae,* a dull purple striped with white and green, in the bottom of which sparkles a drop of water, a liquid diamond dropped from the casket of Aurora, which the sun is in the act of dissolving in the fire of his rays.

Church's picture corresponds to this description not only in mood and attractiveness but also in its careful scientific observation; it is the outdoor study of a botanist. What is fascinating is that Marçoy's description turns abruptly on the reader in a tactic reminiscent of Ishmael's in "The Mast-Head" chapter of *Moby-Dick* ("Heed it well, ye Pantheists!"):

> This charming little haven, which the reader might admire upon the faith of our description, and whose waters, always calm, seem to invite the stranger to taste the pleasures of the bath, is a dreadful haunt of alligators. There the voracious monsters lurk behind the pendant branches, some half-concealed by the rank vegetation, some sunk in the water, apparently insensible to everything, but with ears open to the slightest sound, and only waiting for a favourable moment to spring upon their prey. O dreamer, O poet! whom your instinct might draw into this pleasant haven, to dream at your ease and string rhymes at your pleasure, avoid its deceitful shades![37]

We can only guess as to whether Marçoy was the inspiration for Church's vision. Nonetheless, in this last of Church's great tropical works, the sinister

Figure 4.5. Frederic Church, *Jungle Scene* (1891). Courtesy of the New York State Office of Parks, Recreation and Historic Preservation, Olana State Historic Site, Taconic Region.

undertones of the swamp emerge in the heart of the tropics. The apparition, arising from the remains of the broken synthesis of knowledge and faith, evokes the desperate struggle for survival at the core of nature. Church's own struggle for survival along with that of the fated Romantic ethos of nature, as the nineteenth century came to a close, seems to be represented by a very late (1891) oil sketch (Figure 4.5) which pictures a white bird floating toward a barely perceptible opening to the sky from the dim and tortuous recesses of a jungle interior. Likewise, the 1870s and 1880s marked a dramatic reversal in the interests of the American art public and with it came a drastic decline in the fortunes of America's leading landscape painter.

The Penetration of the Jungle

Again and again in the many accounts of voyages to the tropics that appeared in periodicals and travel books in the 1850s, a striking pattern recurs. As the perspective of the traveler changes from the panoramic to bodily immersion, the nature of the experience is also altered. This might seem to belabor the obvious were it not that the transition from image to environment – so dramatic in itself – was full of fascinating symbolic implications. Eden, seen from close up, was apt to seem more like Gehenna. As a vista, tropical mountain scenery appeared utterly resplendent:

> There were the grand mountains of Costa Rica ever within sight – oftentimes within pistol-shot – glittering in their dark-green and purple glory, from the rising to the setting of each sun, and at night deepening with their majestic forms the darkness of the sky. Pictures of shadowy deep ravines – great leafy branches over-arching them, their walls trickling with moisture, and a full stream, cold and bright, bounding over rocks, plunging into green transparent basins which the sunshine veined with gold, and then with a smooth swiftness widening off between two strips of sand and pebbles – the fragrance of flowers and the notes of birds, the most beautiful and wonderful on earth, pervading all – such were the appeasing pictures which those mountains ceaselessly suggested.[1]

To most travelers at mid-century, the landscape represented a larger-than-life spectacle, existence teeming with possibility, beauty unsurpassed.[2] Explorers like Church were inspired to record its natural wonders. Others like Louis Agassiz went to study its scientific curiosities. The volcanoes of Latin America, fulfilling the aims of both aesthetic and geological pursuits (as evidence of nature in process), held forth the allure of natural meccas. Most Americans, of course, were not of the reverent, pilgrimaging sort. They came to the tropics in order to exploit their resources, especially minerals. The seductive vision that greeted everyone, often upon the first sight of land, rose like a mirage before their eyes. Yet its charms quickly subsided when entering the far less welcoming interior.

The same writer who surveyed the prospect just quoted later had an entirely different experience, in his effort to reach the volcano of Chiriqui. He and his party made their way

> through mountains so wild and lonesome, in such appalling rains as fall there, over rivers such as thunder through these solitudes, in the midst of dismaying perplexities to which such dark tracts of forest oftentimes give rise – day after day advancing through the undisturbed domain of the wild beast and reptile, between dawn and sundown ascending and descending thousands of feet with torn hands and swollen ankles, lying down for the night under a roof of woven palm-branches, with Indian followers snoring and steaming to the right and left of you, and a pile of green logs crackling and sputtering, and slug-gishly rolling up a smothering cloud of smoke, through which the bat and fire-fly never cease to flit. . . . [3]

The tropical environment mounted an almost overwhelming assault on the senses. Observing the tropical growth along the Chagres River in Panama, Bayard Taylor provided a typical catalogue of natural abundance:

> Blossoms of crimson, purple and yellow, of a form and magnitude unknown in the North, are mingled with the leaves and flocks of par-oquets and brilliant butterflies circle through the air like blossoms blown away. Sometimes a spike of scarlet flowers is thrust forth like the tongue of a serpent from the heart of some convolution of unfold-ing leaves, and often the creepers and parasites drop trails, and stream-ers of fragrance from boughs that shoot half-way across the river. Every turn of the stream only disclosed another and more magnificent vista of leafs, bough and blossom. [4]

N. P. Willis, that tireless devotee of the picturesque, admitted: "It curiously enlarges one's world to be surrounded with an entirely new multitude of trees and flowers. . . . Everything grows differently from the vegetation in our cli-mate. The branches oftenest seem to have put forth with passionate irregu-larity, and are wholly without the orderly symmetry which Nature maintains at the North." [5]

It was the intensity with which nature worked, "producing, in close groups, every form of vegetable life," [6] that gave it its unusual beauty but that also might easily inspire fear. The density of growth was frequently impenetrable. When not mired in the boggy floor of the jungle, travelers were likely to find themselves entangled in its prolific vegetation. They were open to attack from numberless insects. And even when they avoided these encroachments on the flesh, they still had to contend with the visual and aural bombardment. They were bewildered by the richness and splendor of all that met the eye while, for most hours of the day or night,

> A universal hubbub wild
> Of stunning sounds and voices all confused,

> Borne through the hollow dark, assaults the ear
> With loudest vehemence . . . ,

as one writer in *The Atlantic* quoted Milton's description of chaos.[7]

At this point, the amazing superabundance of life, far from being a blessing, became a liability. Existence consisted of a constant struggle, "an undying competition for light and life, among both plants and animals," in which the human interloper became only one participant. Confronting the primeval forest, the writer just cited was reminded of "life in a crowded city, where the excessive abundance of supplies for human wants imported from the surrounding country causes a still greater superfluity of population, and produces a struggle for livelihood more severe than in any rural district of gravel and boulders."[8] Becoming philosophical, the author of "The Unexplored Regions of Central America," which appeared in *Putnam's* (1868), concluded:

> But with all this wealth of teeming earth around him, man feels that he is here only as an accident. The part which he plays is so insignificant, that he seems hardly requisite to the general harmony of the creation. He struggles through the dark old forests like a pygmy, the impotent challenger of constantly occuring obstacles. It is in these vast solitudes that the enigma of human existence first presents itself to the mind. Nothing here accords with the ideas implanted by education and developed by pride, and the traveller cannot help reflecting for how many centuries have these forests given shade and vegetation without at all profiting those beings who arrogate to themselves the dominion of the world![9]

The concentration of life in the jungle generated a world of uncanny contrasts. Traveling in Brazil with her husband the renowned scientist, Mrs. Louis Agassiz recounted how one excursion took her party up a lake

> through a strange, half-aquatic, half-terrestrial region, where land seemed at odds with water. Groups of trees rose directly from the lake, their roots hidden below its surface, while numerous blackened and decayed trunks stood up from the water in all sorts of picturesque and fantastic forms. Sometimes the trees had thrown down from their branches those singular aerial roots so common here, and seemed standing on stilts.[10]

In the jungle, evil and beneficence, the beautiful and the fearful, were intricately meshed: "The sight of the fairest flowers and the most beautiful insects and birds only renders one more keenly sensitive to the frightful discords that startle and the perils that surround him."[11] Everywhere beneath the appearance of sensual and exotic beauty lurked the threat of sudden and horrible destruction. The most loathsome and terrible creatures crouched in the gorgeous vegetation, coiled in the arabesques of vines, or were disguised in the flowers.

The ambivalence of the tropical environment did not, however, depend merely on the presence of dangerous animals. It was inherent in its peculiar ecology. So rapid were the processes of natural growth and decay that produced the remarkable conditions of the jungle that they could actually be seen at work. In his evocation of "Natural Scenery in Jamaica," a correspondent for *The Crayon* drew attention to the way in which life and death existed side by side in this landscape:

> The trees of the forests (some of which are of immense size) are begirt and encumbered with the wild tendrils and running vines of parasites, which often hang suspended like huge ropes from their highest branches. I have seen them coiled like a snake, for rods, around the roots of trees, and then, gradually ascending, wind themselves around the trunks, until they cut through the bark, and stopped the circulation of the sap – killing them in their deadly folds, much as a boa constrictor would a man![12]

The decay and death by strangulation observed in this passage, often juxtaposed with allusions to wild sensual beauty, undermined the identity of the tropics as an elaborate natural paradise and substituted something more subtle but ultimately more compelling. Because of such associations, the jungle offered the often sardonic intuitions of those looking inward, exploring the primitive self beyond the province of social institutions and conventions. The intensity of the tropical experience, its failure to meet expectations, the ambiguity of its implications, militated against any clear-cut message. These qualities not only reflected the shift from moral to psychological landscapes beginning to take place in the 1850s; they also were instrumental in bringing about this shift. They encouraged the distillation of some significant content within the self that, in place of old beliefs and ideologies, could give new coherence to the image.

If the spiritually inclined sought new sources of conviction in the face of declining religion, society as a whole, especially the emergent middle class, needed new reservoirs of power – of relation to the world – as it confronted an increasingly impersonal environment. At least one wellspring of power was uncovered in the exploration and eventual exploitation of primitive cultures. But even more pertinent to our concerns than this colonialist motive was a corollary of exploitation: The American reading public could participate vicariously in the ordeals undergone by the explorers and adventurers in their initial encounters with alien lands.

Though referring to twentieth-century France, Claude Lévi-Strauss placed this consequence of colonialism in a perspective that applies to American society of the 1850s as well, a society also laboring under its own kind of collective ennui:

> Society shows complete indifference to what might be called the rational outcome of such adventures. They neither involve new scientific discoveries, nor make any new contribution to poetry and literature, since the accounts are, for the most part, appallingly feeble. What counts is the attempt in itself, not any possible aim . . . a young man who lives outside his social group for a few weeks or months, so as to expose himself . . . to an extreme situation, comes back endowed with a power which finds expression in the writing of newspaper articles and bestsellers and in lecturing to packed halls.[13]

In the numerous accounts of the tropics that appeared in the middlebrow literature of the 1850s and 1860s, a revealing pattern emerges. On the one hand, these accounts offered a fund of experience that could invigorate the readers' awareness of the world, exciting their own sense of adventure as well as other feelings not usually aroused by the common sentimental fare of the day. Narratives of immersion in the unknown, of exposure to the darker side of nature, had always served in this way. Allusion to the primitive elemental struggle could be cathartic, as it relativized the web of normative values that had ensnared middle-class America by contrasting it with the drama of survival. On the other hand, the appropriation of the primitive that such exploration and colonialism involved abetted its destruction in the name of civilization. Invariably, accounts of traveling in the tropics paused to take note of the boundless possibilities for material exploitation. Railroad and mining interests were most often served, but commentators usually imagined a future in which the jungle would be turned into a domestic haven where "life may be maintained with as little labor as in the Garden of Eden."[14] As Lévi-Strauss concluded (to return again to the context of twentieth-century colonialism):

> The fact is that these primitive peoples, the briefest contact with whom can sanctify the traveller, these icy summits, deep caverns and impenetrable forests – all of them august settings for noble and profitable revelations – are all, in their different ways, enemies to our society, which pretends to itself that it is investing them with nobility at the very time when it is completing their destruction, whereas it viewed them with terror and disgust when they were genuine adversaries.[15]

In view of the discovery of darkness at the heart of the tropical world, it seems possible that the experience of the jungle would have become linked in many minds with the North American swamp – so similar to it psychologically as well as physically – which, as we have seen, was gaining new recognition in the same period. Here too was a primordial vitality, despite the swamp's age-old association with death. A writer in *Picturesque America* noted that along the swampy banks of the Mississippi, one could see "the constant creation seemingly under your eyes. From water to ooze, to mud, to soil; from grass to shrubs, to ferns, to forest trees."[16] A correspondent for *Putnam's,* surveying the same landscape, had his thoughts carried "back to the early geological periods": "The gloomy surroundings remind one of those old chaotic times, when the earth first began to emerge from the sea."[17]

The illustrations of Louis Figuier's *The World Before the Deluge* (1867) showed a series of idealized swamps inhabited by bizarre reptiles, reinforcing the idea that in its earliest phases the whole earth had been swampy. These perceptions and imaginings coincided with evolutionary thought, which had its own version of the relationship between life and death, as adopted by the author of "Wonders of the Deep," which appeared in *Putnam's* in 1869. Alluding to the ceaseless "murder and maddest conflict" going on below the surface of the ocean, he told his readers that "immeasurable hatred dwells in

Figure 5.1. A. R. Waud, *Bear Hunt in a Southern Canebrake. Harper's Weekly Magazine,* October 22, 1870.

those cold, unfeeling waters – and yet for a good purpose, since it is only through this unceasing destruction and change that life can be maintained in a crowded world that dwells in the 'waters below the earth!' "[18]

The close interweaving of life and death in the swamp invited ambivalent associations comparable to those of the tropics. For the swamp too involved an endless struggle for survival, a continual process of death and renewal. T. Addison Richards, for instance, noticed this ecological character in "The Landscape of the South," written for *Harper's Monthly* (1853): "The giant cypresses, edging on either side as far as the eye may penetrate, the bed of a deep channel in these dark jungles, interlace their branches and form grand cathedral aisles, gorgeously adorned by the pendant vines and flowering shrubs. Life and death are locked in close embrace, as the budding flowerets cling around the rotting *debris* of former vegetation."[19]

There remained, of course, differences between associations with the swamp and with the tropics. Whereas, the tropics were manifestly a land of plenty where food was often (although not always) within hand's reach, the swamp was a virtual wasteland. One traveler to Central America pointed out that the party of Lieutenant Strain, which had explored the region earlier and had gone for some time without food, would have perished in the swamps of Pennsylvania.[20] The desolation, though not the stagnation, traditionally attributed to the swamp was without parallel in the tropics. But with the convergence of the two images in the 1850s, the plenitude of the swamp and the dynamism of its ecology were beginning to appear as part of the landscape's symbolic importance.

Its growing association with the tropical world helped the swamp gain attention. Americans of the antebellum period were expanding their horizons both at home and abroad. They awakened to the exotic world that lay at their feet at least partially as a result of having looked thousands of miles away for a novel experience of nature. By the postwar period, a number of artists – including Martin Johnson Heade, Meyer Strauss, and Granville Perkins – were attracted indiscriminately to the North American swamps and the Latin and Central American jungles. Although the spirit of exploration entered the swamp through its association with the exotic landscape of the tropics, the psychological implications of desert places were in turn helping to transform the notion of exploration itself.

Integral to this new dimension of exploration was a different orientation toward the archetypal journey expressed by certain Americans in the antebellum years. They conceived of it less as a pilgrimage than as a quest. Church's great dome in the heart of the Andes is, as Theodore Winthrop said, a mecca sought by the pilgrim who would kneel at one of the "holiest shrines of Nature."[21] The perspective is religious. The emphasis falls on the goal in view. The process of the journey is subsumed by its end. The quest, on the other hand, is defined by Webster as "a journey in search of adventures." It also involves a destination, but one that is not known. It stresses process and end together, a crucial aspect, as we saw, of Porte Crayon's account. The context is therefore established in which nature is no longer approached as a holy shrine but is confronted as a profane antagonist. The shift gives rise to a growing concern with the penetration of nature and to the identity of the hunter so closely linked to the vocation of the symbolist (Figure 5.1).

American Nature Writing in the Mid-Victorian Period: From Pilgrimage to Quest

The two different orientations to the journey, as pilgrimage and as quest, were linked to distinct symbolic modes. The symbolism of the pilgrimage was emblematic or typological, having primarily religious and moral references. An example of this relationship appears in an account of a pilgrimage to the summit of Mount Carmel in "Memoirs of the Holy Land" by Jacob Abbott, serialized for *Harper's Monthly*. Describing the return from the convent atop the mountain, Abbott points out that "the visitor is somewhat restricted in respect to the range that he can safely take, by fear of the wild beasts that infest the jungles and thickets that grow densely on the declivities of the mountain, and around the base of it. . . . "[1] No effort is made to explore this forbidding terrain, only to bring alive its terrors, for it is an emblem of moral waywardness. Travelers must keep rigorously to the path. Even then they are subject to attack from the wild beasts who inhabit the wilderness through which it winds. Abbott relates an anecdote about a panther who once attacked a servant of the convent and, instead of killing him outright, "began to play with him as a cat plays with a mouse which she has succeeded in making her prey."[2]

The man was eventually rescued, wrested, presumably, as much from the prospect of moral dissolution as from death itself. We are reminded of the panther attack in Charles Brockden Brown's *Edgar Huntly*. Indeed, the incident is a common motif in American Romantic literature relating to the wilderness. It evokes the fear of mental and moral disintegration in the midst of nature's disorder, symbolized by the literal tearing apart of the body by a ferocious creature. But whereas Abbott's context is explicitly Christian, Brown's has definite psychological overtones.

The limits to which the emblematic and typological vision of the American landscape was taken are indicated by Charles Lanman's *Letters from a Landscape Painter* (1845). Lanman wrote of being caught in a terrible thunderstorm in the Catskills:

Presently a peal of thunder resounded through the vast profound, which caused the mountain to tremble to its deep foundation. And then followed another and another, as the storm increased, and the rain and hail poured down in floods. Thinking it safer to expose ourselves to the storm than remain under the pine, we retreated without delay, when we were suddenly enveloped in the heart of a cloud, only a few rods distant; a stroke of vivid lightning blinded us, and the towering forest monarch, even upon his proud throne, was smitten to the earth. We were in the midst of an unwritten epic poem about that time, but we could not then appreciate its beauties, for another peal of thunder, and another stroke of lightning, attracted our whole attention. Soon as these passed, a terrible gale followed in their wake, tumbling down piles of loose rocks, and bending to the dust, as if in passion, the resisting forms of an army of trees, and a glorious rainbow spanned the mountain like that distinguishing circle around the temple of the mighty and holy, as portrayed by the painters of old. The commotion lasted for an hour, when the region of the Bear Bank became as serene as the slumber of a babe. A silent and holy prayer seemed to be brooding over that scene of marvelous loveliness, and with a shadow of thoughtfulness at our hearts we resumed our upward march.[3]

Lanman's exultation in immersing himself in nature is the ultimate in Romantic heroic sentiment. His immersion is controlled, however, by the definite meaning with which he invests nature. Exposed to the fury of the elements, he confronts the divine majesty much as if he were Moses standing before God on Mt. Sinai. The Almighty is veiled in storm clouds and speaks with the wrath of thunder and lightning; he demonstrates his power by striking down a "towering forest monarch." The witness to this theophany is riveted, blinded. The display is followed by a gale that shadows forth the Apocalypse. But in its wake appears an emblem of hope: "a glorious rainbow spanned the mountain like that distinguishing circle around the temples of the mighty and holy."

It is as if Lanman had projected himself into the Old Testament. He feels that he is "in the midst of an unwritten epic poem." The orotund qualities of his rhetoric ("resounded through the vast profound") affirm his own exalted position. A latter-day prophet, he bears testimony to the coming millennium. For Lanman, as for Church confronting the Andes, the mountain scenery is the symbolic manifestation of God's chosen land, and Lanman's typology is consistent with the doctrine of Manifest Destiny. This concept united the eternal dimension of salvation with the temporal course of human history and awaited the imminent thousand-year reign of Christ in the New World. Typological method mediated the brilliant light of Christ's advent with the shadows – the persons, places and actions – of the Old Testament.[4]

Lanman's perception of nature relates closely to the American tradition of the picturesque that dominated the cultural establishment throughout the first half of the nineteenth century, reaching its culmination in the publication in 1872 of Picturesque America. In 1852, a group of writers including Washington Irving, William Cullen Bryant, James Fenimore Cooper, and Bayard Taylor contributed to a collection entitled The Home Book of the Picturesque, which celebrated the charms of the American landscape and included engravings based on the work of the Hudson River school painters.

In the opening essay, "Scenery and Mind," E. L. Magoon equated the character of the American landscape with the promise of the national destiny. Magoon began by stating that "God made the human soul illustrious, and designed it for exalted pursuits and a glorious destiny. To expand our finite faculties, and afford them a culture both profound and elevating, Nature is spread around us, with all its stupendous proportions, and Revelation speaks to us of an eternal augmentation of knowledge hereafter, for weal or woe."[5] Like Lanman, Magoon was convinced that of all things in nature, "mountains exert the greatest and most salutary power."[6] He declared that "all vigorous souls prize most highly that healthy and expansive exercise of mind which is attained chiefly by traversing rugged paths and scaling celestial heights, in order to breathe pure and bracing air."[7]

A temperament like Lanman's could hardly be expected to find in the swamp an object of veneration or even exploration. There is, in fact, an example in Lanman's work of how he viewed this landscape. Predictably, he regarded it as an emblem of death and an occasion for meditation. In a sketch entitled "Death in the Wilderness," included in his *Adventures in the Wilds of North America* (1853), Lanman describes "one of the largest and most forbidding of tamarack swamps," located midway between the St. Louis River and Sandy Lake, in the territory of Minnesota:

> From time immemorial it has been a thing of dread, not only to the Indians, but also to the traders and voyagers. . . . It is so desolate a place as to be uninhabited even by wild animals, and hence the pleasures of travelling over it are far from being manifold . . . we cannot wonder that it should frequently be the scene of mishaps and accidents. We distinctly remember to have seen evidence to prove this, when once crossing the swamp, for all along the trail were the skeletons of canoes, which had been abandoned by their owners, together with broken paddles and the remnants of camp furniture.[8]

Lanman goes on to recount a legend connected to a solitary grave in one corner of this wilderness. It has to do with a mysterious stranger, a Frenchman, who after eating a quantity of poisonous sweet flag he finds in the swamp, falls fatally ill. As death approaches, he ritualistically prepares himself, divesting himself of clothes and belongings, which are then burned. He breathes his last at sunset. Told without commentary from Lanman, the story stands as a solemn warning against penetration into the unknown and absorption into the elemental.

The shift from emblematic, allegorical, and typological frames of meaning to a concentration on the subjective and asocial perception of nature emerging in the 1850s is the point of departure for a symbolic mode with a largely psychological context. Opposed to the Old Testament perspective, emotional inflation, and tendentious imagery of Lanman's treatment of the Catskills are Melville's open-ended stories about the Galapagos Islands, "The Encantadas or Enchanted Isles," and Thoreau's *Cape Cod*. In the exotic world that Melville portrays, any link between nature and a distinct meaning is impossible, as over its vistas and through its sultry atmosphere, perception is fooled. Appearance pertains not to the reality of things but to the viewer's relation to the thing viewed. This fact is responsible for the enchantment from which the islands take their name:

> Ere ascending, however, to gaze abroad upon the Encantadas, this sea-tower itself claims attention. It is visible at the distance of thirty miles, and, fully participating in that enchantment which pervades the group, when first seen afar invariably is mistaken for a sail. Four leagues away, of a golden hazy noon, it seems some Spanish Admiral's ship, stacked up with glittering canvas. Sail ho! Sail ho! Sail ho! from three masts. But coming nigh, the enchanted frigate is transformed into a craggy keep.[9]

Similarly, in *Cape Cod,* the beach becomes a mirage of objects that constantly change size and shape before the viewer as he draws near them:

> Objects on the beach, whether men or inanimate things, look not only exceedingly grotesque, but much larger and more wonderful than they actually are. Lately, when approaching the seashore several degrees south of this, I saw before me, seemingly half a mile distant, what appeared like bold and rugged cliffs on the beach, fifteen feet high, and whitened by the sun and waves; but after a few steps it proved to be low heaps of rags, – part of the cargo of a wrecked vessel, – scarcely more than a foot in height.[10]

Thoreau's experience on the Cape, like Melville's in the Galapagos, is based on movement through the environment (developing beyond the eighteenth-century static or "picturesque" view) and involves a deflation of heroic participation with nature through attention both to the distinctness of the local landscape, with its dwarfed trees and beach refuse, and to the conditions of perception, so often distorted. The dissolution of "objective" perception (underlying the validity of moral judgment) expressed by these writers is akin to the ambiguous vision suggested by the swamp. Moreover, the accent on the evocative qualities of light in landscapes of the 1850s – usually termed *luminist* by historians of American art – may reflect a tendency among the more antinomian artists and writers to rely directly on the inner light of the gospel, without mediation by Old Testament symbols. In abandoning the Old Testament, artists and writers deserted a community of shared meaning for the labyrinths and vortices – we might say the jungle – of inward vision.

There are hints of this change in orientation toward nature even among figures steeped in traditional attitudes. In contrast with the elaborate stage setting of Lanman's nature sketches is Theodore Winthrop's experience of climbing Mount Katahdin in *Life in the Open Air* (1863). Winthrop's tone is whimsical and buoyant, even though while making the heroic ascent, he finds nature distinctly uncooperative. His party awakens on the day they intend to climb the mountain to find Katahdin veiled in thick clouds: "When a mountain is thus in the sulks after a storm, it is as well not to disturb him: he will not offer the prize of a view."[11] Undaunted, nevertheless, they set forth only to find that, as their journey proceeds, the mistiness persists. Near the top, the panorama below sparkles in the sunlight, but the mist above their heads, like "an unwelcome parasol," makes their August a "chilly November":

> Besides what out eyes lost, our minds lost, unless they had imagination enough to create it, the sentiment of triumph and valiant energy that the man of body and soul feels upon the windy heights, the highest, whence he looks far and wide, like a master of realms, and knows that the world is his; and they lost the sentiment of solemn joy that the man of soul recognizes as one of the surest intimations of immortality, stirring within him, whenever he is in the unearthly regions, the higher world. (pp. 103–4)

Still, they are enticed away from the vista below by the mysterious prospect of the thickening fog above. They proceed "from sunshine and Cosmos into fog and Chaos" (p. 104). Where they arrive, finally, they do not know: "It was a top, certainly: that was proved by the fact that there was nothing within sight." Having thus reached the "height of their folly," they begin the descent, only to be mocked when they arrive back at the bottom by the mountain's towering summit, now clear of mist: "The rascal evidently had only waited until we were out of sight in the woods to throw away his night-cap" (p. 106).

Had Theodore Winthrop been Charles Lanman, the mist would surely have cleared within moments of his arrival at the top (or he would have waited hours for the event to occur), revealing the spectacular glow of the sun among the clouds. By renouncing the stage management of the theatrical mode, however, Winthrop is willing to accept nature's intransigence and to make the best of it by philosophizing. Speaking of Katahdin, he says, "We began to forgive him, to disbelieve in any personal spite of his, and to recall that he himself, seen thus, was far more precious than any mappy dulness we could have seen from his summit" (p. 107).

By the time his account was published in *The Atlantic* in December 1862, Winthrop was dead, one of the earliest casualties of the Civil War. It is tempting to see his failure of vision on the heights of Mount Katahdin as a premonition. It is at least typical. Winthrop's discretion in not projecting his domineering personality on nature but, instead, in allowing its capriciousness to prevail is representative of the new generation of American interpreters of nature.

In the years before and during the Civil War, figures as diverse as Winthrop and Thoreau in nature writing and Church and Martin Johnson Heade in landscape painting reflected to varying degrees the transformation of American culture that John Higham characterized in *From Boundlessness to Consolidation*. Higham sees a "quest for order" in the period, following the radical anti-institutionalism of the age of Jackson and Emerson. As Americans grasped the dangerous implications of romantic boundlessness, they tried to enclose "the freedom, movement, and diversity . . . associated with nature within an intricate but a fundamentally stable pattern."[12] Higham quotes Herbert Spenser to indicate that attitudes during this period became increasingly complex: "Everywhere the change [is] from a confused simplicity to a distinct complexity . . . from a relatively diffused, uniform and indeterminate arrangement, to a relatively concentrated, multiform, and determinate arrangement" (p. 5).

This development reflected the growing urbanization, industrialization, and modernization taking place during the Mid-Victorian period. Because of the changing social structure, traditional ways of interpreting nature no longer were sufficient. The emerging vision of the landscape revealed Americans' loss of faith as a result of the greater difficulty of reconciling science and religion. Although Higham centered his attention on the growing empiricism through which nature was viewed by figures as diverse as Thoreau and Church, we might extrapolate from his thesis to conclude that as civilization competed more and more with nature, the increasingly problematic relationship had to be accommodated by a more complex symbolic mode, one generated by the resistance, not the harmony, between image and meaning.

Though some chroniclers of nature fell into a merely factual presentation, there is evidence that others met the challenge in a more positive spirit. Higham found a new emphasis on institutions and professionalism in the period, a simultaneous acceptance of "the practical needs of business" and a "taste for elegance of social life" (p. 1). Seemingly paradoxically, the spirit of the age could also be characterized as one of continuing outward exploration and, in the face of the Victorian compromise, a greater responsiveness to the emotional needs of the inner self among the more sensitive members of American society.

Such a paradox will arise only if we confuse this rising cosmopolitanism, and the new individualism expressed in the arts of the 1850s, with the earlier ferment of democratic hopes and transcendental expectations. In fact, the phenomena are quite different. What Higham calls *boundlessness* refers to a series of conscious aspirations that aligned artists and writers with society as a whole. The 1850s, by contrast, witnessed the first real alienation of the artist in America: Here was a situation in which, increasingly though still uncommonly, art and literature were concerned not with conscious communal aspirations but with the unconscious and with anxieties and ambiguities that struggled for articulation but remained largely implicit. One corollary of boundlessness, as Higham mentioned, had been the need for a strong individual conscience that excluded all subversive influence (p. 13).[13] The new emphasis on the unconscious during the period of consolidation suggests that the necessity for inner defense had diminished, perhaps because of the reassertion of institutional controls, allowing for greater openness to new experience.

Attempting to find a basis for the role of social and psychological factors in the creation of imaginative forms, John Cawelti concluded that such forms (like the Western) persist "not because they embody some particular ideology or psychological dynamic, but because they maximize a great many such dynamics. Thus, in analyzing the cultural significance of such a pattern . . . we must show how a large number of interests and concerns are brought into an effective order and unity." He sees one important way of looking at this process in "the dialectic of cultural and artistic interests."[14]

Cawelti's approach to the relationship between art and what is generally thought of as the collective or political unconscious corresponds to my own sense of how the swamp as an image changing meaning and gaining significance in the 1850s is culturally revealing. He distinguishes between the "mimetic" impulse in literature that "tends toward the bringing of latent or hidden motives into the light of consciousness" and the "escapist" impulse that "tends to construct new disguises or to confirm existing defenses against the confrontation of latent desires."[15]

The presence of this dichotomy between artistic and popular interests in the 1850s is confirmed by Henry Nash Smith, who, in discussing popular resistance to the work of Hawthorne and Melville, spoke of "the prevailing common sense philosophy that took for granted the existence of a stable extramental universe completely independent of consciousness yet accurately knowable by all normal observers."[16] Smith thus defined the problem as any attempt to relate the explorations of unrepresentative artists and writers to the Mid-Victorian popular imagination, which on the surface remained intransigent when confronting the implications of the unconscious. "The new articulate middle-class . . . craved not challenge but reassurance. The unstated and probably unrecognized common purpose of the best-selling novels of the 1850s was to relieve the anxieties aroused by rapid upward mobility, especially the fear of failure, and to provide assurance that the universe is managed for man's benefit."[17]

The new cosmopolitanism manifested in the same constituency – evident in the enormous success of *Harper's Monthly* as well as in the spate of travel books that appeared at this time – demonstrated a similar need for escape from an increasingly troubled and claustrophobic environment. If most Americans refused to deal directly with the unconscious, might there not be ways of gauging its impact on culture in terms of the available modes of escape from that culture? Such an escape was to become explicitly linked to the swamps of the South only after the Civil War. In the meantime, the jungles of Latin and Central America would help provide it. Despite being ostensibly at odds, there was indeed an underlying connection between the incipient cosmopolitanism of middlebrow society and the concurrent interest among artists and writers in desert places as a means of inward exploration.

A Loss of Vision:
The Cultural Inheritance

Cultural change and the presence of unfulfilled needs and contradictory attitudes and values do not in themselves fully explain the alteration of meaning that the swamp and related images underwent in the Mid-Victorian period. Another factor is the character of the images themselves, their potential for suggesting new meanings and correspondences. While cultural tensions and social anxieties exerted pressure on the signification of these images from above the sphere of conscious volition, their peculiar character at the physical and expressional levels provided its own ongoing challenge from below. An iconological approach must therefore be supplemented by a phenomenological one. As we have seen, the impact of science and travel, propelling a new aesthetic of close observation, brought swamp, jungle, and related landscapes into sharper focus and gave them new dimensions of meaning. But there was an internal process that also contributed to the erosion of the traditional moralistic tillage of nature and worked to open up new channels through which its signification could be extended, leading eventually to the flood of transformation.

The problem posed by immersion in the unknown, whether in the context of exploration or of representation, was tied to a tacit reappraisal of epistemological assumptions. This realignment of the basic terms of knowledge was bound to upset the prevailing attitudes toward nature. As nature gradually lost its objective status, moral allegory and even accepted modes of representation came to seem more and more irrelevant.

It is thus important to understand the aesthetic and epistemological frameworks in which American writers and artists of the early nineteenth century perceived nature and that were influenced by not only social and economic forces but also the phenomenology of the newly examined images themselves. Here again we must deal with a complex dialectical interaction between the meaning immanent in the image itself and the capacity of the available cultural models to give it shape and in turn be shaped by it.

The following three chapters are an attempt to establish the aims and assumptions determining such concerns as composition, expression, and style (in both visual representations and verbal texts) and then to suggest the complex interplay between these changing formal aspects of vision and the evolving content of the image itself (that aspect of it remaining largely untrammeled by established cultural schema) as it posed new and unforeseen pressures from its immanent form.

This approach seeks to demonstrate the instrumentality of images in cultural evaluation while taking into account their interpretive dimension. This dimension is made up of both the traditional assumptions about how we know the world and the mode of seeing itself. What this mutuality of influence implies is a highly uncertain, often ironic progression in which conscious motives and concerns frequently have unpredictable and generally contradictory results. In any case, the distinction between conception and content is impossible to draw clearly, just as the connection between matter and spirit is indissoluble.

The dominant epistemology in America throughout the first half of the nineteenth century derived from the British empirical school. As numerous literary and art historians have shown,[1] the apprehension of the landscape reflected in the work of American artists and writers of the early Romantic period drew, on the one hand, on Edmund Burke's formulation of the sublime (as opposed to the beautiful) and, on the other, on the associationism of Archibald Alison and the moral sense and rhetorical sensibility of the Scottish Common Sense school (Thomas Reid, Dugald Stewart, Lord Kames, and Hugh Blair, in particular). Although they were attracted to Burke's emphasis on terror in the experience of the sublime, Americans shied away from his tendency – based on a curiously naive sensationism – to separate aesthetic experience from moral and religious insight. Alison's associationism, on the other hand, because it centered perception not in the senses but in experience and culture, offered a formulation of the harmony between beauty and truth that constituted the central aim of eighteenth-century aesthetics. As Alison declared:

> Had organic enjoyment been the only object of our formation, it
> would have been sufficient to establish senses for the reception of
> these enjoyments. But if the promises of our nature are greater; if it is
> destined to a nobler conclusion; if it is enabled to look to the Author
> of Being himself; and to feel its proud relation to *him* then nature, in
> all its aspects around us, ought only to be felt as signs of his provi-
> dence, and as conducting us, by the universal language of these signs,
> to the throne of the *deity*.[2]

Furthermore, Burke's repudiation of the tradition of *ut pictura poesis* – his insistence that language not be seen in terms of imitation, the proper domain of painting (proleptic of Coleridge's far more developed view) – was ignored in America in the wake of the pervasive Common Sense attitude that stressed the act of seeing.[3]

The commonsense connection between material vision and moral intuition was, for instance, made explicit by the influential Scottish Presbyterian minister James McCosh:

The mind perceives matter at once, but it also perceives benevolence, and perceives it to be good as clearly as the eye perceives objects to be extended. In brief, in all our cognitions, our intuitive convictions carry their own evidence and authority; adopt any other theory, say idealism, and make the mind add to things as it perceives them, or phenomenalism, which makes us know mere appearances, and we shall find ourselves ever knocking against intuitive conviction as against facts facing us as rocks.[4]

Such an inherently "visual" understanding of moral and metaphysical as well as material worlds lay behind the pervasive assumption in America of the early nineteenth century – codified in the Sister Arts doctrine – that painting and poetry, despite the dimension of time that gave the poet an advantage, functioned analogously – descriptively, that is. Indeed, given the primacy allotted to vision by the empirical tradition, the visual even gained priority over the verbal. The image was characterized as natural, whereas words were supposed to be a matter of convention.

This conviction militated against any truly expressive conception of art, and as I shall argue at least implicitly throughout the ensuing discussion, it tied vision to a material basis expressed in the metaphoric parallel drawn between seeing and owning. Vision became a matter of appropriation, an extension of having "property" in something, a prospect, for instance. Emphasis on seeing underscored the distinction between subject and object rather than working to join the two in a mutual exchange of values. Such a reification of observer and observed followed the designs of mercantile and capitalistic acquisition, laying the foundation for the motives for colonization and imperialism.

This tendency to appropriate applied especially to the picturesque which, framing the world as a series of pictures, directly recalled the Sister Arts idea, out of which it evolved. Moreover, the etymological connection between "property" and "propriety" further exposes the ideological underpinnings of the picturesque as it dominated American taste throughout the antebellum period. At stake here is not only a mimetic rather than an expressive sensibility but also the persistence of an aristocratic bias (or at least one that is implicitly elitist) in the cultivation of landscape. This bias is reflected in the aesthetic criteria organized around a culturally conditioned notion of what is "proper" that tends to limit the relationship with nature to a matter of embellishment, idealization, and control.[5]

In keeping with its original status as an intermediate category between the beautiful and the sublime, the picturesque was characterized by a balance between the human and the natural. It demonstrated the effort to improve on wild nature through the mediation of specifically pictorial values, including chiaroscuro, gradation, connection, variety, and harmony. These values were meant to support the unity of effect, and their presence confirmed the virtue of what was generally termed *congruity,* defined by Samuel F. B. Morse as the "consistency or propriety of objects or circumstances with each other."[6]

According to Henry Home, Lord Kames, on whom Morse relied for his definition, "We are, indeed, so framed by nature, as, among things so connected, to require a certain suitableness or correspondence, termed *congruity* or *propriety;* and to to be displeased when we find the opposite relation of *incongruity* or *impropriety.'*[7] Such an appeal to decorum masked as common sense signals the conservative ideological position invested in the picturesque. Iconography reflects the assumption of a uniformity of perspective. There is a "necessary" connection among certain motifs, values, and affective states that is in turn brought into the sphere of constituted social discriminations by being deemed proper.

As Martin Price showed, the picturesque originally was shaped by the formulations of William Gilpin, Uvedale Price, and Richard Payne Knight as an amoral aesthetic category. They emphasized the stimulation of the mind to playfulness, which developed the link with associationism. "Interest" and "curiosity" were the motives that compelled a response to picturesque effects, and these motives implied a certain lack of moral commitment and an air of emotional detachment.[8]

Price pointed to Wordsworth and Ruskin as figures in the British tradition who reclaimed the picturesque for oral and religious purposes. He explained: "Once the appeal of the picturesque is given moral or religious grounds, the picturesque moves toward the sublime." The picturesque, in Price's view, had been an unstable term that looked back "to the earlier discussions of wit and forward to later conceptions of imagination. Its very instability is important, for the aesthetic detachment it represents allowed a new sensibility to reclaim for artistic attention what had previously been neglected."[9] Richard S. Moore, drawing on Price's argument, delineated the pressures in American culture "to conflate the moral picturesque and the moral sublime in a politically expressive aesthetic vision."[10] The continuity between picturesque and sublime that is seen in a moral and political perspective is too often overlooked in discussions of American painting and literature of the early Romantic period.

Despite the conservative foundations of the picturesque aesthetic, it contained some of the seeds of its own destruction. These derived from the dualistic nature of its epistemological framework. To the intuitive realism of the Common Sense perspective, Alison's associationism added an expressive and subjective element that was inherently at odds with it. Alison acknowledged that nature is different to different people because "the original constitutions of their minds has led them to different habits of Emotion . . . their imaginations seize only those expressions in nature, which are allied to their prevailing dispositions."[11] This suggests that truth might not be so self-evident after all.

In Chapter 9 we shall consider the career of associationism (expressed through the metaphors of infection and contagion) in an American environment succumbing to a pluralism of perspective that Alison could hardly have imagined. Commonsense assumptions would be exploded. Alison, however, never really explored the implications of his associationism, for while rejecting the uniformity of perspective of Burkean theory, he still assumed enough cultural stability and homogeneity to hold subjectivism in check. His associationism naturally lent itself to the development of sentimental culture, with its moral platitudes and mannered expressions of romance and nostalgia. These in turn could counterbalance any excesses of associationism by providing familiar and organic frameworks around which the associations could group.

There was another reason for the relatively conservative application of Alison's aesthetic and psychological thought. For all its ability to transform the quality of experience, the metaphors defining associationism confined this faculty within the perimeters of what Coleridge called "fancy," conceived of as "a mechanical faculty combining particles of ideas." Herein lies a crucial if rather subtle distinction. Associationist theory falls short of any full-fledged appropriation of the organic metaphor as the basis for the revolutionary theory of the imagination envisioned by Coleridge. M. H. Abrams pointed out just where so many interpreters of Coleridge have erred. The Coleridgean Imagination is not associative in any sense; it is creative. It does not work – as John Stuart Mill, for instance, presumed – through the combination of particles of ideas or images with some dominant feeling. But as "the plant transmutes the fixed air and the elementary base of water into grass or leaves" (in Coleridge's own words),[12] it produces something different from what was originally assimilated. Without this creative capacity of the mind, reality remains essentially self-evident, lacking any truly mental basis.[13]

An associationism invested with the antivisual bias stemming from the Burkean sublime and Romantic theory generally would result in the irrational world of, for example, "The Fall of the House of Usher," a world of disorganized and antagonistic sense impressions. The organic theory of Imagination on the other hand, would show the way to transform the irrational energies of the unconscious into transcendent insight. Though this prospect of reinstituting a direct intuitive connection with the godhead might prove to be just another mirage, art and literature would nonetheless be dramatically reshaped by the possibility.

With the exception of the Transcendentalists and the essentially orthodox theologian Horace Bushnell, the insights of Coleridge and German Idealism did not fully enter the mainstream of critical discussion in America before the Civil War.[14] As William Charvat established, Common Sense theory was fostered in the United States during the first third of the nineteenth century, by an economically dominant class that was concerned with the need for social control and that consequently wished to give art a judicial and moral tone, sustained against the "seductive wiles" of imagination and technique.[15]

With the flourishing of romantic sensibility in the 1820s, 1830s, and 1840s, writers and artists like James Fenimore Cooper, William Cullen Bryant, and Thomas Cole exploited the subjective energies of natural images along the lines of Alisonian associationism. This associationism, however, never threatened the rationalistic, universalistic premises onto which it was grafted. Although such categories as the sublime and the picturesque were invoked to organize and energize experience – and, indeed, Cooper and Cole were masters at investing natural description (in either words or paint) with these expressive dimensions – their efforts were limited to religious and communal contexts of meaning.

Ultimately, even the sublime worked to stabilize and totalize the response to nature. Natural imagery embraced predictable categories of thought and feeling. Thus Cooper's descriptions of wilderness in *The Pioneers* (1822) opposed the various symbols of civilization and were motivated by a thematic concern with finding a middle ground between thought and feeling. In this

Figure 7.1. Thomas Cole (American, 1801–1848), *Landscape with a Dead Tree* (oil on canvas, 26 × 32¼ in., 1828). Walter H. Kimball Fund, Museum of Art, Rhode Island School of Design, Providence.

middle ground, psychological and aesthetic harmonies were subsumed by and in turn reinforced a social and political equilibrium embodied by the pastoral ideal and panoramically represented in the opening description of the book.

The evocation of an idealized "middle" democracy – a blueprint for a society consisting of yeoman farmers who respect nature even while they transform it – echoes Alison's own evocation of the moral influence of natural scenery in "ages of civilization and refinement" in which there is a "union of devotional sentiment with sensibility to the beauties of natural scenery" through the artifacts of human improvement. As Alison sets the scene, "the columns of the temple, or the spire of the church, rise amid the ceaseless luxuriance of vegetable life, and by their contrast, give the mighty moral to the scene. . . ."[16]

For Alison, reminders of death and the life hereafter are the mediating influence in this landscape of natural vitality. They attest to a religious understanding that dovetailed with the social and political notions of the first generation of American Romantics. Preoccupation with human mortality was the principal value bestowed by the humanistic tradition and shared by the Enlightenment and evangelical culture in America. It propelled the central themes and stylistic orientation of American artists and writers who subscribed, on the one hand, to the Sister Arts ideal (with all that it implied about the mimetic nature of representation) and, on the other hand, to a cyclical view of history and of life in general. This view led not only to meditations on death like Bryant's "Thanatopsis" but also to common and persistent fears of impending apocalypse, as expressed in Cole's series of paintings *The Course of Empire* (1831–5) or in Cooper's novel *The Crater* (1847). A concern with the dangers of human pride and ambition was the corollary of this preoccupation with mortality. It supported a distrust of democracy (a fear of the excesses of both individualism and conformity), and it generated the characteristic iconography associated with the American picturesque tradition.[17] Paradigmatic of this early Romantic orientation to the landscape is Thomas Cole's *Landscape with a Dead Tree* (ca. 1828) (Figure 7.1).

Here, the canvas is split into light and dark halves, suggesting an almost Manichean struggle between the forces of sunlight and storm. The moralistic propensities of this chiaroscuro arrangement are likewise explored in the gigantic blasted tree of the foreground, the key formal element of the entire composition as both a framing device and a way of accentuating the scene's primary division. This tree serves as a kind of *memento mori*. Its gigantic form, resembling a cross, is echoed in the diagonal lines that shape the background. Rooted to the earth yet seeming to reach toward the spiritual realm, it encapsulates the human condition. It infuses the entire scene with a terrific anthropomorphic energy. It is an expression of aspiration reflecting Cole's desire to leave the earthly realm. His concern was not to rest in the image, to inhabit the world imaginatively in the manner of a Thomas Wentworth Higginson, but to ensure that the image would point to its justification in the imperium of the sky. The transcendence of earth, of death, at the center of the painting's message is symbolized by the peak, occupying the upper left half of the picture, touched by sunlight and surrounded by blue. The breathtaking hurtle of space from foreground to background calls to mind the leap of faith in religious conversion and brings to bear the idea of aspiration and the sense of the sublime essential to it. Formal and thematic elements thus work throughout the painting, energized by a single hyperbolic gesture, a powerful vertical thrust. All the expressive constituents of the natural scene – the autumn foliage, for example, that alludes to the cycle of decay and regeneration – can be shaken out into a symmetrical skein of values.

In his journal, Cole indicated how his conception of nature is structured as a meditation on time and eternity, impressing on the poet and votary of the landscape the lesson of the transcendence of death by faith. Describing a walk in the hills outside Athens, New York, he evoked a scene reminiscent of *Landscape with a Dead Tree*:

> The south wind blew strongly, and dark masses of cloud moved
> across the twilight sky, the heralds of approaching storm. A leaden
> hue overspread the vale, the woods, and distant mountains. How con-
> tagious is gloom! A flow of melancholy thoughts and feelings over-
> whelmed me for a time. I thought of the uncertainty of life; its
> bootless toil and brevity. The south wind, I thought, would still con-
> tinue to blow, and bring up its dark clouds for ages after my works,
> and all the reputation I might gain had faded away, and become as

though they had never been, – swept by the wing of time into oblivion's gulf.

Having reached this nadir in his brooding on human mortality, Cole's thoughts suddenly force themselves into a characteristic upturn which, in a roundabout way, justifies his pursuit of artistic fame:

And shall it be? Shall the spirit, that mysterious principle, unknown even to itself, that vivifies this earth, and generates these thoughts, sink also into the gloomy gulf of non-existence, nor feel again created Beauty, nor see the Nature that it loved so much? It cannot be. The Great Originator, the Mighty One, the Unspeakable, hath not created for purposes vain and useless this power of conceiving, – this wish and "longing after immortality," – this hope, – this faith which gives an energy to virtue, and raises in the breast these lofty aspirations, – this fear of sinning, of deception and delusion. No! There are no fallacies with God. To prove that, if not to disprove all existence, would be to render all things doubtful.[18]

It is as if the painter-poet were listening to the divine monologue voiced through the landscape. Clearly shared by both painting and journal passage is an oratorical sensibility that betrays Cole's (and his contemporaries') debt not only to the rhetoricians of the Scottish Enlightenment – most notably Kames and Blair with their concern with promoting picturesque and sublime language – but also to the seminal link between rhetoric and the sublime. This link was first discussed in classical times by Longinus in his *On the Sublime* and reflected centuries later in such sentimental meditations on the past and the picturesque decay of earthly grandeur as Constantin Volney's *Ruins* and Washington Irving's "Westminister Abbey."[19]

The appeal to nature itself – to its cycle and the lesson it teaches – is the lowest common denominator here. But a distrust of the visual image is as much a motivating factor. The dominant mode is verbal. The necessary linguistic shaping force ensures proper and ultimately spiritual understanding. Oratorical theory sought to recapture the power and natural eloquence of a universal primitive language and the energy of such picturesque diction (or "fossil poetry," as Emerson later called it) was channeled by rhetorical motives and tropes which, in their expressiveness, evoked the spontaneous gestures of the body. Such "natural" language was believed to be effective precisely because it was so natural, so universal. Far from inviting subjective responses through its materiality, the image was presumed to be self-evident in import and accordingly functioned as an agent of social harmony and solidarity. Commensurate with this view were those shared emotional responses – pathos, nostalgia, pride – that worked to consolidate and mobilize the group spirit.

Crucial to the effectiveness of the oratorical mode was the presence of sonority, of the orotund – reflecting the congruity of sign and thing signified that was native to a tradition still dominated by the spoken word. The reverberating o's of Charles Lanman's rhetoric, as in the passage on the Catskills quoted in the last chapter, show an effort to hold on to the unitary and resonating world whose prototype is in the Old Testament. Its latest manifestation is in the ideal of community promoted by such an eminent arbiter of culture and scion of New England as Daniel Webster, whose voice and appearance were those of a biblical prophet. Conservative Whigs like Webster and Rufus Choate were apt to be the most powerful orators on the American scene, and their oratorical skill could be attributed to their ability to recreate a communal past through picturesque description as well as their filiopietism and social organicism.[20] It is no accident that Burke, the most forceful advocate of the sublime, also became an eloquent defender of tradition.

In restructuring the experience that the swamp allows us to glimpse, this domineering synthesis of oral culture, patriarchal religion, conservative political ideals, and commonsense epistemological assumptions should be seen in relation to the kindred aesthetic categories of the picturesque and the sublime, both of which presupposed a sense of "presence" – whether the presence of the past, the presence of the word, or simply the visible presence of an object. And we should not forget the legacy of history painting, a reflection of the same sensibility, with its aristocratic assurance and didactic condescension. Cole's early landscapes in particular can be seen as an adaptation of natural forms to the theatricality and closed meaning that dominated the historical mode. To the extent that all these categories of response to nature could not be modified and adapted to less unitary patterns of experiencing the world in mid-nineteenth-century America, they were bound to become irrelevant.

Though Cole's work is especially amenable to this kind of moral and religious interpretation, the conceptions of other members of the Hudson River school (for instance, Asher B. Durand, John Casilear, Sanford Gifford, and John Kensett and their literary "kindred spirits," Irving, Bryant, and Cooper) also use dramatic sweeps and pleasing or instructive associations, betraying an inheritance from history painting and oratory.[21] Such touchstones promoted a message – whether historical or emotional, typological or allegorical – that was officially encoded and thus reinforced communal identity. It served as both warning (as in Cole's *Course of Empire* series) and inspiration (as in Frederic Church's grandiloquent natural visions) in the formulation of the nationalistic enterprise.

Coleridgean Imagination, by contrast, opened the way for the liquidation of all such rational structures, by means of an unconscious response to immersion in nature. Instead of invoking familiar, often downright anthropomorphic, patterns by which individuals could orient themselves simultaneously in the chaotic world of nature and in the potentially unstable social sphere, it required reliance on what Keats termed "Negative Capability": the faculty whereby "a man is capable of being in uncertainties, Mysteries, doubts, without any irritable reaching after fact & reason. . . ."[22] It pointed toward a greater willingness to imaginatively inhabit images rather than anxiously seeking to go beyond them.

Thomas Cole was led by trees in the forest "to reflect upon the fine effects they produce" which spring "from some resemblance to the human form." Cole found "an expression of affection in the intertwining branches, – of despondency in the drooping willow."[23] The actual coalescence of subject and object that Coleridge sought, by contrast, eschewed this intervening framework of unsubstantiated comparison between the human and the nonhuman, this reliance on what Ruskin called the "pathetic fallacy."

It is no wonder that facing for the first time in his life the swamps of Florida, the young John Muir had to admit feeling alienated: "Everything in earth and sky had an impression of strangeness; not a mark of friendly recognition, not a breath, not a spirit whisper of sympathy came from anything about me, and of course I was lonely."[24] In a sense, empathy is never more replete than in the confrontation with the swamp or jungle, and this loss of balance – the preternatural aliveness realized by the projective imagination in these environments – is acknowledged in Aldous Huxley's censure of Wordsworth's rationalized pantheistic worship of nature: "Wandering in the hot-house darkness of the jungle, he would not have felt so serenely certain of those 'Presences of Nature,' those 'Souls of Lonely Places,' which he was in the habit of worshipping on the shores of Windermere and Rydal."[25] According to Huxley,

> The Wordsworthian adoration of Nature has two principal defects. The first . . . is that it is only possible in a country where nature has been nearly or quite enslaved by man. The second is that it is only possible for those who are prepared to falsify their immediate intuitions of Nature. For Nature, even in the temperate zone, is always alien and inhuman, and occasionally diabolic.[26]

Huxley's focus on the hostility of nature extends one ramification of Coleridge's discovery in the realm of "primary" consciousness. Investigating Coleridge's references to the phenomenon of "double touch," John Beer traced the development of the poet's conviction that there exist two poles (vital and organic) in human consciousness – "an outer sense of touch and an inner which was in direct communication with the inner life-forces of the universe" – and that a loss of equipoise between these two poles, constantly working in tandem in normal consciousness, is responsible for such extreme bodily experiences as nightmare, nausea, hypnotic trance, and orgasm. Whereas the infant's relationship to the mother is one of "single touch," the adult's relation to the world comes about through a series of "delicate alignments" in which, in Beer's words, the individual is required

> to magnetise himself to particular people and places where the warmth and affection could still combine with accumulated experiences of knowledge by touch to make him feel "at home." If the adult were suddenly to be plunged back into a pure state of "single touch," on the other hand, the abrupt withdrawal of his or her magnetisation to the known and familiar landscape might well induce a state of utter terror.[27]

This condition parallels the experience of being lost in the jungle, an existential equivalent of the submission of will to spontaneous process, which for Coleridge was essential to both the act of imagination and the greatest enemy to the integrity of the self, an ambivalence he had personally endured. It looks forward to the "defamiliarization" sought by modern art. Under the traditional religious regime, the experience of being lost or entrapped in the jungle had been symbolic of the wayward path. With the faltering of religion and the establishment, among the most radical Romantics, of a new religious myth founded on Imagination, it led to a novel sense of authenticity.

For most Americans the apparent subjectivism of Coleridgean Imagination (provided they were even capable of understanding it) was a fearful prospect. Religious orthodoxy rejected outright the whole idea of communion with nature, not to mention intercourse with landscapes like the swamp which imaged the worst pitfalls of the uncontrolled imagination. Less extreme positions still revealed a positive distrust of sensualism. Nevertheless, a submerged countertendency is evident, if only in the posture of defensiveness adopted by the proprietors of culture. Increasing scientific knowledge, gratifying the materialism of the American public, and the social processes behind secularization – urbanization, industrialization, commercialization – were forcing the need to reconstitute a religious faith that would accommodate the larger private and affective sensibility resulting from social atomism.

Emersonian Transcendentalism, as I shall argue in chapter 10, pointed the way to this secularized version of faith, but in its most authentic form, it remained inaccessible to all but a few. In the meantime, what traditional religion had always attempted to sublimate into the proper devotional mood now posed as the threat of a displaced subjectivity, a subjectivity that could no longer clearly be distinguished from religious inspiration but that might even take the form of an unsettling animism or fetishism.

The persistent efforts in the Romantic period by artists and cultural spokespersons to establish art as a prophetic mode rather than a form of idolatry were in the end stymied as art production became enmeshed in a world of commodities. It was this condition in the material world that defeated the Romantic project of sustaining a balanced, mutually regenerative relationship between matter and spirit, empirical fact and human aspiration. To varying degrees, the problem of distinguishing between religious inspiration and mere subjectivism embraces most of the spectrum of American culture at mid-century. Its presence is best perceived, however, in the influence and misapprehension of John Ruskin's ideas.

In asserting the dictum of "truth to nature," Ruskin himself had grappled with the distinction between inspiration and subjectivism, trying to return the question of symbolic perception to an organic social order in which the conditions of work and productivity retained their holistic function against the fragmenting and mechanizing tendencies of capitalism. He also imaginatively reinhabited a thought world that healed the split among the literal, historical, and symbolic realms. On the whole, however, Americans failed to reinstate this context in their attempts to bring together the aesthetic and the prophetic. American misunderstanding of Ruskin's credo of "truth to nature" thereby reflects the failure of thought to give intuition any reliable objective status.

The 1850s witnessed the ascendancy in American art of a new synthesis that provided a neutral ground between the battle lines of an orthodox repudiation of nature and a transcendental communion with it. Roger Stein demonstrated how the aesthetic system set forth by John Ruskin in the volumes of *Modern*

Painters gave Americans the basis for unifying religion, nature, and art under a single coherent system.[28] Wedded to neoclassical standards of beauty but also wooed by the psychology of Romantic poetic theory, Ruskin attempted to render irrelevant what to him seemed the dangerous subjectivism of Alisonian associationism, on the one side, and the well-worn categories of the sublime, the picturesque, and the beautiful, on the other. In their stead he proposed the confusing criterion of "truth to nature" (as distinguished from the "general" nature of Sir Joshua Reynolds and other neoclassical theorists), justified by a romanticized typology that accorded with American religious aspirations to see in the landscape the Deity.

Conceiving of beauty as the reflection of God's nature in visible things, Ruskin distinguished between beauty that was "Typical" and beauty that was "Vital."[29] Typical Beauty was a beauty of order (consisting of such attributes as infinity, unity, repose, symmetry, purity, and moderation) and served as the *raison d'être* of the whole system. It contrasted with Vital Beauty – the "felicitous fulfillment of function in living things" – which corresponded to the Romantic conception of beauty as emotion. Although the latter was essential to the sympathy and unconscious aesthetic response that, from the human point of view, gave life to natural forms, it was the former that stood for the permanent, objective aspect of beauty and that expressed the nature of God. Ruskin subordinated Vital Beauty to Typical Beauty.[30]

In defining the faculties that respond to Typical and Vital Beauty – which Ruskin termed, respectively, "Theoretic" and "Imaginative" – he sought to establish the independence of the former from merely aesthetic apprehension: "The first of these, or the Theoretic faculty, is concerned with the moral perception and appreciation of ideas of beauty. And the error respecting it is, the considering and calling it Aesthetic, degrading it to a mere operation of sense, or perhaps worse, of custom; so that the arts which appeal to it sink into a mere amusement, ministers to morbid sensibilities, ticklers and fanners of the soul's sleep." Conversely, he was concerned with aligning the Imaginative faculty with ultimate truth:

> The second great faculty is the Imaginative, which the mind exercises
> in a certain mode of regarding or combining the ideas it has received
> from external nature, and the operations of which become in their
> turn objects of the theoretic faculty to other minds. And the error re-
> specting this faculty is, in considering that its function is one of false-
> hood, that its operation is to exhibit things as they are *not* and that in
> so doing it mends the works of God.[31]

George P. Landow contended that although Ruskin feared the subjectivity of associationism – what Ruskin called the "pathetic fallacy" – and the violent emotion evoked by the sublime, he was forced to accommodate both in his theory, especially after the loss of his religious faith in 1858 when he began turning from the study of nature to social criticism.[32]

In the end, Typical Beauty represented an atavistic position untenable in the post-Romantic era. However, what concerns us in evaluating the influence of Ruskin's aesthetic thought on Americans is the appeal of his classicist theory of beauty, not its erosion in his own mind. Referring to the function of the artist in "guiding the spectator's mind to those objects most worthy of its contemplation" – based on the standard of Typical Beauty – Ruskin maintained that the artist

> not only *places* the spectator, but *talks* to him; makes him a sharer in his own strong feelings and quick thoughts; hurries him away in his own enthusiasm; guides him to all that is beautiful; snatches him from all that is base, and leaves him delighted – ennobled and instructed, under the sense of having not only beheld a new scene, but of having held communion with a new mind, and having been endowed for a time with the keen perception and impetuous emotion of a nobler and more penetrating intelligence.[33]

Ruskin's conception of visual forms as language, besides being congenial with American commonsense assumptions, transformed the neoclassical theory of imitation into a communion with the expressive dimension of natural scenery. Thus, in analyzing the biblical expression "He bowed the heavens," Ruskin resorted to a literal-typological reading:

> The expression either has plain meaning or it has *no* meaning. Understand by the term "Heavens" the compass of infinite space around the earth, and the expression, "bowed the Heavens," however sublime, is wholly without meaning; infinite space cannot be bent or bowed. But understand by the "heavens" the veil of clouds above the earth, and the expression is neither hyperbolical nor obscure; it is pure, plain, and accurate truth, and it describes God, not as revealing Himself in any peculiar way to David, but doing what He is still doing before our own eyes day by day. By accepting the words in their simple sense, we are thus led to apprehend the immediate presence of the Deity, and His purpose of manifesting Himself as near us whenever the storm-cloud stoops upon its course. . . . [34]

In this way, Ruskin could invoke the authority of history and revelation in order to sanction a symbolic perspective. Moreover, intrinsic to Ruskin's literal-historical typological reading of nature was an analogy between the proper forms of nature and "the noble characters of man in his association with his fellows." According to this anthropomorphism, "What grace of manner and refinement of habit are in society, grace of line and refinement of form are in the association of visible objects. What advantage or harm there may be in sharpness, ruggedness, or quaintness in the dealings or conversations of men; precisely that relative degree of advantage or harm there is in them as elements of pictorial composition."[35]

Much of what Ruskin had to say, including the dictum of truth to nature, received independent formulation by American writers on art like Asher B. Durand. In his influential " Letters on Landscape Painting" (1855), Durand advised budding artists that with art, "if abused and adulterated by the poisons of conventionalism, the result will be the corruption of veneration for, and faith in, the simple truths of Nature, which constitute the true Religion of Art, and the only safeguard against the inroads of heretical conventionalism."[36] Similarly, Ruskin had spoken of "those artists [who] worked entirely on conventional principles, not representing what they saw, but what they thought would make a handsome picture. . . ."[37] Yet we should realize that Durand's admonition to avoid conventionalism stemmed from a typological orientation that was well established in America before the advent of *Modern Painters* and that Ruskin's system served merely to confirm and embellish.

Reflecting the commonsense perspective, Durand conceived of the motive to study nature early in life as deriving from its influence on the mind and heart:

> The external appearance of this our dwelling-place, apart from its wondrous structure and functions that minister to our well-being, is fraught with lessons of high and holy meaning, only surpassed by the light of Revelation. It is impossible to contemplate with right-minded, reverent feeling, its inexpressible beauty and grandeur, for ever assuming new forms of impressiveness under the varying phases of cloud and sunlight, time and season, without arriving at the conviction
>
> > – "That all which we behold
> > Is full of blessings" –
>
> that the Great Designer of these glorious pictures has placed them before us as types of the Divine attributes, and we insensibly, as it were, in our daily contemplations,
>
> > – "To the beautiful order of his works
> > Learn to conform the order of our lives."[38]

Durand was simply adding his voice to a familiar doxology in America and allying art with "scientific" truth. The system of natural theology, with its cornerstone in William Paley's dictum that "there cannot be design without a designer . . ." had conditioned Americans to use induction to ascertain the connection between the natural revelation and the Maker. The Baconian ideal, which was documented by Theodore Dwight Bozeman and Herbert Hovenkamp as the fundamental principle in the reconciliation of science and religion in antebellum America, could be adapted to aesthetic practice after all.[39]

The emphasis on such congruent principles as truth to nature, the literal-historical typological mode of interpretation, and the inductive method in science perfectly meshes with the commonsense worldview. Such attempts to eradicate the distinction between subjective perception and objective truth while maintaining the preeminence of the personality of both God and humanity rest on the assumption of a hermetic universe subsumed by revelation and based on analogous and homologous relationships among all the different orders of being.[40]

Surveying humanity and nature, James McCosh, for example, found "on the one hand, a power of reading the symbols, and, on the other, a wondrous book spread out before us full of the highest instruction. The consequence to man is, that instead of being a stranger, a wanderer, and an outcast . . . he feels himself to be so much at home. . . ."[41] The possibility that nature might be ambiguous, that its meaning might be open to different and irreconcilable interpretations, had no place in this scheme. Science served to elucidate providence, and any lack of clarity could be traced to an insufficient number of facts. There was no hint in this worldview that human knowledge might exceed the bounds of a rigorous empiricism.

This predisposition toward the empirical might well have led to the distortion of Ruskin's ideas on both sides of the Atlantic. At any rate, there were certain revealing problems with the comprehension of Ruskin in America. In avoiding interpretation and hypothesis, scientific realism resulted in sterility. Similarly, while denying the necessity of interpretation, aesthetic realism ironically ended up in some cases by overturning the very relation to the world it had originally been intended to reflect. In fact, the appeal to nature as merely an empirical principle satisfied Ruskin himself as only one stage on the way to the inspired representation of nature that projected the "greatest number of the greatest ideas"[42] and that was exemplified by the work of the English artist Joseph Mallord William Turner.[43]

Ruskin eventually condemned the failure of the Pre-Raphaelites to move beyond the minute specification of natural detail.[44] By the same token, after his initial enthusiasm, he rejected photography.[45] Thus a writer in *The Crayon*, the American art journal of the latter half of the 1850s devoted to propounding Ruskin's ideas, answered his own question correctly according to the Ruskinian gospel when he wrote: "Is the eye of the artist but a mere inlet through which outward nature literally reflects herself on his canvas? Not at all. Man, the artist, in loving contact with outward nature, generates a thing of beauty, which, while partaking of both, is different from both, and marks a progression on the ascending scale of beauty; otherwise it is not imitation, and not yet Art."[46] Elsewhere in the same journal, Brownlee Brown pointed to the perfect balance of inward and outward principles that was the core of the Ruskinian synthesis: "Idealism and naturalism are the soul and body of Art: without the one it is a clod, without the other a phantom. In the union of the two we recognize our strong, serene, inspiring guide and companion."[47]

For many, however, Ruskin's subtle distinction between imitation and truth to nature created a confusion that only fully surfaced in the controversy over the work of George Inness. At this point, questions of artistic technique became entangled with those of iconography. The realism that Ruskinianism fostered established parallel hierarchies of value both for what was to be depicted and for how it was to be depicted. The Ruskinian critic James Jackson Jarves supported Inness against the editors of the Pre-Raphaelite – inspired journal of the 1860s, *The New Path*,[48] arguing that in painting, the thought should predominate and the forms would flow from it. *The New Path* urged the opposite, objecting to the practice of informing nature, in a work of art, with the artist's personal associations and emotions.[49] The artists who supported *The New Path* characteristically produced natural still-life paintings notable for their objectivity and meticulous detail.[50] The extraordinary influence of photography on American landscape painting in this period indicates the wide currency of this aesthetic of close observation. In approaching nature, many looked for nothing more than what was thought of as photographic accuracy.[51]

The problem was that Ruskin's own words could be invoked in support of either interpretation: "The moment [the artist] can make us think that *he* has done nothing – that moment he becomes ennobled, he proves himself great. As long as we can remember him, we cannot respect him."[52] But in

Figure 7.2. William Trost Richards (American, 1833–1905), *In the Woods* (charcoal and white chalk on paper, 1865). Purchased with funds from the Charles E. Merrill Trust given in memory of Brigadier General William L. Plummer. High Museum of Art, Atlanta.

view of the distinction between Typical and Vital Beauty that is behind this statement, Ruskin's position is clear. He was attacking subjectivism but not interpretation per se.

The Pre-Raphaelites, in rejecting the emotional investiture of nature, were also leaving out the transcendent spiritual perspective of the truly God-enraptured artist with which they confused it. Too often they portrayed only "vital" beauty and appealed merely to the aesthetic sense. Jarves was much closer to the meaning of the master. But Henry T. Tuckerman, the influential critic of the 1860s, came closest to understanding Ruskin's desire to eliminate the distinction between subjective and objective, when he noted: "This suggestive in contrast with the literal aim in landscape has caused a decided partisan tone in criticism; on the one hand, we are told that painters like Church are scientific, and painters like Inness soulful; but the diversity is greatly exaggerated; the two styles often approach each other, and not infrequently mingle in the same work."[53]

What is interesting about this issue is that it reveals a susceptibility within American art circles to undercut unintentionally the Ruskinian reconciliation

Figure 7.3. David Johnson, *Brook Study at Warwick* (oil on canvas, 25⅞ × 39⅞ in., 1873). Munson–Williams–Proctor Institute, Utica, N.Y.

of art with religion, morality, and science by allowing the objectified natural image to assert its own autonomy. An artist like William Trost Richards, who once wrote: "Every day I feel the strong influence of inanimate nature over heart and brain; I go to Wordsworth with a fresher sense of all he meant . . . "[54] could nonetheless devote himself to depicting nature with such clarity that it took on a surreal effect, as in the charcoal and chalk drawing *In the Woods* (1865) (Figure 7.2). Although Richards's hyperrealism is, of course, conceptual, it bespeaks a relation to the natural world different from that reflected in the traditional Romantic vision.

Regardless of Ruskin's efforts, there was no longer a basis in common understanding for the absolute identity of subjective and objective enabled by the literal-historical tradition of typology. American art confronted this fact in the 1870s and 1880s with the rejection of the alliance between painting and photography and the ascendancy of Hegelian critical standards – which saw spirit gradually freeing itself from the objective – when photographic realism was given up for tonalism, impressionism, and symbolism by the most representative artists. But meanwhile, the misunderstanding of Ruskin (the partisan tone that Tuckerman noticed) indicated cracks in the monolithic structure of natural revelation and faith supporting American painting in the pre–Civil War period.

Well before the advent of Ruskin in America, Thomas Cole had warned: "Take away from painting that which affects the imagination, and speaks to the feelings, and the remainder is merely for sensual gratification, mere food for the gross eye, which is as well satisfied with the flash and splendour of jewelry."[55] Cole was particularly concerned with the tendency of contem-

Figure 7.4. William Trost Richards, *Ferns in a Glade* (1859). Private collection.

porary art to forsake its main object for the study of technicalities, but that is just how later commentators like Jarves also saw the problem of mere slavish imitation.

For Jarves, "Nature is not to be exhausted by the utmost diligence of exploration; nor can we hope by the finite to render her infinite. The higher law of art is interpretation; imitation is secondary. Those artists who exalt the latter above the former of necessity fail, because life or spirit is something more than color and form."[56] Writing of Inness, Henry T. Tuckerman likewise declared that "the artist seeks to cover, to harmonize details with the central idea; to carry the mind from the objective fact to the subjective thought. Thus emphasis is put upon no specific detail; device or trick for effect is scorned; forms suggest ideas, and one feels rather than sees. . . . "[57] The earlier identification of seeing with feeling, based in Common Sense philosophy, seemed to have been effaced in Tuckerman's mind, despite his sensitivity to its implications.

If Cole, Jarves, and Tuckerman all demanded a landscape viewed through the alembic of the artist's or poet's vision, those American artists who accepted the Pre-Raphaelite creed at face value, adhering to a "mechanical" accuracy of representation, groped toward a different kind of interiority that tapped the ability of the newly conceived image to radiate a sense of otherness that had nothing to do with the artist's spiritual intent. This tendency extended to both the selection of suitable subject matter for painting and the delineation of detail and matters of technique. In an implicit way, the objective, fragmentary still-life images of artists associated with Pre-Raphaelitism, like William Trost Richards or David Johnson and Aaron Draper Shattuck (Figures 7.3 and 7.4) – whose work was dominated by an immaculate conception of natural detail – are linked to the understated technique and innovative iconography of swamp and jungle encountered in the work of Martin Johnson Heade.

This imagery gains its preternatural aliveness largely through the conflict between an energizing fidelity to the myriad detail of the natural world and the traditional need to see some overall design in the midst of it, a conflict that signified the mind's effort to control what was finally uncontrollable. Gone is the rich patina of the picturesque. In suggesting so much more than what the mind could cast into coherent and meaningful patterns, such imagery retains only the most tenuous connection, if any at all, with the religious concerns that had dominated American art for decades.

8

A Loss of Vision:
The Challenge of the Image

Having considered the predominant aesthetic and epistemological assumptions held by Americans in the first half of the nineteenth century, it is now time to consider how the phenomenology of swamp and jungle landscapes (particularly as the two images tended to merge) might have undermined such assumptions and, in so doing, contributed to the restructuring of experience during a period of cultural crisis and transformation. Swamp and jungle landscapes presented features that set them apart from other types of landscape familiar to mid-nineteenth-century Americans. Here we must take care to distinguish between matters of vision and actual features in the landscape that are factors in determining vision. Of course, even phenomenology in the Bachelardian sense may be construed as an aspect of the image's social construction – to just what extent remains an open question. Surely, in any case, it emerges from levels of the unconscious that are less accessible to historical change than are the more conceptual categories that we have been examining.

The ensuing discussion is an effort to delineate these relatively innate features (not forgetting that the faculty of sight, from which vision primarily derives, is itself interpretive) and to pose this phenomenology of the landscape against the basic schema for seeing and understanding the world provided by cultural norms. I shall use this method to probe the ideological premises that determine such schema and to assess the culture's capacity to alter these premises. Because I shall try to isolate the image itself here, my focus at the beginning will be primarily on pictorial concerns, especially compositional devices and formalistic elements.

Much that I have to say is applicable also to literary considerations of the image. In the Romantic period in America, literary and painterly approaches went hand in hand with the social construction of the image. But I submit that the momentum for such social construction, at least initially, came more readily from painting. This at least was the basis for what Donald Ringe called the "pictorial mode."[1] We should also keep in mind that although the phenomenological approach requires that we be sensitive to individual variations in the experience of an image, we can eventually relate these variations to more stable cultural patterns. Indeed, divergence from the norm in isolated instances is precisely what makes these patterns dynamic.

My phenomenological analysis begins with visual awareness – always revealing a certain fragmentation of the individual consciousness as well as isolation from the object in view – and proceeds to aural and tactile awareness. From the image (that is, a painting or verbal description) I move to the sense of an actual environment along a continuum of progressive absorption into the body of the landscape. The upper layers of culture disappear as the relatively stable conceptual orientation imposed by the visual gives way to the volatile space of sound. Increasingly dominant sensorimotor and kinesthetic sensations pace the movement into the realm of unconsciousness, and tactile immersion completes the process.

In recapitulating this regressive movement, the examples I have chosen necessarily reflect an expanding time depth. The iconography of the landscape is subject to periodic change as the conceptual apparatus of seeing responds to cultural reconstruction. The visualization of the image thus is highly responsive to current theories of perception and imagination and the interrelated conventions of artistic composition (while influencing them in turn). Far more constant are the aural and tactile dimensions that carry us into the realm of folklore and repetitive drama that underlies all expression. Here the landscape is condensed and transmogrified, often assuming the form of a grotesque or ferocious creature who lives in the swamp and who threatens to devour its victims or tear them into pieces.

Finally, whereas the prospect of being consumed by the swamp (that is, sinking into the mire, being eaten by monsters, becoming hopelessly lost amidst the bewildering vegetation) stands for the physical pole of total assimilation of the self to the environment, the spiritual or psychic pole is most fully realized in the atmosphere of the swamp, with its power to infect. The swamp's mephitic atmosphere (to be examined in the next chapter) takes us beyond the boundaries of the sensorium and brings into play the most primitive fears with the most sophisticated trajectories of consciousness.

There is a revealing comparison with the question of sexual differentiation to be drawn here which thus far has only been implicit to my argument. The romantic, essentialist, and symmetrical account of sexual differentiation discussed at the end of Chapter 3 in terms of the "Great Mother" archetype, positing an original state of undifferentiation from "mother nature" that is later replaced by feelings of antagonism and fear as the self seeks individuation, may be opposed to a Lacanian version of sexual differentiation as semiotic and asymmetrical. The basis for such a "skewed" differentiation, according to Jane Gallop, is an invidious distinction between sight and smell:

Freud articulates the "discovery of castration" around a sight: sight of a phallic presence in the boy, sight of a phallic absence in the girl, ultimately sight of a phallic absence in the mother. Sexual difference takes its actual divisive significance upon a sighting. The privilege of the phallus as presence, the concomitant "disappearance" of any female genitalia under the phallic order, is based on the privilege of sight over other senses.

She then pointed out that Freud linked the privilege of sight to the degradation of smell and suggested that the latter has instead a privileged relation to female sexuality. Female sexuality is an "immediate" mode from which emanates an "odor di femina." This in turn may be linked at least generically to those feelings of anxiety elicited by the threat to a stable means of representation (made possible by the status of the phallus as a "signifier") which we find mobilized in confrontation with the swamp and immersion in it. As Gallop stated (paraphrasing Michèle Montrelay): "The 'odor di femina' becomes odious, nauseous, because it threatens to undo the achievements of repression and sublimation, threatens to return the subject to powerlessness, intensity and anxiety of an immediate, unmediated connection with the body of the mother."[2] Though I have found little reference to the stinks of the swamp in American culture, the immersive and atmospheric (not to mention potentially repugnant) quality of smell is roughly coextensive with the aural and tactile aspects of the environment, which tend to undermine the controls exercised by the visual and to unmask its sublimations.

The asymmetry of sexual differentiation suggested by the castration complex (fear of being lost in the jungle is a metaphor for this psychological dynamic) is accordingly revealed to be a function of the process of signification, not something absolute or substantialist (as Jung, for instance, with his theory of a collective unconscious, would have it). It points to the symbolic fabrication of "the subject" which ultimately leaves the female in an alienated relationship to language. An impassable chasm is opened up, in other words, between the nature of female sexual desire (linked to the sense of smell) and a language generated by the signifying function of the phallus (and tied to sight).

The problematic and fluid relationship between language and the world resulting from this rift will be considered in terms of the "atmospheric analogy" and in the concluding chapter through an examination of texts, not surprisingly, by two women: Emily Dickinson and Katherine Anne Porter. We may view the shift in psychological metaphors – from a romantic or archetypal relationship between the sexes based on complementarity to one that underlines the subjugation of female to male that is a consequence of the signifying process – as designating the point at which awareness pivots into an acceptance of the linguistic or fictive character of social constructs. This enables sensibility to be transformed and thus to right the situation: The female does indirectly gain a voice. Such a change in awareness can come about only by confronting the failure of language to accommodate experience whose demands for expression have become imperative.

The distinction "between a more immediate, primitive, olfactory sexuality and a mediated, sublimated, visual sexuality"[3] (to quote Gallop) thus helps us anticipate what in my account will end in a transcendence of the sensorium as the locus of intercourse with the world. This is signaled by the advent of atmospheric agency which collapses the normal antinomies of thought into one another and which is increasingly identified not with the physical but with the linguistic.

At this point, an approach incorporating deconstructive and semiotic perspectives becomes helpful, as they can aid us in identifying the insights whose sequence leads us to the most radical tendencies in the culture itself, culminating in the extraodinary adumbration of the Postmodernist narrative that Melville achieved in *The Confidence-Man,* to be discussed in Chapter 9. The revision of an essentialist view of the relationship of identity to the image (involving metaphoric substitution) to a semiotic view (involving metonymic contiguity, as in the literary technique of *The Confidence-Man*), comes close to reconstituting the seemingly paradoxical situation that has guided my argument: It is only through greater immersion in the image that thought eventually escapes its limited grounding in the empirical.

But the change I am suggesting here is perhaps more easily reached through the metaphor of decomposition suggested to me by the ecology of the swamp. Decomposition of the physical or substantialist conception of the world releases a material emanation – atmosphere or miasma – that (being both material and aeriform) in effect deposes the traditional polarity between material and spiritual and initiates an ambiguity between the two that effectively emphasizes the medium itself, detached from any consistent referent. In other words, only through reversion to the primitive conditions of existence in which animism or the "omnipotence of thought" freely reigns can the means be found to move thinking in its most sophisticated (and alienating) directions. This is the "logic" of cultural transformation at stake in the impact of the swamp on sensibility. With this logic in mind, let us now turn to the question of the sensorium and the effect of the image on the available schema for organizing, representing, and figuring it.

It is the unusual demand that intimacy with the swamp or jungle landscape places on perceptual awareness that makes it so arresting and evocative. This demand begins with the extreme visual density and intricacy of these landscape images. The composition of semitropical or tropical forest is like a puzzle. The compact, disjointed quality of the vegetation resists the powers of discrimination. It is difficult to see how the various components of the image fit together into a whole, as they are so entangled.

Alexander von Humboldt observed of the Latin American jungle:

> In the midst of this abundance of flowers and leaves, and this luxuriantly wild entanglement of climbing plants, it is often difficult for the naturalist to discover to which stem different flowers and leaves belong; nay, one single tree adorned with Paulliniae, Bignoniae, and Dendrobia, presents a mass of vegetable forms which, if disentangled, would cover a considerable space of ground.[4]

And referring to the jungle along the Chagres River in Panama, Bayard Taylor found:

> All the gorgeous growths of an eternal summer are so mingled in one impenetrable mass, that the eye is bewildered. . . . All outline of landscape is lost under this deluge of vegetation. No trace of the soil is seen; lowland and highland are the same; a mountain is but a higher swell of the mass of verdure. As on the ocean, you have a sense rather than a perception of beauty. The sharp, clear lines of our scenery are wanting. . . .

Figure 8.1. Martin Johnson Heade (American, 1819–1904), *Orchids and Hummingbird* (oil on canvas, 14½ × 22¼ in. [36.8 × 56.5 cm.], n.d.). Gift of Maxim Karolik for the Karolik Collection of American Paintings, 1815–1865. Courtesy, Museum of Fine Arts, Boston.

While it overwhelmed the mental faculty, the jungle made its singular appeal, at once sensuous and mystical. As Taylor continued, "You gaze upon the scene before you with never-sated delight, till your brain aches with the sensation, and you close your eyes, overwhelmed with the thought that all these wonders have been from the beginning – that year after year takes away no leaf or blossom that is not replaced, but the sublime mystery of growth and decay is renewed forever."[5]

With its network of vines and the unabashed color of its birds and flowers, the jungle offered absorption into the realm of the senses. Martin Johnson Heade's numerous studies of the hummingbirds of Brazil, commissioned by the Emperor Dom Pedro during the 1860s, exemplify this possibility. A painting like *Orchids and Hummingbird* (Figure 8.1) may well have provoked the charge of a critic like James Jackson Jarves against a meretricious fidelity to natural detail. In his brief review of Heade in the *Book of the Artists*, Henry T. Tuckerman praised the artist's landscapes as "clever and novel." "None of our painters has," he added, "a more refined sense of beauty, or a more delicate feeling for color." But then he characterized Heade above all as "an accurate and graceful illustrator of natural history."[6]

There was simply no other category available at the time with which to make sense of these images. The hummingbird paintings reflect a startling manipulation of landscape conventions. In Heade's formula, contrary to canonical practice, the minutely perceived foreground – in which looms the faintly sinister orchid with its lascivious contours and garish coloration – takes prec-

Figure 8.2. Caspar David Friedrich, *Oak Tree in Snow* (1829). Staatliche Museen Preussischer Kulturbesitz, Nationalgalerie, West Berlin.

edence over the background, swathed in heavy mist and replete with enigmatic forms, pendulant and sinuous. By focusing all the energy of the composition on the single prominent element of the flower, seen out of all proportion to its customary place in the landscape, Heade captured an effect similar to what the German Romantic painter Caspar David Friedrich achieved in his "portraits" of individual trees which stand out against the landscape as if Totemic (Figure 8.2).

Heade's tropical landscapes demonstrate a radical new solution to the iconographic problem faced by those who would depict such densely foliated scenery. Density and intricacy are formal characteristics, of course, which precede the evocation of mood or character – the appearance of the landscape as "vigorous" or "desolate," for instance. The challenge to painters in depicting jungle scenery was evolving expression out of what struck the nineteenth-

century eye as a hopelessly monotonous prospect. To a large extent this challenge was endemic to the more general challenge of the American wilderness,
as revealed in Worthington Whittredge's comments on returning to his native
land after ten years abroad:

> It was impossible for me to shut out from my eyes the works of the
> great landscape painters which I had so recently seen in Europe, while
> I knew well enough that if I was to succeed I must produce something
> new and which might claim to be inspired by my home surroundings.
> . . . I hid myself for months in the recesses of the Catskills. But how
> different was the scene before me from anything I had been looking at
> for many years! The forest was a mass of decaying logs and tangled
> brush wood, no peasants to pick up every vestige of fallen sticks to
> burn in their miserable huts, no well-ordered forests, nothing but the
> primitive woods with their solemn silence reigning everywhere.[7]

Similarly, a writer in *The Crayon,* recounting the experience of traveling
down an American river, complained of the lack of those features that impart
to the landscape a sublime or picturesque effect:

> An occasional birch, yellow in the first autumn changes, or a deli-
> cately-leaved mountain ash relieved slightly the monotonous green,
> but the monotony of foliage nothing relieved. There were no bold
> crags or wild passages, no clefts through the living rock which should
> give a picturesque variety – nothing but the deep, dark river winding
> through sombre forests, into which the eye could not pierce a boat's
> length.[8]

Nineteenth-century descriptions of the swamp again and again emphasized
its sameness. We have seen how narratives like the opening passage of "The
Fall of the House of Usher" or Porte Crayon's Dismal Swamp account –
exploiting the dimension of time – found a use for monotony by placing it in
the larger context of a psychological transformation. Painters, however, limited to a single moment in time, had to betray a truism of their art if they
conveyed anything of the monotony of the swamp landscape.

In his "Letters on Landscape Painting," Asher B. Durand pontificated: "For
Nature, indeed, abhors monotony as she does a vacuum, and perhaps it is to
this feature above all others that we may ascribe the unpleasantness of a dull,
cloudy day." Durand prescribed sunlight – often notably absent in the swamp's
interior – in order to avoid the somnolence that would ensure "from the
contemplation of a surrounding mass of unvaried color, as soon as from the
most somnific monotony of sound or motion."[9]

But the swamp was just as likely to cause irritation as to induce sleep.
According to the theory of the picturesque, irritation derived from roughness
and variation, both of which the swamp possessed in abundance, once the
perspective is shifted toward closer observation. Here again the jungle fell
short of the visual harmony demanded by the presiding conventions. Without
the spatial sweep necessary to provide a sense of the sublime, it also failed to
promote repose and continuity, qualities that Uvedale Price, one of its leading
expounders, had required of the picturesque: "if the whole . . . were to be

covered with sharp projecting ornaments, the eye would be harassed and distracted, and there would be a want of repose. . . . ."[10]

Price believed the essence of the picturesque to reside in contrast: "Discords in music, which are analogous to sharp and angular objects of sight, are introduced by the most judicious composers, in their accompaniments to the sweetest and most flowing melodies, in order to relieve the ear from that languor and weariness which long continued smoothness always brings on."[11] But he would have agreed with Sir Joshua Reynolds – that leading authority on the neoclassical principles of painting so influential in America – who stated that "contrast, in the same manner, when it exceeds certain limits, is as disagreeable as a violent and perpetual opposition; it gives to the senses, in their progress, a more sudden change than they can bear with pleasure."[12]

Behind this criterion of harmony was the need for a unitary effect which Anton Ehrenzweig termed a "good Gestalt."[13] The desire for some logical or perceptual clarity of arrangement which for centuries had dictated the developing practices of composition and representation – while abetting the organization of art for the purposes of formal communication – was at odds with heretical feelings and wayward impulses that demand expression through more sensory and instinctive modalities. As Herbert Read contended, "There intervenes between our experienced reality and our representation of reality, a mental function to which the psychoanalysts have given the name *superego:* it is a conscious form or structure given to the otherwise amorphous life of feeling and desire." Conscious structure answers to "an ever-present desire to stabilize the area of consciousness, of intellectual awareness . . . [which] stimulates thought and leads to the evolutionary development of Weltanschauung. . . ."[14]

This motive for idealistic aesthetics constitutes the bedrock of a patriarchal and logocentric ideological orientation that might well be further illuminated by considering its grounding in a traditional aural-oral culture, as opposed to an emergent print culture. We should not forget the degree to which the rise of the penny press and the proliferation of print culture, along with the development of new techniques of reproducing visual material, were helping revolutionize sensibility in the Mid-Victorian period.[15] Revelation and enlightened opinion gave way to "information" as journalism was transformed.

In an age of mechanical reproduction, the boundary separating works of art and literature from commodities inevitably blurred, leading to the further confusion of art and idolatry. Moreover, a far more open-ended relationship between the growing reading public and the text or reproduction impinged on the proprieties of the picturesque mode and the oratorical style to which it was tied. Surely, the relaxation of conventional means of controlling response to the image shared by both the rhetorical tradition and the picturesque aesthetic opened up the possibilities for projective or otherwise unsanctioned meaning in a way that could only threaten hegemonic, largely patriarchal patterns of thinking and feeling. The expansion of chirographic and print culture inevitably weakened the "presence" of the Word. And one may actually trace an awakening self-consciousness regarding the problematic relationship between text and picture in the art of illustration which increasingly operated along lines diverging from the picturesque.[16] We might say that the balance shifted away from idealism toward expressionism.

Echoing terms we have already encountered in Ruskin, Read interpreted the history of art as a dialectic of expressionism and idealism, the first being an externalization of feeling in which the primary value is vitality, and the second a containment of feeling within a harmonic form defined by the reigning standard of beauty. Whereas the latter is a stabilizing factor, the former functions as a way of making new insight evident to the senses, as "an instinctive response to any challenge from across the threshold of knowledge, from the numinous void. . . ."[17] According to these terms, the progress of modern art represents a disintegration of formal patterns and the concurrent emergence of "gestalt-free" structures on the canvas, as in the "jungle" of Jackson Pollock's abstract expressionist works. Although the break away from the tyranny of illusionism was consummated in the plastic arts only in the twentieth century, Read found an awareness of it in Romantic poetic theory with its discovery of and commerce with the unconscious.

Although I do not mean to suggest that the realistic representation of the jungle by nineteenth-century American painters bears any formal relationship to the technique of modern art, the actual encounter and grappling with the jungle interior certainly encouraged a subtle reorientation toward the idealism seminal to the established conventions of representation. Whereas the picturesque convention was a compromise with the idealism of neoclassicism, the impact of the jungle on consciousness was to overturn idealism; or more exactly – as in the case of Coleridgean theory – to force a closer integration of idealism with reality, a more complex reconciliation of the opposites art and nature. This is a position less radical than the "anarchy" of perception seen in "drip" paintings by Jackson Pollock. But it can be found in a few works (those of Heade are the outstanding examples) that seem to express a more projective relationship to nature than had high Romantic art in America.

The limitation of associationism in this regard becomes evident in Archibald Alison's remark that "there is no man of common Taste, who has not often lamented that confusion of expression which so frequently takes place, even in the most beautiful scenes of real Nature and which prevents him from indulging to the full, the peculiar emotion which the scene itself is fitted to inspire."[18] Alison's desire for a unitary effect placed a hedge around the subjectivist propensities of his theory, making him very much a man of his age and entirely acceptable to the conservative critical establishment in America, which took for granted the world's hierarchical structure. The problem with the jungle was that as an image it refused to gratify the desire for a "peculiar emotion" around which subordinate associations could be grouped, thus forming "character" and "expression."

From this perspective, Alison belongs to the same world as does Sir Joshua Reynolds, champion of history painting and the authority of the academy. Reynolds summed up the significance of idealism when he declared in *Discourse IX*: "The mind is continually labouring to advance, step by step, through successive gradations of excellence, towards perfection, which is dimly seen, at a great though not hopeless distance, and which we must always follow because we never can attain. . . . " And this truth, for Reynolds, teaches another:

> Our art, like all arts which address the imagination, is applied to somewhat a lower faculty of the mind, which approaches nearer to sensuality; but through sense and fancy it must make its way to reason; for such is the progress of thought, that we perceive by sense, we combine by fancy, and distinguish by reason: and without carrying our art out of its natural and true character, the more we purify it from everything that is gross in sense, in that proportion we advance its use and dignity. . . . [19]

Nowhere else do we find the problem with imagination more clearly presented, along with the justification for hierarchy and the selective imitation of nature that distinguished neoclassical aesthetics. Reynolds's all but wholesale rejection of the material, of the body, stands in opposition to the material and bodily associations of the swamp as well as to the specificity of vision it encouraged: "But the beauty of which we are in quest is general and intellectual; it is an idea that subsists only in the mind; the sight never beheld it, nor has the hand expressed it: it is an ideal residing in the breast of the artist. . . . "[20]

The political implications of the neoclassical tradition to which Reynolds is pivotal was discussed by John Barrell, who saw this tradition in the context of the waning of the "public" virtues singled out by the tradition of civic humanism in eighteenth-century England. Reference to such values as "independent life," "integrity of office," and, above all, "a passion for the commonweal" was being superseded in discourse on painting by a preoccupation with virtues formerly regarded as "private": "prudence, temperance, frugality, industry, assiduity, enterprise, dexterity" – those virtues, in other words, by which people make themselves "serviceable to themselves" and are enabled to promote their own interest.[21] As these private virtues gained a new status in the social arena, the type of painting they fostered changed in order to accommodate a larger affective dimension, reflecting the interests of a rising mercantile class which were competing more and more with those of the landed aristocracy (as evidenced even in the transition in Reynolds's *Discourses* over the thirty or so years in which he delivered them).

Eventually, history painting, with its appeal to the heroic, its didactic tone, and its theatrical trappings, yielded to the popular modes of melodrama, genre, and landscape. The growing middle-class patronage made irrelevant the old neoclassical hierarchy of genres and the values with which it intermeshed. We may extrapolate from Barrell's argument in order to speculate on the economic and political dimension of the further "privatization" of painting represented by the developments taking place in landscape representation in America in the 1850s. As I suggested in Chapter 2, productive culture, including mercantile culture, was beginning to give way to a culture of consumption in which social virtues such as discipline, temperance, and prudence seemed less imperative than before. Conversely, there was a greater tolerance of sensual exuberance and formal dissonance. Consumerism and materialism propelled the aestheticism flourishing by the 1870s. Here was the final triumph of an idolatrous image that could take its proper place in a world of commodities.

Along with the picturesque, other traditional modes of thinking about nature began to lose their hold on Americans by mid-century. The basis for the typological "reading" of nature also rested on the positing of a visual hierarchy that reflected the relation of spirit and matter enjoined by both Platonism and Christianity. The assumption was that nature presented a regular gradation of entities and occurrences, much in the same way that there was a "Great Chain of Being" running from the simplest, most humble organic species up to the Almighty. The Linnaean categorization of species that was part of the natural theology of the first half of the nineteenth century was the scientific counterpart of this typological perspective distributed along a vertical axis. According to the values of "higher" and "lower," mountains represented spiritual aspiration and worldly striving, valleys the opposite. In the words of the Reverend Abiel Silver, valleys "denote the most base and grovelling affections of the natural mind."[22]

As one of the "low places of the earth," the swamp had naturally been associated with evil; its negative connotations were compounded, moreover, by the resistance of the jungle itself to any rational organization or human habitation. The conditions of tropical growth produced an anarchic effect on space – especially when viewed from the ground level. Opposed to the technique of massing forms essential to the picturesque desiderata of unity of effect, chiaroscuro, connection, gradation, and variety, the interlacing of vegetation almost ensured that equal emphasis be given to all the elements of the image at once.

The tremendous variety of textures and leaf forms struggled against the imposition of a visual hierarchy and consequently a clear indication of moral values. As one writer remarked:

> When, on entering the forest, the single leaves become distinguishable, even the last traces of harmony disappear. Here they are delicately feathered, there lobed; here narrow, there broad; here pointed, there dark and arid as if decayed with age. In many, the inferior surface is covered with hair; and as the wind plays with the foliage, it appears now silvery, now dark green, now a lively, now a melancholy, hue.[23]

In asserting its own autonomy, the image substituted an organic dynamic for one that had been histrionic. An observation of Rudolph Arnheim, a psychologist of vision, is pertinent here: "The winding, twisting, swelling shapes of tree trunks, branches, leaves, and flowers retain and repeat the motions of growth. . . . Thus nature is alive to our eyes partly because its shapes are fossils of the events that gave rise to them. The past history is not merely inferred intellectually from clues, but directly experienced as forces and tensions present and active in visible shape."[24] The jungle presented awareness with the overwhelming energy of growth.

This hyperanimation of the organic might have appealed to those increasingly sensitized to a nature in process that was coming into view through the offices of contemporary science, but it disturbed Ruskin as much as it had Alison. Following Alison, Ruskin gave the picturesque a moral dimension derived from his insistence that variety must be subsumed under a larger unity, that it must, in other words, be a "harmonious and chordal variety." Ruskin called for the massing of forms in order to evoke a sense of vastness, of infinity, that was morally and spiritually exalting: "A forest of all manner of trees is poor, if not disagreeable in effect [in a footnote, Ruskin pointed out that Edmund Spenser's "various forest is the Forest of Error"]; a mass of one species of tree is sublime."[25]

The expression of character through the landscape could link nature to the highest form of religious insight. On the other hand, contemporary descriptions of semitropical and tropical landscapes dwell on the various types of densely interspersed trees and plants, a textual feature that in itself must have produced an atonal effect on the reader. The paratactic syntax alone illustrated the flattening out of values that was anathema to any rhetorical communication of the presence of the divine.

Similarly, in his concern with regeneration through nature, Ruskin distrusted "too great fondness of wandering luxuriance in vegetation, associated with decay."[26] He warned against the deceptive allure of flower and leaf patterns that could be scrutinized:

> But the leaves of the herbage at our feet take all kinds of strange
> shapes, as if to invite us to examine them. Star-shaped, heart-shaped,
> arrow-shaped, fretted, fringed, cleft, furrowed, serrated, sinuated; in
> whorls, in tufts, in spires, in wreaths endlessly expressive, deceptive,
> fantastic, never the same from foot-stalk to blossom; they seem per-
> petually to tempt our watchfulness, and take delight in outstripping
> our wonder.[27]

The jungle image, charged with the kinetic energy of its multitudinous visual patterns, was nearly as resistant to the shaping force of the artist's subjective vision as it was to the theological superstructure that, in the more conservative aesthetic theory, was supposed to transfigure the artist's vision. In this respect, the apprehension of the jungle image suggests a variation on what Ortega y Gasset called "distant vision":

> Instead of fixing a proximate object, let the eye, passive but free, pro-
> long its line of vision to the limit of the visual field. What do we find
> then? The structure of our hierarchical elements disappears. The ocular
> field is homogeneous; we do not see one thing clearly and the rest
> confusedly, for all are submerged in an optical democracy. Nothing
> possesses a sharp profile; everything is background, confused, almost
> formless.[28]

This point parallels Emerson's observation in *Nature*: "When I behold a rich landscape, it is less to my purpose to recite correctly the order and superposition of the strata, than to know why all thought of multitude is lost in a tranquil sense of unity. I cannot greatly honour minuteness in details, so long as there is no hint to explain the relation between things and thoughts. . . ."[29]

Distant vision and the apprehension of the jungle image share a tendency toward homogeneity of the ocular field. But whereas in the former case, visual elements lose their tactile resonance along with their sharp profile, the jungle encourages the preservation of tactile resonance and forces the eye to contend constantly with a plethora of sharply distinguished contours, as we see in the

photograph *Las Nubes, Delia Falls* by Eadweard Muybridge (Figure 8.3) or in
Frederic Church's preliminary sketches of tropical vegetation (see Figure 4.4).

It is again worth considering the political and ideological implications of
landscape composition, to see the readiness with which eighteenth-century
commentators alternated between the natural and the political spheres. This
is indicated by Uvedale Price when he observed in his discussion of the picturesque that "the mutual connection and dependence of all the different ranks
and orders of men in [England]; the innumerable, but voluntary ties by which
they are bound and united to each other . . . are perhaps the firmest securities
of its glory, its strength, and its happiness." He then made an even more direct
link between visual harmony and social harmony:

> Freedom, like the general atmosphere, is diffused through every part,
> and its steady and settled influence, like that of the atmosphere on a
> fine evening, gives at once a glowing warmth, and a union to all
> within its sphere: and although the separation of the different ranks
> and their gradations, like those of visible objects, is known and ascer-
> tained, yet from the beneficial mixture, and frequent intercommunica-
> tion of high and low, that separation is happily disguised, and does
> not sensibly operate on the general mind.

Price went on to warn that "should any of these most important links be
broken; should any sudden gap, and distinct undisguised line of separation be
made, such as between noble and roturier, the whole strength of that firm
chain (and firm may it stand) would at once be broken."[30]

In Price's mind, hierarchical ordering that preserves easy communication
among the various levels of the visual field (as in a picturesque vision) is equal
to a liberal social organicism favorable to peace and prosperity. By extension,
homogeneity of the visual field, as in distant vision, naturally suggests comparison with a "dangerous" political democracy. As the hierarchical ordering
weakened, the atmosphere believed to suffuse the organic community became
displaced; losing its mellow and mellifluous qualities, it was transformed into
a radically unstable medium that began to substitute itself for the message it
had previously served to transmit.

If the homogeneity of the visual field created in distant vision offers an
analogue to political democracy, the jungle might be said to reveal the dark
half of the democratic principle: the anarchic conflict of equally insistent impulses. Moreover, if distant vision, effecting "a perfect unity of the whole
visual field" (in contrast with the duality of proximate vision), relates to what
has been called American "luminist" painting – with its democratic and tran-
scendentalist implications[31] – the experience in the jungle carried those implications one step further in just the direction that conservatives feared they
might lead. As opposed to the submergence of the objective factor in the
subjective during a pantheistic moment,[32] it promoted a separation of the two,
but in a new key, different from the traditional duality of subject and object
assumed by mere proximate vision.

The preservation of sharp outlines in distant prospects (atmosphere now in
a sense becoming "airless") in the more "surreal" luminist landscapes – those
above all of Heade and Fitzhugh Lane – implies the same thing: the apparition

Figure 8.3. Eadweard Muybridge, *Las Nubes, Delia Falls* (photograph). *Photographic Studies of Central America and the Isthmus of Panama* (San Francisco, 1876). Courtesy of the Department of Special Collections and University Archives, Stanford University Libraries, Stanford, Calif.

Figure 8.4. Martin Johnson Heade (American, 1819–1904), *Brazilian Forest* (oil on canvas, 20¹/₁₆ × 16 in., 1864). Gift of Mr. and Mrs. Richard Steedman, Museum of Art, Rhode Island School of Design, Providence.

of a "world out there" that has become a "world in here" only to grow alien again at the very moment of transcendental embrace.

A comparison of Heade's *Brazilian Forest* (1864), (Figure 8.4) or *View from Tree-Fern Walk, Jamaica* (1887) (Figure 8.5) in which minute delineation is exploited to the utmost, with Church's *Evening in the Tropics* (1881) (Figure 8.6), in which the artist considerably mutes the intricacy of tropical foliage through a flaccid and generalized treatment, highlights the evocative possibilities in the more positivistic approach to tropical vegetation. Why Church tended to fall back into an almost Claudian rendering of the tropical landscape late in his career remains an interesting question.[33]

Figure 8.5. Martin Johnson Heade (American, 1819–1904), *View from Tree-Fern Walk, Jamaica* (1887). Mr. and Mrs. Patrick A. Doheny, Los Angeles County Museum of Art.

Figure 8.6. Frederic Church, *Evening in the Tropics* (1881). Bequest of Clara Hinton Gould, Wadsworth Atheneum, Hartford, Conn.

As tokens of the new intimacy with nature, the close-up visions of swamp and jungle scenery that began appearing in the 1850s and 1860s shared an affinity with the popular image of the secluded forest bower or glade. These images picture nature from the inside, as it were, evoking a series of subjective impressions. According to a writer in *The Crayon,*

> To the student of Nature's interior, her outward forms do not appeal merely to the senses, but solicit the utmost refinement of thought built upon thought, giving an expansion to the human mind, which lends new interest to all its observations, and increased force to its conclusions. The whole study becomes subjective, and all outward delineations are used to subserve the purpose of a psychical development.[34]

A favorite subject of the Hudson River school painter Asher B. Durand, the forest glade recalls the poetry of the English Romantics and behind them the sensibility of the eighteenth century. Such poetry was pastoral, envisioning humans embosomed in nature. Durand's compositions hark back to Claudian and seventeenth-century Dutch conventions, often including the typical *repoussoir* element in the foreground.

Sunset in a Swamp (Figure 8.7) by the French-born painter François Regis Gignoux, whose work was fashionable during the 1840s, represents the adaptation of the swamp subject to this benign formulation. James Henry, in much the same spirit, asserted: "It is the fulfillment of a law which has always been a mystery, when the imagination dwells among trees of a venerable

Figure 8.7. François Regis Gignoux (b. France, 1816–1882), *Sunset in a Swamp* (oil on canvas, 31¼ × 47 in. [79.4 × 119.4 cm.], n.d.). Bequest of Henry Herbert Edes. Courtesy, Museum of Fine Arts, Boston.

growth and cypress gloom.''[35] In Gignoux's painting, the forlorn and gro-tesque character of natural forms is softened by the lush, rutilant sky reflected in the lake. The open space of the lake controls the encroachment of the dense forest, and the trees that frame the composition complete the picturesque effect. The work may be compared with the seventeenth-century Dutch painter Jacob van Ruisdael's handling of the swamp (Figure 8.8). In both cases, the overtones of stagnation are exploited merely for the pungence they lend to an essentially harmonious and idyllic conception.

Durand's compositions evoke the aura of a woodland sanctuary or chapel. The open sky visible beyond the forest suggests a relationship between inner and outer realities. As Ruskin observed, ''the landscapist dares not lose himself in forest without a gleam of light under its farthest branches, nor ventures out in rain unless he may somewhere pierce to a better promise in the distance, or cling to some closing gap of variable blue above: Escape, Hope, Infinity . . . the desire is the same in all, the instinct constant. . . . ''[36] The possibility of penetration to the sky beyond ensures the moral dimension of intimacy with nature. The secluded forest bower, with its welcoming space and familiar attributes, is a human place, a home. Although its recesses bring to mind an inner world, its contours yield easily to rational understanding. It embodies the inwardness of meditation, a deliberate, probing movement of the mind. The true landscape, according to Durand, ''becomes companionable, holding silent converse with the feelings, playful or pensive – and, at times, touching a chord that vibrates to the inmost recesses of the heart, *yet with no unhealthy*

Figure 8.8. Jacob van Ruisdael, *Oak by a Lake with Water-Roses* (n.d.). Staatliche Museen Preussischer, Kulturbesitz, Gemaldegalerie, West Berlin.

excitement [emphasis mine], but soothing and strengthening to his best faculties."[37]

The momentum toward greater naturalization, encouraged by Ruskinism and demonstrated particularly by those who adopted the Pre-Raphaelite credo, worked against this pastoral motive. The most cursory comparison of Durand's *The Beeches* (1845) with his *In the Woods* of ten years later (Figures 8.9 and 8.10) reveals this artist's striking move from European pastoral conventions and toward a less monitored rendition of the American landscape. Worthington Whittredge's *The Old Hunting Grounds* (1864) (Figure 8.11), which depicts a woodland interior with a decaying birchbark canoe, represents an even greater contrast with Durand's earlier pastoral vision.

Durand's canvases were always meant to be entered imaginatively. "That is a fine picture," he declared, "which at once takes possession of you – draws you into it – you traverse it – breathe its atmosphere – feel its sunshine, and you repose in its shade without thinking of its design or execution, effect or color."[38] Whittredge's interior, however, tends to preclude the viewer's entry into it to bask there. It is circumscribed by densely clustered birch trees that block the view of the sky and present a nearly abstract pattern, like an ice stencil on a window. This visual effect is reiterated in the high contrast between the dark foreground and luminous background. Durand also used this effect, immersing the foreground in shadow while the prospect opened out to the sunny fields beyond the forest. But Whittredge reconfigured this formula by drastically constricting

Figure 8.9. Asher B. Durand, *The Beeches* (1845). Bequest of Maria De Witt Jesup. The Metropolitan Museum of Art, New York.

Figure 8.10. Asher B. Durand, *In the Woods* (1855). Gift in memory of Jonathan Sturges by his children, 1895. The Metropolitan Museum of Art, New York.

Figure 8.11. Worthington Whittredge, *The Old Hunting Grounds* (1864). Reynolds House, Museum of American Art, Winston-Salem, N.C.

the space and superimposing the outlines of the foreground trees not on simpler contours but on an even more detailed series of lines.

Design (albeit a complex and seemingly arbitrary design) gains slightly on illusion; the scene is less the background for human activity, more an image in its own right. Even though Whittredge's composition includes the framing device in the trees of the left foreground, these have lost some of their clearly defined spatial orientation. The picture is structured according to a series of skewed planes that subtly push against one another in their disequilibrium. Whittredge, still essentially a Hudson River school painter, has begun to test the potential of the American wilderness that he lamented on his return from Europe. The decaying birchbark canoe in the foreground of his painting, drawing attention to the cycle of generation and decay, testifies to what is immanent throughout the canvas: the unyielding force of nature even in the face of human artifacts.

Visions of the American landscape in the 1850s and 1860s commonly suggest impenetrability as the point of view becomes more intimate. David Johnson's *Brook Study at Warwick* (1873) (see Figure 7.3), for instance, affronts the viewer with a wall of moss-covered rock and multitextured vegetation, completely filling the canvas. Thomas Moran's *Slaves Escaping Through the Swamp* (1865) (see Figure 3.4) presents its emotionally and psychologically charged subject in an avalanche of baroque vegetation and Salvatoresque blasted tree trunks, an ironic inversion of the older, now irrelevant, props.

The scenes of jungle interior painted by Frederic Church, Martin Johnson Heade, and others in these years allude to impenetrability not only in the vegetation depicted but also in the mists and hazes that shroud the backgrounds of their paintings. If light should pierce the murkiness, even if it is intended to have religious overtones, it is modulated by accents that make it seem eerie and portentous. The combination of unkempt vegetation and light-transfixed mists could result in a singularly interior vision – a "landscape from the other side of the moon" – as in Heade's *South American River Scene* (1868) (Figure 8.12) or Herman Herzog's tonalist *Moonlight in Florida* (dating from the latter part of the century) (Figure 8.13).

In these works, regardless of technique, any moral perspective has been destroyed, and the same quiescent remoteness presides as must have presided in the primordial beginnings of the world and can be expected to preside again at its end. The boat that makes its way up Heade's Latin American river (Which way is it going? – we don't really know) seems bound not for the pinnacles of moral insight but merely into the unknown. Paintings like *South American River Scene*, Church's *Tropical Scenery at Night* (Figure 8.14), or Granville Perkins's *Florida Landscape* (see Figure 2.9) seem to offer a window on the world, suggesting a perspective from within the mind itself.

The persistent association of the swamp with moonlight, a shimmering tonality that does not penetrate as does the light of the sun but that suffuses an environment, is invoked again and again during the 1870s, 1880s, and 1890s in the works of painters seduced by the vogue for depicting swamp and tropical scenery. Washington Allston's prophetic *Moonlit Landscape,* Thomas Cole's *Desolation* (the last stage in his *Course of Empire* series), and James Hamilton's watercolor *Bayou in Moonlight* (see Figure 1.4) are prototypes for this kind of reverie.

But if the attraction to moonlit swamp and jungle scenes drew on the Romantic stock-in-trade, the post-Romantic visions often replace the elements of pathetic fallacy or allegory that generally mediated the reverie in the earlier instances (Allston's work is the purest example), with an intensity at times bordering on the surreal. *Moon over Lake Nicaragua* (Figure 8.15), by the San Francisco artist Fortunato Arriola, gains its extraordinary intensity from the contrast between the diffuse tonality of the moonlight and the sharply etched forms of the silhouetted palm trees and century plants. Similarly, in Heade's late paintings of Florida swamps, such as *The Great Florida Marsh* (1886) (see Figure I.3), the sense of desolation – a traditional category of feeling – is reinvigorated and psychologized by being merged with its opposite, a tropical vitality expressed by dense, twisted growth, intricate leaf patterns, and vibrant colors.

Thus, in a variety of ways, the propensity of swamp and jungle landscape to test or sabotage accepted ways of perceiving and experiencing nature that had been embodied in high Romantic iconography and long-established pat-

Figure 8.12. Martin Johnson Heade (American, 1819–1904), *South American River Scene* (oil on canvas, 26 × 22½ in. [66 × 57.1 cm.], 1868). Gift of Maxim Karolik for the Karolik Collection of American Paintings, 1815–1865. Courtesy, Museum of Fine Arts, Boston.

terns of composition (based on clearly demarcated intervals of space and on a vertical axis of moral value) resulted in several new solutions that suggest not a communal and religious relationship to nature but one that is deeply personal and occult.

A case could be made for understanding the landscapes of a high Romantic artist like Thomas Cole in terms of a psychological relationship to nature.[39] Certainly there is a powerful affective element in Cole's pyrotechnic displays of natural beauty that takes them far beyond their allegorical moorings. But analysis of the psychological dimension of Cole's work must rely, I contend, almost totally on Freudian analysis, because the psychological aspect of his

Figure 8.13. Herman Herzog, *Moonlight in Florida* (late 1800s). Whereabouts unknown.

paintings is confined to the relatively reductive instinctual drama of containment and release, repression and wish fulfillment (often symbolized by the
abrupt leap of space between composed foreground and distant mountain and
by the chiaroscuro division of the canvas).

There is no hint in Cole's canvases that he used the numinous effects of
nature to create a world truly apart, a symbolic alternative to the repressive
demands of civilization building. Cole's fantasies are never confrontations with
the demonic or communions with the unknown. His anthropomorphism is
always intact; his spiritual aspirations make him too impatient to rest in the
image for its own sake, to inhabit it imaginatively and to integrate its otherness
into his own sense of being. His "bewilderment,"[40] experienced after becoming
lost one night in the Catskills and falling into a gorge out of which he had to
find his way, is just that: a struggle with nature's dark side that never becomes
a mode of intercourse, never is resolved into implicit form. Cole does not
have the interior resources from which he can cast his experience into any
pattern of self-transformation; he lacks the unconscious awareness that can
transcend the physical limitations of the self and reconcile spiritual and material

Figure 8.14. Frederic Church, *Tropical Scene at Night* (n.d.). Anonymous loan, The Fine Arts Museum of San Francisco.

realities, as in the Jungian notion of individuation. In relation to nature, this could come only after a willed blurring of the distinction between self and environment.

Beyond the visual aspect of the swamp, writers drew attention to a level of experience relating to sound that extended the meaning of the environment, especially as it pertained to the unconscious. We think first of the passage in *Walden* in which Thoreau contemplates the call of the hooting owl: "It is a sound admirably suited to swamps and twilight woods which no day illustrates. . . . " It suggests to him "a vast and undeveloped nature which men have not recognized." Owls, he says, "represent the stark twilight and unsatisfied thoughts which all have."[41]

Typically, sound comes into its own in the swamp only after dark, when the visual image is obscured. As an image of the dark side of nature, it was natural that the swamp (neither land nor water) should be associated primarily with twilight and nighttime, and especially with twilight which, like the swamp, represents an in-between state. During the day the swamp (unlike the

Figure 8.15. Fortunato Arriola, *Moon over Lake Nicaragua*. Private collection.

tropical jungle which is nearly always noisy) is usually silent. It is the contrast
of isolated sounds with the enveloping silence in the swamp that makes them
so ominous. But with the coming of night, as Thoreau noted, a transformation
takes place: "All day the sun has shone on the surface of some savage swamp,
where the single spruce stands hung with usnea lichens, and small hawks
circulate above, and the chickadee lisps amid the evergreens, and the partridge
and rabbit skulk beneath; but now [at night] a more dismal and fitting day
dawns, and a different race of creatures awakes to express the meaning of
nature there."[42]

The shift in sensory focus from sight to sound both results from and deepens
the immersion in the landscape. Walter Ong discussed at length the differences
between the experiences of sound and sight. Sound surrounds the self. It is a
transitory experience, locked in a single moment in time but incapable of being
arrested in space and thus preserved for scrutiny at a later time. It consequently
relates to a more spontaneous and immediate mode of being than does sight,
which lends itself to the abstraction and preservation of experience as knowledge. As Ong pointed out, "Sound is more real or existential than other sense
objects, despite the fact that it is also more evanescent. Sound itself is related
to present actuality rather than to past or future. It must emanate from a source
here and now discernibly active, with the result that involvement with sound
is involvement with the present, with here-and-now existence and activity."[43]

Because of its timelessness, sound is capable of awakening reverberations
from beyond the realm of culture, of creating an I–Thou relationship between
the self and the reality beyond the threshold of human knowledge. Yet just
as this relationship can heighten the sense of religious communion, it can also

awaken the sense of victimization at the hands of the diabolic: The experience of sound is far less stable than that of sight.

Sound accentuates the most disorienting effects of the swamp. In this environment it is often difficult, even with the aid of sight, to locate accurately the origin of sounds, to judge their direction and distance. The medium creates a multidimensional space whose contours constantly shift, in contrast with the relative stability of visual and especially pictorial space. Because of its atmospheric quality as well as the human ability to imitate many of its manifestations, sound presents the prospect of both immersion and absorption into the realm of otherness.

Hence Thoreau found the hooting of the owl melancholic. It reminded him of the dying moans of a human being, "some poor weak relic of mortality who has left hope behind, and howls like an animal, yet with human sobs, on entering the dark valley, made more awful by a certain gurgling melodiousness." In his own effort to duplicate this sound, he found himself beginning with the consonants *gl,* "expressive of a mind which has reached the gelatinous mildewy stage in the mortification of all healthy and courageous thought."[44] There is perhaps an ironic allusion here to Keats's "Ode to a Nightingale," to identification with the immortality of the bird (whose singing is a continual dying to the world in which beauty and truth are separate) through immersion in the rich environment of its song:

> Now more than ever seems it rich to die,
>   To cease upon the midnight with no pain,
>   While thou art pouring forth thy soul abroad
>   In such an ecstasy!

Listening to the hooting of the owl at close hand, Thoreau thought of madness: "It reminded me of ghouls and insane howlings." However, the answering call from the distance suggests mainly pleasing associations, as the subject – object relationship has been reestablished. Keats must confront his inevitable falling away from the painful happiness of empathic union with etherialized nature:

> Still wouldst thou sing, and I have ears in vain –
>   To thy high requiem become a sod.

Thoreau's more cautious and skeptical approach keeps him within the physical world, embedded in a more temperate relationship to experience.

Sound amplifies the sense of both the unknown and the danger commonly experienced in the swamp. It mobilizes the impression of alien forces encroaching the boundaries of the self. John Lawson's early eighteenth-century description in his *History of North Carolina* is typical of those occurring down through the ages:

> When we were all asleep in the Beginning of the Night, we were
> awakened with the dismalist and most hideous Noise that ever pierced
> my Ears. This sudden surprizal incapacitated us to guessing what this
> threatening Noise might proceed from: but our Indian Pilot, (who
> knew these Parts very well,) acquainted us, that it was customary to

hear such Music along the Swamp side, there being endless Numbers
of Panthers, Tygers, Wolves, and other Beasts of prey, which take
this Swamp for their Abode in the Day, coming in whole Droves to
hunt the Deer in the Night, making this frightful Ditty till Day appears, then all is still as in other Places.[45]

In this case, the surrounding darkness takes on the quality of nightmare; fear
derives less from the sense of absorption than from the prospect of being
devoured.

Another instance of this situation was recounted in *Harper's Monthly* (1853)
in a piece entitled "Ibis Shooting in Louisiana." The anonymous author wrote
of being lost in the bayou:

> With night came new voices – the hideous voices of the nocturnal
> swamp; the qua-qua of the night-heron, the screech of the swamp-
> owl, the cry of the bittern, the el-l-uk of the great water-toad, the tin-
> kling of the bell-frog, and the chirp of the savanna-cricket – all fell
> upon my ear. Sounds still harsher and more hideous were heard
> around me – the plashing of the alligator, and the roaring of his voice;
> these reminded me that I must not go to sleep. To sleep! I durst not
> have slept for one single instant. Even when I lay for a few minutes
> motionless, the dark reptiles came crawling round me – so close that I
> could have put forth my hands and touched them.[46]

Immersion here is about to reach the point of actual contact with the flesh.
With tactile experience, the somatic focus shifts from the center within (sought
in the silence and integration of meditation) to the skin. The swamp environment attacks the surfaces of the body. Touch is repelled by coldness, sliminess,
and other unpleasant sensations provoked by the slightest movement.

In the forest glade or bower, the limited perspective engenders a sense of
intimate enclosure. The bower is a felicitous space inducing reverie or quiet
contemplation. The extreme density of tropical vegetation, on the other hand,
carries enclosure to the point that it becomes frightening. But the protectiveness
of the bower's space, its sanctuary, may also create a feeling of imprisonment.
Intimacy becomes claustrophobic, even suffocating. Whereas the bower offers
its occupant a relaxing stillness, the impenetrable density of the jungle enforces
immobility. Movement through the jungle is at best arduous, and usually
treacherous and debilitating. It requires an aggressive if not a combative stance.

Adventurers hack their way through jungles, destroying nature's bounty
at every step. They pursue their routes awkwardly into mud-choked waters,
stepping gingerly over bridges of decaying matter. As John Muir remembered
toiling through the Florida wilderness: "Frequently I sank deeper and deeper
until compelled to turn back and make the attempt in another and still another
place. Oftentimes I was tangled in a labyrinth of armed vines like a fly in a
spider-web. At all times, whether wading or climbing a tree for specimens, I
was overwhelmed with the vastness and unapproachableness of the great
guarded sea of sunny plants."[47]

To move from forest bower to jungle interior is to leave behind a relationship to nature that is traditionally conceived of as poetic and to enter into

a dramatic conflict, an exposure to hostile elemental forces. The moment passes, we might say with Gaston Bachelard, when "being is 'cast into the world.' "[48] Nature is no longer a clear bell, a sonorous and integrative agent; instead it poses the ever-present threat of disintegration. Humans become actors in the cosmic drama of survival rather than salvation. Being lost, devoured, or trapped are the stakes as the self achieves self-consciousness and progressively senses its separation from the surrounding universe.

The transition from the romantic to the naturalistic world involves an initiation that awakens repercussions from the stage of personal development when the individual first begins to distinguish itself from the mother. In the words of Erich Neumann:

> During the phase when consciousness begins to turn into self-consciousness, that is, to recognize and discriminate itself as a separate individual ego, the maternal uroboros [the snake who devours his own tail, symbolizing the primordial condition of oneness] overshadows it like a dark and tragic fate. Feelings of transitoriness and mortality, impotence and isolation, now color the ego's picture of the uroboros, in absolute contrast to the original situation of contentment.[49]

In this transition, the locus of reality moves from the soul to the mind, from communion to confrontation. In this context, we understand the ethic of social Darwinism, the determination and no-nonsense view of nature canonized, for instance, in the histories of Francis Parkman and the wilderness watercolors of Winslow Homer. The artist-seer is succeeded by the hunter as the representative communicant with the natural world. Having lost his innocence, the hunter must exorcise his guilt by turning his aggression outward. Yet at the same time, naturalism retrieves the Calvinistic sense of alienation from nature which is likely to bring with it the conservative-organicist notion of social organization. Institutions, not nature, now define the limits of human behavior.

But before such naturalistic experience received social and doctrinal rationalization in the institutions and thought systems that came with the Civil War (and especially in the ethic of the strenuous life),[50] it was reflected in the cautionary fantasies of regression encountered in folklore and popular literature.

The trauma of entrapment in the swamp was portrayed in the anonymous piece just cited, "Ibis Shooting in Louisiana."[51] The narrator, telling of his search for the rare scarlet ibis, begins unassumingly enough with an account of the bird and its natural habitat, the bayou country of Louisiana. His search leads him into "a solitary region, with marshes stretching as far as the eye could see, covered with tall reeds" (p. 102). Struck by the sense of being the first ever to enter these dark waters, he is overcome with curiosity and eventually finds himself at the end of an oblong lake, a mile or so in length: "It was deep, dark, marshy around the shores, and full of alligators. I saw their ugly forms and long serrated backs, as they floated about in all parts of it, hungrily hunting for fish, and eating one another; but all this was nothing

new, for I had witnessed similar scenes during the whole of my excursion"
(p. 103). Then, upon the shore of a small islet, he finds the object of his search.

In the excitement of shooting and bagging one of the scarlet ibis, he forgets
to fasten his skiff which floats off, leaving him imprisoned on the islet. Only
after a minute does he realize his peril. Reflecting on the slim possibility of
being missed by someone, he concludes there is no hope. Notwithstanding
his despair, he shouts involuntarily: "I shouted loudly and fiercely: my answer
– the echoes of my own voice, the shriek of the osprey, and the maniac laugh
of the white-headed eagle" (p. 206).

Eventually, succumbing to the burden of his solitude, he totters to the
ground – "I lay in a state of stupor – almost unconscious . . . " – later awakening
from this condition to find himself surrounded by "dark objects of hideous
shape and hue."

> Reptiles had been before my eyes for some time, but I had not seen
> them. I had only a sort of dreamy consciousness of their presence; but
> I heard them at length: my ear was in better tune, and the strange
> noises they uttered reached my intellect. It sounded like the blowing
> of great bellows, with now and then a note harsher and louder, like
> the roaring of a bull. This startled me, and I looked up and bent my
> eyes upon the objects: they were forms of the *crocodilidae,* the giant
> lizards – they were alligators. (p. 107)

With hindsight, he attempts to reconstruct his state of mind at this point:

> I have been in a gloomy prison, in the hands of vengeful guerrilla
> banditti, with carbines cocked to blow out my brains. No one will
> call that a pleasant situation – nor was it so to me. I have been lost
> upon the wide prairie – the sea-land – without bush, break, or star to
> guide me – that was worse. There you look around; you see nothing;
> you hear nothing: you are alone with God, and you tremble in his
> presence; your senses swim; your brain reels, you are afraid of your-
> self; you are afraid of your own mind. Deserted by everything else,
> you dread lest it, too, may forsake you. There is horror in this – it is
> very horrible – it is hard to bear; but I have borne it all, and would
> bear it again twenty times over rather than endure once more the first
> hour I spent on that lonely lake. Your prison may be dark and silent,
> but you feel that you are not utterly alone; beings like yourself are
> near, though they may be your jailers. Lost on the prairie, you are
> alone; but you are free. In the islet, I felt that I was alone; that I was
> not free: in the islet, I experienced the feelings of the prairie and the
> prison combined. (pp. 106–7)

The shrinking of the world to the conditions of solitude and imprisonment
in otherness opens up the prospect of pure unconsciousness, an existential state
unmediated by the mind. Our informant's tenure on the island was an ordeal
of exposure and starvation. He engaged in a desperate struggle with himself
to keep awake. If unconsciousness should steal upon him again, he would be
sure to be devoured by the alligators, who fearlessly rubbed against his body:
"I was startled by the touch of something cold and half-stifled by a strong

musky odor that filled the air. I threw out my arms; my fingers rested upon an object slippery and clammy: it was one of those monsters – one of gigantic size" (p. 110).

The self is almost completely hypostatized by the landscape, creating an aura of nightmare, and the sensations of immersion and suffocation promote a sense of incest with the world of primordial matter.[52] The preceding account may be contrasted with the sensual nocturnal swim of Thomas Wentworth Higginson examined in Chapter 2. Although both experiences involve a loss of control – entrance into a world of intense projection – Higginson's feelings are erotic and energizing. Whereas the "ibis" account offers a situation of victimization accompanied by a warning, Higginson demonstrates his relative autonomy. His loss of control is an inviting release, and the eroticism he feels is a measure of his self-conscious choice.

A revolution in sensibility intervened between the consciousness of the ibis hunter (who is dominated by a fear of the unconscious) and the self-consciousness of Higginson (who heartily embraces the unconscious). The former is much closer to the folk imagination. The typical characteristics of the swamp – repulsiveness, cannibalism, encroachment, and violation – take on an aggressive form when embodied in its saurian denizens. Snakes, in particular, aroused feelings of fear and repugnance.

Relating his escape into the "Great Pacoudrie Swamp," the former slave Solomon Northrup pictured himself surrounded by snakes:

> I saw hundreds of moccasin snakes. Every log and bog – every trunk of a fallen tree, over which I was compelled to step or climb, was alive with them. They crawled away at my approach, but sometimes in my haste, I almost placed my hand or foot upon them. They are poisonous serpents – their bite more fatal than the rattlesnake's. Besides, I had lost one shoe, the sole having come entirely off, leaving the upper only dangling to my ankle.[53]

The myriad snakes might be likened to the profusion of vines and tendrils in the swamp. Northrup's sense of vulnerability is based on a real danger, of course: The snakes are poisonous. But there is an instinctive repulsion beneath this knowledge. As an article in *Harper's Monthly* (1855) assured its readers: "This terror [of snakes] is one of the most defined instincts of human nature, for it exists without having been founded upon any direful experience, and can not be overcome by reason."[54] Significantly, the serpent, like the swamp, evokes a contradictory response; it is at once enticing and forbidding: "Of all animated life, the serpent at first sight, is the most repulsive; and yet, with the species, there is such a combination of the beautiful, the terrible, and the mysterious, that the beholder, in spite of himself, is attracted by their appearance."[55]

This thinking along the lines of synechdoche – representing a total environment in concentrated, animate form through a single one of its aspects – is typical of folklore which is largely anti-imagistic, presenting its lessons through dramatic episode or humorous anecdote rather than scenery.[56] The folklore of the Great Dismal Swamp signals its taboos in parables of ghostly enchantment or mysterious disappearance. It abounds in spirits, witches, fair-

Figure 8.16. Anonymous American, *A Louisiana Swamp* (oil on canvas, 30 × 24 in., 1845). Gift of Edgar William and Bernice Chrysler Garbish, New Orleans Museum of Art.

ies, natural hoaxes, and unnameable creatures, but there is little description of the actual place.[57]

Two examples of this folklore were recorded by Robert Arnold in his reminiscences of growing up near the Great Dismal Swamp. One is about a man hunting in the swamp who suddenly found snakes coming at him from every direction. Looking in front of him he saw a lump of them as large as a barrel:

> He supposed there must have been as many as five hundred, all so interwoven that they looked like a ball of snakes. He said he was too close on them to shoot so stepping back he fired both barrels of his gun at the bunch. An untangling at once commenced, and he said "consarned if he ever saw so many snakes before." Upon going to the place where he had shot he found 150 snakes dead, and as many more wounded. He carried some of the largest of the dead out, procured a ten-foot rod, and on measuring found that it measured twenty-three feet.

This little story clearly serves as a parable of the human need to derive order out of chaos.

The other anecdote was told by a gentleman who had seen the fabled phantom fisherwoman of the Dismal Swamp. Standing one morning near the lake, he was astonished to see "come out of the woods at a point so thick with reeds, bam-boo and rattan, that you could not get three feet from the shore, a beautiful, finely dressed lady; she walked out on a log about twenty feet into the Lake, with a fishing pole in her hand. I saw her bait her hook and throw it out into the Lake."[58] The man watched at the same place for several days and each day witnessed the same apparition.

From another source we learn that the lady had been a bride whose prospective husband had gone hunting in the swamp on their wedding day and never appeared for the ceremony. During the wedding feast she too slipped away into the swamp, presumably in search of him, never to return. Frequently appearing to the locals along the south shore of Lake Drummond, she was believed to be either a beneficent deity or an evil spirit who lured lost hunters to their doom in the swamp.[59]

There is a primitive painting in which the lady is pictured fishing in a swamp copied directly from the engraving of the Dismal Swamp after John Gadsby Chapman (Figure 8.16).[60] A somewhat sinister-looking gentleman in a top hat spies on her from behind a tree. Naturally, the swamp offered a hospitable retreat for the devil and his minions. Hordes of evil spirits lurked in its depths or glimmered from its obscurities.[61] Forsaken spirits were condemned to wander about its dusky recesses. Prevalent belief in the presence of supernatural forces nourished the growth of an elaborate network of spirit controls that informed the speech patterns of the local inhabitants for the sake of both protection and spite.[62]

But the most widespread belief pertaining to the malevolent influence of the swamp – one adopted by medical opinion as well as surfacing spontaneously in the folk and popular imagination – was the traditional wisdom that fevers (typhoid, malaria, yellow fever) were caused by *miasma,* an infectious air that emanated from swamps and marshes: "This noxious effluvium . . . was variously assigned to decaying vegetable matter, to stagnant water, to decaying bodies on battlefields, or to plain putrefying animal matter."[63]

As we shall see in the next chapter, belief in infectious air, with the grounding in ancient superstition, formed the basis for a metaphor that had the most wide-ranging application in American antebellum culture but that was also affiliated with the most extreme and sophisticated patterns of Romantic thought. Linked to the process of spiritual decomposition I have been tracing, the metaphor of infectious air gives us a sense of what might happen were associationism to be unleashed from the control of culture without being stabilized and transfigured by any transcendental categories of thought. For our purposes, it relates the swamp to a pattern of imagery that was offered as a primary conduit into the molten core of subjectivity to be recast into new social and cultural patterns and to help transform the conception and function of language itself.

Infection and Imagination: The Swamp and the Atmospheric Analogy

The crucial twenty-third chapter of Melville's *The Confidence-Man* (1857) develops an analogy between the linguistic wiles of the latest avatar of the Confidence-Man (or Devil) and the imagery of infectious atmosphere. The chapter opens with a flood of allusions to an insidious agent hidden in the air, carrying infection and threatening death: "At Cairo, the old established firm of Fever & Ague is still settling up its unfinished business; that Creole grave-digger, Yellow Jack – his hand at the mattock and spade has not lost its cunning; while Don Saturninus Typhus taking his constitutional with Death, Calvin Edson and three undertakers, in the morass, snuffs up the mephitic breeze with zest."[1] Eyeing the "swampy and squalid domain" that lies before Cairo, the Missourian, Pitch, peers through the "dubious medium" of a "dank twilight, fanned with mosquitoes, and sparkling with fire-flies" and revolves in his mind an earlier conversation with the P.I.O. man, who, only moments before, had induced him to pay money for a promised boy servant. He begins to suspect he has been conned.

Somehow Pitch had been moved to suspend "that general law of distrust systematically applied to the race," allowing the man with the plate to take his money on a mere promise. Now he wonders how a man like himself may wake up "very wise and slow" and yet, before nightfall, find himself duped "by like trick of the atmosphere" (p. 129). The association here between the casuistical language of the Confidence-Man (at one point, Pitch accused his adversary of being a "punster of ideas") and a parody of the conversion experience it has just brought about in the Missourian[2] materializes in the imagery of infectious atmosphere, the very medium of trickery. This convergence of words and ideas with the image is critical to the passage's meaning, which carries all the weight of Melville's own skeptical encounter with Romantic culture.

I would like to acknowledge my substantial indebtedness in this chapter to Angela Miller, professor of art history at Washington University. My conversations with her were crucial to my formative thinking about this chapter, and she also generously offered me a number of the references that I have cited.

In a narrative structured as a dense vine of intertwining and increasingly resonant puns, the seminal pun of *The Confidence-Man* is surely that on the Word itself. On the authority of the Gospel of John, merging linguistic and christological frames of reference (Christ as the Word made flesh), words in the naturalistic sense extend by analogy to the supernatural. Language and faith achieve equivalence, accordingly, when the material aspect of the word (the *letter* or, in the terminology of postmodernist criticism, the *signifier*) is sacrificed. But where in the Christian scheme the mortification of the body unstops the springs of eternal life, in Melville's transmogrification of religion, the sacrifice of the physical issues is nothing other than the release of poisonous air. Rather than spiritual transformation, in other words, there is simply putrescence and its attendant exhalations. The "joke" of *The Confidence-Man* is that the divine afflatus ironically turns out to be only a mephitic breeze.

In tying the power of words to the power to infect, Melville at one level reproached a fluid, increasingly atomistic "mass" society whose members interacted with one another on the basis of mere professions of sincerity – mere words – as signified by the claims to honesty of the various confidence men. Manipulation of appearances, not stable values and reasoned discourse, were the order of the day.

At another level, Melville undercut the Promethean tendencies of self-declared prophets of all kinds, especially religious and literary, who relied on language to incarnate what was supposedly eternal truth. Accordingly, the name Don Saturninus Typhus, cited at the outset of this chapter, suggests an ironic inversion of the pretenses of the Confidence-Man in its oblique reference at the same time to the artist – a figure "born under Saturn," filled with the urge to realize the infinite yet frustrated by his physical limitations – and to the symptoms of an epidemic disease. Typhoid fever manifests itself as a delerious stupor which here stands for the transformation of language from its traditional function as reasoned discourse to the slippery and irrational "chain of signifiers" it was becoming in an age of consumerism and advertising.[3]

In each case we confront an aspect of "the mystery of human subjectivity" that Pitch ponders as he peers through the dense haze rising from the "villainous bank" that the P.I.O. man has just left. It is associationism gone crazy. Traditional adversaries that Romantic culture and mass society are, they here are subtly implicated in each other: At the least, both dismantle objective guideposts in the spread of infectious atmosphere.

But before pursuing further this parallel and its implications in Melville's text, I want to discuss the context in which such a paradoxical linkage becomes possible. Probing this dialectic between Romanticism and mass society along the nexus provided by the metaphor of infectious atmosphere allows us to detect the reverberations from the problem of language that arises when the spiritual aspect of the word loses its priority over the material aspect. The discovery of the resulting instability is, I believe, what ties Romanticism, if anything does, to the subsequent unfolding of Modernism and Postmodernism.

To trace this discovery in the American cultural context is to begin to understand the innovative and radical thrust of the American Romantic movement, as shown in a book like *The Confidence-Man* and in the proliferation of imagery relating to the swamp. In applying the atmospheric analogy specifically to words, Melville brought to culmination a mode of thought that is at the core of American Romantic culture and that indicates – to turn the metaphor back on itself for a moment – the decay and phosphorescent glow of the logocentric principle intrinsic to the tradition of humanism and patriarchy in Western thought.

To conceive of language as infectious is to acknowledge its slippage from the moorings to which eighteenth-century philosophy and discourse had sought to tie it. The effort to determine "the proper and strict meaning of words"[4] stemmed from John Locke's concern, vis-à-vis what he called *general terms,* "to avoid the inconveniences of obscurity and uncertainty in the signification of words: without which it is impossible to disourse with clearness or order concerning knowledge. . . . "[5] Though arguing that words have only a conventional, not a natural, relationship to their referents, Locke was interested in pinning words to simple ideas, to sensible things. Even abstract significations were to be taken from "the operations of sensible things," for instance, *"Spirit,* in its primary signification, is breath; *angel,* a messenger. . . . "[6] The primary legacy of this essentially idiographic version of language to America came through the influence of the Scottish Common Sense school of philosophy.

Locke's effort to tie words to things, to stabilize language, was, as Paul de Man and others showed, ultimately unsuccessful.[7] Along with its failure to establish an ontological certainty beyond merely symbolic language, Locke's model of the mind raised a crucial and difficult epistemological problem regarding the question of active power. This problem is evident in the failure of Common Sense philosophy, reflecting Locke's failure to account for the language of agency.

In his *Essays on the Active Powers of the Human Mind* (1788), for example, the influential Thomas Reid was forced to admit that words such as *cause* and *effect, action,* and *active power* could be defined only by "synonymous words which need definition as much."[8] Reid managed to avoid the upsetting implication of what amounted to an endless chain of signifiers by rejecting the Lockean premise that "all our ideas are ideas of sensation and reflection" and by simply asserting that in regard to the question of agency, we know what we know – a typical commonsense solution. "It is certain that we can conceive no kind of active power but what is similar or analogous to that which we attribute to ourselves; that is, a power which is exerted by will and with understanding."[9] The only problem left at this point is to show how will (the active power) in uncorrupted natures always follows the dictates of reason and conscience.

This commonsense perspective, having disposed of the epistemological issues opened up by empiricism, was the underpinning of the dominant mode of moral philosophy in early nineteenth-century America. The notion that signification should avoid ambiguity by being tethered to the sensible world and the conviction that agency should derive from the dictates of conscience were embedded in the ideology of the cultural establishment. A course in moral philosophy, required of all college seniors, was regarded as the capstone of the American educational experience.[10]

The commonsense perspective was even accepted in transfigured form (vitalized by the latest organic psychology from England and Germany) by the New England Transcendentalists. These thinkers traced their intellectual roots to both Europe and native American Unitarianism, a religion whose rationalistic and commonsense bias they never abandoned.[11] Hence Emerson could speak as convincingly as had Thomas Jefferson about self-evident truth, and he echoed Locke on the need to relate words to sensible things. We should note, though, that these propensities were at odds with another important part of Emerson's linguistic reflections, namely, his quest for a "fluxional" use of symbolic language (to be discussed in the next chapter).

It is against this background of commonsense assumptions – of a uniformity of perspective and of a language conceived of as basically descriptive – that the metaphor of infection achieves significance. Indeed, it emerges dialectically from the repressions of the commonsense worldview. The point here is that such a worldview had isolated the medium of words, of signs, from the source of agency; it had therefore precluded a dynamic mode of signification, a vital or "symbolistic" interaction between words and things. The image of infectious atmosphere, as I hope to show, came to serve a variety of American writers and thinkers as a way of imagining just this possibility. As such, it represents a kind of "revenge of the repressed," a recrudescence of energies suppressed by the monolithic structure of inherited thought that was less and less able to impose order on social, political, economic, and linguistic processes gone wild in a nation becoming modernized.

We begin to find in the early nineteenth century the peculiarly American inflection of the metaphor of infectious atmosphere in this distinctive relationship between Romantic ideas and social factors. Universal truths and the ideal of staid and reasoned discourse made little sense in a culture experiencing the impact of such forces as democratization, with its undermining of traditional hierarchy and hegemony; the rapid advance of capitalism, in which the expanding market economy was fueled by speculation and the disappearance of reliable monetary values; and the rise of industrialism and urbanization, uprooting masses of people and eventually remolding the contours of the self, as determined by its increasingly complicated relationship to others, time, and space. Perhaps the most devastating of all these forces was that of consumerism, generating a spate of semiotic manipulations and transformations.

All these disruptions of the relatively stable values of the eighteenth century sprang from the release of emotional or otherwise irrational forces, which attested to the inherent divisiveness and unpredictability of the self and its various means – above all, language – of inscribing itself on the world. The notion of infectious atmosphere was a way of identifying these forces imagistically. It helped reincarnate what Michel Foucault called "the living being of language," a property lost with the advent of the "Classical age" in the seventeenth and eighteenth centuries.

Language in the pre-Classical age, according to Foucault, made no distinction between words and things. The world appeared as a vast system of resemblances and their signs (signs manifesting the hidden knowledge contained in resemblances) under which there was presumed to run an original text, an ultimate revelation. Yet in this nondistinction between observation and language, which was the corollary of this "order of things," language could simply accumulate to infinity. Signs and similitudes, discourse and graphics, presented a kind of writing that demanded interpretation (rather than observation or demonstration) as the way to knowledge. But significantly, there was no closure in the system; the world simply continued to unfold in permutations of commentary; commentary on commentary.[12] The significa-tion of signs "did not exist, because it was reabsorbed into the sovereignty of the Like"; instead, "their enigmatic, monotonous, stubborn, and primitive being shone in an endless dispersion."[13]

The dynamic component here was resemblance itself, a middle term be-tween the sign or mark and what it signified. By removing this middle term from its conception of the sign, the Classical age was able to stabilize forms: "Language, instead of existing as the material writing of things, was to find its area of being restricted to the general organization of representative signs."[14]

Foucault saw literature as perhaps recalling the memory of the being of language that was lost with the establishment of this new *episteme,* as it forsakes the representative or signifying function given to words in the Classical age. In supposing only a conventional connection between the word and what it signified (not one mediated by the potentialities of resemblance), the Classical age separated the visual and verbal modes, a separation (upheld, paradoxically, by the Sister Arts idea) that remained at odds with any fully symbolistic sensibility. We shall see how the metaphor of infection figures in the recon-solidation of visual and verbal that resulted in the breakdown of representation in the nineteenth century.

Charged with the energy of what was alienated, the metaphor of infection did not simply reflect the social forces that seemed out of control to those of a conservative bent. It also became an agent for consolidating and defining energies that contained all the doubleness of the uncanny, of what was at once unfamiliar and familiar, threatening and beneficent.

This doubleness – paralleling that of the swamp, often the putative source of infectious air – helps explain the ambiguity with which all values became invested as they were reenvisioned in the Romantic period. I mean to suggest, on the one hand, a reemergence of long-buried mythic patterns of thought, along with the resurgence of the primitive self as traditional controls slackened and, on the other hand, the continuing alienation of these patterns and energies, as they were no longer mediated by their original ritualistic and social contexts. Without a coherent social and cultural structure to give them stability, these patterns and energies became subject to continual reconfiguration and to ma-nipulation through language in contexts as diverse as advertising, philan-thropy, and religious revival – as reflected by *The Confidence-Man's* attack on such phenomena.

In this light, it is germane to see the metaphor of infectious atmosphere as a multivalent metaphor, to discuss its relevance not only to literary explorations but also to such seemingly disparate but ultimately homologous cultural phe-nomena in the first half of the nineteenth century as epidemiology – the popular idea of the "atmosphere" of the home and of woman's "influence" that arose with the cult of domesticity – and the vogue for mesmerism, with its assumption of a "universal fluid" pervading all matter. Though lacking any explicit connection to the conception of language, these beliefs and modes of thought helped colonize an elastic realm of intersubjectivity within which language could reconnect itself to agency and within which words could become both things and actions and primarily such.

Although this development can also be traced in Europe, I claim its particular relevance to American culture, owing to the more radical nature of modernizing social trends in the nineteenth century and to the inner dynamic of the "romance" tradition, which will be sketched out later. These factors provide the context for the self-conscious linguistic awareness of Melville as well as for the psychological explorations of Poe, Hawthorne, Brockden Brown, and others.

What unites these beliefs and modes of thought and brings them into play with the ideology of Romanticism is that they all are founded on the idea of atmospheric agency. They rely, that is, on the assumption that the source of what happens in the world is not personal but environmental. Action, in other words, derives not from a divine or human actor but from the surrounding atmosphere.

In his "grammar of motives," Kenneth Burke distinguished a "pantheistic moment in philosophy [that], by producing a merger of personal and impersonal principles . . . can serve as a bridge leading from theology to naturalism."[5] The ascendancy of the atmospheric analogy in early nineteenth-century America denotes just such a collapse of the personal into the impersonal, leading toward a deterministic world in which action (*drama* in Burke's terms) is reduced to the motion of natural forces. In such an atmosphere, human motivation becomes behavioristic, a matter of stimulus–response transactions having nothing to do with conscious interiority (the commonsense assumption, for instance, that will naturally follows the dictates of understanding).

In this pantheistic merging of scene and agent, it becomes impossible to distinguish the realm of freedom from that of necessity. In the Romantic quest-narrative, for example, the freedom represented by imagination blurs into the compulsion of mysterious inner forces, as in the idea of following one's genius or demon. In this transitional moment, the imagination and the unconscious become, respectively, the locus and the source of agency, raising for the first time the prospect of overdetermination; the sense, that is, that insidious, unnameable spirits or influences are about, a kind of animism that infuses the atmosphere and is the effect of an inner world projected on the outer. It is here that we locate the metaphor of infection, with its momentum away from theological and dramatistic explanations of events and toward the naturalistic and materialistic worldview in which truth is no longer to be discovered in the outside world but to be made and endlessly remade through the medium of words, a medium now seen to be severed from its metaphysical roots.

What this movement finally suggests is an end to the traditional antinomies of culture, not only that between scene and agent – in which the outer world collapses into the inner world of the poet (a condition we shall explore in "The Fall of the House of Usher") – but also that between intellect and emotion, matter and spirit, and even word and referent. In the process, the distinction between good and evil becomes problematic.[16]

I have suggested that the notion of infection was a metaphor for exploring human consciousness and communication as it took shape beyond the limits prescribed by the official cultural boundaries in late eighteenth-century and early nineteenth-century America. Because of its identification with marginal aspects of culture, the metaphor generally carried negative connotations; indeed, it was charged with the urgency of danger. What was so frightening about it was that the identification of self with environment that Romantics normally found to enlarge perspective and invigorate the faculties was apt to give way to a loss of control. By their very intangibility, atmosphere and what it breeds have the capacity to expand without limit. We think, for instance, of the gloomy fog, with its overtones of pestilence, that is associated with the endless litigation and its corruptions in Charles Dickens's *Bleak House*.

Fear that order and reason could be supplanted by the manic energies of unconscious response found an analogy in the literal meaning of infection. During the first half of the nineteenth century, Americans commonly continued to believe that epidemic fevers were caused by miasma, an infectious air said to emanate from decaying matter and swamps and marshes.[17] Every summer, for example, those who could afford to do so left the South Carolina low country for Charleston in order to escape contamination from the overheated swamps. In a letter to the *New York Mirror*, William Gilmore Simms told of packing his family off to the city: "The season is fast approaching when the rank vegetation of our swamps becomes fatal to European and Atlantick [*sic*] life;" he wrote, "and we natives of the seaboard find it a timely precaution to depart before the middle of June."[18] This belief was not limited to Americans. Describing the onset of fever while he traveled in Chagres, Panama, the German traveler Julius Froebel wrote: "I think I knew the very moment when the fetid miasmata, rising from the neighbouring swamp and mixing with the air at the fall of night, took effect upon my constitution."[19]

Though Europeans also believed that epidemic disease was caused by infectious atmosphere, the presence of infectious air was commonly identified from at least as early as 1802, as a peculiarly American phenomenon.[20] In an oration that began with the familiar tribute to American uniqueness and promise, Charles Caldwell, M.D., listed the reasons for "the super-abundance of *marsh miasma* in the United States, compared with most parts of Europe. . . ."[21] Caldwell recommended that swampy land, which made up the better part of the southeastern seaboard region, be drained and cultivated: "A neglect of this rational, salutary, and lucrative practice, subjects thousands in the United States to the malignant action of marsh miasma, who would otherwise escape this deleterious poison."[22] Nonetheless, he concluded, even though we make war on beasts of prey and insects that ravage crops, "we are strangely supine and inattentive, in the adoption of measures to secure ourselves against the ravages of disease."[23]

For all the common sense of Caldwell's proposal, it is not hard to detect the metaphoric dimension in this typical opposition between "rational, salutary, and lucrative" practice and the ravages of disease. Indeed, at the bottom of Caldwell's thinking, as with most thought about epidemic disease in this period, lies the moral issue of self-control and loss of control which was bound to have powerful reverberations in a country where so many were committed to the Protestant ethic and Republican virtue, both of which were concerned with discipline, sobriety, industry, and the like. It is clear that the notion of controlling infection, when wielded even literally, reflects a conservative and pessimistic bias against perceived forces of disintegration. Federalists and Conservative Whigs were the most likely to adopt the metaphor.

What is crucial and highly suggestive about all this is the extent to which moral and mental as well as physical problems were attributed to the contraction of cholera and other fevers. That certain individuals, due to moral and mental laxity, were predisposed to infection (and here the poor as well as the debauched were the most likely victims) was an assumption shared by doctors, jeremiahs, and the public alike.

This notion seems to have been particularly strong in New England. Writing to George Bancroft in 1832, George Ticknor noted proudly of his native Boston: "The apprehension of the approach of cholera excites very little sensation here. We are such a moral, cleanly population, that, if we have it at all, we must have it very lightly."[24] By the mid–1850s, the connection between the moral and biological realms had become no less forceful for being merely metaphoric in the mind of Charles Eliot Norton:

> The miasma that broods over Carolina in the summer seems to me
> but the emblem of the invisible, unrecognized, blindly guessed at
> moral miasma that rests over the lands where slavery exists. If I ever
> write against slavery, it shall be on the ground not of its being bad for
> the blacks, but of its being deadly to the whites. The effect on
> thought, on character, on aim in life, on hope, is, . . . plainly as sad as
> anything can be. . . . [25]

This confusion persisted even among doctors. According to Charles E. Rosenberg, "The doctrine of predisposing causes went completely unquestioned by the medical profession. Even the moderate report of the American Medical Association's Committee on Practical Medicine and Epidemics reasoned that cholera could not be contagious, for a debauch or a drinking bout had never been known to cause a contagious disease."[26] The use of the word *contagion* here indicates that the confusion between the moral and physical realms extended to the influence among individuals as well. In 1832 during the first cholera epidemic to sweep the United States, those doctors who believed that the disease was contagious (communicated from person to person, that is) were far outnumbered by others who were convinced that its cause lay in the atmosphere. Nevertheless, the connotations of the words *infection* and *contagion* were nearly identical, and there is evidence that in the early nineteenth-century etiology of disease, the concepts they referred to were commonly conflated (an example of the collapse of the personal into the impersonal that colored thinking in general).[27]

The failure to discriminate between the moral and physical spheres at the source of the atmospheric analogy is virtually ageless and is embedded, as Angus Fletcher noted, in the etymology of the Greek noun, *miasma,* which originally stood for any pollution or polluting agent and thus with its Latin equivalent, *inficere,* subsumes the basic element of impurity.[28]

Not surprisingly, however, the notion of disease not as punishment for but as a sign of evil – something mental, intrinsic to human motivation – gained ascendancy only with the American and French revolutions, as typified by the remark of Gouverneur Morris in Paris in 1789 that "Republicanism is absolutely a moral Influenza from which neither Titles, Places, nor even the Diadem can guard their possessor . . . the Lord preserve us from a hot summer."[29] On the other hand, the implicit, even unconscious reference of the words *infection* and *contagion* to kinds of communication, whether baneful or not, is rooted in sixteenth- and seventeenth-century English. As Sir Toby Belch said of the gulling of Malvolio, "His very genius hath taken the infection of the device, man."[30]

As either unintentional or devious ways of translating opinion or conveying various emotional states of mind (for example, we speak of panic or laughter as "contagious"), the linguistic referents of contagion and infection were distinguished from deliberative discourse and helped establish the presence of an uncertain because unconscious realm of human motivation and signification. Most important to the gradual realization of this unconscious realm is the circumvention of the will, of intention, that might take place at any point in the communicative process and that occasioned in turn an inherent moral instability, an emerging determinism. The association of these words with the benign operation of example and especially of sympathy – a form of human interaction that came into its own with the advent of sentimentalism in the eighteenth century[31] – existed alongside the darker implications of impure contact. A quick look at prominent theoretical formulations of child rearing, mesmerism, and spiritualism in the mid-nineteenth century suggests how the use of the atmospheric analogy both reflected this instability as a reality in American culture and consolidated and advanced its influence on fundamental ways of thinking.

As late as 1861 the distinction between rationalistic and patriarchal models of communication, on the one hand, and an unconscious intersubjectivity based on the atmospheric analogy, on the other, was exploited by the American theologian Horace Bushnell in his epoch-making book on child-rearing practices and family life, *Christian Nurture.* In discussing child rearing, Bushnell contrasted "the law of simple contagion," as he called it, with "influence," which for him denoted "a persuasive power, or a governmental power, exerted purposely and with conscious design to effect some result in the subject." The law of contagion, by contrast, rested on "the organic unity of the family" and referred to "a power . . . exerted by parents over their children, not only when they teach, encourage, persuade, and govern, but without any purposed control whatever. The bond is so intimate that they do it unconsciously and undesignedly – *they must do it* [emphasis mine]. Their character, feelings, spirit, and principles must propagate themselves, whether they will nor not."[32]

According to Bushnell, the intimacy of the close-knit "organic" family would allow for "unconscious influence" from parent to child and militate against the individualism and social disruption entailed by the evangelical "crisis" conversion, the dominant mode of initiation in America against which he posed his new model. Influenced by Romantic psychology, Bushnell conceived of "contagion" functioning in the family as an atmosphere consisting of "the manners, personal views, prejudices, practical motives, and spirit of the house . . . which passes into all and pervades all, as naturally as the air they breathe."[33]

But although Bushnell's concept of "unconscious influence" provided a way of stabilizing family life relative to threatened social upheaval, for the truly traditional and organic society he sought to reinstate, he had to acknowledge the loss of control. The enemy had sneaked through the gates inside the Trojan horse of the atmospheric analogy, which carried the burden of the displaced subjectivity resulting from social change. It is revealing that in changing his focus from the voluntary to the involuntary, Bushnell was forced to recognize that there was nothing to guarantee that "the spirit of the house" daily breathed into the child's nature would be a positive influence. To that extent, his formulation of "nurture" succumbed to the unconscious determinism latent in the notion of atmospheric agency itself. Although they might unconsciously nurture the child to virtuous habits and inclinations, the parents might just as easily "propagate their own evil in the child, not by design, but under the law of moral infection. . . . The airs and feelings and conduct of idolatry are back of all choice and memory."[34]

Such subtle influences bypassed any professed moral code or expression of will and raised the nagging question of the parents' sincerity. In the Puritan tradition to which Bushnell clearly belonged, the struggle to reconcile inner conviction and outward behavior, the attempt to see the internal through the external was nothing new; it continued the issue of "visible sainthood." But with an increasingly complicated social fabric, the viability of sincerity had suffered, all the more in a culture raised on the complacencies of the Common Sense philosophy with its effective denial of subjectivism[35] (hence we find Melville attacking the cult of sincerity in his play on the ambiguous relationship between "confidence" and " conmanship"). And it is precisely at this juncture between the Common Sense worldview and social change that the concept of sincerity merges with that of sympathy as an attribute of the self vulnerable to the deleterious effects of moral infection. In sharing a basis in atmospheric agency, both concepts lost their boundaries, which threatened the common-sense perspective itself.

Still another primary conduit into the molten center of intersubjectivity from which sincerity and sympathy were crystallized was the mid-nineteenth-century vogue for mesmerism. It takes little imagination to perceive the relationship between the atmospheric analogy and the basic assumptions of mesmerism – at once pseudoscience and pseudoreligion – that Bushnell's religious orthodoxy and political conservatism led him to condemn but with which his stress on the aeriform nature of sympathetic response has an affinity.

Mesmerism was founded on the presumed existence of a "universal fluid," invisible of course, that circulated throughout the universe and between the outer world and the human organism. Restoration of the proper proportion of this fluid in the body was seen as the requirement for health, and the idea was easily extended to society as a whole.[36] Utopia might be achieved as the result of the harmonious flow of universal fluid among individuals, constituting a "magnetic chain of sympathy." J. Stanley Grimes, in an interesting explanation of mesmerism, identified this universal fluid with the ether of science and traditional cosmology, whose motions were attributed to such physical phenomena as gravity, heat, electricity, magnetism, and light but which he also extended to the "animal and human motions" exerted in mesmerism. As he put it, mesmeric manifestations occurred simply through "the diversion of etheral force from its normal and constitutional avenues."[37]

Numerous repercussions originate from the widely held notion of a universal fluid, ether, or some other type of atmospheric agent acting as the medium for the communication of subjective messages between one being and another or for the exchange of energy between mental and physical, material and spiritual. For example, consider the interesting responses to this idea in the years before the Civil War. Because of its silent, undynamic character, the power of atmospheric influence offered an alternative to the violent, revolutionary developments Americans saw taking place in Europe. An 1848 article in the *Univercoelum, and Spiritual Philosopher* (an organ for the promotion of mesmerism and spiritualism) on "The Late Revolution in France" cautioned that if Americans did not heed the "still small voice of Nature . . . she will by-and-bye speak with the voice of earthquake and thunder. . . ." The writer went on to express the hope that Heaven would "grant that the lowering thunder clouds which darken our own social firmament . . . equalize themselves by the gradual process of electrical induction, and not by violent and destructive explosions!"[38]

A general appreciation for unconscious influences is perhaps the key to the quiescent mood that takes over in American "luminist" landscape painting, involving an interest in the palpable presence of light, following the preeminence of the Hudson River school (and especially Thomas Cole), whose representation of scenery was characterized by the theatricality of the Burkean sublime. The ambiguity of this influence may even account for the disturbing undertones in the work of Martin Johnson Heade and Fitz Hugh Lane. In the emptying out of rhetorical and dramatic content in these paintings, we are left with something of the visual equivalent of Melville's "dumb blankness, full of meaning."

Bushnell himself, in his sermon "Unconscious Influence" (1859), used an analogy between the influence of parents on their children and what goes on in the natural world: "Behind the mere show, the outward noise and stir of the world, nature always conceals her hand of control, and the laws by which she rules. Who ever saw with the eye, for example, or heard with the ear, the exertions of that tremendous astronomic force which every moment holds the compact of the physical universe together?"[39] In shifting emphasis from such highly perceptible natural manifestations as thunder and lightning to the silent but abiding and far more profound influence of gravity or light, Bushnell presumed to account for an agency in life more intrinsic and far more powerful than whatever surface convulsions might attract attention.

The loss of the boundary between the physical world and the mental and spiritual worlds in mesmerism was explicitly entertained by the German writer J. H. Jung-Stilling, whose *Theory of Pneumatology* appeared in translation in the United States in 1851 and who tied spiritualism to the mesmeric trance in terms of just this loss of distinction between the phenomenal and the noumenal. During the trance, the senses are at rest, and the body is "as it were dead. . . ." Accordingly, the "inner man enters into a more elevated, and agreeable state, which gradually increases, the more frequently magnetizing or stroking according to certain rules is repeated." The "exaltation of the inner man" may reach such intensity that the medium comes into contact with the invisible world wherein are revealed "hidden mysteries, and also remarkable things, which are taking place at a distance, or will shortly happen."[40]

This continuity between the here and now and the beyond is not limited for Jung-Stilling to the case of the mesmeric trance. There is also the example of light (with obvious relevance to the iconography of nature in this period), which is regarded as matter yet has properties completely opposed to the nature of all other matter: "Light is the connecting link between visible and invisible worlds," he explained, "The transition from one to the other is through its medium."[41] Having established the monistic implications of the "atmospheric" medium of light, with its resonances from the New Testament, Jung-Stilling is ready to take the momentous next step of connecting this essence (again taking his cue from Scripture) to the specifically linguistic realm: "The whole universe consists entirely of created beings, each of which is an expressed and really existing *word* [emphasis mine] of God."[42] It is no accident that this assertion reminds us of Poe's visionary sketch entitled "The Power of Words," for Poe's ideas had a similar genesis.

Clearly, mesmerism, as its impact was felt in the United States during the first half of the nineteenth century, was one way in which the Romantic psychology (as opposed to the dominant materialistic model of mind stemming from Locke) could make its way into popular culture. Jung-Stilling was expressly concerned with refuting materialism. Yet in the end, and here is the dilemma, such efforts to tie together spirit and matter could wind up promoting simply a more subtle type of materialism and determinism, as is obvious in the analogy drawn by J. Stanley Grimes between the human will that directs *ethereal* force and the capacity of an electric eel to discharge *electric* force.[43] An essential materialism is certainly evident in the thought of Poe, whose attempts to see matter and spirit as ultimately the same thing – simply poles of a spectrum in which ether occupied an intermediate position (in such pieces as "Mesmeric Revelation," "The Power of Words," and *Eureka*) – reflect not only mesmerist theory but also his close ties with eighteenth-century physicotheology (and his consequent rejection of Coleridge's theory of Imagination). Poe's adventures in cosmology are the background for his inability to get beyond the belief that the way to achieve the Ideal was nothing more than a matter of managing the right effect.[44]

The materialism of Poe's approach to both art and life has been related to his fascination with death and decay.[45] Obviously, matter unimbued with spirit is bound to decay and putrefy. Here we encounter the key to the meaning of the miasmic atmosphere of "The Fall of the House of Usher." But before considering this question, we should further clarify the relationship of sincerity and sympathetic response to the developing sphere of Imagination. It was in the tradition of the American romance that this relationship began and where the paradox to which it gave rise was most sensitively developed and probed.

Charles Brockden Brown, perhaps the first important American novelist, had been concerned in his fiction with exposing the inherent contradictions between the dual commitment in the sentimental mind to common sense (which gave priority to objective reality), on the one hand, and to sincerity, sympathetic response, and imagination (all expressions of subjectivity), on the other. The problem, for Brown, lay with the inner world of the self, in all its volatile potentiality. For instance, Edgar Huntly's persistent efforts (in the novel of the same name) to be sincere, both in responding to the demonic Clithero – a dark alter ego who fascinates him – and in telling his story, are what propel him into a world in which his commonsense assumptions are exploded and his presumption of sincerity ends up a sham. Moreover, Huntly's unconscious identification with Clithero continues to delude him in his assessment of the latter's character and points to the pernicious control, whether willful or not, of one person (Edgar) by another (Clithero) through the most nebulous of means (not unlike the moral infection exerted by "bad" parents on their children, which for Bushnell represented the liability of "unconscious influence").

To relate conduct to what was at bottom an elusive psychological process rather than to a tangible doctrinal source of authority was indeed to unveil the insidious, uncontrollable forces of moral infection, through which a person's perception of the world became increasingly relative and subjective if not actually vulnerable to outside control and deception. The dangerous undertones of this metaphor are apparent in the declaration of an English publication of 1851, *The Parents' Great Commission,* concerned with child rearing: "The miasmata of contagion, the particles which carry odour, are not so subtle, so pervading, so penetrating, or so inevitable, as are the immaterial emanations which infect the heart with the quality of its neighbor."[46]

Most of the ingredients of the metaphor of infection I have been analyzing are at least implicit here: Along with the subtlety, pervasiveness, and penetration of the "immaterial emanations," their inevitability charges the notion of infection with the threat of loss of control and the dissolution of personal boundaries. The notion that a person is able to direct such unconscious energy only underscored its negative accents. Surely, the loss of autonomy in the mesmeric medium that Hawthorne feared (we think of Westervelt and Priscilla in *The Blithedale Romance* or of Hawthorne's letters to his wife warning her to beware of mesmerism) or the psychological control of the *Pequod*'s crew by that consummate "mesmerist" Ahab are only the most striking examples of the manipulation of unconscious energies that accompanies the dissolution of constituted hierarchical structures and the growing ineffectuality of reasoned discourse. The reorientation from mesmerism to hypnotism stemming from the discovery in 1843 of "suggestibility" as the basis for mesmeric phenomena little affected the explanatory power of mesmeric influence that continued on in the popular imagination in the concept of animal magnetism, with all its sexual overtones.

In the evolution of the American romance tradition, it is easy to trace the expanding role of the metaphor of infection as it interacted with the ideas of sympathetic response and imagination. The rise of sentimentalism in the eighteenth century had naturally given a big boost to this kind of volatile rapport, evident, for example, in the seduction of Isabella by Mercutio in James Butler's *Fortune's Foot-ball* (1797), in which Isabella's heart, "tender as the orb of sight, had caught the sweet infection . . . with a sudden tremor, which thrilled like lightening through the deepest and most intricate recesses of it."[47]

Such loss of control could spell only disaster in the long run, and we indeed see the dark side of imaginative response in the work of Brockden Brown. The plague that rages in *Ormond* (1798) is explicitly related to the delusions of imagination in the case of Baxter, the husband of Constantia Dudley's friend Sarah, who dies of yellow fever merely (as the narrator surmises) because he *believes* he has been assailed by the "noisome effluvia" while witnessing the burial of a neighbor who, in turn, he only *assumes* has been struck down by it. The narration concludes: "His case may be quoted as an example of the force of imagination. He had probably already received, through the medium of the air, or by contact of which he was not conscious, the seeds of this disease. They might have lain dormant, had not this panic occurred to endow them with activity."[48]

If a susceptible imagination or lax moral standards (the two usually went together) made one especially liable to infection, it is not surprising that the chaste and demure "Puritan" maiden Hilda, in Hawthorne's *The Marble Faun*, should not dread the summer atmosphere of Rome, "although [it was] generally held to be so pestilential. She had already made trial of it, two years before, and found no worse effect than a kind of dreamy languor, which was dissipated by the first cool breezes that came with autumn."[49]

Nor, by the same token, is it surprising that that "little American flirt," Daisy Miller, as a direct consequence of her innocent if scandalous unconventionality, should breathe the same atmosphere (albeit more than two decades later) during a late-night jaunt to the Colosseum in the company of an Italian gentleman of questionable motives, contract the fever, and die.

The apparition of the ancient ruin by moonlight induces Winterbourne to murmur some famous lines from *Manfred*, "but before he had finished his quotation he remembered that if nocturnal meditations in the Colosseum are recommended by the poets, they are depreciated by the doctors. The historic atmosphere, scientifically considered, was no better than a villainous miasma."[50] Ruinous seduction by the alluring but corrupt European past is reserved for less guarded epicureans of romance than the bloodless Winterbourne. James here simply echoed Hawthorne, according to whom "the feverish influence . . . haunts those beautiful lawns and woodlands around the suburban villas" of the Roman Campagna: "What the flaming sword was to the first Eden, such is the malaria to those sweet gardens and groves. We may wander through them, of an afternoon, it is true, but they cannot be made a home and a reality, and to sleep among them is death. They are but illusions, therefore, like the show of gleaming waters and shadowy foliage in a desert."[51]

The psychological basis for the supernatural in American romance may in fact be said to originate from this connection between infection and the imaginative distortion of "reality," as exemplified by Washington Irving's account of the mysterious effect of a painting on the sensibility of the "nervous gentleman" in *Tales of a Traveller* (1822). It is not the painting that is the source of the weird sensations he experiences in its presence: "The faintly lighted apartment had all the qualifications requisite for a haunted chamber. It began in my infected imagination to assume strange appearances – the old portraits turned paler and paler, and blacker and blacker; the streaks of light and shadow thrown among the quaint articles of furniture gave them more singular shapes and characters."[52] Far from resorting to the convention of the "explained Gothic" in concluding the tale, Irving stressed the possible subjective origins of the supernatural by retaining to the end of the story the ambiguity of whether the painting in question is in fact the one known to be haunted. In any case, he made a general observation on the nature of sympathetic or imaginative response that proved prophetic: "Whoever has been in a state of nervous agitation, must know that the longer it continues the more uncontrollable it grows."[53]

This principle of uncontrollable growth is also the peculiar law of Roderick Usher's universe. It is exemplified by the miasmic atmosphere that comes from the tarn at the foot of Usher's house and that, having "no affinity with the air of heaven," reeks "from the decayed trees, and the gray wall, and the silent tarn – a pestilent and mystic vapor, dull, sluggish, faintly discernible, and leaden hued." We are alerted near the outset of the story to the possibility that this atmosphere has no objective reality. The narrator admits that his first impressions of Usher's realm have so worked on his imagination that he is ready "to believe that about the whole mansion and domain there hung an atmosphere peculiar to themselves and their vicinity. . . . "[54] His initial sense of gloom and oppressiveness had been heightened by his first glance into the mirrorlike waters of the tarn. Now he wonders whether his "superstition" (as he calls it) is somehow self-generating. The acceleration of its increase dictates the steady accumulation of atmosphere surrounding the house of Usher until the fatal climax of the story on the tempestuous evening when the Lady Madeline wreaks her revenge on her brother.

From his first encounter with the house, the narrator finds himself struggling to retain rational control of his experience as he is submerged in a world that, as the tarn itself reveals, has no concreteness. Impressions here have nothing to do with "a mere different arrangement of the particulars of a scene"[55] (a reference to Locke's objective world). The arbitrariness of the real has been usurped by the tautology of subjective vision.

The accumulation of infectious atmosphere in Usher's universe is paralleled by the growing contagion that is the agent in the intercourse between Usher's mind and that of the narrator, who remarks at one point. "It was no wonder that [Usher's] condition terrified me – that it *infected* me [emphasis mine]. I felt creeping upon me, by slow degrees, the wild influences of his own fantastic yet impressive superstitions."[56] The notion of influence is paramount here: not an influence that is tangible but one that is terrifying because it cannot be comprehended, because it is covert and insidious. Usher, as Leo Spitzer explained, lives in a deterministic world in which causality is atmospheric. It would be ridiculous, therefore, to expect him to resist what is endemic to his nature.[57] Naturally, it is superstition and not some more theistic religious conviction that is the message of this infectious medium. Usher pulls the narrator into a world of primitive forces and fears, where the omnipotence of thought rules all. There is no longer any clear distinction between subject and object.

In Usher's domain the energies of sympathetic response and of imagination, as embodied in the infectious atmosphere, directly reflect the materialism of Poe's worldview mentioned earlier. The disintegration of his world results from the divorce of matter and spirit as Usher attempts to deny nature – the sensible world – in his megalomaniacal striving to reach the Ideal. Predictably, according to the logic of the "revenge of the repressed," Usher's effort to escape from matter ends up making him its victim. The consequence of his dissolution of sensibility, naturally enough, is the decay of "dead" matter (matter no longer invested with spirit) that in turn unleashes the miasma that haunts Usher and anticipates the release of now uncontrollable imaginative and unconscious energies in the breakdown of the normal synergy of the self. The inevitable consequence of Usher's status as the god of his own universe is the reduction of that universe to the conditions of sheer materialism.

This is the point at which the exploration of the metaphor of infectious atmosphere in America departs from corresponding developments in English and European Romanticism. Shelley's poem "The Sensitive Plant" (1820) pictures such a materialistic world as well, but only after the death of the maiden (representing the spiritual aspect of love, the logocentric principle) who tends the garden. As Harold Bloom noted, "She is 'a ruling Grace' in the garden; she is to the flowers 'as God is to the starry scheme.' "[58] Until her death, signifying the approach of winter, the sensitive plant had received the beneficent influences from the world around it, much as if it were a mesmeric medium:

> The quivering vapours of dim noontide,
> Which like a sea o'er the warm earth glide,
> In which every sound, and odour, and beam,
> Move, as reeds in a single stream;
>
> Each and all like ministering angels were
> For the Sensitive Plant sweet joy to bear,
> Whilst the lagging hours of the day went by
> Like windless clouds o'er tender sky.

After the maiden dies, however, the garden, in effect having lost its soul and become a merely material creation, succumbs to decay:

> And agarics and fungi, with mildew and mould
> Started like mist from the wet ground cold;
> Pale, fleshy, as if the decaying dead
> With a spirit of growth had been animated!

This decomposition in turn generates poisonous exhalations (malevolent, animistic forces), and so the organic cycle from sympathetic harmony to dangerous infection is complete:

And hour by hour, when the air was still,
The vapours arose which have strength to kill:
At morn they were seen, at noon they were felt,
At night they were darkness no star could melt.

The putrescence of the garden, turning the air to poison, is likened to the decay of the maiden's corpse, the smell of which, "cold, oppressive, and dank," is "Sent through the pores of the coffin plank."[59]

With the maiden's removal from the garden, Shelley dramatized the elimination of the personalistic and spiritual element from the natural setting. This moment signified nothing less than the end of Idealism. The presence of the maiden had focused the energy of a spiritual order of being integral to physical existence that, with the deterioration of a theological worldview, was lost (though there is, at one level, an allegory of winter here, suggesting a cyclical return to the resurgence of spring).

In order to perceive the concrete link between the metaphor of infectious air and the development from a teleological worldview to one of arbitrary determinism, one need only think of the organic cycle of infection, disease, death, putrefaction, and the resulting infectious air that most Americans and Europeans of the Romantic period took for granted as an explanation for epidemic fevers. But whereas Shelley offered simply a depersonalized meaning, Poe gave it a psychological meaning, in placing Usher at the center of the story as the god of his own universe. And the thrust of this psychological variation on the metaphor pushes toward the linguistic realm itself. Usher lives in a world characterized by (in Allen Tate's suggestive phrase) "the Dark Night of Sense,"[60] and it is only appropriate that the story should unfold primarily as the intensification of a mood, not as a narrative in which things especially happen.

An aspect of this lack of drama in the tale is the narrator's failure at the outset to put his finger on just what he is feeling. The mood that engulfs him continues to elude the denotative power of language. It is precisely this disjunction between rational and irrational, denotative and connotative, that opens the way for the reversal of terms through which language is to be seen and finally used as atmospheric. Here is where the indeterminacy of the physical at the heart of the swamp experience in mid-nineteenth-century America exerts its most fundamental and far-reaching effects on literary and cultural sensibility. It is no surprise that Poe himself later linked the reverse metaphysic entailed by the collapse of spiritual into physical to the action of words themselves, thus reuniting language – at least in theory – with the agency from which the Enlightenment had severed it.

In "The Power of Words" (1845), Poe extended the analogy between atmosphere and consciousness to include the notion that every word is "an impulse on the air." The "physical power of words" – the motion of impulses in the ether that pervades the universe – has its source in the thought of God. In this postapocalyptic sketch, Agathos, Poe's disembodied spirit, explains that each imperishable thought emanating from God has infinite results; that "it is indeed demonstrable that every such impulse *given the air,* must, *in the end,* impress every individual thing that exists *within the universe"*; and that mathematics offers a species of analysis by which all remote undulations might be traced "upward and onward for ever in their modifications of old forms" until found to be reflected, "unimpressive at last – back from the throne of Godhead."[61]

This postulation of a means of reaching divine insight while circumventing the physical world – the source of analogy – by relying on algebraic calculations (a means perfected only by God, though also exercised by the host of angelic intelligences) looks beyond the practice of language as magic – as an active agent in the creation of the world – to the possibility that a language susceptible to a certain calculus might simply wind up sterile. The infectious atmosphere of "The Fall of the House of Usher" offers this paradoxical prospect of Poe's metaphysic, whose full implications were left unexplored in his more speculative pieces.

A language in which spirit and matter have become one is, by the logic of the atmospheric analogy, paradoxically also a language cut off from "thingness," hence from the source of productivity. It is important to keep in mind here the basic dynamic of Kenneth Burke's "grammar of motives," for it allows us to see how values based on the fiction of substance can change places or can simply collapse into the source of meaning where all distinctions disappear.[62] With the effective end of any "living" distinction between spirit and matter, the tension allowing words to mean something specific and at the same time to mean nothing in particular that had sustained their "symbolistic" freedom surrendered to a condition in which everything becomes a matter of finite calculation.

Such control of the domain of language, as envisioned in Poe's prophecy of a mathematical accuracy in determining the original impulse for a word, would confine language to being an agent in a world defined by deterministic or mechanical forces. The condition of determinism can in turn be seen as a direct consequence of the world of reified objects created by industrial capitalism and its attendant consumerism. It owes its existence to the chasm between ideas and sensuous activity, between "seeing" and "being" (to adopt Carolyn Porter's term), which was the fundamental "dissociation of sensibility" engendered by the American economic system as it came into its own before the Civil War.[63]

A world in which everything is in the process of becoming a commodity is a world in which language too loses its power to transform social life and becomes simply an agent in the system's stereotyping and manipulative processes. Words become mere empty things, ready to conform to any message the system finds it profitable to broadcast. The chain of signifiers is endless. This is the point at which American Romanticism – as defined by an idealistic metaphysics and aesthetics – becomes implicated in the rise of mass society. It is a truism I hardly need repeat, that the age that saw the advent of the masses also saw the advent of the individual. The difference in sensibility between observing the world and participating in its remaking was one that the great American Romantic writers – Emerson, Thoreau, Whitman, and Melville – all confronted and managed to bridge with varying success.

In the final section of this book, I shall be concerned with the role of the swamp and other desert places in enabling certain figures to bridge the gulf between themselves and the physical and social world around them or (to change my metaphor to a more appropriate dynamic one) to wrestle more effectively with the impact of capitalist alienation on their modes of thought. Immersion in the physicality of the swamp could function as a way of bringing body and soul back together again and, through this self-consolidation, could then engender a metaphoric and productive use of language that might at least point toward a transformation of the social realm. The incarnation of this revolutionary perspective on the world was at best a delicate one, however, and we find evidence of it only fleetingly in the American literary tradition – most clearly, I believe, in Thoreau, for whom Emerson pointed the way. For the most part, immersion was experienced not in the more physical aspects of the swamp but, as we have seen, in the atmosphere emanating from it, always giving the mental factor an upper hand over the physical. The primacy of mental agency in the metaphor of atmosphere eventually shut out any sense of alterity from a world of domineering projection, of sometimes hallucinatory intensity.

It is this world that Melville both heralds and bemoans in his ingenious jeremiad. Poe's duality of language brings us back to Melville's *The Confidence-Man,* in which the active power of language is released from logic and the commonsense world, to ricochet between the poles of infinite possibility and its foreclosure before settling by the latter, in which nearly every aspect of American Romantic culture – imagination, sincerity, sympathy, and Pauline faith – is finally turned inside out. By the time he wrote the novel, Melville had lost faith in the American enterprise, in religion, in the power of words to do anything but seduce and fool the auditor, and in reality, and his writing drags behind it the burden of the commodification of everything wrought by the totalizing system of capitalism.

To return to the action of Chapter 23 of Melville's *The Confidence-Man:* As he ruminates on his exchange with the P.I.O. man before the "villainous bank" where the latter has just disappeared, Pitch is led to speculate on the man's motives, "incomprehensible under the laws of logic" ("Two or three dirty dollars the motive for so many wiles?") (p. 130). Then the figure of the P.I.O. man appears before his mental vision, and Pitch discovers a more productive line of thought: "The doctrine of analogies recurs." This is a "fallacious enough doctrine when wielded against one's prejudices" (p. 130), as it was by the P.I.O. man who, Pitch recalls, had used it to con him. Now, however, he realizes that "in corroboration of cherished suspicions," the doctrine of analogies might indeed be useful. In his mind's eye – and this is the crucial moment of insight – the image of the P.I.O. man coalesces with its dark meaning. "Analogically [Pitch] couples the slanting cut of the equivocator's coat-tails with the sinister cast in his eye; he weighs slyboot's sleek speech in the light imparted by the oblique import of the smooth slope of his worn bootheels; the insinuator's undulating flunkyisms dovetail into those of the flunky beast that windeth his way on his belly" (p. 130).

Pitch is the only passenger on the *Fidèle* to see through the Confidence-

Man's masquerade. In reaching this insight, he returns to the world of literal meaning and concrete perceptions (indeed, his name suggests "stickiness," as opposed to the "slipperiness" of the Confidence-Man's name) from which he had been seduced by the P.I.O. man's sophistical analogies. Besides rejecting the false reasoning, Pitch also rejects the pretense of congeniality that the con man had played on and that later in the book is associated with drunkenness. Drunkenness dissipates the attitude of skepticism or distrust, blurs normal distinctions, and promotes intersubjectivity (as in the conversation between the Cosmopolitan and Charlie Noble). It intensifies a willingness to draw connections among different aspects of the world not on the basis of common sense or rational judgments (properly conditioned by "distrust") but on the basis of the fluid, provocative but patently conventional medium of words themselves. The elaborate punning exploited by the various avatars of the Confidence-Man both stands for and enacts the manipulation of reality by language that has become detached from "natural" and ethical realms. The lapse of logic and denotation and the consequent riot of connotative meanings and analogies produced by words that in effect have become mere signs determine reality aboard the *Fidèle,* a vessel descending into a region with the unmistakable figuration of hell. This reality, constituted purely by language, is imaged by the deepening twilight and tainted air along the banks of the Mississippi through which Pitch attempts to peer.

Behind the imagery of infectious atmosphere lies that of the swamp that is its source, and the presence of this symbol at the heart of the novel underscores the dialectic of the two levels of Melville's allegorical attack, on mass society and on Romantic striving. The swamp in Melville's day was both a supposed source of infection and, as we have seen, a common image of alienation and melancholy. In its function as a symbol in the complex semantic mosaic of Melville's writing, it therefore merges nominal opposites: on the one side faith, to be aligned with sincerity and with fever, and on the other side skepticism, a shift back to concrete, commonsense distinctions.

This collapse of faith and skepticism into their common source is borne out in the text when Pitch paradoxically perceives the true nature of the Confidence-Man just as if he were contracting a fever. We take our cue from the title of the chapter: "In Which the Powerful Effect of Natural Scenery Is Evinced in the Case of the Missourian, Who, in View of the Region-Round About Cairo, Has a Return of His Chilly Fit." The expression "Chilly Fit" does double duty here by referring not only to the symptom of fever but also to the restoration of the Missourian's habitual attitude of "cold" skepticism, as opposed to "warm" sympathy and faith, precisely that condition under which he had been duped. The implication, in other words, is that infection, though not always a truthful or effective means, is necessarily the only means by which the world is ever to be known.[64]

In his bewilderment, the doctrine of analogies is Pitch's only recourse. Even the idea that this means of gaining insight is effective only if "wielded against one's prejudices" is cast into doubt, for we are left to wonder whether Pitch's analogical reasoning does not itself partake of the linguistic element – as in "the undulating *flunky*isms" that "dove-tail into the *flunky* beast that windeth his way on his belly." Is this merely the author's rhetoric? We have little sense of even his presence. In this confusion between picture and word, author and text, Melville signaled the absence of distinction between visual and verbal that had been enshrined in early nineteenth-century American culture and that, in the form of the Sister Arts idea, had been the bulwark of the tradition of descriptive language left by the Enlightenment.[65]

It may appear here that we have made a circle around the question of analogy, and indeed we have. But given this circularity, we can now appreciate the elusiveness of the distinction Melville seems to have been trying to make. The difficulty of drawing this distinction kept him from resolving his own deepest conflict, between the will to believe and the need to doubt. The problem pertained to the ambiguous relationship between matter and spirit in a world conditioned by mass society in which the relatively stable hierarchies of value were fast disappearing. In such a world, the question of faith also devolved into a question of language.

In approaching the Romantic doctrine of Imagination with ambivalence and distrust, Melville and other American romancers reacted to a paradox that I characterize as the central problem of American Romantic culture, the paradox of competing apprehensions of reality, inner and outer truth, sincerity and commonsense.[66] In regard to language, this paradox addressed the fact that words were both finite and infinite, sign and signified, bounded in meaning by their denotative function and part of an endless chain of signifiers.

In a fundamentally theological worldview in which the otherness of spirit remained inviolate – as with the Puritan doctrine of the absolute sovereignty of God – this paradox might be sustained and inhabited in all its delicate and excruciating tension. But as theology gave way to naturalism, via a momentary pantheistic fusion of matter and spirit, the constituent elements of the paradox were bound to fly apart. Words were either demoted to the status of inert and finite counters, not expressing anything beyond themselves, or they expanded into a miragelike haze of indeterminate meaning. In this dissociation we perhaps find, in its own internal structure, the clue to the culmination of Romanticism in America and its momentum in altered form into the twentieth century. It is no wonder that the final passages of *The Confidence-Man* enact an ironic parody of Revelation and that Melville leaves us with only the final assurance that "something further may follow of this masquerade."

PART THREE

The Circuit of Death and Regeneration

Therefore we ought to abandon the idea that it is a mere matter of accident that an actual phenomenon of the external world is chosen to furnish a shape thus conformable to truth. Art does not appropriate this form either because it simply finds it existing or because there is no other. The concrete content itself involves the element of external and actual, we may say indeed of sensible manifestation. But in compensation this sensuous concrete, in which a content essentially belonging to mind expresses itself, is in its own nature addressed to the inward being. Its external element of shape, whereby the content is made perceptible and imaginable, has the aim of existing purely for the heart and mind. This is the only reason for which content and artistic shape are fashioned in conformity with each other. The mere sensuous concrete, external nature as such, has not this purpose for its exclusive ground or origin. The birds' variegated plumage shine unseen, and their song dies away unheard, the torch thistle which blossoms only for a night withers without having been admired in the wilds of southern forests, and these forests, jungles of the most beautiful and luxuriant vegetation, with the most odorous and aromatic perfumes, perish and decay no less unenjoyed. The work of art has not such a naive self-centered being, but is essentially a question, an address to the responsive heart, an appeal to affections and to minds.

> G. W. F. Hegel, *Introduction to the Philosophy of Fine Art*

The imagination will be refined into a chaste and sober view of unveiled nature. It will be confined within the bounds of reality. It will no longer lead the way to insanity and madness by transcending the works of creation and, as it were, wandering where God has no power to protect it; but finding a resting place in every created object, it will enter into it and explore its hidden treasures. . . . When there shall be a religion which shall see God in everything, and at all times, and the natural sciences not less than nature itself shall be regarded in connection with him. . . .

> Sampson Reed, *Observation on the Growth of the Mind* (1826)

10

Immersion and Regeneration:
Emerson and Thoreau

One of the earliest traces of an imagistic awareness of the swamp occurs in William Byrd's *History of the Dividing Line* (1728). It is noteworthy that Byrd, as a commissioner for Virginia to establish its border with North Carolina, remained on the outskirts of the Dismal Swamp. His impressions are second-hand, worked up from notations in his diary (the "Secret History") that were based on accounts by members of the surveying party that actually entered the swamp.

Comparison of the "official" history (which the author never got around to publishing) with the diary indicates the extent to which Byrd developed the original observations, weaving them into a dramatic scenario. On the edge of the swamp, Byrd and his associates are harangued by one of the local inhabitants: "Ye have little reason to be merry," he tells them; "I fancy the pocosin you must struggle with tomorrow will make you change your note and try what metal you are made of. Ye are, to be sure, the first of the human race that ever had the boldness to attempt it, and I dare say will be the last."[1] The swamp's neighbors have no idea, however, of what really lies within its precincts. They are full of idle stories about lions, panthers, and alligators. Not to be daunted, Byrd's men resolve that there is "no intelligence of this *Terra Incognita* to be got but from our own experience" (p. 188).

This spirit of exploration transforms Byrd's treatment of the swamp, which becomes for him a sprawling gallery of natural anomalies. He notes how the surveyors, venturing into the morass, found the soil "so spongy that the water oozed up into every footstep" (p. 191) and that it was "an easy matter to run a ten-foot pole up to the head in it without exerting any uncommon strength . . ." (p. 190). He comments that in the swamp's sweltering heat, it was "a little provoking to hear the wind whistling among the branches of the white cedars . . . and at the same time not to have the comfort to feel the least breath of it" (p. 189). Such details offer an inchoate wisdom. They have about them something of the uncanny, the talismanic. The swamp is a "land of the dead," so putrid that not even turkey buzzards will fly over it. Yet curiously, its one beauty derives from the source of its pollution: "The moisture of the soil preserves a continual verdure and makes every plant an evergreen; but at the same time the foul damps ascend without ceasing, corrupt the air, and render it unfit for respiration" (p. 194). Whether subversive or oppressive, the landscape defies understanding, anticipating its opposition to normal assumptions.

In our own day David Wagoner tells of "Wading in a Marsh" in images that exude a kindred if richer atmosphere (see the Appendix for the entire poem):[2]

> My rake-handle staff goes first, searching
> For footholds in the moss under the water,
> In the soft debris of needles and spikerush
> And mud and the good lost lives of burreeds,
> And my feet follow, slow as the spawn of tree-frogs.
> The water-logged hemlock logs give way
> Underfoot as easily as the earth they've turned to,
> And my staff, at times, reaches down to nothing
> As deep as I am tall. I don't go there.

Separated by the better part of American history, Byrd and Wagoner both awaken to the impulsive energies of elemental life. Their encounters with the swamp convey a message all the more urgent for being inarticulate, seething at the touch of things. In the swamp's "hand-me-down" light, Wagoner wades "Uncertain of every surface preoccupied / By milfoil and watercress. . . ." Images exist as pure potentiality, like the "water starwort whose leaves allow / No reflection of mine, not even their own." Something about their presence nevertheless hints at revelation.

What charges Wagoner's awareness is his immersion in a dense, dynamic, and unfamiliar medium. In the swamp the exchanges between skin and enveloping matter, the synaptic response of nerves to the myriad signals in the surrounding space, and the overburdening of mind with the onrush of uncatalogued perceptions all initiate the dissolution of the self. As self-consciousness relaxes, instinctual energies surge. And here the analogous experience of sexual excitation is often implicated. We think of Whitman's glorification of the female form which attracts "with fierce undeniable attraction." His imagery creates an association with the rampant growth and lubricity of the swamp:

> Mad filaments, ungovernable shoots play out of it, the response
> likewise ungovernable,
> . . . .
> Ebb stung by flow and flow stung by the ebb, love-flesh swelling and
> deliciously aching,
> Limitless limpid jets of love hot and enormous, quivering jelly
> of love, white-blow and delirious juice,
> Bridegroom night of love working surely and softly into the prostrate
> dawn,

Undulating into the willing and yielding day,
Lost in the cleave of the clasping and sweet-flesh'd day.

We have only to turn from this passage in *I Sing the Body Electric* and from the celebration of procreation that unifies the *Children of Adam* series of poems to the homoeroticism of *Calamus* to measure the exhilaration – teetering on the edge of self-immolation – that Whitman feels in the presence of the female. By contrast, the *Calamus* poems, though at times sexual, are restrained. The poet pursues "paths untrodden, / In the growth by margins of pond-waters, / Escaped from life that exhibits itself. . . . " From "prairie-grass dividing" he demands the spiritual correspondence of "the most copious and close companionship of men." Words, acts, and beings, he asserts, must reflect "the open atmosphere" which is "coarse, sunlit, fresh, nutritious. . . . "

As physical circumstances come alive in the swamp, they push into the spiritual sphere. The self experiences transfiguration. Thus for Whitman, "Bodies are all spiritual. . . . " Similarly, Wagoner's movement into the swamp first creates a "man-made silence" that then gives way as "three wrens at once from three directions / Burst into songs as beautifully interwoven / As white water crowfoot tripling itself in shade." The process of organic empathy – in which the synergy of the environment finally comes to image the functioning of the body – is paradoxically a spiritual regeneration. Such is the fertility of otherness, of the unknown, always a female essence.

The fecundity of physical imagery – to shift from experience to expression – was discussed by Kenneth Burke (he used the term *concrete*) in relation to the "greenhouse" poems of Theodore Roethke. Burke proposed the maxim "a minimum of 'ideas' a maximum of 'intuitions.' " And he offered a more specific formulation: "Severedness, dying that is at the same time a fanatic tenacity; submergence (fish, and the sheer mindless nerves of sensitive plants); envagination as a homecoming."[3]

Roethke's purification of language aims at a childlike simplicity of diction, words that speak from aboriginal awareness of the physical and forsake the geometry of the latinate for the rawness of the saxonism. The need, expressed recurrently throughout the proliferation of civilization, is to get away from abstraction, to counteract the forces pulling apart mind and body, the forces generating technology and the crucible of time. Roethke's greenhouse is no swamp (Burke remarked on the artificial aspect), but its essence is close to that of the primordial world. In the encounter with both greenhouse and swamp, language strives to go beyond the descriptive. Words immersed in sense recover the intensity of action. As Whitman put it in his extravagant way, "A perfect writer would make words sing, dance, kiss, do the male and female act, bear children, weep, bleed, rage, stab, steal, fire cannon, steer ships, sack cities, charge with cavalry or infantry, or do anything, that man or woman or the natural powers can do."[4]

Such awareness is present in all of Whitman's greatest poetry and is revealed in all its lyricism at the end of "Out of the Cradle Endlessly Rocking," in which "the low and delicious word death" acquires an animate form as the waves of the sea and becomes the poet's lover:

... edging near as privately for me rustling at my feet,
Creeping thence steadily up to my ears and laving me
softly
    all over,
Death, death, death, death, death.

Whitman's willingness to conceive of sexuality in other than genital terms, his conception of sexual intercourse as immersion, is crucial here, as it allows the erasure of the boundaries between self and other. By the last line of the poem, by means of a grammatical ambiguity, Whitman has become the expression of the word *death* he himself enunciates: "The sea whisper'd me." This eroticization of death, of the otherness of physical life, achieved through the spoken word that in turn "speaks" the poet, is the consummation of the merging of life and death forces to which the natural world attests and that challenges the sentimentalist Victorian values expressed (as we saw in Chapter 1) in a morbid flight from death.

Predictably, Whitman just as drastically disagreed with the myth of infectious atmosphere influencing the language of mere convention and manipulation that we considered in the last chapter. In "This Compost" (1856), he directly denied the polluting effects believed to emanate from decaying vegetable matter:

What chemistry!
That the winds are really not infectious,
That this is no cheat, this transparent green-wash of the sea which is
               so amorous after me,
That it is safe to allow it to lick my naked body all over with its
               tongues,
That it will not endanger me with the fevers that have deposited
               themselves in it, . . .

For Whitman, the ability of decomposition not to produce death-dealing poison but to grow "such sweet things out of such corruptions" is simply one manifestation of a pervasive potential that in "When Lilacs Last in the Dooryard Bloom'd," his great elegy on the death of Lincoln, is embodied in the swamp:

I fled forth to the hiding receiving night that talks not,
Down to the shores of the water, the path by the swamp in
  the dimness,
To the solemn shadowy cedars and ghostly pines so still.

The potential of death for Whitman is the potential for an endlessly dynamic and interactive relationship to life. It is the benign fermentation that produces the ever-new forms of life and language.

William Byrd delimits this potential, seeking stability rather than dynamic interaction with the swamp environment. Although his language captures the fascination of the swamp, it does not breathe its redolence. Bemused, reasonable, and a member of the Royal Society, Byrd writes about the swamp as if he were collecting its images as "natural curiosities." Indeed, his keenness for specimens matches his desire to see the swamp drained and turned into arable land (p. 202).

To Byrd's eighteenth-century mind, the swamp is a desert place. His application of the term implies that the biblical drama takes precedence in his awareness over the actual qualities of the landscape. Byrd draws a somewhat cavalier comparison between his situation in the wilderness and that of the wandering children of Israel. He repeatedly emphasizes both his own superior manliness and moral rectitude, in contrast with those of the slatternly commissioners from North Carolina (not to mention the local inhabitants), and his abiding faith in God's providence.

One of the badges of the new order that he and his men form, the Order of the Maosti ("signifying in the Saponi language a turkey's beard"), portrays in gold a wild turkey with wings expanded, as well as a collar engraved on which the motto *vice coturnicum* ("in place of quail") alludes to the food that God fed to the starving Israelites (Exod. 16:13). Byrd pointed out: "As most orders have been religious in their original, so this was devised in grateful remembrance of our having been supported in the barren wilderness so many weeks with wild turkeys instead of quails" (p. 139).

Tracing the source of the American idea of the wilderness in the Old Testament, Roderick Nash established its significance as a place "in which to find and draw close to God" and as "a testing ground where a chosen people were purged, humbled, and made ready for the land of promise."[5] In keeping with this biblical frame of reference, Byrd described the swamp primarily as a landscape of ordeal, into which passage is hindered by thickly interwoven reeds and briars. An even greater obstacle is the cypresses blown down by the wind and heaped on top of one another. On their limbs are sharp snags, "pointing every which way like so many pikes." With perhaps moralizing intent, Byrd observed that these trees, "being evergreens and shooting their large tops very high, are easily overset by every gust of wind, because there is no firm earth to steady their roots" (p. 191).

The swamp is repeatedly referred to as filthy and noisome, full of aguish exhalations. In these respects, the experience of the surveyors was little different from that of the New England settlers depicted by the Puritan Edward Johnson in his *Wonder-working Providence* (1650). Traveling through "unknowne woods" and "watery scrampes," these servants of Christ pass through thickets "where their hands are forced to make way for their bodies passage"; where their feet "clamber over crossed trees, which when they missed they sunke into an uncertaine bottome in water"; and where they wade "up to their knees, tumbling sometimes higher and sometimes lower. . . . " Their perseverence is a testament to their faith. What pulls them through are their "thirsting desires . . . to plant [Christ's] Churches."[6]

Johnson, however, while making vivid the toils of faith through sensuous imagery, saw the swamp only insofar as it affected the body. He thus concentrated on the settlers' bodily punishment, the blood trickling from their torn flesh, their fainting from the heat. The swamp held no interest for Johnson beyond its moral function as an epitome of this world's evils. Byrd, on the other hand, as Richard Slotkin asserted, was a "peculiar kind of mediator between civilization and savagery."[7] Byrd's obvious sympathies for the wilderness determined his comparatively greater appreciation for the distinctive qualities of the landscape itself, its imagistic possibility.

What is more, Byrd was not insensitive to the congenial aspects of the wilderness at the levels of biology and sex. The landscape engenders a struggle for survival that, for all its hardship, is quickening. It provokes a recrudescence of animality; as Byrd explained, the swamps and marshes "made such beavers and otters of us that nobody caught the least cold" (p. 186). He finds instinctual gratification in the constant hunt for food. The Virginians, unlike the timid Carolinians who accompany them, rely largely on food they can kill. And now and then Byrd enjoys a dalliance with a "copper-colored" maiden (though always protesting his restraint).

Despite its repugnance, the swamp thus beckons, appealing to the sense of adventure. And despite the dire forecasts at the outset, Byrd's men clamber to be included in the party entering the swamp. They hope to gain the immortal reputation of being the first to enter the "Great Dismal." Hercules, Byrd observed, "would have as soon sold the glory of cleaning the Augean stables..." (p. 188). The simile is telling. It uncovers Byrd's unconscious assumption that bound up with the chance for instinctual release is the prospect of purification, of enjoying the certitude of discipline. The landscape poses a challenge, calling on selfhood to refurbish its battlements. The flow of energies is thus mastered, ritualized. Byrd described the penetration of the swamp in a peculiar but pregnant image:

> Thus, like Norway mice, these worthy gentlemen went right forward, without suffering themselves to be turned out of the way by any obstacle whatever. We are told by some travelers that those mice march in mighty armies, destroying all the fruits of the earth as they go along. But something peculiar to those little animals is that nothing stops them in their career, and if the house happen to stand in their way, disdaining to go an inch about, they crawl up one side of it and down the other. (p. 209)

Although the motive of self-discipline fulfills the biblical precedent in which one sought the wilderness as a means of purification, Byrd's manifest delight and curiosity in the swamp – his observent eye – constitute a departure from the traditional pattern. This pattern, according to Roderick Nash, admitted no fondness for the wilderness itself. To Byrd the swamp is more than a desert place, and his experience in it is more than simply an ordeal. This discrepancy prompts us to note a distinction between symbolic attitudes that is relevant to the genesis of sensibility. Aside from the problem of survival, which has its own, largely moral implications at the symbolic level, we need to account for the swamp's specific and often imagistic or aesthetic qualities that point beyond the meaning inherent in the wilderness, generic and conceptual as it is. Byrd's sensitivity to these qualities may have something to do with his sanguine personality and instinctual ease, in contrast with Johnson's Puritan settlers. The desire for adventure and exploration makes the essential difference. Such awareness begins the process toward a more complex and ambiguous meaning.

Comparing Byrd with Wagoner, we are impressed by the effects of this process. Byrd's purpose in the swamp, for all his adventurousness, is essentially to secure the self, that representative figure that constitutes a covenantal identity. Wagoner aims instead at self-transformation, and the self for him has become far more individualized. Byrd defined his selfhood according to the desert; his response is reflexive, tightening rather than relaxing his defenses. Wagoner groped toward life-giving forces; he is both absorbed and absorbent. Byrd, though not insensitive to the ambiguity of his moral censure of the swamp, confronted what he believed to be a natural embodiment of death. Wagoner's awareness enters more deeply into the being of the landscape. Although the marsh that holds him is "the climax of a lake, shallowing, dying," it is at the same time

> Filled with the best endeavors of pondweeds,
> The exploring and colonizing shapes of a world
> Too good at living for its own good . . .

Byrd protects the self by means of potent associations that control the stimuli of the environment, arranging them into coherent patterns. Meaning is preordained, almost wholly intentional. For Wagoner, the balance has shifted away from this ritualistic and representative pattern to a more open commerce between meaning and sense.

Jaded by the depredations of science and technology, Wagoner learned "the underlying answer / Of swamps as unforgettably as my name." He knows far more than the danger of the landscape:

> To stand is to sink, to move is to rise
> Again, and nothing at all has died in the winter
> Without being reborn.

The swamp presides over Wagoner's spiritual regeneration as well as his physical survival. The answer he seeks – avoiding a definite formulation – hides behind the danger that stirs him. In acknowledging the "sacredness" of the swamp, Wagoner recognizes its organic coherence and thus gives it a power that Byrd's swamp lacks. For Wagoner, "I learn why I came here / Out of order: in order to find out how to belong / Somewhere. . . . " And this reordering, for all its spiritual significance, turns back on physical immersion: " . . . to change where all changing / Is a healing exchange of sense for sense." The swamp holds a secret to be ascertained only by unraveling the tightly knotted ambiguity of sense and "sense." One attempts solution by hazarding the swamp's revenge. Yet somehow the riddle, remaining unsolved, may be lived. That is why, in the swamp, Wagoner must keep moving. If he stands still to listen, he will begin to sink.

This axiom is no less true for Byrd, but in the physical sense alone. Beneath the layers of cultural sensibility reside the facts of existence. The self may have to endure severe physical hardship in the swamp: exposure, starvation, and the ever-present threat of death. One can be devoured by wild animals or become hopelessly lost. If in the span from the seventeenth to the twentieth century, several revolutions of thought intervene, there is a constant frame of reference in the conglomerate of sensations and rudimentary emotions that, if not unique to the swamp, are closely associated with it: slipperiness, entanglement, suffocation, sinking, and the dread or panic that result. This welter can destroy entire universes of discourse, like Whitman's female form, "all falls aside but myself and it, / Books, art, religion, time. . . . " At this physical level, the swamp exacts the same vigilance from Wagoner as from Byrd. Wagoner's realization that he must draw a limit resounds in his terse declaration, "I don't go there."

But Wagoner faces a more intangible though no less formidable risk in the swamp, one that Byrd does not, at least consciously, recognize. In the swamp, space tends to condense into matter. Under extreme contraction, spirit may lose all reflex to rebound, hence the physical death or the reversion to animality that Byrd allows. Yet if charged by contact with matter, spirit may rebound out of all proportion. Thus for Wagoner the swamp's menace reaches through the body into the structures of the mind. Spiritual regeneration is achieved despite the peril of madness.

Wagoner's insight into the problem of orientation in the swamp – his realization that the swamp offers regeneration, even permits survival, only to those who move through it, never standing long enough to sink – has a metaphoric dimension. Here we touch on an ancient truth. Similarly, Nick's decision to avoid the swamp, in Ernest Hemingway's "Big Two-Hearted River," accords in its psychological resonance with far less self-conscious intuitions. The swamp's association with the derangement of the mind originates in myth and folklore. The extension of the swamp's influence, whether salvific or demonic, to modes of seeing and understanding derives, indeed, from primitive apprehensions – apprehensions that Byrd, and eighteenth-century culture in general, did not admit. During the nineteenth century, these apprehensions were reconstituted as a conscientious vision, a symbolic mode that has become a legacy to the twentieth century.

Practically a manifesto of this symbolic mode is Thoreau's essay, "Walking, or the Wild" (1862), published at the end of his life.[8] "When I would recreate myself," asserted Thoreau, "I seek the darkest wood, the thickest and most interminable and, to the citizen, the most dismal swamp. I enter the swamp as a sacred place, a *sanctum sanctorum*. There is the strength, the marrow, of Nature" (p. 228). Life, he declared, "consists with wildness." And this fact is bound to the urge to move: "One who pressed forward incessantly and never rested from his labors, who grew fast and made infinite demands on life, would always find himself in a new country or wilderness, and surrounded by the raw material of life." He would be climbing "over the prostrate stems of primitive forest trees" (p. 226). For Thoreau, it went almost without saying that this walk through the actual world "is perfectly symbolical of the path which we love to travel in the interior and ideal world" (p. 217).

Thoreau's conviction that the swamp is antithetical to humans as "citizens" was similarly voiced by Emerson who, in *English Traits* (1856), thought of the swamp in attempting to describe America to an English friend:

There, I thought, in America, lies nature sleeping, overgrowing, almost conscious, too much by half for man in the picture, and so giving a certain *tristesse,* like the rank vegetation of swamps and forests
seen at night, steeped in dews and rains, which it loves; and on it man
seems not able to make much impression. There, in that great sloven
continent, in high Allegheny pastures, in the sea-wide sky-skirted
prairie, still sleeps and murmurs and hides the great mother, long
since driven away from the trim hedge-rows and overcultivated garden of England.[9]

Emerson's reconciliation with the savagery of nature in the New World opposed the long-established accusations of Europeans who pointed to the swamp
as proof of the New World's decadence, of its inferiority to the Old.[10] It
contrasted, moreover, with the traditional theological interpretation of the
swamp expressed, for instance, by Horace Bushnell in *Nature and the Supernatural* (1858). Illustrating the general principle "that the world is linked to
man and required to represent him to himself," Bushnell connected the swamp
with the consequences of sin: "The earth itself displays vast deserts swept by
the horrid simoon; muddy rivers, with their fenny shores, tenanted by hideous
alligators; swamps and morasses, spreading out in provinces of quagmire, and
reeking in the steam of death."[11]

Walking and wildness had long been the two central metaphors of Thoreau's
life. The mode of discovery and the source of inspiration were complementary
aspects of his seminal motive of self-regeneration. Walking was a way of
bringing body and spirit back together: "I am alarmed when it happens that
I have walked a mile into the woods bodily without getting there in spirit. . . . In
my walks I would fain return to my senses" (p. 211). By walking Thoreau
meant not traversing the country on a highway but striking out into the woods,
allowing himself to get lost for a while. This transcendence of the self's normal
patterns was the common term in his association of walking with the spirit
of chivalry (that is, *sainte terre*), of the self-sacrifice that contrasted with the
mercenary preoccupations of most of his Yankee neighbors.

The curative effect of walking on the self derived from its assimilation of
that proportion that "the night bears to the day, the winter to the summer,
thought to experience" (p. 210). And Thoreau brought the integration of
mental and instinctual – the salvation of the outdoor life – into contemporary
perspective by contrasting it with the prevailing ethos of sentimentalism:
"There will be so much more air and sunshine in our thoughts. The callous
palms of the laborer are conversant with the finer tissues of self-respect and
heroism, whose touch thrills the heart, than the languid fingers of idleness.
That is mere sentimentality that lies abed all day and thinks itself white, far
from the tan and callus of experience" (p. 210). He saw the necessity of living
in harmony with life's fundamental rhythms: the continual alternation of light
and dark, waking and sleeping, knowledge and ignorance. To understand these
rhythms in their proper relation, to traverse from the natural to the symbolic,
was to pivot on what was an even more decisive division of the day's process,
that between confinement and walking.

To the townspeople who confined themselves in their shops and houses all day, three o'clock in the afternoon might as well be three o'clock in the morning. Their power of endurance was astonishing. Confinement in effect erased the rhythms of life and collapsed its symbolic dimension into the literal. For those individuals who spent their afternoons behind store counters, darkness supplanted the light of day; walking was tantamount to sleeping; and knowledge was just another kind of ignorance. For walkers, however, the rhythms were compounded, and walking required no endurance, for it involved periodic renewal through the infusion of the natural into the metaphoric. Whereas confinement involved the persistence of the commonplace, walking repeatedly confronted the novel and strange. Thus walkers enjoyed a pastime more restorative than sleep; entering into the unfamiliar, they assumed an ignorance that was really knowledge. The transvaluations of the polarity of confinement and walking were parallel but pointed in opposite directions, one toward literal understanding and the other toward metaphoric intuition. Either one continued to occupy a finite space, or one proceeded (Thoreau's use of the gerund in his title stressed the processual) toward the infinite.

Thoreau's essay began as a lecture entitled "The Wild," first delivered in 1851 and subsequently reworked and augmented until it was eventually split into two parts, with the new part called "Walking." Not until just before his death, when he decided to publish the essays in the *Atlantic Monthly*, did he put them back together.[12] It is interesting to see how the juxtaposition of the essays, after their respective topics had been developed individually, transformed the meaning of the whole. Viewed separately, the two are relatively straightforward. Brought together, their imagistic and metaphoric patterns blend. The opening section on walking gives complex and dynamic nuances of meaning to the later sections on wildness. Although each part incorporates the basic structure and meaning of the whole, their interaction emphasizes the most radical implications of Thoreau's message: the interdependence of movement and immersion in the constant renewal of apprehension that constitutes atonement with creation.

At the outset, Thoreau engages the subject of walking literally. Although he elaborates metaphorically, his concern is still with actual movement through space. He remarks that his walks follow the outline of a parabola (or cometary orbit), returning him to a different point from whence he began. He invokes traditional associations, such as with pilgrimage. The walk is, like the crusades of old, a journey to the holy land, the *sainte terre* from which derives the verb *to saunter* (in Thoreau's fanciful etymology).

Hence place becomes verb: The pun prefigures the conversion of terms in the latter part of the essay. Wildness Thoreau equates with the West and with the future, with the promise of America. Westward (or southwest) his way wends, drawn by a "subtle magnetism in Nature, which, if we unconsciously yield to it, will direct us aright" (p. 216). Only the mind's interference causes indecision over which direction to proceed. Thoreau testifies to the westering of spirit as the basic creative impulse of all culture, pointing to the myths of the islands of Atlantis and the Hesperides. "We go eastward," he says, "to realize history and study the works of art and literature, retracing the steps of the race . . . " (p. 218). Eastward he is induced only by force, but westward he goes freely. East he equates with the light of the mind, West with the fruit of experience.

In the section on wildness, Thoreau shifts away from images that emphasize the opposition of movement and confinement at the physical level to images of inhabiting that combine the two at the symbolic level. Yes, he says, "though you may think me perverse, if it were proposed to me to dwell in the neighborhood of the most beautiful garden that ever human art contrived, or else of a Dismal Swamp, I should certainly decide for the swamp" (p. 228); or "A town is saved not more by the righteous men in it than by the woods and swamps that surround it." This imagery of settlement is supplemented by that of cultivation: "A township where one primitive forest waves above while another primitive forest rots below – such a town is fitted to raise not only corn and potatoes, but poets and philosophers for the coming ages" (p. 229). Thoreau finds the farmer "stronger and in some respects more natural" than the nomadic Native American because he "redeems" the meadow. The task of the American is to work the virgin soil. The Native American instead wears out his lands.

Thoreau has added a twist to the simple opposition between walking and confinement with which he began. His praise of the farmer seems to conflict with earlier statements such as "I would have every man so much like a wild antelope, so much a part and parcel of nature, that his very person should . . . remind us of those parts of nature which he most haunts" (pp. 224– 6). Apparently even more contradictory is his contention, in the opening section of the essay, that those who seek to possess the land rather than simply walk over it, who deform it with human "improvements," turn a heaven into hell. Thoreau played here on a contrast between his own paean to wildness and the swamp's traditional associations:

> I saw . . . some wordly miser with a surveyor looking after his hounds, while heaven had taken place around him, and he did not see the angels going to and fro, but was looking for an old post-hole in the midst of paradise. I looked again, and saw him standing in the middle of a boggy Stygian fen, surrounded by devils, and he had found his bounds without a doubt . . . I saw that the Prince of Darkness was his surveyor. (p. 212)

We are perplexed unless we realize that as the essay develops, Thoreau is not opposing two terms – wildness and society – but is seeking to find a balance between them in a third. The cultivation of the farmer is analogous to the activity of the walker, despite what many of Thoreau's contemporaries would have seen as an alternative between responsibility and vagrancy. In regard to this point, it is important to keep in mind, as Sherman Paul made clear, that Thoreau was no anarchic individualist; "he was antisocial only in the sense that he wanted to change society."[13] Thoreau rejected society only insofar as it was "exclusively an interaction of man on man. . . . " A civilization based on this principle was "destined to have a speedy limit" (p. 237).[14] Thoreau saw that vagrancy, that walking, was indeed the way to responsibility.

Thus the wise farmer knows that he must allow his fields to run to meadow and woods so that they will eventually produce to their fullest potential.

What resolves the apparent paradox in Thoreau's argument is that his essay, in unfolding, has risen to a higher metaphoric level, to a level of understanding capable of reconciling even the distinction between substance and action. The metaphors of inhabiting and cultivation merge the stability of confinement with the energy of walking. Thus the miserly farmer of the Stygian bog is contrasted with the later example of a farmer, at one time "actually up to his neck and swimming for his life in his property," who remarks to Thoreau, "true to his instincts, that he would not part with [this swamp] for any consideration, on account of the mud which it contained" (p. 230).

Thoreau's essay, in other words, progresses to the suggestion that one does not simply spend four hours or so a day walking in the wild, as originally proposed; every aspect of life should take on the virtue of walking through swamps. In the essay's increasingly symbolic atmosphere, walking on the earth becomes equivalent to realizing one's true nature in the earth, through analogy with it. Like the earth, Thoreau reasoned, the greater part of the human should lie fallow, "as meadow and forest, not only serving an immediate use, but preparing a mould against a distant future, by the annual decay of vegetation which it supports" (p. 238). This metaphoric relation of human and earthly, in which immersion becomes dynamic, is based on the realization that "we have a wild savage nature in us . . . " (p. 237) that awakens in sleep, anger, passion, and inspiration – those states of being that transport us outside the province of the "citizen" selves represented by our names. Such intuition – a "wild and dusky knowledge" or "mother-wit" (p. 238) – knows as a matter of principle that there can be "an excess of informing light" (p. 238).

It is the degree to which Thoreau experienced life metaphorically that seems to have eluded even Emerson and led to the persistent misunderstanding between the two men. In his journal of 1858, Emerson pondered his disagreement with Thoreau over the meaning of a real-life parable: "I hear the account of the man who lives in the wilderness of Maine with respect, but with despair. . . . " Emerson doubtlessly was referring to the character mentioned by Thoreau in "Allegash and East Branch," "a sort of hermit . . . who spent his time tossing a bullet from one hand to the other, for want of employment. . . . "[15]

Thoreau had mused that "this sort of tit-for-tat intercourse between his two hands, bandying to and fro a leaden subject, seems to have been his symbol for society." Having talked with Thoreau about his recent outing in Maine, Emerson admitted feeling the beauty of the wilderness spectacle, "the impression of broken land and water. . . . " But he insisted that "Henry's hermit" could not be important "until we know what he is now, what he thinks of it on his return, and after a year." There was always the chance, Emerson thought, that the man would find it in retrospect "foolish and wasteful to spend a tenth or twentieth of his active life with a muskrat and fried fishes." He told Thoreau "that a man was not meant to live in a swamp, but a frog. If God meant him to live in a swamp, he would have made him a frog."[16]

The disagreement calls to mind Thoreau's complaint about another occasion: "Talked, or tried to talk, with RWE. Lost my time – nay, almost my identity. He, assuming a false opposition when there was no difference of opinion, talked to the wind – told me what I knew – and I lost my time trying to imagine myself somebody else to oppose him."[17]

It seems that the nuances of Thoreau's fable of the hermit escaped Emerson because of his belief that an experience must be assessed in a social context; the hermit must at least return to tell. Yet Emerson was simply opposing society and wilderness – confinement and freedom – whereas Thoreau tried to combine them at a higher level of intuition. It was not that Thoreau rejected society in the concrete. This was where Emerson's relative literalism misled him. Thoreau was rejecting simply what society in America had come to represent: confinement. It is true that in "Circles" Emerson wrote: "The one thing which we seek with insatiable desire is to forget ourselves, to be surprised out of our propriety. . . ."[18] But his choice here of the word *propriety* is in itself telling. It points equally to his own self-consciousness, of which he was well aware, and to his conception of the symbol as idea. Both contributed to his inability to be surprised.

Emerson's comments on Thoreau's hermit reveal the heart of his differences with his younger disciple. At the risk of treading a beaten path first brilliantly laid out by F. O. Matthiessen,[19] it is relevant to our theme to pursue somewhat further this contrast of perspectives, for it highlights the crucial connection between immersion in nature and the metaphorical transformation after which Emerson harkened but whose essence he never seemed to have grasped.

That Emerson was unusually sensitive to the spontaneity and plenitude of physical life is clear from his journals. One summer day in the early 1850s, while walking with Ellery Channing in one of the swamps near Concord, Massachusetts, he was impressed by Channing's young dog who "scampered and dived and swam at such a prodigal rate that one could not help grudging the youth of the universe [the animals] their heaven." He wondered at "how much more the dog knows of nature than his master, though his master were an Indian. The dog tastes, snuffs, rubs, feels, tries everything, everywhere, through miles of brush, grass, water, mud, lilies, mountain and sky."

It is just as noteworthy, however, that Emerson brought home the contrast between feral and human natures. He was sure that the animals "think us poor pedants in petticoats. . . ."[20] The image reminds us of the poet's compulsion to dress his verses in the decorative garb of a still rather neoclassic diction and prosody. In a journal entry in 1856, Emerson commented on the contrast with poignant self-consciousness: "How the landscape mocks the weakness of man! it is vast, beautiful, complete and alive; and we can only dibble and step about, and dot it a little. The gulf between seeing and doing is a symbol of that between faith and experience."[21]

Emerson's admitted failure here to merge faith and experience is commensurate with his general inability to match theory and practice. He foundered on an inherent diffidence toward nature. He knew that "the swimmer standing on the land dreads the plunge, yet, having plunged, enjoys the water" and that this fact had a deep spiritual significance: "The living fear death, yet, dying, enjoy the new life."[22] One wonders, however, how often, if ever, he brought himself to make the plunge. For contrast, we might think of the often quoted passage in Thoreau's journal in which he asks, "Would it not be a luxury to stand up to one's chin in some retired swamp for a whole summer's day, scenting the sweet-fern and bilberry blows, and lulled by the minstrelsy of gnats and mosquitoes?"[23] Thoreau continues, asking, "Cold and damp, – are they not as rich experience as warmth and dryness?"

The sense of propriety that characterized Emerson's temperament – keeping him from making the plunge – has its conceptual counterpart in his philosophical concern with the Ideal. This static construct clearly had a constricting effect on his poetry. As David Porter said of Emerson the poet, "The crucial conversion process at the center of the concept and the verse, continually pressuring reality into ideal forms, making natural law rhyme with moral law, could not but dissipate poetic power."[24]

By the same token, Carolyn Porter stated that Emerson's reliance on Spirit, the active form of the Ideal, led him to enact in the social realm the reification of the subject–object distinction that his formulation of causality in nature had tried to overcome. As she put it, "the new authority of Spirit upon which Emerson relied to free him from the world's objectively fixed appearance by revealing its human mediation, returns to haunt his rhetorical project, for when you break free of the world's static appearance, you are always acting in accord with a predetermined teleological plan." Porter went on to point to the notorious "transparent eyeball" passage in *Nature* as exemplifying the split between "the I who sees nature and the I who inhabits it." Emerson's figure expresses not only "the desire to reunite man with himself" but also "the less obvious and more telling desire . . . to absent one's self from the world as physical being in order to view the world from the vantage point of the disembodied eye."[25]

To adopt a somewhat different but corresponding view of this matter: Emerson saw the problem of spiritual unfolding primarily in the patriarchal terms of the penetration of facts by the intellect. In *The Conduct of Life* (1860), he defined fate as "unpenetrated causes." And he voiced the conviction that "every jet of chaos which threatens to exterminate us, is convertible by intellect into wholesome causes."[26] The first two chapters of his book, "Fate" and "Power," echo an inherent duality and are the basis for all that follows: "On one side, elemental order, sandstone and granite, rock-ledges, peat-bog, forest, sea and shore; and, on the other, thought, the spirit which composes and decomposes nature – here they are, side by side, god and devil, mind and matter, king and conspirator, belt and spasm. . . . "[27]

Emerson's assurance that power will prevail, however, is less a matter of experience than of faith; less a question of doing than of seeing. It is his consistent stress on seeing, at the expense of the other senses, that betrays Emerson's project, for it is sight that is responsible for the rationalistic and illusory division of the world between subject and object. Emerson never escaped from this typically eighteenth-century tyranny. His dualistic premises are evident early on in *Nature,* when he sees the world in terms of the "Me" and the "Not-Me."

His stress on the penetration of the world by intellect places Emerson at variance with Thoreau, who, in "Walking," declared, "My desire for knowledge is intermittent, but my desire to bathe my head in atmospheres unknown to my feet is perennial and constant" (p. 240). That he sought a different experience for his head than that of his feet is testimony to Thoreau's transcendental proclivities. Yet Thoreau here represents his mode of transcendence not as penetration but as immersion. The difference marks a shift away from thought toward sense, away from knowledge toward "Sympathy with Intelligence," not so much seeing as feeling and breathing. As Matthiessen pointed out: "What separates Thoreau from Emerson is his interest in the varied play of all his senses, not merely the eye. . . ."[28]

Thoreau's is accordingly a far more porous symbolic mode than is Emerson's, one that relied more on the surfaces of things to generate its transformations than on the particular "ocular" perspective taken by the subject. The patriarchal metaphor of penetration, allied to the traditional tropes of vision and light, gives way in Thoreau to a metaphor that engages the body as a whole, both the individual body of the percipient and the world's body. Thoreau shares with Melville, and particularly with Whitman, this opening up of the sensorium, undermining the hegemony of sight and creating a far more participatory relationship to the world. Thoreau nonetheless stops short of Whitman's concern (and of Melville's too, though more subtly) with exploiting the erotic potential inherent in such a surrender to the "polymorphous perverse."

Even if only a matter of degree in its departure from Emerson, this difference is significant. Emerson was an ardent proponent of the evanescence of the symbol. His "waking knowledge" assumed that all results are new beginnings.[29] He wrote in "Circles": "In nature every moment is new; the past is always swallowed and forgotten; the coming only is sacred. Nothing is secure but life, transition, the energizing spirit."[30]

Yet though the quest for a "fluxional" symbolism permeates Emerson's work, there is nothing about it that approaches Thoreau's radical notion of "higher knowledge" as perhaps nothing more "than a novel and grand surprise on a sudden revelation of the insufficiency of all that we called knowledge before, – a discovery that there are more things in heaven and earth than are dreamed of in our philosophy" (p. 240). Even Thoreau's phrasing in this statement bespeaks the dispersal of energies and sensitivities that characterized his sensibility. Whereas Thoreau methodically collected observations that might unexpectedly yield a meaning beyond themselves, Emerson actively pursued ideas. Emerson could not be surprised because he was too impatient.

What I am trying to differentiate here is not simply a matter of emphasis and temperament. Unlike Emerson, Thoreau represents a different attitude toward both faith and social action. Thoreau's faith was masked by a skepticism that is more assertive than any of Emerson's reservations about experience. Thoreau felt that

> with regard to Nature I live a sort of border life, on the confines of a world into which I make occasional and transient forays only, and my patriotism and allegiance to the state into whose territories I seem to retreat are those of a moss-trooper. Unto a life which I call natural I

would gladly follow even a will-o'-the wisp through bogs and sloughs unimaginable, but no moon nor firefly has shown me the causeway to it. Nature is a personality so vast and universal that we have never seen one of her features. (p. 242)

What Thoreau suggests here is not skepticism at all but simply a more complex and dynamic faith than that constituted by Emerson's stable center, away from which expand the concentric circles of meaning. Sherman Paul said of Emerson: "As the center of the circle, God (through his sympathetic correspondence with Him) provided him the fixity and centrality he needed when nature became an ever-changing screen of 'slippery sliding surfaces. . . .' "[31] Thoreau's faith did not shun contact with such surfaces. Moving through the swamp, it adjusted to ever-changing circumstances, assimilating to them rather than forcing them into some predetermined design.

Whereas for Emerson there was always the difficult gap between faith and experience, seeing and doing – a gap measured by his own nagging self-consciousness – Thoreau explored a region of sensibility in which faith and experience combine in an unconscious awareness that actively restructures the basic response to the world, breaking through any tendency to commodify it. If Emerson struggled earnestly against an American society in which things "were in the saddle," it was Thoreau who managed to overcome the reification of the world in an age of expanding capitalism.

Thoreau's shift away from a preoccupation with transcendental insight in the 1850s may stand for a movement into naturalism only insofar as the delicate symbolic mode by which he was trying to live could slip imperceptibly into dry empiricism accompanied by a personal loss of buoyancy. But whereas others have emphasized the deflation of Thoreau's powers in his later work, I point to his renewed sense of wonder on discovering a piece of phosphorescent wood in his campfire during the summer of 1857. The wood's effect on him indeed seems emblematic of a mode of perception that had long been his but that then suddenly crystallized:

It was a dense and damp spruce and fir wood in which we lay, and, except for our fire, perfectly dark; and when I awoke in the night, I either heard an owl from deeper in the forest behind us, or a loon from a distance over the lake. Getting up some time after midnight to collect the scattered brands together, while my companions were sound asleep, I observed, partly in the fire, which had ceased to blaze, a perfectly regular elliptical ring of light, about five inches in its shortest diameter, six or seven in its longer. . . . It was fully as bright as the fire, but not reddish or scarlet like a coal . . . a white and slumbering light, like the glowworm's. I could tell it from the fire only by its whiteness. I saw at once that it must be phosphorescent wood, which I had so often heard of, but never chanced to see. . . . [32]

Thoreau asserted that he could hardly have been more thrilled if the phosphorus had taken the form of letters or the human face. He had little thought, he stated portentously, "that there was such a light shining in the darkness of the wilderness for me."[33]

The context in which Thoreau placed this discovery is even more significant: "I exulted like 'a pagan suckled in a creed' that had never been worn at all, but was bran [*sic*] new, and adequate to the occasion." And he developed an opposition between belief and knowledge, between the sense of oneness with the animistic world and the methods of science:

> I let science slide, and rejoiced in that light as if it had been a fellow-creature. I saw that it was excellent, and was very glad to know that it was so cheap. A scientific *explanation,* as it is called, would have been altogether out of place there. That is for pale daylight. Science with its retorts would have put me to sleep; it was the opportunity to be ignorant that I improved. It made a believer of me more than before. I believed, that the woods were not tenantless, but chokefull of honest spirits as good as myself any day, – not an empty chamber, in which chemistry was left to work alone, but an inhabited house, – and for a few moments I enjoyed fellowship with them.[34]

For Thoreau, this animistic awareness is true religion. He would go not to the missionary to learn it but to the Native Americans. Yet it is all the more revelatory that after keeping the little chips of phosphorescent wood and wetting them the next night, he found that they emitted no light. He had chosen a difficult faith whose flickerings were furtive at best, a faith requiring a continual renewal of commitment and concentration. In an entry in the journal of his Maine venture during the summer of 1857, he declared:

> I am interested in an indistinct prospect . . . a mere suggestion often, revealing an almost wholly new world to me. I rejoice to get, and am apt to present, a new view. But I find it impossible to present my view to most people. . . . Heat lightning flashes, which reveal a distant horizon to our twilight eyes. But my fellows simply assert that it is not broad day, which everybody knows, and fail to perceive the phenomena at all.[35]

His interest in the indistinct prospect, the mere suggestion, ties Thoreau to the pragmatism of William James and to James's prophetic formulation of the "stream of thought," to the great value he places on the penumbra of suggestiveness that could bring the world alive in a perpetual self-renewal. Thoreau's example of concentrated vision, of metaphoric transformation, effectively cut him off from the world of social construction. As Carolyn Porter concluded, "If Emerson argued the merits of a detached vision, Thoreau argued the virtues of a detached life."[36] But as she went on to point out, Thoreau remained unswerving in his position; there was no essential contradiction at the heart of his thinking, as there surely was with Emerson. Thoreau had always been willing "to pass for a fool in [his] often desperate, perhaps foolish, efforts to persuade them to lift the veil from off the possible and future, which they hold down with both their hands, before their eyes." This is simply the price paid by the latter-day evangelist who knew that "the most valuable communication or news consists of hints and suggestions."[37] If Thoreau's difficulty anticipated the arid subjectivism that has beset twentieth-century culture, it also reinstated the ebb and flow of the anxious but passionate faith of the Puritans at the heart of an enduring American tradition.

11

The Identification with Desert Places: Martin Johnson Heade and Frederick Goddard Tuckerman

Two who might well have heeded Thoreau's evangel were the painter Martin Johnson Heade (1819–1904) and the poet Frederick Goddard Tuckerman (1821–73), figures who, though they never met each other or knew each other's work, can be considered kindred spirits in their unusual identification with desert places, including swamps. Notwithstanding the distinctions entailed by the different media in which they worked as well as disparities of character and temperament, the vision of the poet from Greenfield, Massachusetts, and that of the peripatetic painter from nowhere in particular bear comparison.

Born and raised in Lumberville, Pennsylvania, Heade traveled throughout his life, living as far afield as California, Brazil, and Florida. Much of his important work, however, was done in Rhode Island and Massachusetts and is a response to the singular charms of the regional landscape. Moreover, Heade's art, besides having affinities with the work of Thoreau and Tuckerman, relates to that of such other New England writers as Thomas Wentworth Higginson and the historian Francis Parkman. Though he is often characterized as a "luminist,"[1] Heade's personality and artistic sensibility place him among those breaking with the American emblematic and typological tradition best represented by Thomas Cole and Frederic Church. Tuckerman's inner biography, as it emerges in the sonnets he began writing in 1854, shows a similar departure from contemporary norms of seeing nature. His subtle probing eventually led him to develop a more complex symbolic mode than that given him by his cultural background.

Heade's obsession with desert landscapes like swamps, jungles, marshes, and uninhabited beaches points to an inward exploration. This psychological relation to nature not only distinguished the artist from the emblematic and picturesque tradition; it also alienated him (as I suggested in Chapters 7 and 8) from the predominantly Ruskinian cultural establishment in America that promoted landscapes with "character." What is more, the artist's taut symbolic visions reveal intuitions beyond even the limits conceived by Emersonian Transcendentalism, with its doctrine of "correspondence" and dedication to Truth. It has been argued that there is a close relationship between luminism and Transcendentalism, based on Emerson's pronouncements about the ameliorative effect of light on natural forms.[2] But the link with Emerson fails to explain the disturbing accents in many of Heade's paintings, for instance, in such a clearly luminist work as *Lake George*.

Heade's tensest images offer an implicit critique of Emerson's blithe announcement in "Self-Reliance" that " 'if I am the Devil's child, I will live then from the Devil.' No law can be sacred to me but that of my nature. Good and bad are but names very readily transferable to that or this; the only right is what is after my constitution; the only wrong what is against it.'"[3] A painting like *Lake George* may be seen as subverting such an attitude, as warning against it. The artist's own adherence to radical individualism taught him, it appears, to distrust it. As William Ellery Channing realized, "Thought frees the old bounds to which men used to confine themselves. . . . Undoubtedly this is a perilous tendency. Men forget the limits of their powers. They question the infinite, the unsearchable, with an audacious self-reliance. . . . "[4] It appears that Heade explored the implications of Emerson's antinomianism and discovered – if not altogether consciously – the terror at the heart of pure faith. His quest paralleled that of Melville, whose "Whiteness of the Whale" unveiled the "colorless all-color of atheism."

The structure of *Lake George* (1862) (Figure 11.1) images the Emersonian quest to reach the "further shore" and behind it the more general American myth of innocence, progress, and achievement that encouraged such popular causes as social reform and Manifest Destiny. The foreground of the painting is energized by the repeated diagonal accents of the rocks jutting from the shore. The shoreline underscores and even seems to impel the man strenuously pushing the boat as if pursuing the faraway mountains. In contrast with the foreground, the background looks soft and miragelike. The distance over the lake is indeterminate, and the mountains appear both to recede before the parallel thrust of boat and rock and to push toward it, causing the plane of the lake to bow convexly. The contrast of sharp and soft forms in the lower part of the picture is echoed in the sky in which cumulus clouds are broken by horizontal spearlike clouds – probably portents of a storm to be unleashed by the billowing thunderhead on the horizon. The diffuse but intense light (in contrast with the chiaroscuro of the picturesque), along with the low horizon, imparts a sense of heightened consciousness. But combined with the conflict of sharp and soft forms, hints of storm, and warping of space over the lake, it seems ominous.[5]

Unlike the iconography of Thomas Cole's paintings of the wilderness or the sentimental imagery that was losing its grip on the popular imagination by the 1850s, Heade commented on the energetic striving, so much a part of American myth and character, from a position inside its motivational matrix. He understood what he criticized and acknowledged its attraction while warning against it.

As Theodore Stebbins pointed out, Heade chose the pen name Didymus, referring to Doubting Thomas, for his articles in the sports magazine *Forest*

Figure 11.1. Martin Johnson Heade (American, 1819–1904), *Lake George* (oil on canvas, 25 × 49¾ in. [66 × 126.3 cm.], 1862). Bequest of Maxim Karolik. Courtesy, Museum of Fine Arts, Boston.

and Stream. Heade's skepticism owes its character to an urge to master nature. The contrast between this identity and the pose of a figure like Charles Lanman as enraptured artist-prophet is startling. Although little is known about Heade's life and the artist wrote nothing of consequence,[6] we surmise a spirit in keeping with the new "tough-minded" individualism of his age, personified by the vigorous protagonists of Francis Parkman's histories.[7]

Heade's love of hunting and his preoccupation with stricter game laws (particularly in his later years) reveal an attitude of ritual antagonism to nature; his numerous articles in *Forest and Stream,* written in the 1880s and 1890s, attest to this. The artist commonly indulged in unrepentant accounts of his killing sprees:

> After one or two failures I picked up my "Fox" one day, an hour be-
> fore dinner, and took a walk just back of an orange grove near the
> house, and stumbled on an innocent bevy, but as they failed to notify
> me of their intention to rise I only got one, but marked them down in
> a patch of dwarf palmettoes and thick grass, where I found them so
> nicely scattered that I put them up singly and shot down ten, but the
> next one selfishly got behind a tree and got off with all his feathers.[8]

Yet paradoxically, Heade also complained about the wanton shooting of animals: "It would be a scandalous libel upon the craft of sportsmanship to picture it as made up of such lust for blood, such devilish cruelty, such fiendish enjoyment of the death agonies of inoffensive creatures as pervades the pages of these Florida 'rustlings.' "[9] It appears that Heade was deeply concerned with enacting a rigorous code of sportsmanship, a patterned response to nature, in order to achieve control in the absence of prophetic vision.

A precedent for this ethic is certainly Francis Parkman's experience in the wilds of New England and northern New York during his college days. Parkman's journals of his youthful excursions stress their initiatory character: "My chief object in coming so far was merely to have a taste of the half-savage kind of life necessary to be led, and to see the wilderness where it was as yet uninvaded by the hand of man. I had some hope of shooting a moose. . . . "[10]

Arriving at a precipice overlooking a lake around which nature lay in dis-array – after climbing through "tangled woods and steep sunscorched ledges" – Parkman was moved to discharge his gun, "Satan," into the gulf.[11] He prided himself on his ability to endure pain and physical discomfort. Assailed by swarming mosquitoes and "no-see-ems," he laughed at his companion's agonies while "a million red-hot needles were gouged into hands, faces, every-where. . . . " But at last his philosophy gave way, "and the utmost point of my self-command was to suffer in silence."[12]

Heade's ritual combativeness with nature was characteristic of the new heroes of the age, "adventurers," in John Higham's words, "loose in a hostile or indifferent environment."[13] Typically, Heade wrote of the tropical Chagres River, "I was warned that danger lurked in the dampness of the early morning, and was cautioned against going out till the sun had dissipated the fog and dew; but I heeded not the wise advice." He ignored the threat of fever: "I felt that it was a dangerous game to play, but it was so beautiful and the birds and flowers were so interesting, that I was blinded to the risk."[14]

Heade's exposure to nature was motivated by a desire for sensual gratification, not moral insight – reflecting a failure of trust. Far from symbolizing the divine monologue, nature was for him evasive if not duplicitous. In this respect, his work looks forward to Winslow Homer's watercolors done in the tropics at the end of the nineteenth century and the beginning of the twentieth. Homer's mastery of the watercolor medium – the vibrancy of color and the extraordinary control he achieved – enabled him to produce jungle images that culminated the line of imagery Heade may be said to have inaugurated (Figures 11.2 and 11.3).

Heade's visits to Latin America in the early and mid-1860s provided him with images for the impenetrability of nature to human understanding and for the spirit of conquest that it challenged. *Brazilian Forest* (1864) (see Figure 8.4) envisions the themes later expressed in his writings on hunting in the tropics. This jewel-like work has an intricate delineation of surface detail, a richness of tonality and texture, that captures the most suggestive possibilities of tropical vegetation. Vertical in format, it presents a vortex among the hills at whose bottom is a reflectionless pool. The top of the vortex opens to the light of a cloudy sky, but its bottom lies deep in shadow, as if in a "heart of darkness." Here the hunter crouches expectantly. What will emerge from the dense foliage?

We are reminded of Ishmael's premonition in "The Spirit-Spout": "For a time, there reigned, too, a sense of peculiar dread at this flitting apparition, as if it were treacherously beckoning us on and on, in order that the monster might turn around upon us at last in the remotest and most savage sea."[15] The painting rouses our instinctive fear of "nameless, lurking forces"[16] associated with swamp and jungle. It depicts a confrontation with the deepest self. The nearly reflectionless pool reveals nothing, not even a narcissistic image. Indeed, the depths offer only further mystery and the threat of annihilation. In this realm the hunter becomes the hunted.

Frederick Goddard Tuckerman defined, more directly than Heade did, his relationship to nature in the context of Romantic assumptions. His poetry reflects a loss of Transcendental faith, conceived of as the Wordsworthian visionary gleam of youth:[17]

> Yet wear we on, the deep light disallowed
> That lit our youth; in years no longer young
> We wander silently, and brood among
> Dead graves, and tease the sunbreak and the cloud
> For import: were it not better to fly,
> To follow those that go before the throng,
> Reasoning from stone to star, and easily
> Exampling this existence? (series I, ix)

Tuckerman too explored his inner self through an identification with desert places. In an early poem, "A Sample of Coffee-Beans,"[18] he speaks of how he shunned

> The world, and, reckless of
> mosquito

Figure 11.2. Winslow Homer, *Homosassa Jungle* (watercolor over graphite on white paper, 14 × 22 in. [35.2 × 55.1 cm.], 1904). Gift of Mrs. Charles S. Homer in memory of the late Charles S. Homer and his brother Winslow Homer. Fogg Art Museum, Cambridge, Mass.

Figure 11.3. Winslow Homer, *In the Jungle, Florida* (watercolor over pencil, 13⅞ × 19¹¹⁄₁₆ in. [35.1 × 50.0 cm.], 1904). Museum Collection Fund and Special Subscription, The Brooklyn Museum, New York.

By pond-hole dark, and weedy drain,
Sequestered swamp, or grassy side-hill,
Would linger, breathing dull disdain
In many a rustic ode and idyll.

In "Twilight," he indicated his association of such places with a past which
continually haunted him:

So, to this stranger stream
And its still woods, come drifting in,
Thoughts, memory, doubt, and dream,
Of the noble hearts that sailed with me:
Here to this desert spot
Come their dim ghosts, where they, indeed,
Were known and nurtured not.

Through his identification with the neglected side of nature, Tuckerman
pondered how "Nature daily through her grand design/Breathes contradiction
where she seems most clear" (i,xxvi). Furthermore, he critically engaged the
assumption of Transcendental correspondence and eventually proceeded beyond it to personal integration derived from a less-monitored experience of
nature.

It is first of all in his sense of isolation from nature that Tuckerman – botanist
and astronomer as well as poet – is Heade's kindred spirit. In the sonnets
written from 1854 to 1872 and in his masterpiece, "The Cricket" (composed
sometime in the 1860s), Tuckerman is overwhelmed by nature's secrecy:

But vain, O vain this turning for the light,
Vain as a groping hand to rend the dark –
I call, entangled in the night, a night
Of wind and voices, but the gusty roll
Is vague, nor comes their cheer of pilotage. (I, vi)

The attitude sets the poet apart from the majority of his American contemporaries. There is much that distinguishes him from Heade as well, not least
the almost-Keatsian richness of diction and emotion displayed here. Born in
Boston into an upper-class family, he attended Harvard and moved to Greenfield, Massachusetts, after marrying. There, except for two brief visits to
England in the early 1850s, he spent his days working quietly at his desk and
in his laboratory. A tiny legend of reclusiveness grew up around him.[19]

We are struck by the contrast with Heade's nomadic life. Although Heade
approached nature aggressively, hunting and traveling widely, Tuckerman
stayed at home. He was a diligent scientist, scrutinizing nature through microscope and telescope. He delighted in herbariums. Moreover, unlike Heade,
he was steeped in tradition: his characteristic diction; the inspiration and friendship of Tennyson, whom he met on his second trip abroad; the age-old topos
of death in life at the center of his vision; and his Puritan-like faith. Hearing

him describe his spiritual condition by way of swamp imagery, we think of
Edward Taylor:

> Dank fens of cedar, hemlock branches gray
> With trees and trail of mosses, wringing-wet,
> Beds of black pitchpine in dead leaves set
> Whose wasted red has wasted to white away,
> Remnants of rain and droppings of decay,
> Why hold ye so my heart . . . ? (I, vii)

There is no such religious lyricism in Heade, whose vision originated in the
understated idiom of folk art.

It is most of all melancholy that saturates Tuckerman's poems and contrasts
with the emotional deflation of Heade's landscapes. The poet is overcome with
the loss of something that Heade apparently never even possessed:

> Yes, though the brine may from the desert deep
> Run itself sweet before it finds the foam,
> O what to him, whose deep heart once a home
> For love and light, is left? to walk and weep:
> Still, with astonished sorrow, watch to keep
> On his dead day. (II, iii)

That Tuckerman's melancholy was constitutional is clear from the first series
of sonnets, predating the tragic death of his wife in 1857, on which the second
series is a dirge.[20] The poet fulfills William James's classic characterization of
the "sick soul" yearning for rebirth:

> Now there are some subjects whom all this leaves a prey to the pro-
> foundest astonishment. The strangeness is wrong. The unreality can-
> not be. A mystery is concealed, and a metaphysical solution must
> exist. If the natural world is so double-faced and unhomelike, what
> world, what thing is real? An urgent wondering and questioning is set
> up, a poring theoretic activity, and in the desperate effort to get into
> right relation with the matter, the sufferer is often led to what be-
> comes for him a satisfying religious solution.[21]

Tuckerman's early sonnets adumbrate the religious solution as a flight of
faith:

> No more thy meaning seek, thine anguish plead,
> But leaving straining thought and stammering word,
> Across the barren azure pass to God:
> Shooting the void in silence like a bird,
> A bird that shuts his wings for better speed.

Actually, as we shall see, Tuckerman found the cure to his soul sickness not
in such spiritual flight but otherwise.

Despite this fundamental divergence in temperament, the similarity between
Tuckerman and Heade is impressive, especially when the poet turns to relatively straightforward description:

And I have stood beneath Canadian sky
In utter solitudes, where the cricket's cry
Appalls the heart, and fear takes visible shapes;
And on Long Island's void and isolate capes
Heard the sea break like iron bars. And still
In all I seemed to hear the same deep dirge
Born in the wind, the insect's tiny trill,
And crash and jangle of the shaking surge,
And knew not what they meant, prophetic woe?
Dim boding wherefore? Now indeed I know. (II,xxx)

Heade's art may lack the sadness of Tuckerman's poetry but not the aware-ness of estrangement from the inhuman embodied by "utter solitudes" or "void and isolate capes." Humans in Heade's paintings seem indifferent to the omens all about them. See, for instance, *Approaching Storm* (1859), *Low Tide* (1860), *Thunderstorm over Naragansett Bay* (1868).[22] Without a sense of loss, these paintings present an emotional vacuum; they lack pathos as much as they lack ebullience. Unrelieved by catharsis, nature's fearful side grows in the absence of rapport between humans and the environment. In *Twilight, Spouting Rock Beach,*[23] a barrel tossed aimlessly on the beach accentuates the randomness, the lack of hope, inherent in the prospect.

Such an opposition of mystery and fact suggests the narrative of Thoreau's *Cape Cod,* especially in the opening chapter about a shipwreck. In the midst of this disaster, the diligent work of aggrandizement proceeds undisturbed. Thoreau's juxtaposition of nature's inscrutable course and such mundane of-fices – underscoring the gulf between the two – was envisioned by Tuckerman as well:

But Nature in her mood pushes and pulls
At her caprice; we see what is not shown
By that which we behold, nor this alone;
To commonest matters let us fix a bound
Or purport, straight another use is found
And this annihilates and that annuls.
And every straw of grass, or dirt, or stone,
Has different function from the kind well-known:
Commerce and custom, dikes and watermills.
Not to the sea alone, from inland earth,
The stream draws down its freight of floats and hulls,
But backward far, upwinding to the north,
The river gleams, a highway for the gulls
That fly not over land, into the hills. (III,ii)

Tuckerman's subdued reminder that nature has functions other than the normal human ones (those of "Commerce and custom, dikes and watermills") hints at sacred primordial meanings: "backward far" and "to the north" where the river that "gleams" winds its way "into the hills." The river fulfills an ancient covenant with the unreasoning gulls, "That fly not over land"; a pristine sympathy beyond human ken.

The meeting of land and sea is for Tuckerman a telling image of alienation:

> Ay! once I trod these shores too happily,
> Murmuring my gladness to the rocks and ground
> And, while the wave broke loud on ledge and reef,
> Whispered it in the pause, like one who tells
> His heart's dream and delight! And still the sea
> Went back and forth upon its bar of shells,
> Washed and withdrew, with a soft shaling sound,
> As though the wet were dry and joy were grief. (III, vi)

The effectiveness of this passage gains from the approximation of form (note the rhythm, alliteration, and onomatopoeia of the last three lines) to content, imparting immediacy and movement to the scene. The poet attempts to project his feelings on the sea only to be baffled by its ceaseless movement. Inner and outer worlds do not merge. A raw sensuous power denies every meaning Tuckerman seeks to impose on nature.

Another seashore vision, this time from "The Cricket," signifies the same ineffectual effort to inform nature with meaning. Throughout the early sections of this meditation (which lapses fitfully into reverie) the poet ruminates on the cricket's song:

> Might I but find thy knowledge in thy song!
>   That twittering tongue,
> Ancient as light, returning like the years.

His first inclination is to pursue the absolute knowledge he feels the crickets must possess: the knowledge of death, the absorption that their song conveys. But through the process of the poem he resolves his yearning, realizing in the final lines that to understand nature's message would divest it of mystique and joy:

> For larger would be less indeed, and like
> The ceaseless simmer in the summer grass
> To him who toileth in the windy field,
> Or where the sunbeams strike,
> Naught in innumerable numerousness.

He learns to content himself with nature unsubordinated to knowledge, hence to accept the death of loved ones:

> But failing this, the dell and grassy dike,
> The water and the waste shall still be dear,
> And all the pleasant plots and places
>   Where thou has sung, and I have hung
>   To ignorantly hear.

Before this resolution, however, Tuckerman ponders his association with the cricket's song. He identifies the myriad insect voices, lulling him into a half-sleep, with a sense of immersion that recalls the sea and death. Thus he tries to keep the mind moving in a particular direction. The passage is reminiscent of Heade's painting *Approaching Storm: Beach near Newport* (Figure 11.4). Apostrophizing the cricket, Tuckerman muses:

Figure 11.4. Martin Johnson Heade (American, 1819–1904), *Approaching Storm: Beach near Newport* (oil on canvas, 28 × 58¼ in. [71.1 × 147.9 cm.], 1859). Gift of Maxim Karolik. Courtesy, Museum of Fine Arts, Boston.

Figure 11.5. Martin Johnson Heade (American, 1819–1904), *Salt Marshes, Newport, Rhode Island* (oil on canvas, 15½ × 30¼ in. [39.4 × 76.8 cm.]). Gift of Maxim Karolik for the Karolik Collection of American Paintings, 1815–1865. Courtesy, Museum of Fine Arts, Boston.

Night lover too; bringer of all things dark
And rest and silence; yet thou bringest me
Always that burthen of the unresting Sea,
The moaning cliffs, the low rocks blackly stark;
These upland inland fields no more I view,
But the long flat seaside beach, the wild seamew,
    And the overturning wave!

The "upland inland fields" carry associations comparable to those in Heade's marsh scenes, to be examined later: a joyful inner world linked to lost childhood. But Tuckerman's handling of the seashore is especially interesting in relation to Heade. The descriptive phrases "moaning cliffs," "low rocks blackly stark," "long flat seaside beach," and "overturning wave," if not literally applicable to Heade's painting, evoke a similar lugubriousness mingled with foreboding. Furthermore, Tuckerman shares Heade's economy of expression when he treats the various elements of the scene as discrete entities apprehended sequentially. Unlike the sonnet just quoted (III, vi), in which the sensorium is focused on sound rather than sight, there is no immediacy here. A volatile scene has been rendered motionless and abstract.

The tension between static and dynamic in both Tuckerman's description and Heade's depiction is a highly suggestive affinity. For Tuckerman, the cricket's song calls to mind not only "all things dark/And rest and silence" but, simultaneously, "that burthen of the unresting Sea." Through his meditation, the constant motion of the sea comes to stand for unmoving eternity. Tuckerman unites flux and motionlessness in order to become reconciled to death. Accordingly, the sight of the overturning wave brings him back to the song of the cricket and to death: "Thou bringest too, dim accents from the grave."

Similarly, the waves in *Approaching Storm* appear stationary. This suspended animation is partly a vestige of Heade's early training as a folk painter. Vernacular form afforded a means of transmuting dynamic experience into stable patterns (a kind of homemade classicism). The scene is also characteristic of the seashore around Newport, Rhode Island. We are apt to forget that Heade's vision merges inwardness with verisimilitude; it is still very much a response to the actual landscape. This tension between subjective and empirical also appears in the eerie-looking, rocks along the shore, transformed by the livid light of the storm. Whatever its source, it is essential to the symbolic nature of *Approaching Storm*. The painting contrasts with certain other seashore scenes by Heade, in which the power of the sea is directly experienced but the point of view is simply outward. The unusual energy of *Approaching Storm* derives less from its dramatic subject than from a transvaluation of the visual: the apparent animation of the sharply defined rocks and the solidity of the breaking waves.

It is essentially the effort to assimilate outer world to inner that generates the melancholy of Tuckerman's poems and the sinister overtones of many of Heade's paintings. Both men attempted in some way to control nature: Heade as hunter, Tuckerman through science. But it is the ability of both to look critically at the will to know, to grasp its limitations, and then to relinquish it that constitutes their truest identities and significantly links them. Both artist and poet ultimately forsook the external stability imposed by the mind for a stability of the psyche.

The moments of tension in *Brazilian Forest, Lake George,* and *Approaching Storm* fall within the context of Heade's lifelong pursuit of inner equilibrium, a quest that led to the sensual luxuriance of his marsh scenes and tropicals. By the same token, the development of Tuckerman's sonnets is toward the resolution reached in "The Cricket." The fifth and final series of poems contains an imagery of personal fulfillment. Gone is the hopelessness that earlier haunted him. Whereas Heade appears to have returned instinctively to the state of well-being awarded by a naive apprehension of the image, such an awareness was a long-sought achievement for Tuckerman.

Renouncing the moral allegory of the previous generation of American landscapists (Cole and Durand, for example), as well as avoiding the studio interpretation advocated by the Ruskinian critic James Jackson Jarves, Heade freely portrayed the vibrations of nature – its melodious arabesques, rhythms, and echoes and the expressive features of color and light. These qualities encouraged not activity but repose.

According to T. W. Higginson, the most exuberant champion of this sort of thing: "Nature is not didactic, but simply healthy. . . . The waterfall cheers and purifies infinitely, but it marks no moments, has no reproaches for indolence, forces to no immediate decision. . . . "[24] The lengthy series of marsh scenes that Heade painted in the vicinity of Newburyport, Massachusetts, and Newport, Rhode Island, epitomize this sensuality. The marshes are desert places in a special sense: seductive, not repelling; pastoral, but with a difference. No doubt they express a message from the depths of the soul. For Heade, this obsessive vision was like Ishmael's "insula Tahiti," an inward retreat from the world of economic enterprise and moral endeavor. For us it is, in Gaston Bachelard's phrase, "the land of Motionless Childhood."[25] The sanctuary deep within – the domain of reverie – relates to both the stillness and the narcissism characteristic of luminist painting.

Heade explored the many apparitions of the marshes.[26] The sky in these paintings may be covered with dense clouds, play host to a passing storm, or (especially at sunset) stretch forth limpid and quiescent. Dominant is the pulse of ever-elusive light through the landscape: light deflected by clouds and sparkling on the marsh grass; shadows and the reflections of hayricks in streams and ponds. *Salt Marshes, Newport, Rhode Island* (ca. 1865–70) (Figure 11.5) offers a scene orchestrated by light and echoing forms. The eye follows the zigzag of hayricks from foreground into distance. The luminous clouds covering the sky give the illusion of a vast chamber, like the resonating inner space of childhood. Sunlight transfixes all. The contrast of light and dark is nearly supernatural in many of these scenes. The hayricks assume occult power through their lack of intelligibility. Here the utilitarian is transmuted almost imperceptibly into the beautiful.

Higginson surely had such a landscape in mind when he wrote of summer: "There are moments when the atmosphere is so surcharged with luxury that every pore of the body becomes an ample gate for sensation to flow in, and one has simply to sit still and be filled." In this setting,

> The soul is like a musical instrument; it is not enough that it be
> framed for the most delicate vibration, but it must vibrate long and
> often before the fibres grow mellow to the finest waves of sympathy.
> I perceive in the verry's carolling, the clover's scent, the glistening of
> the water . . . there are attainable infinitely more subtle modulations of
> thought than I can yet reach the sensibility to discriminate, much less
> describe.[27]

Tuckerman, too, after a long struggle, arrived at this awareness: that it is above all the poet's receptive attitude, his suspension of preconceptions, which allows him to commune with nature. Thus he learned to "glean" the harvest of wastelands:

> Yet in such waste no waste the soul descries,
> Intent to glean by barrenest sea and land.
> For whoso waiteth, long and patiently,
> Will see a movement stirring at his feet –
> If he but wait nor think himself much wise. (V, ii)

Though his temperament did not share the spontaneous sensuality of Heade or Higginson, Tuckerman certainly approached the spirit of their vision. Intriguingly, his awakening in the final sonnet series is linked to the swamp:

> Nay, from the mind itself a glimpse will rest
> Upon the dark; summoning from vacancy
> Dim shapes about his intellectual lamp,
> Calling these in and causing him to see;
> As the night-heron waking in the swamp
> Lights up the pools with her phosphoric breast. (V, ii)

Vision, Tuckerman now realizes, issues from the mind itself. The connotative power of images submerged in the poet's unconscious produces "Dim shapes about his intellectual lamp" (similar to Higginson's "infinitely more subtle modulations of thought"). Vision has to do not with direct but with reflected light, with tonality. This "phosphoric" light (recalling Thoreau's epiphany in the Maine woods) comes through the heron's waking, a harbinger of dawn, though, significantly, a not-altogether natural dawn. Phosphorous is the gleam of decayed wood but may be associated with the morning star. It implies rebirth from the obscurity of night and swamp.

The swamp, too, is an ambiguous image that evokes both begetting and destroying. To Tuckerman, the swamp signifies a force that he must assimilate if he is to achieve vision. The light by which he sees is lambent, enigmatic. It challenges his sensitivity, the theme enunciated at the beginning of the series:

> But Nature where she gives must give in kind,
> Grant to the rich and from the poor withhold;
> And much that we in manifest behold
> Is faint to some, while other some still find

Truths – that to our sense may be veiled and furled –
Published as light, notorious as wind. (V, i)

Tuckerman has accepted nature's mystery. He beholds in its image something other than the "published" truths. His new identity, more than faintly Whitmanesque, embraces nature's dark side: "Whilst I in dim green meadows lean and lag" (V, v).

Tuckerman drew a distinction between word and image that is analogous to the contrast he saw between the mind that pries into and exploits nature and the soul content to relax and enjoy it. A man "finds his vaunted reach and wisdom vain,"

Lost in the myriad meaning of a word
Or starts at its bare import, panic-stirred:
For earth is hearth or dearth or dirt,

But, "The sky heaved over our faint heads is heaven"(V, iv). The stability of faith in heaven is opposed to what one can know of earth – reflecting a loss of faith in science and reason. Words, our basic tools for making meaning, vary endlessly. But the faith sought by the poet at the end of the first sonnet series and conceived as spiritual flight has come full circle to an identification with the stabilizing relation to the image. Matter and spirit, life and death, unite. Tuckerman intuited what the depth psychologist Erich Neumann saw as the connection between *uroboros* and *mandala* (both circular forms): the infantile unconscious and adult individuation.[28]

Tuckerman reached this insight as his inner journey led him back to the childlike vision he had longed for in the sonnets following his wife's death. In the third sonnet of the final series, he described his own moment of epiphany, a personal integration of individual origins and eternity:

And yet tonight, when summer daylight dies,
I crossed the fields against the summer gust
And with me, rising from my feet like dust,
A crowd of flea-like grasshoppers, like flies
Presaging dry and dry continuance; yet
Where they prefigure change all signals must
Fail in the dry when they forbode the wet . . .
I know not. All tonight seems mystery:
From the full fields that pressed so heavily,
The burden of the blade, the waste of blowth,
The twinkling of the smallest life that flits
To where, and all unconsciously, he sits:
My little boy, symbolling eternity,
Like the god Brahma, with his toe in his mouth. (V, iii)

Here once more is the passive response: Immersion is an open field whose dustiness – in keeping with Tuckerman's ascetic personality – reveals the "desert." The paradox and confused syntax of lines 5 through 7 show the mind bewildered by nature's contradictions. Then in the eighth line, thought suddenly relaxes. The poet declares, "I know not" and allows nature to impress itself on his being through a mellifluous orchestration of sight, sound, and touch. Dust and insect life suggest regression. Tuckerman is lulled by the hypnotic rhythm of the flitting insects; his experience, coinciding with their oblique paths, reenacts the unconscious responsiveness of the child. "My little boy," sitting with his toe in his mouth, like "the god Brahma," brings to mind the self-consuming oneness of the *uroboros* (the snake devouring its own tail). In thus inhabiting the unconscious, the poet assumes the child's narcissism and repossesses a divine knowledge.

It is no surprise that in his appropriation of the primitive, Tuckerman should recall the Hindu, not the Christian, deity. In this choice, he anticipates a growing receptivity of thoughtful Americans to the religious sensibility of so-called primitive or alien cultures that culminated in the vogue for things Asian toward the end of the century and that had one of its most outlandish devotees in Lafcadio Hearn. As we shall see, the relationship between Hearn's predisposition to Asia and his exuberant reaction to the jungle is not inconsequential.

Religion, Science, and Nature: Sidney Lanier and Lafcadio Hearn

In an article on the philosophy of art that appeared in a New Orleans newspaper in November 1878, a young journalist named Lafcadio Hearn offered some trenchant speculations. He took note of the growing rift between science and religion and concluded. "The skepticism of the Nineteenth Century is of a description which renders the resubjugation of a whole people to any one pre-existing religious idea [as advocated by men like James Anthony Froude] impossible. . . . " This state of affairs did not bode well for the arts which, Hearn believed, depended for their continuing vitality on a solid religious basis: "A new art-period in the world's history can follow only upon a new religious period in that history." Hearn did, on the other hand, foresee unlimited progress in science and mechanical skill: "We must expect that nations will seek less and less after outward appearances and more and more after latent practical power."[1] The only hope for art thus was the prospect of a new religious revelation somehow delivered by science itself.

Hearn was uncompromising about the terms for such a reconciliation between knowledge and faith. Seven years later, in a review for the New Orleans *Times-Democrat,* he took John Fiske to task for allowing expressions of personal faith to interfere with the logical sequence of his argument, in holding that the "omnipresent energy" immanent in evolutionary process was (quoting Fiske) "in some way anthropomorphic or quasi-personal" and that the "orderly progression of events is toward *a goal recognizable by human intelligence."* Then Hearn attacked the gist of Fiske's confusion. "The pantheism of evolution is not . . . incompatible with the idea of personality; and Mr. Fiske believes in a being to be prayed to, and a soul to be immortal."[2]

Fiske's argument for a new religious idea would stand little chance against the incisive reasoning of a book like Morton Prince's *The Nature of Mind and Human Automatism* (whose title speaks for itself). For Hearn, as he developed his interests in the new scientific revelations, the failure of systems like Fiske's sprang from their adoption of a "humanly-ethical point of view." "Nature has kindnesses indeed," Hearn admitted; "but she is frightfully merciless; – she possesses supreme beauty and yet creates extremes of hideousness; she manifests indeed the justice of an unsparing judge, but of a judge whose code is framed very differently from the code which regulates the manners of mankind."[3]

Given his tough-minded stance on the central artistic issue of the day (though one would not have known it from reading the poetry being produced at the time), one wonders how Hearn would have reacted to a poem that first appeared anonymously in *A Masque of Poets*. The publication of Sidney Lanier's "The Marshes of Glynn" (written in the summer of 1878) coincided almost exactly in time with Hearn's call for an art based on a religious attachment to the world envisioned by advancing science. Had he seen the poem (and he may well have), Hearn would probably have responded positively, for it represented a new departure if not an altogether successful solution to the crisis of values initiated by Darwin's theory. "The Marshes of Glynn" marked a personal and artistic breakthrough for Lanier at a time when, wracked by the tuberculosis that would kill him within three years, he was beginning to be filled with the presentiment of death.

Obviously, Lanier was well aware of nature "red in tooth and claw," and he was prepared to make much of the indifference and amorality of the natural world that was becoming an inescapable fact of life. The apparent injustice of nature occupied him in the late poem "The Cloud" (1880):

> Cold Cloud, but yesterday
> Thy lightning slew a child at play,
> And then a priest with prayers upon his lips
>
> For his enemies, and then a bright
> Lady that did ope the door
>   Upon the stormy night
> To let a beggar in, – strange spite, –

Yet beneath this seeming willfulness Lanier sensed a larger purpose. The little poem "Opposition" (1879) formulated a veritable credo of Darwinian theory, with direct application to the question of poetic inspiration:

> The dark hath many dear avails:
>   The dark distils divinest dews;
> The dark is rich with nightingales,
>   With dreams, and with the heavenly Muse.
> . . . .
> Of fret, of dark, of thorn, of chill,
>   Complain thou not, O heart; for these
> Bank in the current of the will
>   To uses, arts and charities.

The emergence of good out of evil, the reconciliation of opposites in the expansiveness of nature, and the return to childhood innocence were the central themes of "The Marshes of Glynn," which might be seen to recount the moment when nature's true significance first struck Lanier. This significance – the begetting of good from evil – pertained to the rhythmic pulsation that unified all life. Here, in effect, was where Lanier brought science into alignment with the supernal world to which he aspired. In his *Science of English Verse* (1878), in which he argued for what he saw as the analogy between music and verse, Lanier cited Poe's image in *Eureka* of the rhythmic beating of the heart of God as the underlying principle of both nature and creativity. And if rhythm was the basis for the central creative act of the universe, was such rhythm not also a kind of antagonism?

Lanier could point to no less an authority than Herbert Spencer in support of the proposition that "where opposing forces act, rhythm appears," as in "the two motions which carry the earth towards, and away from, the sun and so result in the periodicity of the earth's progress and others." In developing the analogy between music and poetry, Lanier went so far as to extrapolate an intrinsic link between the physical and the moral:

> When we compare what one may call the literal rhythm which rules throughout physical nature with the metaphorical rhythm or proportion which governs good behavior as well as good art; when we find that opposition in the physical world results in rhythm, and that so opposition in the moral world – the fret, the sting, the thwart, the irreconcilable me as against all other me's, the awful struggle for existence, the desperate friction of individualities, the no of death to all requests – may also result in rhythm; when we perceive that through all those immeasurable agitations which constitute both moral and physical nature this beautiful and orderly principle of rhythm thus swings to and fro like the shuttle of a loom and weaves a definite and comprehensible pattern into the otherwise chaotic fabric of things: we may be able to see dimly into that old Orphic saying of the seer, "The father of metre is rhythm, and the father of rhythm is God."[4]

Coming near the end of the poet's life, this resolution reflects a quest for certainty that, however, contradicts much of Lanier's earlier thinking and brings up the specter of conflict and paradox that beset so many of his contemporaries also seeking reconciliation with an impersonal universe. Indeed, Lanier's failure to integrate his Wordsworthian yearnings for communion with nature and his push for certitude in a fractured and diminished world illustrate the philosophical and temperamental inconsistency pinpointed by Lafcadio Hearn.

Only since 1874, with the composition of "Corn," had Lanier really begun finding himself as a poet. At this point, he had determined to revolt against the "trim smugness and clean-shaven propriety" of conventional poetic form.[5] His reading of Emerson helped lead him to nature as the truest locus of poetic concern.[6] Then, through his friend Bayard Taylor, he discovered Whitman in February 1878.

Leaves of Grass struck Lanier "like rude salt spray" in the face.[7] Despite protesting that he disagreed with Whitman "in all points connected with artistic form," Lanier found in the older poet confirmation of his own experimental attitudes in prosody. His spiritual quest to understand poetry in terms of music (he was a highly accomplished musician who played first flute for the Peabody Orchestra in Baltimore) soon culminated in his *Science of English Verse*. Lanier's main affinity with Whitman lay in a different direction, however. Shortly after reading his work, Lanier wrote the poet: "It is not known to me where I can find another modern song at once so large and so naive: and the time needs to be told few things so much as the absolute personality of the person, the sufficiency of the man's manhood to the man, which you have propounded in such strong and beautiful rhythms."[8] Whitman's Romantic egotism appealed to Lanier as the way to independence from nature.

The relationship between matter and spirit had long been on Lanier's mind. In 1873 he communicated to his brother Clifford the one general principle, distilled after much reading and reflection, by which he could live:

> Whilst there is a remarkable parallelism between the phenomena of
> Mind and the phenomena of the nervous system (a parallelism which
> Herbert Spencer has detailed with a wonderful insight and supported
> by a prodigious number of illustrations), yet it is always unsafe to as-
> sert... anything like a *dependence* of mind upon matter; much more to
> erect a theory that mind is made of matter, in any way.[9]

Lanier's rejection of materialism led to his insistence on the autonomy of the artist's creative personality in the face of the innocent yet terrible injustice of nature pictured, for instance, in "The Cloud" (1880):

> Awful is Art, because 'tis free.
> The artist trembles o'er his plan,
>   Where men his Self must see.
> Who made a song or picture, he
> Did it, and not another, God nor man.
> . . . .
>
> Oh, not as clouds dim laws have plann'd
> To strike down Good and fight for Ill,
>   Oh, not as harps that stand
> In the wind and sound the wind's command:
> Each artist – gift of terror! – owns his
> will. . . .

Lanier's concept of personality represented an altogether different tangent from the attempt to see in rhythm the unity of science and religion. Yet strands from both ideas – unraveled as they were – were so entangled with each other that they almost formed a separate fabric.

Insisting on the autonomy of artistic personality was a way of breaking with the definite, with the one-dimensional terms of theology or science. Traveling in Florida (in order to gather information for his guidebook of 1875) helped Lanier refine his sense of the infinite suggestiveness of nature that carried the soul beyond the scope of the knowable and definable. While in Tampa, Lanier jotted down some sentiments that appeared almost unedited in the introduction to his guidebook and that looked forward to the meditative communion with the live oaks in "The Marshes of Glynn":

> In among the trees in Florida. Here walking one presently finds a host
> of contrasts exhaling from one's contemplation of the forest, one

glides out of the idea that this multiform beauty is familiar, that it is a clump of trees and vines and flowers: No, it is Silence, which, denied access to man's ear, has caught form, and set forth its fervent appeal to man's eye: it is Music, in a siesta; it is Conflict, dead, and reappearing as Beauty: it is amiable Mystery, grown communicative: it is Nature, with her finger on her lip, – gesture of double significance, conveying to one, that one may kiss her, if one will say nothing about it: it is Tranquillity, suavely waving aside men's excuses for wars, ... it is Trade, done into a flower, and blossoming as perfect type of honest *quid pro quo,* in the lavish good measure of that interchange whereby the undersides of leaves use man's breath and return him the same in better condition, paying profitable usuries for what the lender could not help loaning: it is a Reply, in all languages, but untranslatable in any, to the multitudinous interrogations ... of students who dimly behold the unknowable world of the something unexplainably sweet beyond the immediate field of thought. ... [10]

This passage gathers together most of the themes that interested Lanier. The inexpressible mystery was a sanctuary from the world of endless monetary transaction and futile material gain. It hovered in the silence and repose that blessed the primordial wilderness, and access to it came chiefly through poetry, which had the power to modulate into a new key the conflict that seemed everywhere immanent, not only in trade but in nature as well. Lanier was becoming fascinated with the delicate nexus between sound and silence, a fleeting yet eternal moment he attempted to capture in the late poem "Sunrise" (1880). At the sight of the first appearance of the sun on the horizon, he exclaimed:

> Oh, what if a sound should be made!
> Oh, what if a bound should be laid
> To this bow-and-string tension of beauty and silence a-string, –
> To the bend of beauty the bow, or the hold of silence the spring!
> I fear me, I fear me yon dome of diaphanous gleam
> Will break as a bubble o'er-blown in a dream, –

Music, whose rhythms were resolved through the interplay of sound and silence, came closest to communicating the mystery of the unknown. This dance of sound and silence was simply a more rarefied version of the mating of matter and spirit that was the source of poetry in general. When nature and the human soul came together in metaphor, a "beautiful One" was created.[11] In the nature metaphor, as Lanier had written in early 1872, "soul gives life to matter and Matter gives Antaean solidity to soul."[12]

Lanier dismissed any clumsy linking of the two in the service of some preconcerted meaning, some didactic piety. Rather, he proclaimed "that strange and manifold transfusing of human nature into physical nature which has developed the most interesting phasis of modern culture and which constitutes the most characteristic of modern art."[13] He saw nature and soul "each complementing the other's significance, each *meaning* the other in such will-o'-wisp transfigurations as the mind cannot easily analyse." God himself had decreed this "correlative intersignificance of man and man's earth."[14]

For the poet, music proved to be the most efficacious means of reaching toward the ineffable. Rejecting the new doctrine of art for art's sake, Lanier reasserted the central role of art – of poetry and music and of poetry as music – in the human spiritual quest. Above all, this was a quest for love, for an emotional bondage with what lay beyond the definite. In an essay entitled "From Bacon to Beethoven" (1876), Lanier determined just where he left science behind. Spencer had offered the possibility for a partial relation to the infinite in the sphere of cognition. But there remained the more important sphere of emotion, and here music provided much closer access to the supernal.

We find a singularly Lanier-like sensibility in Lafcadio Hearn when in 1883 Hearn described the Têche country of Louisiana as "The Garden of Paradise." Hearn begins with the contrast between the ancient fancy that "somewhere above the fir-belts, above the roar of the cascades, above the reach of human endeavor" there lies "some mysterious summit whose whiteness is not of snow, but of Divinity . . . " and his conviction that in the swampy country of the Têche, "Heaven is not . . . above reach, – one may drift dreamily into it with a waft of orange-scented wind. . . . " There is something more here, Hearn felt, than "even in those Arcadian vales peopled by a race who called themselves Proselenoi, or older than the moon."[15] Yet Lanier would never have gone so far, surely, as to accept this pantheism.

When he sought glimmerings from across the interval between silence and sound, Hearn looked no farther than the kaleidoscopic intercalations of sensation and fancy in his own surroundings. His description of the moss of the Têche had advanced a long way beyond the stock characterizations of writers earlier in the century, and it represents nothing less than the aestheticization of nature:

> It is the moss that forms the *theme* of the scenery – if a musical word may be used descriptively. It constitutes the character of the landscape. It is omnipresent and omnipotent in effect. It streams from the heads and limbs of the oaks; from the many-elbowed crypress skeletons it hangs like decaying rags of green. It creates suggestions of gibbets and of corpses, of rotten rigging, of the tattered sails of ships "drifting with the dead to shores where all is dumb." Under the sunlight it has also countless pleasant forms – the tresses of slumbering dryads, the draperies flung out upon some vast woodland-holiday by skills of merry elves. Under the moon, losing its green, every form of goblinry, every fancy of ghastliness, every grimness of witchcraft, every horror of death, are mocked by it. A weird and wonderful morning seems to droop over the plains; – all the woods and groves, the lily-kissed pools, the shadow-reflecting bayous, – appear to lament some incalculable bereavement, some vast and awful death. It is as though this land were yet weeping for Pan, – as though all the forests and streams had not ceased after more than a thousand years to lament the passing away of the sylvan gods and nymphs of the antique world.[16]

There is much, to be sure, of the pathetic fallacy in Hearn's description, but it is spun out in a kind of spiritual vacuum that, though we are reminded of some of Lanier's prose descriptions of Florida, stands opposed to the spiritual striving of the southern poet. Although he might have identified in large part with Lanier's relationship to nature, Hearn would have found much in Lanier's concept of the preeminence of artistic personality to criticize. Lanier's unfortunate predilection for the pathetic fallacy in his nature imagery – his "sweet" and "dear" woods – springs from the same root as this reconstituted idealism and disrupts his quest for reconciliation with the ethereal in the world around him. Moreover, there is no mistaking the poet's heartfelt Christianity, especially in the poem outlines he wrote toward the end of his life for the series *Hymns of the Marshes:*

> O Science, wilt thou take my Christ,
>   Oh, wilt thou crucify him o'er
> Betwixt false thieves with thieves' own pain,
>   Never to rise again?
>
> Leave me this love, O cool-eyed One,
>   Leave me this Saviour.

Such sentiment would have struck Hearn as so much sediment at the bottom of Lanier's glass.

Lanier's poetic surge during the last years of his life squeezed through a breach in the scientific understanding of the world. Addressing science, the poet commanded:

> Tear me, I pray thee, this Flower of Sweetness-of-Life petal from
> petal, number me the pistils, and above all, above all, dear Science,
> find me the ovary thereof, and the seeds in the ovary, and save these.
>   Thou canst not.

On another occasion, Lanier defined the difference between Darwin's and Beethoven's approaches to nature:

> Our Darwin boldly takes hold of Nature as if it were a rose, pulls it
> to pieces, puts it under the microscope, and reports to us what he saw
> without fear or favor. Beethoven, on the other hand, approaching the
> same good Nature – from a different direction, with different motives
> – and looking upon it with the artist's – not the scientist's eye, finds it
> a beautiful whole; he does not analyze, but, pursuing the synthetic
> process, shows it to us as a perfect rose, reporting his observations to
> us in terms of harmony.[17]

In realizing the limitation of scientific knowledge, Lanier found grace. Here was the license for, if not the source of, the poetic rapture on nature that readied him intellectually, emotionally, and spiritually for death. What was left after science and after moral judgment was, it turned out, everything.

This was Lanier's message in "The Marshes of Glynn" which, like "Sunrise," its companion piece of two years later, is built around the psychological transformation from enclosure to expansion. All day long, the poet secreted himself among the "Glooms of the live-oaks" whose "Wildwood privacies" recall the penitential meditation of the secluded monastery. These "closets of lone desire" are

> Cells for the passionate pleasure of prayer to the soul that
> grieves,
> Pure with a sense of the passing of saints through the wood,
> Cool for the dutiful weighing of ill with good; –

But this retreat away from men, the stroke of the scythe and the trowel of trade, is only a preparation of the self, until the spirit has grown "to a lordly great compass within" so that it can awaken to the sublime openness of the marshes beyond the forest. Although the oaks are treated as lovers whom the poet physically embraces, they also image the self entangled in a physical world in which judgment and melancholy are the ruling realities, as suggested by the poem's opening lines:

> Glooms of the live-oaks, beautiful-braided and woven
> With intricate shades of the vines that myriad-cloven
> Clamber the forks of the multiform boughs, –
> Emerald twilights, –
> Virginal shy lights,

Now, however, as evening approaches, the soul has overmastered doubt and "knows that it knows." Moral questions have given place to a sense of spiritual serenity. Physical entanglement is superseded by identification. Lanier is able to embrace without fear the vastness and mystery of the marshes, the fullness of emptiness, the apotheosis of silence and space. Here lies the freedom of the soul "From the weighing of fate and the sad discussion of sin" that has occupied him all day long.

As with Martin Johnson Heade's paintings, the marshes are a vision of childhood wholeness and harmony:

> Sinuous southward and sinuous northward the shimmering band
> Of the sand-beach fastens the fringe of the marsh to the folds
> of the land.
> Inward and outward to northward and southward the beach-
> lines linger and curl
> As a silver-wrought garment that clings to and follows the firm
> sweet limbs of a girl.

Lanier's return to innocence is a way of bringing

> God out of knowledge and good out of infinite pain
> And sight out of blindness and purity out of a stain.

This return is made possible through identification with the landscape which in turn has been brought about by the transformation of the scene, effecting an expansion of the soul. The poet's regression allows him to become what he sees and to gain "a hold on the greatness of God" through the intermediary of the environment he inhabits. His merging with nature is evoked in some of the best lines of the poem:

As the marsh-hen builds on the watery sod,
Behold I will build me a nest on the greatness of God:
I will fly in the greatness of God as the marsh-hen flies
In freedom that fills all the space 'twixt the marsh and the skies:
By so many roots as the marsh-grass sends in the sod
I will heartily lay me a-hold on the greatness of God:
Oh, like to the greatness of God is the greatness within
The range of the marshes, the liberal marshes of Glynn.

The poet's return to origins is paced by the setting of the sun. The ushering in of night brings on the rise of the tide which covers the marshes. We are prepared for the imageless vortex that lies on the farther side of childhood. The final stanza, enigmatic and unexpected, hurries into conjunction the sleep, unconscious awareness, and intimations of death that are the origin of the poet's utterance and that pose the final question of the unknown accompanied by all its subliminal reverberations:

And now from the Vast of the Lord will the waters of sleep
Roll in on the souls of men,
But who will reveal to our waking ken
The forms that swim and the shapes that creep
Under the waters of sleep?
And I would I could know what swimmeth below when the tide comes in
On the length and the breadth of the marvellous marshes of
Glynn.

In transcending the Darwinian and Spencerian view of nature through personal faith, Sidney Lanier simply opted out of a dilemma that nagged all Romantics in an emphatically post-Romantic world. Lanier is, indeed, not guiltless of the charge leveled at him by Southern agrarians like Robert Penn Warren, who concluded that he "never understood the function of the idea in art"; hence his poetry "performed an arbitrary disjunction . . . between the idea and the form in which the idea might be embodied."[18]

Lafcadio Hearn achieved a more successful resolution of the new science and unmistakably Romantic sensibility. As his career testified, Hearn was capable of wholeheartedly embracing the anarchy of nature. The exhilaration in his declaration of personal freedom extends to his review of "The Life of Stars" for the *Times-Democrat:*

"Nature's calm" is a fiction. The infinite roars with the parturition of
nebulae pregnant with solar systems – rages with the agonies of dying
suns; and all the while that monstrous belt of blazing sphere to which
our own system belongs is changing shape like smoke, is rolling up
like a scroll, is tearing its seething way through unknown deeps of
darkness with the rapidity of lightnings, – though we, like the creatures wriggling within a drop of water beneath a microscope, may not
be conscious of sounds too vast for our tiny brains to comprehend.[19]

In such vastness, human life was reduced to "one vibration of an everlasting force."

By 1888 this cosmology had taken fictional shape in Hearn's retelling of the legend of "L'Île Dernière" in *Chita*. In 1856 a tremendous Gulf storm had destroyed Last Island, a fashionable resort area on the beach below New Orleans, killing hundreds of vacationers whose frivolity on the very evening of the catastrophe underlined the ironies of the human failure to grasp nature's power and mystery. In what is surely one of the most extraordinary descriptions of nature in American prose, Hearn recreated the gradual, furtive, yet ineluctable rise of tension in the gathering storm which draws on an unseen but palpable malevolence in the "heaven's blue dream of eternity":

> To one who found himself alone, beyond the limits of the village and
> beyond the hearing of its voices, – the vast silence, the vast light,
> seemed full of weirdness. And these hushes, these transparencies, do
> not always inspire a causeless apprehension: they are omens sometimes
> – omens of coming tempest. Nature, – incomprehensible Sphinx! –
> before her mightiest bursts of rage, ever puts forth her divinest witch-
> ery, makes more manifest her awful beauty. . . . [20]

Like Lanier, Hearn was not above personifying nature, but there is nothing here of the Southern poet's sentimentalism.

The influence of Thoreau's *Cape Cod* is everywhere in the opening sections of *Chita*. We recall in particular Thoreau's own peculiarly passive, noneditorializing response to the shipwreck which throws a disquieting pall over the account of his first and subsequent excursions to the Cape. Whereas Thoreau's narrative hints strongly of the naturalistic context, Hearn had at hand a concerted theory, a model of natural process, with which to press his case. Hearn saw in nature the Darwinian struggle for survival, the continuing cycle of destruction and recreation evident in this primordial holdout of the tropical world. In "Torn Letters" he made this view explicit in commenting on the sight of birds voraciously attacking fish:

> Enormous slaughter! – appalling cruelty! – destruction symbolizing
> grimly the great contests of human life in which the fiercest and
> strongest and swiftest survive to exemplify Nature's mystic and mer-
> ciless law, – symbolizing, too, the stranding of myriad ambitions in
> the terrific race for wealth, the stranding of countless lives upon the
> sands of Illusion, – symbolizing, likewise, the loss of unnumbered
> precious things desperately won only to be wrested brutally from the
> winner by superior strength and cunning and ferocity in that eternal
> Battle of Success which is also a tearing-out of hearts. . . . [21]

Hearn explored the region where the teeming anarchy of the natural world intersects with the interior civil war that had obsessed Poe, in whom he found a spiritual father: the fascination of decay and disintegration, the crucial ellipsis of the link in the chain of logic, the revel in the putrescent and the macabre. In *Chita* Hearn described the vortex of sensation that funnels downward into madness:

> The gulls fly lower about you, circling with sinister squeaking cries; –
> perhaps for an instant your feet touch in the deep something heavy,
> swift, lithe, that rushes past with a swirling shock. Then the fear of

the Abyss, the vast and voiceless Nightmare of the Sea, will come upon you; the silent panic of all those opaline millions that flee glimmering by will enter into you also. . . . [22]

Nowhere was this region of terror, which brought one closest to the numinous source of creation, better established than in the Caribbean jungle. If the still-Romantic nature of Sidney Lanier was mirrored in the quiescence of the marsh, Hearn's affinity with the energies at the source of the universe led him to appropriate the cataclysmic cycles of the jungle. Traditional values have changed places. Now it is the jungle that is demonic, whereas the marsh verges on the Edenic. The long passage in Hearn's *Two Years in the French West Indies* (1890) is quoted here in full as it brings to a crescendo the imagery that we have been tracing:

> But the sense of awe inspired by a tropic forest is certainly greater than the mystic fear which any wooded wilderness of the North could ever have created. The brilliancy of colors that seem almost preternatural; the vastness of the ocean of frondage, and the violet blackness of rare gaps, revealing in its unconceived profundity; and the million mysterious sounds which make up its perpetual murmur, – compel the idea of a creative force that almost terrifies. Man feels here like an insect, – fears like an insect on the alert for merciless enemies: and the fear is not unfounded. To enter these green abysses without a guide were folly: even with the best of guides there is peril. Nature is dangerous here: the powers that build are also the powers that putrefy; here life and death are perpetually interchanging office in the never-ceasing transformation of forces, – melting down and reshaping living substance simultaneously within the same vast crucible. There are trees distilling venom, there are plants that have fangs, there are perfumes that affect the brain, there are cold green creepers whose touch blisters flesh like fire; while in all the recesses and the shadows is a swarming of unfamiliar life, beautiful or hideous, – insect, reptile, bird, – interwarring, devouring, preying. . . . [23]

Hearn exulted in human impotence and vulnerability in the midst of this spectacle: "The air itself seems inimical to thought, – soporific, and yet pregnant with activities of dissolution so powerful that the mightiest tree begins to melt like wax from the moment it has ceased to live." Then there is the terrible fer-de-lance, one of the deadliest snakes of the known world: "Even in the brightest noon you cannot venture to enter the woods without an experienced escort . . . at any moment a seeming branch, a knot of lianas, a pink or grey root, a clump of pendant yellow fruit may suddenly take life, writhe, stretch, spring, strike. . . . " The attack precipitates, ironically, the most extreme identification with the environment:

> Necrosis of the tissues is likely to set in: the flesh corrupts, falls from the bone sometimes in tatters; and the colors of its putrefaction simulate the hues of vegetable decay, – the ghastly grays and pinks and yellows of trunks rotting down into dark soil which gave them birth. The human victim moulders as the trees moulder, – crumbles and dis-

solves as crumbles the substance of the dead palms and balatas: the Death-of-the-Woods is upon him.[24]

Yet for Hearn this fantasy of dissolution is only a prelude to a supporting structure of coherence and meaning. His journey harkened not after madness but after a dumb yet serene emotional attachment to that ineffable something uttered in the dazzling light and luxuriant color – the blue and green – of the tropical world.[25] In a letter to his confidant Page Baker, editor of the *Times-Democrat*, Hearn confessed during a visit to Grand Isle:

> I'd like to melt into the water, and move with it lazily, – tumbling sleepily on the lukewarm sand under the big lazy moons; – or become a half-conscious fish to be assimilated by the irresistible stomack of a man-of-war bird. To become a part of the infinite laziness of a man-of-war bird would delight me. Still better to become a cloud floating in the Eternal Blue Ghost and only draw breath at long, long intervals, so enormously lazy have I been.[26]

This physical and moral enervation was, of course, conservative in its political implications. The root of reintegration through stillness and merging with the environment was nourished by the scientific vision that Hearn embraced. From the start, he had been convinced that "all evils tend to correct themselves; even though new evils be afterwards developed by the change; yet the day that visible evil ceases, progress ends."[27] Out of anarchy came the controls that allowed for both equilibrium and development. Nature's monsters and "goblin shapes" had evolved "as destroyers, as equilibrists, as counterchecks to that prodigious fecundity, which, unhindered, would thicken the deep into one measureless and waveless ferment of being. . . . "[28]

Yet beyond the political sphere, enervation was simply a passive sensitivity to the intimations of spirit everywhere immanent in the physical world: "All this sensuous blending of warmth and force in winds and waters more and more suggests an idea of the spiritualism of the elements – a sense of world-life. In all these soft sleepy swayings, these caresses of wind and sobbing of waters, Nature seems to confess some passional mood."[29]

Even when Hearn first, as a young journalist, confronted the spectacle of space, a regressive journey in search of truth seemed to be on the horizon: "Primitive men in worshipping the lights of heaven as *intelligent* being, perhaps came nearer the truth than the hierarchs who founded the faiths that still live."[30] And this animism, in which Hearn founded his religious myth, was never more pronounced than in the tropical forest:

> That beautiful, solemn, silent life upreaching through tropical forest to the sun for warmth, for color, for power, – filled me, I remember, with a sensation of awe different from anything which I had ever experienced. . . . But even here in Guiana, standing alone under the sky, the palm still seems a creature rather than a tree, – gives you the idea of personality; – you could almost believe each lithe shape animated by a thinking force, – believe that all are watching you with such passionless calm as legend lends to beings supernatural. . . . [31]

For Hearn, the personification of nature was not a breach of his scientific perspective, a lapse into anthropomorphism; it was justified by his grasp of the essential truth of the primitive life in harmony with an indifferent world.

There was indeed a far side to the jungle into which Hearn's journey led him. Living in Japan in the last years of his life helped him understand what had kept him pressing toward dissolution in nature and had allowed him to master the inner stability that might offer a way out. In the essay "The Eternal Feminine," he talked of the Japanese inability to comprehend "the Western worship of Woman as the Unattainable, the Incomprehensible, the Divine, the ideal of *'la femme que tu ne connaîtras pas....'"*[32] (Could this ideal have been the mother that Hearn lost at an early age and with whom he sought some kind of symbolic reunion?)

Western art, Hearn felt, had been based on the "nervous analogy" between nature and woman or, rather, "between two modes of pleasurable feeling excited by two different impressions."[33] He implied that his own receptiveness to evolutionary theory had been part of this worship of the Eternal Feminine: "Also it is true that the new philosophy of evolution, forcing recognition of the incalculable and awful cost of the Present to the Past, creating a totally new comprehension of duty to the Future, enormously enhancing our conception of character values, has aided more than all preceding influences together toward the highest possible spiritualism of the ideal of woman."[34] What Hearn realized in confronting Japanese culture, however, was the extent to which the Western vision of nature had been forced abnormally in one direction "by the single emotional idea which has left us nearly, if not totally blind to many wonderful aspects of Nature...."[35]

Here was a refinement of the value of immersion in the unknown that had led Hearn on his quest from Cincinnati to New Orleans to Martinique to Japan. It was a further rejection of any element of abstraction that might interfere with his perception of the richness of nature, of its wonderful multifariousness and irregularity. Such a perception Hearn found in Japanese paintings that reproduced "not only every peculiarity of the creature's shape, but every special characteristic of its motion."[36] The conclusion to Hearn's quest was thus acceptance, a passivity that did not presume to impose on the natural world some obsessive and anthropomorphic pattern that might control meaning and motivate activity but that would reinhabit childlike assurance through the wisdom of the sage: " 'He,' saith the Buddhist text, 'who discerns that nothingness is law – such a one hath wisdom.' "[37] In this final exorcism of the anthropomorphic, Hearn's efforts to bring the metaphysical into relationship with the known might succeed.

Conclusion:
Katherine Anne Porter's Jungle and the Modernist Idiom

In concluding, it seems appropriate to say something more about the relevance of the imagery of swamp and jungle to the quiet but momentous transition from Romantic to Modernist thought beginning in America during the Mid-Victorian period. Throughout this study, I have tried to show some of the ways in which an interest in desert landscapes contributed to the process by which nature lost its objective status and thereby gained metaphoric power and resourcefulness. The dynamic of immersion in the unknown, crucial to the significance of desert places, impelled this process. We might see this as a dissolution of the traditional synthesis of nature and providential history, or of nature and positivistic science, which brought back into play a dynamic and often mysterious and frightening nature that Americans were challenged to reorder and integrate through a new, more dialectical sense of both human nature and human history.

As Georg Lukács explained it from his Marxist perspective:

> History is no longer an enigmatic flux to *which* men and things are subjected. It is no longer a thing to be explained by the intervention of transcendental powers or made meaningful by reference to trand-scendental values . . . the nature of history is precisely that every defini-tion degenerates into an illusion: *history is the history of the unceasing overthrow of the objective forms that shape the life of man.*[1]

The effort in nineteenth-century America to overcome the reification of nature, which involves the reification of human nature and history, has been my fundamental theme. I hope I have established how swamp and jungle imagery both was instrumental in this effort and reflected its successes and failures.

As I suggested in Chapter 9, when considering the question of the miasmic atmosphere believed to emanate from swamps and marshes, the reconfigura-tion of experience in the transition toward Modernist sensibility carries us beyond any particular landscape, as even the terms for an "objective" nature have been called into question through the metaphors of decomposition and infection. This is the point at which the category of desert places vindicates its own asocial meaning and is opened to more general categories of experience, whether literary, artistic, or more broadly cultural.

This vindication resounds most clearly in Thoreau's embrace of the "dismal" without succumbing to the morbidity that characterized most of his contemporaries' approaches to the swamp. But the process I have tried to trace dragged sensibility far beyond the territory indicated by the old labels. The revolution in awareness we confront here led to no less than the emergence of language itself as the lowest common denominator of reality. The medium, in other words, becomes the message, a heresy that most mid-nineteenth-century Americans would not have understood, much less accepted. I have only begun to probe the dynamics of this reconstitution of human experience within a culture whose progressive social processes were, at the time, unparalleled in world history.

Less by way of explanation than as a mode of evocation, an attempt to allegorize the transition with which I have been concerned in order to denote some of its contours and pressures, I would like to end by considering three texts that demarcate moments in the shift away from objectivity. All of these texts are about a confrontation with the fictive nature of reality which leads us to try to find new sources of conviction and power after the explosion of traditional sources of meaning.

In Katherine Anne Porter's "Pale Horse, Pale Rider" (1937), we encounter what amounts to a recapitulation, within the protagonist's personal experience, of the transformation of awareness that stands as the widest ramification of the meaning of swamp and jungle images in nineteenth-century America as I have seen it. Porter's use of jungle imagery in this story must be seen in the context of the story's overall themes in order to bring out all of its nuances. I shall then examine Emily Dickinson's "Further in Summer than the Birds" and Herman Melville's passage on the Mount of the Titans in *Pierre* as representing preliminary steps toward the full-fledged allegory of the undoing of the Romantic self, which I see as Porter's theme.

These texts manifest a growing self-consciousness about the role of the self in constructing its reality which could reach full fruition only in the twentieth century. If neither writer resorts specifically to the swamp or jungle image (Dickinson is writing about crickets, Melville about a mountain – from a traditional point of view the very antithesis of the swamp), the point is simply that the kind of awareness they both express and work to extend no longer requires such a literal focus. It is the structure of their exchanges with nature that enables us to read their experience back into the encounter with the swamp that I have charted.

There is a moment in "Pale Horse, Pale Rider" when Miranda is plunged into an imaginary jungle world at once horrible and exhilarating. Feeling the onset of delirium during an influenza epidemic (based on the great one of 1918), she yearns to escape to the snow-covered mountains from the bleak, claustrophobic city, a modern wasteland in which portents of death by plague accentuate the grim domestic face of World War I. Despite being transported thither in imagination, she is suddenly stabbed by a vision of cold, eternal indifference and soon finds herself longing for warmth. Now her memory roves toward "another place she had known first and loved best," the luxuriant, semitropical world of her native South. She sees it "only in drifting fragments of palm and cedar, dark shadows and a sky that warmed without dazzling," whereas the other – the sky of the mountains – had "dazzled without warming her."[2] Appearing before her as a never-never land, this South is diffused and aesthetically disposed like the repeating motifs on yellowed wallpaper that linger in the memory from a special room one knew as a child.

The landscape Porter recalls is welcoming, sensual, indolent; it is ominous without being threatening. There is "the long slow wavering of gray moss in the drowsy oak shade, the spacious hovering of buzzards overhead, the smell of crushed water herbs along a bank, and without warning a broad tranquil river into which flowed all the rivers she had known." Just as the tranquil river unifies all the rivers of her memory, it is as if the vision as a whole emanated from the very source of her experience. Then suddenly the walls fall away "in one deliberate silent movement on either side" to reveal a ship of fantasy "with a gangplank weathered to blackness" (p. 299) behind which that source stands: a seething jungle.

The gentle wisps of imagery that clouded vision and lulled awareness, wafting resonances from the past, have given way to a sharp-edged, densely packed image that, it seems, has long lurked at the root of consciousness, only now to strike and seize control: "She knew it was all she had ever read or had been told or felt or thought about jungles..." (p. 299). We have seen this transformation before. The ominous notes in her reverie of a southern childhood – the wheeling buzzards and abruptly shifting vistas – have, we realize, prepared us, though partially, for this waking nightmare of sensuality gone crazy, this mingling of the preternaturally alive with corruption and death.

The balance and serenity of a magical past – a past we now know to have been a mirage – slide into the distortion and mania of a largely unconscious world arousing dread and disgust. Whereas all before had "drifted," "hovered," or "wavered" in complacency, experience is now "a writhing terribly alive and secret place of death, creeping with tangles of spotted serpents." The air trembles with "the shattering scream and hoarse bellow of voices all crying together, rolling and colliding above... like ragged storm-clouds...." Her perception, earlier seduced into a drowsy haze, now confronts the visual onslaught of myriad patterns, unabashed colors, and discordant accents: There are "rainbow-colored birds with malign eyes, leopards with humanly wise faces and extravagantly crested lions; screaming long-armed monkeys tumbling among broad fleshy leaves that glowed with sulphur-colored light and exuded the ichor of death, and rotting trunks of unfamiliar trees sprawled in crawling slime" (p. 299).

The projection of the human on the nonhuman augments the uncanny effect of mixing decay and death with life, sensuous beauty with malevolence and violent sound and motion with silent, insidious activity – the emanation of sulphur-colored light, for instance, or the exuding of ichor. Here the pathetic fallacy is enlisted not to domesticate nature by making it seem human but, rather, to render both the human and the natural into something alien by playing on the incongruities generated by the collapse of normal polarities into each other.

Appropriately, Porter's description of the jungle merges naive, picture-book elements – reminiscent of the jungle paintings of Henri Rousseau – with the most repugnant details. Contributing to this effect is Miranda's serene response to this vision, curiously out of kilter with its horror: "Without surprise, watching from her pillow, she saw herself run swiftly down this gangplank to the slanting deck, and standing there, she leaned on the rail and waved gaily to herself in bed, and the slender ship spread its wings and sailed away into the jungle" (p. 299). This flight of fantasy is countered by the raucous voices of the jungle whose cacophony is gradually resolved into two words, *Danger* and *War*, repeated over and over, until Miranda finally awakens to the full sense of her perilous condition.

The shifting back of Miranda's consciousness from detachment to the horror that ends her febrile daydream establishes the pattern of continual transvaluation and self-transformation that supplies the subsequent narrative and symbolic fluidity of the story and accounts for the extraordinary elusiveness of its meaning. Just as in the jungle where normal distinctions blur, things here – self and other, life and death – have an uncanny way of turning into each other. At the narrative level, this is due to the interpenetration of dream and waking realities through the process of projection. Which presents the truer picture? We are finally unable to tell whether Dr. Hildesheim, who tends Miranda, is the salvific figure his profession represents him to be or the German soldier with a naked infant impaled on the end of his bayonet (an agent of the society that oppresses the self) who appears to Miranda in one of her dreams.

It is precisely because of such ambiguity in Porter's narrative that all valuations at the symbolic level are subject to repeated transformation into their opposites. The arena for this constant oscillation between opposed orders of value is created by the dualism of Miranda's consciousness, made emblematic in her romantic memories of a southern childhood. The split takes on a dramatic form in her dream of the jungle: "across an abyss of complaining darkness her reasoning coherent self watched the strange frenzy of the other coldly, reluctant to admit the truth of its visions, its tenacious remorses and despairs" (p. 310). This split – evident at the moment when Miranda waves gaily to herself in bed and then sails off into the jungle – inaugurates what is referred to as the "road to death, a long march beset with all evils." This is the story's central theme, a process in which "the heart fails little by little at each new step, the mind sets up its own bitter resistance and to what end? The barriers sink one by one, and no covering of the eyes shuts out the landscape of disaster, nor the sight of the crimes committed there" (p. 309).

The "landscape of disaster" points us back to the jungle, but the perspective that would characterize it so negatively is at odds with that of the Miranda who sailed off into it. Death is liable to be simultaneously embraced and rejected, and this paradox reflects the tension between a self-conscious and rational mind attempting to master experience and the lure of unconsciousness, the expression of Miranda's death wish. This radical split expresses the divorce in Miranda's sense of the world between seeing and being, between indifferent objectification and vital participation, that is a measure of her entrapment in a system of oppression and commodification from which life is being drained.

Miranda watches herself passively, without any sense of relationship, having forgotten, presumably, that the self is an entity to be made and remade. Yet I should stress the notion of tension here between Miranda's two selves, for it is the existence of such tension that enables her to survive her bout with influenza, which is at one level symbolic of the ravages of the modern waste-land. Her slow journey toward death is marked by a widening perspective on herself as she differentiates herself from both the world of illusion and the world of experience. This self-consciousness awakens in her a sense of irony that eventually permits her to become a maker of fictions. But it is purchased at a terrible cost, for in cutting herself off from the world of experience, she suffers the death of love, at least for the time being.

Miranda is left at the end of the novel with only a confirmation of the state in which she had first found herself shortly after her dream of the jungle: "There were no longer any multiple planes of living, no tough filaments of memory and hope pulling taut backwards and forwards holding her upright between them. There was only this one moment and it was a dream of time . . . " (p. 304). With the loss of an essentialist and organic relationship to the world, she has come to reside in a state of death in life. Emerging from her close encounter with death, she finally says of herself, "Still, no one need pity this corpse if we look properly to the art of the thing." Whereas immediately before her bout with influenza she had been filled with a pressing sense that there was not enough time to be with her lover Adam, once he is gone she feels that (in the final words of the story) "there would be time for everything" (p. 317).

In this respect Miranda differs from Adam, who remains a victim not only of love and the world of experience – it is he who dies, having caught the influenza while tending to the sick Miranda – but of his illusions as well. Unable to perceive the fictions on which social life is based – in particular the fictions of a society in wartime – he lets himself be led like a sacrificial lamb to the slaughter. When Miranda suggests to him that going off to war would be participating in a false cause, he replies: "If I didn't go . . . I couldn't look myself in the face" (p. 295).

Adam's name alerts us to his essential innocence, and Miranda's name like-wise points us to a time when she too was innocent. Not for nothing is she named after the heroine of *The Tempest,* and at the end of "Old Mortality," about an earlier time in her life, we found her "making a promise to herself, in her hopefulness, her ignorance" (p. 221). Miranda begins life thinking that she can reject her past and her family and sets forth on a quest to find truth for herself. What she does not realize is that her self-proclaimed independence is an illusion, and the beginning of "Pale Horse, Pale Rider" shows her still dreaming of her childhood home, still suffocated by her past, still strangled by the family entanglement. As she says to herself, "Too many have died in this bed already, there are far too many ancestral bones propped up on the mantelpieces, there have been too damned many antimacassars in this house . . . and oh, what accumulation of storied dust never allowed to settle in peace for one moment" (p. 269).

Only in her realization that illusion and experience are of a piece and that in the end they both are necessary can she become independent of them, and this is what she learns in her slow march toward death. During her sickness, her dreams and hallucinations culminate in what Porter herself later charac-terized in an interview as her personal experience of the Christian "beatific vision" or the Greek "happy day." Miranda finds herself on the edge of a pit that she knows to be bottomless and becomes aware that "words like oblivion and eternity are curtains hung before nothing at all." She comes face to face with death: "Death is death, said Miranda, and for the dead it has no attributes." She feels as if she lies "like a stone at the farthest bottom of life, knowing herself to be blind, deaf, speechless, no longer aware of the members of her own body, entirely withdrawn from all human concerns, yet alive with a peculiar lucidity and coherence; all notions of the mind, the reasonable inquiries of doubt, all ties of blood and the desires of the heart," have dissolved and fallen away from her. There remains of her "only a minute fiercely burning particle of being that knew itself alone, that relied upon nothing beyond itself for its strength . . . " (p. 310).

Once life is reduced to its essence, this "fiery motionless particle" opens out into a vision of paradise: "It grew, flattened, thinned to a fine radiance, spread like a great fan and curved out into a rainbow." Through this rainbow Miranda glimpses a "deep clear landscape of sea and sand, of soft meadow and sky, freshly washed and glistening with transparencies of blue" (p. 311). Entering the landscape, she finds herself surrounded by pure identities, "and she knew them every one without calling their names or remembering what relation she bore to them" (p. 311).

Yet in "the quietude of her ecstasy" she is troubled by a "vague tremor of apprehension, some small flick of distrust in her joy"; she has the sense that "something, somebody, was missing, she had lost something, she had left something valuable in another country, oh, what could it be?" Then it dawns on her: "There are no trees, no trees here, she said in fright, I have left something unfinished." She asks, "Where are the dead? We have forgotten the dead, oh, the dead, where are they?" (p. 312) As if in answer, the bright landscape suddenly fades, and she returns to her hospital surroundings, to the world of pain and mortality.

Miranda is called back to the living from this disembodied realm, this heavenly vision, by her realization that what is missing that is of value to her is the world of experience that depends on death, the world of love that materializes in the here and now. It is a product of our human condition, of the exigency of time, of the falling short of fulfillment, of the tension between dream and everyday reality, illusion and experience, self-consciousness and unconsciousness, hope and despair. She submits, in other words, to the im-possibility of knowing. Her awareness that there are no trees in this beatific landscape reminds us of the jungle of her earlier vision, with its reference to the force of the natural round, the cycle of degeneration and regeneration.

But in heaven there is no such tension, only the weightlessness of immor-tality. Miranda's vision takes her beyond the veil of mortality. She is enlight-ened to the illusoriness of life, of experience. But she is then only all the more impressed with the value of mortality, its power and necessity. She returns to the world of paradox, a blend of pain and aspiration, in search of Adam, who has been left behind, only to find, ironically and tragically, that he is gone forever, a victim of his own mortality, having died of influenza.

Once back, the fierce particle of light that in her vision had stood for her purity of faith, her desire to live, her will to immortality, remains in her memory, diminishing by contrast all the light of the natural world that now seems drained of meaning and vitality: "There was no light, there might never be light again, compared as it must always be with the light she had seen beside the blue sea that lay so tranquilly along the shore to her paradise" (p. 314). Instead, she is oppressed by a pervasive whiteness, by the white walls of her hospital room and the "colorless light slanting on the snow." We might well think of Emily Dickinson's lines:

> There's a certain Slant of light
> Winter Afternoons –
> That oppresses, like the heft
> Of Cathedral Tunes –

We might even be reminded of Ishmael's meditation on "The Whiteness of the Whale" in which the light of the world, the light of faith deprived of objective status, pales to a blank whiteness, the "colorless all-color of atheism."

I do not casually invoke here two moments at the origin of American Modernism, for Miranda's awakening to an empty world at the end of "Pale Horse, Pale Rider" repeats and enlarges on such moments when the Romantic quest for transcendent meaning, for absolute knowledge, has bottomed out, when the effort to achieve oneness with the divine has resulted in a diminution of the divine, when nihilism is revealed at the heart of pure faith, when the light first turns somber and then flat.

It is possible to see Miranda's journey toward death as the quest of the Romantic self, originally prodded by its alienation from society and the every-day world toward a realization of freedom in the face of nothingness. Miranda's elaborate preparations at the end of the story to mask herself, a Lazarus come back from the dead, and her capacity to summon the ghost of her lover ("more alive than she was, the last intolerable cheat of her heart; for knowing it was false she still clung to the lie, the unpardonable lie of her bitter desire," [p. 17]) point to her new ability to manipulate reality through fictions. She knows now that it is only a matter of time before she will "cross back and be at home again" in the world (p. 317).

Indeed, "The Grave," the last tale of *The Old Order,* gives us a final look at a Miranda ultimately coming to terms with her past, now no longer ro-manticized but opening into the greatest mysteries of life, of identity and sexuality. But the necessary prelude to this awakening was the dying to the old self of "Pale Horse, Pale Rider." This dying to the old self can also be seen as a groping toward the real possibility of choice gained through an identification of experience with illusion which in turn evolves from an aware-ness that the words we use to define experience are themselves fundamentally illusory, from an awareness that absolute knowledge is finally impossible. Behind this insight is Miranda's understanding that to live in a paradoxical and poignant world of mortal striving and endurance is more compelling than to live in a paradise that, after all, may only be an illusion itself, the furthest projection of desire. Miranda's first choice therefore is to return to the world of pain and death.

Before this objectification of experience can take place, however, Miranda must first divest herself of her romantic illusions. Her encounter with the jungle accomplishes this. The benign mask of life – figured, appropriately enough, as the sentimental and aestheticized version of the swamp – is ripped aside. The walls of her reverie of the past fall away, revealing the crucible of unconscious energies: the jungle, a raw primitive intuition unleashed by the destruction of repressive mechanisms. The jungle literally swallows up the pure pleasure-seeking self which then reveals itself as the death wish, the urge to dissolve into the primal chaos of life.

It is this breaking through of the primitive, this moment of destabilization and consequent swift disintegration, that recalls critical moments in the aftermath of the Romantic quest that in turn delineate a pattern in which desert imagery acquires its most far-reaching significance. As Romanticism both generated and decomposed itself, the particularities of certain types of landscape were subsumed by the protean category of the primitive itself. Primitive experience, in its many avatars, worked to dissipate hegemonic and patriarchal patterns of thought, opening up heretical or feminist possibilities whose presence eventually influenced even the status and function of language itself.

One such moment occurs in Melville's novel *Pierre, or the Ambiguities* (written right after *Moby-Dick*) when Pierre, finding himself in a semiconscious or trancelike state, has a vision of the Mount of the Titans. The mount stands both as the embodiment of Pierre's titanic striving – his effort to live according to a cosmic rather than an earthly or relative standard of values – and as the goal of those strivings, a goal that ultimately proves impossible to attain. As a personal symbol, the mount has undergone a transformation in Pierre's mind from "The Delectable Mountain," as it had been styled by "an old Baptist farmer, an hereditary admirer of Bunyan and his most marvelous book," to its austere and portentous characterization by Pierre. As Melville observed: "Say what some poets will, Nature is not so much her own ever-sweet interpreter, as the mere supplier of that cunning alphabet, whereby selecting and combining as he pleases, each man reads his own peculiar lesson according to his own peculiar mind and mood."[3]

Pierre's personal experience of the mountain departs dramatically from the traditional conception of it because he has not viewed it from afar but has actually attempted to approach its summit. From a distance, the view of the mountain evokes the panoramic formula of the Hudson River school of landscape painting. Seen from the piazza of Pierre's baronial manor house, "that sweet imposing purple promise" vindicates the old Bunyanesque title, with its connotations of inspiration, heavenly aspiration, and moral striving.

But then, as if with a zoom lens, Melville abruptly brings us close to the flanks of the mountain, and we find ourselves immersed in a different world: "long and frequent rents among the mass of leaves revealed horrible glimpses of dark-dripping rocks, and mysterious mouths of wolfish caves." In the guise of a hypothetical tourist scaling the mountain's foothills, we are led into a "heart of darkness." As we approach the summit through the lowermost fringe of a hanging forest, we suddenly stop and stand "transfixed, as a marching soldier confounded at the sight of an impregnable redoubt. . . . Cunningly masked hitherto, by the green tapestry of the interlacing leaves, a terrific palisade of dark mossy massiveness" confronts us (pp. 343–4).

"Now you stood and shivered in that twilight, though it were high noon and burning August down the meads." The enveloping landscape is one of elemental destruction and desolation:

> All round and round, the grim scarred rocks rallied and re-rallied
> themselves; shot up, protruded, stretched, swelled, and eagerly
> reached forth; on every side bristlingly radiating with a hideous repel-
> lingness. Tossed and piled, and indiscriminate among these, like
> bridging rifts of logs up-jammed in alluvial-rushing streams of far Ar-
> kansas: or, like great masts and yards of overwhelmed fleets hurled
> high and dashed amain, all splintering together, on hovering ridges of
> the Atlantic sea, – you saw the melancholy trophies which the North
> Wind, championing the unquenchable quarrel of the Winter, had
> wrested from the forests, and dismembered them on their own chosen
> battle-ground, in barbarous disdain. 'Mid this spectacle of wide and
> wanton spoil, insular noises of falling rocks would boomingly explode
> upon the silence and fright all the echoes, which ran shrieking in and
> out among the caves, as wailing women and children in some as-
> saulted town. (p. 344)

Besides being apocalyptic or postlapsarian, the imagery here is unmistakably phallic and Oedipal. The mountains loom above the disordered rows of rock, contorted with a frenzied burst of phallic energy, now a defeated remnant as if in the aftermath of some colossal castration scene. In the midst of these rocks is Enceladus, a huge outcropping of stone named after the most powerful of all the giants, "writhing from out the imprisoning earth; – turbaned with upborne moss . . . still, though armless, resisting with his whole striving trunk, the Pelion and the Ossa hurled back at him . . . " (p. 345). Enceladus is an emblem of the heaven-defying will of Pierre, warring against the powers that be – whether cosmic or social, it finally makes no difference – on behalf of his own vision of the just and true.

As if now rendered impotent, the rock stands drenched by the moisture distilled in the dense mountain fastness, yet "with its unabasable face turned upward toward the mountain, and the bull-like neck clearly defined" (p. 345). In its dignified defeat, it symbolizes Pierre's own fate (his name alludes to his identification with the rock) and also to an archetypal failure of the will to surmount the condition of mortality. Ironically, the effort to mount to the crest, to bask in the pure light of heaven, has plunged the aspirant into the depths of the world's body, just as the heroic, panoramic view of the mountain gives way to immersion in its lowering interior.

The repelling quality of that interior testifies to the alienation of such aware-ness. As in Porter's jungle narrative, the desire for conscious control founders in a world whose allure is a mask: "Stark desolation; ruin, merciless and ceaseless; chills and gloom, – all here lived a hidden life, curtained by that cunning purpleness, which, from the piazza of the manor house, so beautifully invested the mountain once called Delectable, but now styled Titanic" (p. 344). The dramatic alteration in point of view from distant to immediate signals a transformation from the hierarchical ordering of the mind to the anarchy of the unconscious. The apparatus of illusion, of myths and beliefs concerning the world, is dismantled in its midst.

In the book as a whole, Pierre's titanic vision is left to decompose in a "swamp" of ambiguities. His effort to conquer life alters imperceptibly into a death wish that leads him to commit murder and suicide in despair over the endless uncertainty, the meaninglessness of all values. Pierre's fantasy of the Mount of the Titans finally allegorizes the defeat of Romantic striving, the end of the "male" and egocentric quest for absolute knowledge, purity, and self-assertion in the morass of the "female" unconscious.

Unlike Miranda, Pierre's encounter with the jungle (albeit a figurative jungle) is no prelude to constructing a fictive world, for although his romantic illusions are destroyed, he has no deeper confrontation with the illusoriness of experience itself. Still very much the Romantic hero in this respect, Pierre ends his life in a passionate declaration of defiance which attests to his enduring commitment to the substantiality of experience. There is no correspondence to Miranda's corpse in cold cream, her Lazarus come back from the dead, because Pierre never had the chance to take the measure, as Miranda did, of the paradise toward which he so ardently strives.

Melville later explored these limitations, especially in his story "The Piazza" and in *The Confidence-Man,* which is still, as I see it, essentially a protest rather than an endorsement of the identification of experience with fiction. For our purposes, the example of Emily Dickinson is better suited to examining the root of this identification in American literature, for she was the first American writer to abandon the Romantic quest for an organic intuition of life (recreated in Porter's story, as I hope I have shown) and to embrace the making of fictions as her primary *modus operandi.*

In order to point the way to the implications of this identification of experience with fiction in Dickinson's poetry, I shall discuss one moment in her poetic life when the primitive – figured not as a jungle or swamp but as the equally alien world of crickets – breaks through the illusory mask that culture imposes on the world.

In one of Dickinson's greatest poems, "Further in Summer than the Birds" (no. 1068), the end of experience as well as of illusion is implied less in what the words say directly than in their actual function.

> Further in Summer than the Birds
> Pathetic from the Grass
> A minor Nation celebrates
> Its unobtrusive Mass.
>
> No Ordinance be seen
> So gradual the Grace
> A pensive Custom it becomes
> Enlarging Loneliness.
>
> Antiquest felt at Noon
> When August burning low

Arise this spectral Canticle
Repose to typify

Remit as yet no Grace
No Furrow on the Glow
Yet a Druidic Difference
Enhances Nature now

Outwardly, the poem relies on an opposition between words pertaining to traditional religious theology and liturgy – "Mass," "Ordinance," "Grace," "Canticle" – and the connotations of the primitive that resonate from the word "Druidic" and that also evolve from the hidden subject of the poem, the life of crickets, the "minor Nation," of the first stanza. This tension builds in the juxtaposition of the words of religious reference with unexpected modifiers, as in "unobtrusive Mass" or "spectral Canticle." But what modulates the poem into a different key, allowing it to enact the incongruity suggested here, is the way in which Dickinson has all but eliminated both direct reference and linear movement, substituting an organization that internalizes the subjugation of conscious, controlled thought by the unconscious.

Finally the elusive meaning in this poem is approached not through the poem's uncertain logical or syntactic momentum but through the delicate phonal correspondences among the four identical phonemes in the opening line, "Further in Summer than the Birds" – a repetition evoking the "chir" of the crickets, one of the few clues we receive to what the poem is about – and the crucial words "Furrow" and "Difference" in the final stanza.

The equivocal thrust of Dickinson's poem materializes in the competition between two distinct yet interpenetrating orders of meaning in its words. Each word poses its own universe of connotations, along with its denotative meaning, and it also reacts to the words around it and throughout the poem to create a different, even opposite semantic range. In the case of "Furrow" and "Difference," these words in themselves refer to disjunction and in turn evoke the pathos at the emotional center of the poem signaled by "Pathetic" (in reference to the "minor Nation" of crickets). Thus they allude to the smallness of nature (and, by extension, the human) before the remote and impersonal grandeur of the divine which, for the better part of the poem, is merely implied as the object of worship:

No Ordinance be seen
So gradual the Grace
A pensive Custom it becomes
Enlarging Loneliness.

This theme is in keeping with the dominant mood of the poem, the sense of aftermath, of "August burning low" once summer has passed its meridian, the atmosphere of dryness and diminution that characterizes the natural setting.

Yet when the words "Furrow" and "Difference" are seen in relation to their modifiers, different implications can be found. As syntax and some degree of reference come into play, these words oppose each other in meaning. There is *"No* Furrow on the Glow"; that is, no grace is to be remitted. *"Yet* a Druidic Difference/Enhances Nature now." The traditional religious concept of grace, as an encroachment on the impersonal divine, a "Furrow on the Glow," is supplanted by "Druidic Difference."

In other words, anthropomorphic conceptions of the divine activity are deposed through the awareness that otherness is the authentic basis of nature's sacramental value. Something positive having to do with knowledge – "Furrow on the Glow" – is replaced by something negative, "Druidic Difference," announcing above all an absence of knowledge. The latter provides the larger, indeed the infinitely larger, perspective of the primordial bond of awe that breaks through human forms and conventions to assert the profound relationship to the numinous. Intimations of an enlarging loneliness, the result of the "pensive Custom" that creates the poem's mood, are transmuted into a repose typified by the "spectral Canticle" of the crickets that disperses melancholy in offering something – a mood or feeling – less easily defined.

The "Glow" is left intact. Furthermore, in the line "Antiquest felt at Noon," Dickinson's neologism allies the sun with the most primitive sense of time and, by implication, with the origination of words. Still, this is no mere nature or sun worship the poet professes, for in leading us back to the sun of the previous stanza, "Glow" associates itself not only with the glory of the sun at noon but also with its diminution in the aftermath of summer: "August burning low." Indeed, noon for Dickinson held negative associations with commonsense, everyday reality (she may even have had in mind the final words of Lear's fool, "And I'll go to bed at noon"). The effect of this dualism is to preserve the sanctity of otherness – which can never be defined as one thing or another – by continually presenting a paradoxical valuation, a constant transvaluation that can account for both the glory of the sun at its zenith and its subservience to the mysterious natural cycle.

"Further in Summer than the Birds" thus subverts cultural artifacts – life's illusions – in opening out to an apprehension that defies the relevance of these way stations to the infinite; it also offers a radical reordering of the terms of experience itself. It returns us to the uncanny by inhabiting the alien world of the crickets through its use of the pathetic fallacy, the attribution of traditional religious terminology to the life of insects. It also provokes an awareness that experience itself is fundamentally unstable and is merely a function of the artifice of words themselves.

In the space that opens up in the absence of knowledge, Dickinson's fictive universe could shape itself and expand, taking responsibility for the projection of her own desire. In her poem, "By my Window have I for Scenery" (no. 797), Dickinson exercised this fiction-making propensity. Through her window she sees "Just a Sea – with a Stem." If a bird or farmer should call it a "Pine," the "Opinion," she avers, "will serve – for them." This perspective is in stark contrast with the phallocentric organicism of Melville's Pierre. It is surely no accident that Dickinson and Porter, as writers with definitely feminist propensities, share this need to find their own fictive and subversive way. This is how they finally achieve a voice both within and beyond the language of the patriarchal tradition.

I must emphasize, however, that Dickinson proposed to substitute for the patriarchally constituted world no mere collection of "dead" fictions, no defensive disguises, but a series of gestures toward the unknown that are charged with energy derived from a primitive sense of mortality. This is the crucial missing component for Miranda at the end of "Pale Horse, Pale Rider," for at this point she realizes only the negative side of death: her solipsism, the failure of love. Yet as I mentioned earlier, this is not the end of the story.

The last time that we encounter Miranda is in "The Grave," the final tale of *The Old Order*. This story recounts an episode in which Miranda, as a little girl out hunting rabbits and doves with her brother, comes upon the family graveyard, now bereft of the bones of family members, as they were removed to a public cemetery after the land for the graveyard was sold. Peering into the empty graves, the children try to "shape a special, suitable emotion in their minds" but feel "nothing except an agreeable thrill of wonder" (p. 362). Jumping into her grandfather's grave, Miranda finds a silver dove, "no larger than a hazel nut, with spread wings and a neat fan-shaped tail." Her brother recovers a thin gold ring carved with intricate flowers and leaves. Paul prefers the dove, and after a little bickering, brother and sister make a trade. Placing the ring on her finger, Miranda suddenly feels an uncharacteristic urge to go home and make herself feminine: "She wanted to go back to the farmhouse, take a good cold bath, dust herself with plenty of her sister Maria's violet talcum powder . . . put on the thinnest, most becoming dress she owned, with a big sash, and sit in a wicker chair under the trees." This urge is associated with her desire to live as her family did in the past: "She had vague stirrings of desire for luxury and a grand way of living which could not take precise form in her imagination but were founded on family legend of past wealth and leisure" (p. 365).

Instead, however, she resumes playing with her brother. Following him, she finds him kneeling over a rabbit he has just shot. Skinning the animal, the children discover its oddly bloated belly:

> Very carefully he slit the thin flesh from the center ribs to the flanks, and a scarlet bag appeared. He slit again and pulled the bag open, and there lay a bundle of tiny rabbits, each wrapped in a thin scarlet veil. The brother pulled these off and there they were, dark gray, sleek wet down lying in minute even ripples, like a baby's head just washed, their unbelievably small delicate ears folded close, their little blind faces almost featureless. (p. 366)

"Oh, I want to *see*," says Miranda under her breath. She is filled with pity and astonishment yet a certain delight as well. She wants most deeply to see and to know. And now that she sees she feels as if she has known all along. Miranda is initiated into the mysteries of birth, death, and sexuality all at once as she gazes on the dead fetuses: "She understood a little of the secret, formless intuitions in her own mind and body, which had been clearing up, taking form, so gradually and so steadily she had not realized that she was learning what she had to know" (pp. 366–67). "They were just about ready to be born," her brother says, and his voice drops on the last word. Filled with fear at having committed a sacrilege, the children hide the dead rabbit in a clump of sage bushes and resolve never to say a word about the episode. In a few days the whole affair sinks quietly into Miranda's mind, "heaped over by accumulated thousands of impressions" (p. 367).

Only twenty years later is the memory jogged back into her consciousness when, living in Mexico, she is confronted in the marketplace by a vendor who holds up to her a tray of dyed sugar sweets, "in the shape of all kinds of small creatures: birds, baby chicks, baby rabbits, lambs, baby pigs" (p. 267). At the same time, their faint smell of vanilla mingles with the odor of piles of raw flesh and wilting flowers, which is like "the mingled sweetness and corruption she had smelled that other day in the empty cemetery at home: the day she had remembered always until now vaguely as the time she and her brother had found treasure in the opened graves" (p. 267). Faced once again with this awful image of mortality that she had repressed for so long, the incomplete chain of associations that have lain dormant at the bottom of her mind all these years suddenly snaps together, and Miranda undergoes at once an ex-orcism and a revelation: "Instantly . . . the dreadful vision faded, and she saw clearly her brother, whose childhood face she had forgotten, standing again in the blazing sunshine, again twelve years old, a pleased sober smile in his eyes, turning the silver dove over and over in his hands" (p. 268).

Having made her journey to the hithermost reaches of life, having come face to face with death and returned to a loveless world, Miranda now forges a new link with her past, the past she had rejected in "Old Mortality" and "Pale Horse, Pale Rider," once gone but now to be reconstituted. It is not now the illusory past of family legend she had yearned for as a girl and rejected as a young woman. It is a past infused with the currents of a personal experience in which her memory of her brother connects her directly with his own compelling response to the power of the talisman he holds.

The image of him standing in the blazing sunshine, turning the silver dove over and over in his hand, "a pleased sober smile in his eyes," reorders the entire background of the experience: her grandmother's power and independence and heroic efforts to keep the family together through her sheer endurance; the recovery of ring and silver dove (a coffin screw) from the graves and the question of sexual identity they precipitate; and, finally, the vision of the dead rabbit fetuses, evoking the identity of life and death, the ultimate mystery brought home only by the merging of past and present selves, the restitution of childhood unconsciousness to adult consciousness. This vision is no longer horrible; like the lesson of the swamp, it is sustaining, for it reveals an organic link that is not inherited but created and recreated in the depths of the self, the root of fictions not of denial but of prepossessing vitality.

Appendix: "Wading in a Marsh" by David Wagoner

Nothing here in this rain-fed marsh
Has known the sun on the far side of the mountain
Except by the hearsay of the moon
Or the glinting of clouds and snow through cedar boughs,
And by this hand-me-down light I wade,
Uncertain of every surface preoccupied
By milfoil and watercress, the floating
Intricate uncannily green beds
Of water starwort whose leaves allow
No reflection of mine, not even their own.

My rake-handle staff goes first, searching
For footholds in the moss under the water,
In the soft debris of needles and spikerush
And mud and the good lost lives of burreeds,
And my feet follow, slow as the spawn of tree-frogs.
The water-logged hemlock logs give way
Underfoot as easily as the earth they've turned to,
And my staff, at times, reaches down to nothing
As deep as I am tall. I don't go there.

Even with something seemingly lasting
Under me, I sink if I stand still,
Learning the underlying answer
Of swamps as unforgettably as my name:
To stand is to sink, to move is to rise
Again, and nothing at all has died in the winter
Without being reborn. The duckweed
Drifting against my thighs is rootless, unnerved,
Immortal, a cold companion
To be cupped in the palm and then let go
Here in Barr Mountain's permanent shadow.

I see what to say: this marsh that holds me
Is the climax of a lake, shallowing, dying,
Filled with the best endeavors of pondweeds,
The exploring and colonizing shapes of a world
Too good at living for its own good,
But in this man-made silence, while wrens and kinglets
Decide what I am and slowly excuse me
For being a moving object with much less use
Than a stump, I learn why I came here
Out of order: in order to find out how to belong
Somewhere, to change where all changing
Is a healing exchange of sense for sense.

I start to sink, I take a step,
The mud puts up with me momentarily,
And three wrens at once from three directions
Burst into songs as beautifully interwoven
As white water crowfoot tripling itself in shade.
I have to stand still to listen. By the time
I've heard the blue grouse drumming and drumming
Under the wrensongs, vibrant as memory,
I begin to sink. One winter wren
Appears from a literal nowhere: in her beak
A stark-green writhing caterpillar
Airborne ahead of its time. In an instant, she scans
The parts of me still above water,
Then vanishes among a tangle of roots
To feed her young. Far overhead
Sunlight crosses the treetops like crowfire,
And the last snow of a new spring
Melts as it falls, turning to other stars.

Notes

Introduction

1 See especially John Higham, *From Boundlessness to Consolidation: The Transformation of American Culture, 1848–1860* (Ann Arbor, Mich.: William L. Clements Library, 1969).

2 The importance of nature and the American landscape to American antebellum culture need hardly be argued here. Some of the most useful studies are Howard Mumford Jones, "American Landscape" (chap. 10), in *O Strange New World: American Culture: The Formative Years* (New York: Viking, 1952); Leo Marx, The *Machine in the Garden: Technology and the Pastoral Ideal in America* (New York: Oxford University Press, 1964); Perry Miller, "Nature and the National Ego," in *Errand into the Wilderness* (Cambridge, Mass.: Harvard University Press, 1965); Roderick Nash, *Wilderness and the American Mind* (New Haven, Conn.: Yale University Press, 1970); and Barbara Novak, *Nature and Culture: American Landscape and Painting* (New York: Oxford University Press, 1980). For a somewhat opposing view, see Bernard Rosenthal, *City of Nature: Journeys to Nature in the Age of American Romanticism* (Newark: University of Delaware Press, 1980).

3 See Clifford Geertz, "Ideology as a Cultural System," in *The Interpretation of Cultures* (New York: Basic Books, 1973), especially pp. 208–20. Geertz wrote: "And it is, in turn, the attempt of ideologies to render otherwise incomprehensible situations meaningful, to so construe them as to make it possible to act purposefully within them, that accounts both for the ideologies' highly figurative nature and for the intensity with which, once accepted, they are held. As metaphor extends language by broadening its semantic range, enabling it to express meanings it cannot or at least cannot yet express literally, so the head-on clash of literal meanings in ideology – the irony, the hyperbole, the overdrawn antithesis – provides novel symbolic frames against which to match the myriad 'unfamiliar somethings' that, like a journey to a strange country, are produced by a transformation in political life. Whatever else ideologies may be – projections of unacknowledged fears, disguises for ulterior motives, phatic expressions of group solidarity – they are, most distinctively, maps of problematic social reality and matrices for the creation of collective conscience" (p. 220).

4 Victor Turner, *Dramas, Fields, and Metaphors: Symbolic Action in Human Society* (Ithaca, N.Y.: Cornell University Press, 1974), p. 51.

5 Ibid., p. 51.

6 Gaston Bachelard, *The Poetics of Space,* trans. Maria Jolas (Boston: Beacon Press, 1969), p. xv.

7 Gaston Bachelard, *L'air et les songes, essai sur l'imagination du mouvement* (Paris, 1943). Quoted in H. Daniel Peck, *A World by Itself: The Pastoral Moment in Cooper's Fiction* (New Haven, Conn.: Yale University Press, 1977), p. 3.

8 Quoted in David Halliburton, *Edgar Allan Poe: A Phenomenological View* (Princeton, N.J.: Princeton University Press, 1973), p. 25.

9 Angus Fletcher, *Allegory: The Theory of a Symbolic Mode* (Ithaca, N.Y.: Cornell University Press, 1964), p. 17.

10 I hope to avoid here the charge Bruce Kuklick made against the "myth-symbol" school of American studies concerning the lack of empirical grounding for generalizations from literary texts about the American "mind." See Bruce Kuklick, "Myth and Symbol in American Studies," *American Quarterly* 24 (October 1972): especially 444–5.

11 See Erwin Panofsky, "Iconography and Iconology: An Introduction to the Study of Renaissance Art," in *Meaning and the Visual Arts* (Garden City, N.Y.: Doubleday/Anchor, 1955), pp. 26–54.

12 William Bartram, *Travels of William Bartram,* ed. Mark Van Doren (New York: Dover, 1955), p. 138.

13 In referring to the emblem tradition, I have been most influenced by Ronald Paulson, *Emblem and Expression: Meaning in English Art of the Eighteenth Century* (London: Thames & Hudson, 1975). See also Rosemary Freeman, *English Emblem Books* (London: Chatto & Windus, 1948). For suggestive discussions of the relevance of the emblem tradition to the work of certain American artists and writers, see Joy S. Kasson, " 'The Voyage of Life': Thomas Cole and Romantic Disillusionment," *American Quarterly* 27 (March 1975): 42–56; George Monteiro and Barton L. St. Armand, "The Experienced Emblem: A Study of the Poetry of Emily Dickinson," *Prospects: An Annual of American Cultural Studies* 6 (1981): 187–280; Barton L. St. Armand, "Poe's Emblematic Raven: A Pictorial Approach," *ESQ: A Journal of the American Renaissance* 22 (1976): 191–210; Alan Wallach, " 'The Voyage of Life' as Popular Art," *Art Bulletin* 59 (June 1977): 234–41; and Eleanor Wilner, "The Poetics of Emily Dickinson," *ELH* 38 (March 1971): 137–8.

14 In *Languages of Art* (Indianapolis: Hackett, 1976), Nelson Goodman argued for the conventional basis of visual perception and representation and established the difference between visual and verbal in the relative lack of articulation in the former: "Nonlinguistic systems differ from languages, depiction from description, the representational from the verbal, painting from poems, primarily through lack of differentiation – indeed through density (and consequent total absence of articulation) – of the symbol system" (p. 226).

An emblematic rendering, however, substitutes a high degree of articulation and definition for the normal visual continuum, thus aligning picture and word and producing a composite that serves a particular ideological position. My argument concerning the swamp as an image depends a great deal on the potential for uncontrolled meaning in the image itself. I contend, with Goodman, that visualization is essentially a matter of convention; nonetheless, we learn to see something in a particular way. What I offer here is an attempt to trace a departure in the process of learning to see which establishes a relatively open-ended approach to the visual field. For a discussion of the relationship between visual and verbal that assumes that pictures are ultimately like language yet dissents from the semioticians in reserving a sense of difference, see W. T. Mitchell, *Iconology: Image,*

Text, Ideology (Chicago: University of Chicago Press, 1986); see especially Mitchell's discussion of Goodman (pp. 53–74).

15 Panofsky, "Iconography and Iconology," p. 28.

16 Ibid., p. 31.

17 Ann Douglas, *The Feminization of American Culture* (New York: Avon, 1977).

18 Ann Norton called attention to this list of associations in *Alternative Americas: A Reading of Antebellum Political Culture* (Chicago: University of Chicago Press, 1986), p. 56. It appears in a discussion of the influence of the Puritan view of nature on social structures that confined women in Northern political culture before the Civil War, linking them with nature – hence the corporeal, the material, and the unclean.

19 This dialectical formulation of cultural evolution allows us to avoid what Bruce Kuklick termed the "Cartesian view of mind" which regards ideas as platonic, existing "independently of the people who think them," and which he attributes to the work of the "myth–symbol" school. The functionalist nature of iconography that I am attempting to establish preserves the element of intention (to be distinguished from motivation) that lies behind images, symbols, and myths and that again, according to Kuklick, the relative presentism of the myth–symbol school has led it to ignore or discount (see Kuklick "Myth and Symbol in American Studies," pp. 437–8).

20 Daniel Webster, *The Writings and Speeches of Daniel Webster* (national ed.) (Boston: Little, Brown, 1903), vol. 13, p. 434.

21 For a more lengthy discussion of the picturesque, see Chapter 7. The tendency to link the picturesque with the political is evident in the debate between Uvedale Price and Humphrey Repton over the art of landscape gardening and the definition of the picturesque. Repton wrote: "I cannot help seeing great affinity betwixt deducing gardening from the painter's studies of wild nature, and deducing government from the uncontrouled opinions of man in a savage state. The neatness, simplicity, and elegance of English gardening, have acquired the approbation of the present century, as the happy medium betwixt the wildness of nature and the stiffness of art; in the same manner as the English constitution is the happy medium betwixt the liberty of savages, and the restraint of despotic government; and so long as we enjoy the benefit of these middle degrees betwixt extremes of each, let experiments of untried theoretical improvement be made in some other country." Uvedale Price, *A Letter to H. Repton, Esq. on the Application of the Practice as Well as the Principles of Landscape-Painting to Landscape Gardening* (London. 1798, p. 10).

In his reply to Repton's letter, Price offered his own way of seeing the relationship: "A much apter and more instructive parallel might have been drawn between our constitution, and the art you have so much wronged. That art, like the old feudal government, meagre, hard, and gothic in its beginning, was mellowed and softened by long experience and successive trials; and not less improved in spirit and energy. Such indeed is the natural progress of human arts and institutions: the progress from oppression to anarchy, (of which we have seen such an awful example) is not more natural, than from the ease of freedom and security, to indolence and apathy: let England beware; let her guard no less against the one, than against the other extreme; they generate each other in succession, for apathy invites oppression, and oppression is the parent of anarchy" (pp. 103–5).

22 See David Huntington, *The Landscapes of Frederic Edwin Church: Vision of an American Era* (New York: Braziller, 1966); and Katherine Manthorne, "The Quest for a Tropical Paradise: Palm Tree as Fact and Symbol in Latin American Landscape

Imagery, 1850–1875," *Art Journal* (Winter 1984): 374–82. In characterizing the Latin American landscape in the depictions of Church and others as "Edenic," both Huntington and Manthorne ignore the considerable evidence indicating that the image was a good deal more equivocal (see also chapter 5 of this book). Manthorne does acknowledge, in discussing Church's *Morning in the Tropics,* that "the viewer encounters an overgrown opening to a river, a mysterious and almost forbidding vision of the darkest, uninhabited reaches of the Amazon" (p. 381). She provides, however, no context within which to make sense of this departure from the Edenic theme.

23 Herman Melville, *Pierre, or the Ambiguities* (Evanston, Ill., and Chicago: Northwestern University Press and the Newberry Library, 1971), p. 136.

24 Henry David Thoreau, *The Writings of Henry David Thoreau: The Maine Woods,* (Boston. Houghton Mifflin, 1906), vol. 3, p. 242.

Chapter 1

1 David Hunter Strother, "The Great Dismal Swamp," *Harper's New Monthly Magazine* 8 (September 1856): 441–55. See also a reprint of the article in Cecil D. Eby, Jr., ed., *The Old South Illustrated by Porte Crayon* (Chapel Hill: University of North Carolina Press, 1959), pp. 129–52. I discuss only the first half of the article, dealing with the journey to Lake Drummond. The remainder reverts to Porte's usual anecdotal style and includes an incident in which Porte catches a glimpse of a runaway black man.

2 In Freud's suggestive formulation, "an uncanny experience occurs when infantile complexes which have been repressed are once more revived by some impression, or when primitive beliefs which have been surmounted seem once more to be confirmed." See Sigmund Freud, *The Complete Works,* Standard Edition, vol. 17 (London: Hogarth Press, 1953–74), p. 249. Interestingly, as Freud pointed out and as the German *das Unheimliche* (the opposite of "homely") suggests, the uncanny "is in reality nothing new nor alien, but something which is familiar and old-established in the mind and which has become alienated from it only through the process of repression" (p. 241).

3 Gèza Roheim, *Gates of Dream* (New York: International Universities Press, 1952), p. 132. Writing in *The Token* (1831), Orville Dewey offered a typical description of the hypnagogic state: "Fatigued and exhausted, I sought repose at an early hour, – and soon fell into that half sleeping and half waking state, with which the diseased and troubled, at least, are so well acquainted. It is the well known and frequent effect of this state of partial consciousness, to give a mysterious and preternatural importance to everything that attracts the notice of the wandering senses" (p. 20).

Similarly, in our own day, the poet A. R. Ammons spoke of "a descent into the subconscious . . . prepared for not by/blotting out the conscious mind but by intensifying the alertness/of the conscious mind even while it permits itself to sink, /to be lowered down the ladder of structured motions to the/refreshing energies of the deeper self." See A. R. Ammons, *Sphere: The Form of a Motion* (New York: Norton, 1974), p. 40. Finally, Yeats, in "The Symbolism of Poetry," advanced the intriguing notion that the function of rhythm in poetry may be "by hushing us with an alluring monotony, while it holds us waking by variety, to keep us in that state of perhaps real trance, in which the mind liberated from the pressure of the will is unfolded in symbols." See William Butler Yeats, *Essays and Introductions* (New York: Collier Books, 1972), p. 159.

4 See Edgar Allan Poe, "Marginalia," in *The Complete Works of Edgar Allan Poe,* ed. James A. Harrison (New York: Crowell, 1965), vol. 16, p. 88.

5   A technical explanation of Porte's paradoxical process of transformation is provided by Anton Ehrenzweig: "In many ways creativity and mental illness are opposite sides of the same coin. The blocking of creativity through ego rigidity is apt to unleash the self-destructive fury of the superego, which is otherwise absorbed and neutralized by the periodic decomposition of the ego during creativity. An increased measure of the superego's oral and anal aggression against the ego is utilized for deepening the normally shallow oscillation of the ego as it swings down to less differentiated levels. The superego's anal scattering attacks drive the ego inexorably towards an extreme oceanic depth until the process of dedifferentiation even suspends the distinction between ego and superego. Then the ego can shake itself free from the superego's aggression." See Anton Ehrenzweig, *The Hidden Order of Art: A Study in the Psychology of Artistic Imagination* (Berkeley and Los Angeles: University of California Press, 1967), p. 212.

6   See Sigmund Freud, *The Ego and the Id,* trans. Joan Rivière (New York: Norton, 1960), p. 43.

7   During the first half of the nineteenth century, the word *dismal* was generally synonymous with *swamp.*

8   See especially Joseph Campbell, *The Hero with a Thousand Faces* (Princeton, N.J.: Princeton University Press, 1971), pp. 89, 91; and Mircea Eliade, *Rites and Symbols of Initiation: The Mysteries of Birth and Rebirth* (New York: Harper & Row, 1975), p. 66. The pattern is intrinsic to the psychic matrix of creativity.

As Anton Ehrenzweig wrote: "A feeling of oceanic cosmic bliss strangely contrasts with the imagery of inexorable suffering and death. What seems to matter is that death has first to be faced and the experience of dying worked through before the oceanic-manic level of liberation and rebirth is reached fruitfully." See Ehrenzweig, *The Hidden Order of Art,* p. 189.

9   Cecil D. Eby, Jr., *Porte Crayon: The Life of David Hunter Strother* (Chapel Hill: University of North Carolina Press, 1960), p. vii.

10 Thomas Moore, *The Poetical Works of Thomas Moore,* 2 vols. (Boston, 1874), vol. 2, p. 37.

11 O'Reilly's account is reprinted in Charles Frederick Stansbury, *The Lake of the Dismal Swamp* (New York: Albert & Charles Beni, 1925), pp. 147–72. O'Reilly visited the swamp in 1888. Much material on the Great Dismal Swamp written by visitors over the decades may be found in the North Carolina Collection of the Main Library, University of North Carolina, Chapel Hill.

12 Anonymous, "Feeling and Sentiment," in *The Family Treasury of Western Literature, Science and Art,* ed. Jethro Jackson (Cincinnati, 1854), p. 154.

13 Poe, *Complete Works,* vol. 14, p. 108. The engraving after Chapman's work appeared as the frontispiece of *The Knickerbocker* 13 (May 1839) and probably elsewhere. The connection between Poe and Chapman was explored at length in Burton R. Pollin, "Edgar Allen Poe and John G. Chapman: Their Treatment of the Dismal Swamp and the Wissahickon," in *Studies in the American Renaissance,* ed. Joel Myerson (Charlottesville: University of Virginia Press, 1983), pp. 245–74.

14 William S. Forrest, *Historical and Descriptive Sketches of Norfolk and Vicinity* (Philadelphia, 1853), p. 454.

15 We also think here of James Fenimore Cooper's "Glimmerglass," whose symbolism is discussed in H. Daniel Peck, *A World by Itself: The Pastoral Moment in Cooper's Fiction* (New Haven, Conn.: Yale University Press, 1977), especially pp. 10–12. Peck's observations regarding the relationship of the lake to Cooper's sense of being at home in the world and his apprehension of the "primacy of the image" were an important catalyst in my own thinking. At one point, Peck wrote: "The

circle is unquestionably the basic figure in Cooper's fictional design; its circumference separates the clearing within from the wilderness beyond, and this dialectic of inside and outside embraces a whole range of contrasting values. But the circle also functions as the clearest expression of Cooper's desire to formalize the space of the American woods with 'the beauty of curved lines' and, as we shall see presently, to heighten the theatrical effect of the forest scene" (p. 57).

16 Reprinted in John Keese, ed., *The Poets of America* (New York, 1840), pp. 211–12. Sands's theme relates closely to that of Mrs. Felicia Hemans's in "The Isle of the Founts: An Indian Tradition," in *The Forest Sanctuary and Other Poems* (Boston, 1821), pp. 137–41, which was inspired in turn by William Bartram, *Travels of William Bartram*, edited by Mark Van Doren (New York: Dover, 1955), pp. 47–8. The Indian legend is recorded in B. A. Botkin, *A Treasury of Southern Folklore* (New York: Crown, 1949), pp. 493–4. Botkin tells us that the lake was "effectually concealed by some subtle power of magic in the bosom of the great swamp." Hemans undoubtedly influenced Thomas Holly Chivers's "Nacoochee, or the Beautiful Star" (1837), the setting for which is a lake lying between the Oakmulgee and Flint rivers in Georgia. According to S. Foster Damon, Chivers had originally placed his lost paradise in the Okefenokee swamp but became dissatisfied with this location. See S. Foster Damon, *Thomas Holly Chivers: Friend of Poe* (New York. 1930), pp. 97–8. Chateaubriand's *Atala* also obviously influenced Chivers, being an important prototype for all this sentimental literature.

17 See also Percy Bysshe Shelley's "Alastor, or the Spirit of Solitude," in which swamplike imagery characterizes the transition from loss to disintegration.

18 See, for instance, Thomas Bender, "The 'Rural' Cemetery Movement: Urban Travail and the Appeal of Nature," *New England Quarterly* 47 (June 1974): 196–211. For an illuminating discussion of Whig sentimentalism in relation to the rural cemetery movement and the vogue for melancholy pastoral landscapes, see Blanche Linden-Ward, "Putting the Past Under Grass: History As Death and Cemetery Commemoration," *Prospects* 10 (1985): 279–314.

19 The change from Romantic to Victorian attitudes is discussed in Lawrence Taylor, "Symbolic Death: An Anthropological View of Mourning Ritual in the Nineteenth Century," in Martha V. Pike and Janice Gray Armstrong, *A Time to Mourn: Expressions of Grief in Nineteenth Century America* (exhibition catalogue) (Stony Brook, N.Y.: The Museums at Stony Brook, 1980), pp. 39–48. For a related development in the growing interest in preserving what presented itself as useless, see Henry D. Shapiro, "Putting the Past Under Glass: Preservation and the Idea of History in the Mid-Nineteenth Century," *Prospects* 10 (1985): 243–78. Shapiro argued that preservationists actually validated the "pastness of the past" by stressing its separation from the present and thereby keeping it in its place so that it could not interfere with the march of progress (see especially p. 281). This argument closely parallels my own in the mutually sustaining relationship it sees between nostalgia and civilization building.

20 See Barton St. Armand, "Dark Parade: Dickinson, Sigourney, and the Victorian Way of Death" (chap. 2), in *Emily Dickinson and Her Culture: The Soul's Society* (Cambridge, England: Cambridge University Press, 1984), especially pp. 48–57. On the general topic, see also John Morley, *Death, Heaven and the Victorians* (Pittsburgh: University of Pittsburgh Press, 1971).

21 For a discussion of the relationship between the mid-nineteenth-century vogue for spiritualism and the tendency toward materialism, see R. Laurence Moore, *In Search of White Crows: Spiritualism, Parapsychology, and American Culture* (New York: Oxford University Press, 1977).

22 See Karen Halttunen, *Confidence Men and Painted Women: A Study of Middle-Class Culture in America, 1830–1870* (New Haven, Conn.: Yale University Press, 1982), p. 152.

23 See George Forgie, *Patricide in the House Divided: A Psychological Interpretation of Lincoln and His Age* (New York: Norton, 1979) for a fascinating discussion of the tensions between ambition and the desire of male antebellum Americans to be good sons of the Founding Fathers. Forgie sees sentimentalist rhetoric as founded on the desire to escape from history into a realm of domestic timelessness (p. 49). According to Forgie, men of the postheroic age following the Revolution were faced with the Oedipal problem of reconciling their role in history – their desire to supplant their fathers – with their duty to preserve and venerate the past – their desire to defer to them.

24 For a somewhat different but also relevant analysis of Victorian sexual mores, see Carroll Smith-Rosenberg, "Sex as Symbol in Victorian America," *Prospects* 5 (1980): 51–70. Smith-Rosenberg contended that the Victorian sexual reformers who developed the ideology of sexual purity were responding to a widespread anxiety over social disintegration and the loss of control that was focused on the fear of male orgasm, conceived of as "overpowering, uncontrollable, raging. Rebellious and anarchical, it possessed vast potential for destruction" (pp. 57–8). Behind this fear lay the identification of a growing class of marginalized young males with the collapse of traditional family and institutional structures in the period of increasing urbanization, industrialism, and an expanding market economy.

25 The reversal is discussed by Ann Douglas in "Heaven Our Home: Consolation Literature in the Northern United States, 1830–1880," *American Quarterly* 26 (December 1974): 511.

26 My thinking here was influenced by Norman O. Brown, who identified Freud's "death instinct" with human repression and proposed replacing his instinctual dualism with an instinctual dialectic that restores death to its proper place in the biological process. According to Brown, it is the dualism of life and death that accounts for our neurotic condition: "At the biological level, the death instinct, in affirming the road to death, affirms at the same time the road to life: ripeness is all. At the human level, the repressed death instinct cannot affirm death and therefore must fly from death; death can only affirm itself (and life) by transforming itself into the spirit which always denies life, the spirit of Goethe's Mephistofeles." See Norman O. Brown, *Life Against Death: The Psychoanalytic Meaning of History* (Middleton, Conn.: Wesleyan University Press, 1972), p.103.

27 From "The Pilgrimage of the Saints." I owe this reference to Professor William G. McLoughlin of Brown University.

28 From the story entitled "Drummond," *The Talisman* (1829), p. 268. H. Daniel Peck pointed to the theme of emergence from "the density of the forest into the preferred space of the clearing" at the beginning of Cooper's *The Pathfinder* and *The Deerslayer*. See Peck, *A World by Itself*, p. 48.

29 William Wirt, *The Letters of the British Spy*, 10th ed. (New York, 1832), pp. 105–6.

30 Quoted in Patricia M. Spacks, *The Insistence of Horror: Aspects of the Supernatural in Eighteenth-Century Poetry* (Cambridge, Mass.: Harvard University Press, 1962), p. 107.

31 My ideas about romance owe much to Northrop Frye, *The Secular Scripture: A Study of the Structure of Romance* (Cambridge, Mass.: Harvard University Press, 1978).

32 The probable connection between Frost and Moore was noted by Rosemary F. Franklin in "Literary Model for Frost's Suicide Attempt in the Dismal Swamp," *American Literature* 50 (January 1979): 645–6.

33 See the chapter entitled "Dismal Swamp," in Lawrence Thompson, *Robert Frost: The Early Years, 1874–1915* (New York: Holt, Rinehart and Winston, 1966), pp. 173–89.

34 See ibid., p. 521, note 5.

35 Quoted in ibid., p. 188.

36 Anonymous, "The Dismal Swamp," *Chamber's Edinburgh Journal*, December 14, 1850, pp. 373–5.

37 "The Real Dismal Swamp," *Harper's New Monthly Magazine* 12 (December 1910): 18–23.

38 See "The Dismal Swamp" and "Drummond," in *The Talisman* (1826), pp. 255–86. In a similar vein is William Gilmore Simms's poem, "The War-Eagle of the Dismal Swamp" (1837), illustrated by the engraving after Chapman, which offers a mythical context for the landscape in a legend about the destruction of a tribe of Indians who once inhabited the area. See *The Magnolia* (1837). The poem "Oliatta" (1855), by Howard H. Caldwell, attempts in almost one hundred pages of melodramatic verse to recreate the semimythical event that had inspired a ballad about the Dismal Swamp that was remarkably similar to Moore's and that the author claimed to have heard a young lady sing. See *Oliatta and Other Poems* (New York, 1855).

39 *The Talisman* (1826), p. 256. Although a nearly contemporaneous (April 30, 1830) account in the *Norfolk and Portsmouth Herald* conceded that "the scenery on the canal is rather unique than romantic," the reviewer's solution was to treat the landscape facetiously: "It is delightful to drive along its banks, or skim its surface, in the morning or evening of a summer's day when the sun is just above the horizon: the mirror-like surface below reflecting the trees, whose limbs embrace above, forming unbrageous vistas, beyond which the eye now and then catches a view of an opening to the blue firmament, and the gilding of the sunbeans, relieved by the lengthened shadows of the objects upon which they rest and then, to inhale the delicious fragrance of the jessamine, the laurel, the eglantine and wild rose, and various other aromatic shrubs and flowers with which the swamp abounds – not even the spicy gales of Araby can exceed it, and no effect of the pictorial art can do it justice." Quoted in Jesse F. Pugh, *The Hotel in the Great Dismal Swamp and Contemporary Events Thereabouts* (Old Trap, N.C.: J. F. Pugh, 1964), p. 9.

40 For a very different story of the process through which an image becomes an icon of American national pride and destiny, see Elizabeth McKinsey, *Niagara Falls: Icon of the American Sublime* (Cambridge, England: Cambridge University Press, 1985), especially pp. 37–125. McKinsey showed how the category of the sublime was used to reconcile contradictory feelings about the falls of fear and exaltation and that as this process took place the landscape became a symbol of communal aspirations and self-vaunting.

41 *Complete Works,* vol. 6, pp. 190–2.

42 See T. O. Mabbott, ed., *The Poems of Edgar Allan Poe* (Cambridge, Mass.: Harvard University Press, 1969), pp. 82–4. Rosemary F. Franklin mentioned the possible connection, citing T. O. Mabbott, ed., *Selected Poetry and Prose of Edgar Allan Poe* (New York, 1951), p. 646.

43 Poe, *Complete Works,* vol. 7, pp. 102–5.

44 Edward H. Davidson, *Poe, A Critical Study* (Cambridge, Mass.: Harvard University Press, 1957), p. 94.

45 Poe, *Complete Works,* vol. 7, pp. 102–5.

46 Davidson, *Poe,* p. 96.

47 Herman Melville, *The Piazza Tales and Other Prose Pieces* (Evanston, Ill., and Chicago: Northwestern University Press and the Newberry Library, 1987), p. 7.

48 Geoffrey Hartman, "Romantic Poetry and the Genius Loci," in *Beyond Formalism: Literary Essays, 1958–1970* (New Haven, Conn.: Yale University Press, 1970), p. 330.

49 Even as early as 1838, the *Southern Literary Messenger* reported that "there is a sombre grandeur in the aspect of this dark and gloomy swamp; but even in these solitary morasses, the hand of man is changing the face of nature: many giant-trunked cypresses and junipers have sunk before the stroke of the axe" (vol. 4, p. 261).

50 "The Beginnings of Sentimentalism," in Hoxie Fairchild, *Religious Trends in English Poetry, Volume I: 1700–1740, Protestantism and the Cult of Sentiment* (New York: Columbia University Press, 1939), pp. 205–63.

51 To borrow the phrase of E. Douglas Branch, *The Sentimental Years, 1836–1860* (New York: D. Appleton-Century, 1934), p. 146.

52 Much of my argument in the foregoing rejoins to some extent that of George Forgie's *Patricide in the House Divided.* In probing the psychological sources of aggression and its justification in Northern rhetoric leading up to the sectional crisis, Forgie found that it ironically emerged in the context of regressive fantasies that preoccupied those who dealt with the anxieties of the postheroic age by turning to Burkean and consolidationist political theories that substituted the crucial role of instinct for purely political solutions. In exploiting the cult of domesticity in their call to save the Union, Northern politicians and intellectuals transformed latent Oedipal aggression into fratricidal aggression, thus reconciling the prevailing conflict of the antebellum period between ambition and filiopietism (see note 22).

53 Per Seyersted, ed., *The Complete Works of Kate Chopin* (Baton Rouge: Louisiana University Press, 1969), vol. 2, p. 749.

54 Ibid., p. 749.

55 Ibid., p. 749.

56 Ibid., p. 750.

Chapter 2

1 However, Peter Steinhart, coming from a different perspective, told me that there is strong evidence that "humankind evolved in swampy places, that through most of our history as a species, we lived in such areas, and that most of our great cities grew in swampy areas" (personal correspondence).

2 I owe this reference to Professor Jan S. Emerson of the German department of Reed College.

3 See C. S. Lewis, "Addison," in *Essays on the Eighteenth Century Presented to D. Nichol Smith* (Oxford, England: Oxford University Press, 1945), p. 11.

4 Marjorie Hope Nicolson, *Mountain Gloom and Mountain Glory: The Development of the Aesthetics of the Infinite* (Ithaca, N.Y.: Cornell University Press, 1959).

5 Quotations from Shaftesbury, *Characteristics of Men, Manners, Opinions, Times . . . ,* ed. J. M. Robertson, 2 vols. (London, 1900), vol. 2, pp. 122–3.

6 See Ernest Lee Tuveson, "Space, Deity, and the Natural Sublime," *Modern Language Quarterly* 12 (March 1951): 20–38.

7 Quoted from the description of "What Makes a Slough of Despond," in John Bunyan, *The Pilgrim's Progress.*

8 See, for instance, "Alastor or, the Spirit of Solitude," lines 227–37, and, "Endymion," bk. 2, line 279. These are examples in which the swamp is specifically

mentioned. Of course, both poets use a great deal of imaginary or allegorical desert imagery that could be considered swamplike.

9 Samuel Coleridge, *Biographia Literaria or Biographical Sketches of My Literary Life and Opinions,* ed. George Watson (New York: Dutton, 1975), pp. 137-8.

10 Thomas Carlyle, "Characteristics," in *The Works of Thomas Carlyle* (centenary ed.) (London, 1899), vol. 28, p. 4. The origins and development of the theory of unconscious genius and the metaphor of organic growth in German and English Romantic thought are carefully traced in M. H. Abrams, *The Mirror and the Lamp: Romantic Theory and the Critical Tradition* (New York: Norton, 1953), see especially pp. 202-20.

11 Coleridge, *Biographia Literaria*, p. 46.

12 For the influence of Bartram's book on English writers, see N. Bryllion Fagin, *William Bartram: Interpreter of the American Landscape* (Baltimore: 1933).

13 A case in point is the noted description of a swamp in Charlotte Smith's *The Old Manor House* (1793): "Beyond this the eye was lost in a rich and various landscape, quite unlike any thing that European prospects offer . . . the high cliffs there gave place to a cypress swamp, or low ground, entirely filled with these trees: while on the right the rocks, rising suddenly and sharply, were clothed with wood of various species; the evergreen oak, the scarlet oak, the tulip tree, and magnolia, seemed bound together by festoons of flowers, some resembling the convolvuluses of our gardens, and others the various sorts of clematis, with vignenias, and the Virginia creeper. . . . On this side all was cheerful and lovely – on the other mournful and gloomy: the latter suited better with the disposition Orlando was in; and he reared his little hut on that side next the cypress swamp, and under the covert of the dark fir trees that waved over it." See edition edited by Anne Henry Ehrenpreis (London: Oxford University Press, 1969), p. 384.

It is almost certain that Smith was inspired by Bartram here (as the catalogue of plants indicates). But absurdly, she placed the swamp in the midst of the Canadian wilderness. The swamp itself, moreover, is described only as "mournful and gloomy," in contrast with the landscape juxtaposed to it. The most significant thing about Smith's reference to the swamp is the hallucinatory quality she attributed to the landscape. The hero, Orlando, wakes to the sound of a loud shriek in the middle of the night and, "alive to the keenest sensations of sorrow," looks "perpendicularly down on a hollow, where the dark knots of cypress seemed, by the dim light of early morning, which threatened storms, to represent groups of supernatural beings in funereal habits; and over them he saw, slowly sailing amid the mist that arose from the swamp, two or three of the birds which had so disturbed him" (p. 385).

14 Published in the *National Magazine* 2 (April 1853): 356-8; reprinted in *Travels in the Old South: Selected from Periodicals of the Times,* ed. Eugene L. Schwaab, 2 vols. (Lexington: University of Kentucky Press, 1973), vol. 1, pp. 163-5.

15 Timothy Flint, *Recollections of the Last Ten Years, Passed in Occasional Residence and Journeyings in the Valley of the Mississippi* (Carbondale and Edwardsville: Southern Illinois University Press, 1968), p. 189.

16 In Washington Irving, *Tales of a Traveller,* 2 vols. (London, 1824), vol. 2, p. 451.

17 William Bradford, *Of Plimouth Plantation,* ed. Samuel Eliot Morrison (New York: Modern Library, 1952), p. 84. In *Swallow Barn* (1832), Irving's southern counterpart, John Pendleton Kennedy, also drew on local lore, linking the swamp with the devil in the story of Mike Brown told by Hafen Blok. The folklore occurs at second remove, however, for Hafen – the shiftless vagrant who lives in the "Goblin Swamp" – is the real object of interest. Mark Littleton and Ned Hazard encounter Hafen after losing their way while taking a shortcut through the swamp. Ned

protests that they are bewitched – the place seems so strangely altered – and playfully calls on "Mr. Belzebub" to come to their aid; whereupon there is a rustling of leaves and the grotesque figure of Hafen Blok suddenly appears. "You are well met, Hafen," says Ned. "The devil of the swamp could never have sent us a better man. How are we to get through this bog?" Dryly taunting them at first, Hafen is eventually prevailed on to rescue the young men from their quandary after it becomes apparent that he is concealing a stolen chicken. He then invites himself home for an evening of storytelling, proving in the end to be quite a charming instance of moral turpitude. In Kennedy's idealized plantation world, even the renegade from virtue and the waste land he inhabits have their redemptive value. See John Pendleton Kennedy, *Swallow Barn: A Sojourn in the Old Dominion* (New York, 1852), chap. 28.

18 Francis Parkman, *The Pioneers of the New World, Atlantic Monthly* 12 (August 1863): 230.

19 T. W. Higginson, "My Out-Door Study," *Atlantic Monthly* 8 (September 1861): 306–7.

20 See line 31 of Alfred, Lord Tennyson, "The May Queen" (1832).

21 See Arthur Hallam's review of Tennyson's poems in *The Englishman's Magazine* (1831); quoted in M. H. McLuhan, "Tennyson and Picturesque Poetry," in *Critical Essays on the Poetry of Tennyson*, ed. John Killham (New York: Barnes & Noble, 1960), p. 72.

22 Higginson, "My Out-Door Study," p. 307.

23 Gaston Bachelard, *The Poetics of Space,* trans. Maria Jolas (Boston: Beacon Press, 1969), pp. 159–60.

24 T. W. Higginson, "Water-Lilies," *Atlantic Monthly* 2 (September 1858): 466.

25 T. W. Higginson, *Army Life in a Black Regiment,* ed. Howard N. Meyer (New York: Collier Books, 1969), p. 106. Subsequent page references from this volume are cited in the text.

26 See, T. J. Jackson Lears, "From Salvation to Self-Realization: Advertising and the Therapeutic Roots of the Consumer Culture, 1880–1930," in *The Culture of Consumption: Critical Essays in American History, 1880–1980,* ed. R. W. Fox and T. J. Jackson Lears (New York: Pantheon, 1983), pp. 1–38.

27 Harriet Beecher Stowe, *Dred, A Tale of the Dismal Swamp,* 2 vols. (Boston, 1856), vol. 2, p. 274. For a similar linkage between the South's social condition and the traditional imagery of the swamp, see Frances Anne Kemble, *Journal of a Residence on a Georgian Plantation in 1838–1839,* ed. John A. Scott (New York: Knopf, 1961). Recording her first impressions of the Great Dismal Swamp, Kemble wrote: "It looked like some blasted region lying under an enchanter's ban, such as one reads of in old stories. Nothing lived or moved throughout the loathsome solitude, and the sunbeams themselves seemed to sicken and grow pale as they glided like ghosts through these watery woods. Into this wilderness it seems impossible that the hand of human industry, or the foot of human wayfaring should ever penetrate; no wholesome growth can take root in its slimy depths; a wild jungle chokes up parts of it with a reedy, rattling covert for venomous reptiles; the rest is a succession of black ponds, sweltering under black cypress boughs – a place forbid" (p. 18).

    The context of this passage makes it clear that a comparison with social conditions in the South is on Kemble's mind. For a somewhat different connection between the Southern environment and the Southern culture that proves the persistence of the general attitude into the twentieth century, see W. J. Cash, *The Mind of the South* (New York: Vintage, 1941). Cash wrote: "Moreover, there was the influence of the Southern physical world – itself a sort of cosmic conspiracy against reality in favor of romance. The country is one of extravagant colors, of

proliferating foliage and bloom, of flooding yellow sunlight, and, above all perhaps, of haze . . . " (p. 48).

28 T. W. Higginson, *Out-Door Papers* (Boston, 1863), p. 129.

29 A. R. Waud, "On Picket Duty in the Swamps of Louisiana," *Harper's Weekly,*
May 9, 1863, p. 302.

30 A. R. Waud, "Cypress Swamp in Louisiana," *Harper's Weekly,* December 8, 1866,
p. 769.

31 A. R. Waud, "On the Mississippi," *Every Saturday Magazine,* August 5, 1871,
p. 141.

32 T. Addison Richards, "The Landscape of the South," *Harper's New Monthly Magazine* 6 (May 1853): 721.

33 See Elliott James Mackle, Jr., "The Eden of the South: Florida's Image in American
Travel Literature and Painting, 1865–1900" (Ph.D. diss., Emory University, 1977);
and his "To Find the Phantom Pleasure," in *The Idea of Florida in the American
Literary Imagination,* ed. Anne Rowe (Baton Rouge: Louisiana State University
Press, 1986), pp. 26–43.

34 Fitzhugh Ludlow, "If Massa Put Guns into Our Han's," *Atlantic Monthly Magazine*
15 (April 1865): 508–9.

35 William Cullen Bryant, ed., *Picturesque America: The Land We Live In,* 2 vols.
(New York: D. Appleton, 1872–4), vol. 1, p. 26.

36 Sidney Lanier, *Florida,* in the *Centennial Edition of the Works of Sidney Lanier,* ed.
Philip Graham (Baltimore, Johns Hopkins 1945): VI, 10.

37 Bryant, ed. *Picturesque America,* vol. 1, p. 169.

38 Edward King, *The Great South* (Hartford, 1875), pp. 384, 70.

39 George A. Coulon, *350 Miles in a Skiff Through the Louisiana Swamps* (New Orleans,
1888). A copy of this privately published manuscript, which ends abruptly in mid-
sentence after thirty-odd pages, is in the Louisiana Collection of the Howard Tilton
Library of Tulane University.

40 Julia E. Dodge, "An Island of the Sea," *Scribner's Monthly Magazine* (*The Century*)
14 (September 1877): 658.

41 Quoted in G. W. Sheldon, *American Painters* (New York, 1878), pp. 135–6 (from
Meeker's articles in *The Western,* January–February 1878).

42 Anne Rowe, *The Enchanted Country: Northern Writers in the South, 1865–1910* (Baton
Rouge: Louisiana State University Press, 1978), p. xviii.

43 Harriet Beecher Stowe, *Palmetto Leaves* (Boston, 1873), p. 139.

44 Quoted in Charles Edward Stowe, *The Life of Harriet Beecher Stowe* (Boston, 1889),
p. 468.

45 For a brilliant discussion of the Cavalier myth and its role in antebellum American
culture, see Frederick R. Taylor, *Cavalier and Yankee: The Old South and American
National Character* (Garden City, N.Y.: Doubleday, 1963).

46 Lanier, *Florida,* p. 16.

47 Howard Mumford Jones, *The Age of Energy: Varieties of American Experience, 1865–
1915* (New York: Viking, 1973), p. 262.

48 Quoted in John Tomsich, *A Genteel Endeavor: American Culture and Politics in the
Gilded Age* (Stanford, Calif.: Stanford University Press, 1971), pp. 30–1.

49 In Carolyn Porter, *Seeing and Being: The Plight of the Participant Observer in Emerson,
James, Adams, and Faulkner* (Middletown, Conn.: Wesleyan University Press,
1981). Note in particular Porter's discussion of American "ahistoricism" as continued in the body of critical work on American literature (see preface and chap.
1). Porter's ideas about reification are based on the work of Georg Lukács, especially his essay "Reification and the Consciousness of the Proletariat," in *History*

and Class Consciousness, trans. Rodney Livingstone (Cambridge, Mass.: MIT Press, 1971).

50 It is interesting, in this regard, to note changes in attitudes toward child rearing and education in the period after the Civil War. Daniel T. Rodgers pointed to "a widely noted pedagogical revolt against drill and memory in the name of a more natural, child-centered education" (p. 360). He stated that "this shift from a code of restraints to one of heroic impulse was a quiet, almost unnoticed revolution" (p. 359). See Daniel T. Rodgers, "Socializing Middle-Class Children: Institutions, Fables and Work Values in Nineteenth Century America," *Journal of Interdisciplinary History* 13 (Spring 1980): 354–67.

51 See T. J. Jackson Lears, *No Place of Grace: Antimodernism and the Transformation of American Culture, 1880–1920* (New York: Pantheon, 1981), see especially Preface, pp. xiii–xviii.

52 Ibid.

Chapter 3

1 See the discussion of these terms in the Introduction.

2 See Charles Feidelson, *Symbolism and American Literature* (Chicago: University of Chicago Press, 1969). Feidelson sees the dynamic I am discussing as crucial to the generation of symbolistic technique in the major writers of the American Renaissance. He did not provide a sociocultural context for it, however. In her *Seeing and Being: The Plight of the Participant Observer in Emerson, James, Adams and Faulkner* (Middletown, Conn.: Wesleyan University Press, 1981), Carolyn Porter established a convincing connection between symbolistic technique as Feidelson conceived it and the emergence of a modernist perspective out of the processes of capitalism that achieved relatively free reign in America (in contrast with Europe) during the mid-nineteenth century (see p. 21).

3 Mary Douglas, *Purity and Danger: An Analysis of the Concepts of Pollution and Taboo* (London: Routledge & Kegan Paul, 1978), p. 161.

4 Ibid., p. 142.

5 Lydia Sigourney, *A Young Lady's Offering* (Boston, 1848), p. 247. Subsequent page numbers are cited in the text.

6 See Ann Douglas, *The Feminization of American Culture* (New York: Avon, 1977), pp. 236–8.

7 René Girard attributed this function of symbolic exorcism to the institution of sacrifice in primitive societies: "Nevertheless, there is a common denominator that determines the efficacy of all sacrifices and that becomes increasingly apparent as the institution grows in vigor. This common denominator is internal violence – all the dissensions, rivalries, jealousies, and quarrels within the community that the sacrifices are designed to suppress. The purpose of the sacrifice is to restore harmony to the community, to reinforce the social fabric." See René Girard, *Violence and the Sacred,* trans. Patrick Gregory (Baltimore: Johns Hopkins University Press, 1977), p. 8.

8 William Gilmore Simms, *Poems, Descriptive, Dramatic, Legendary and Contemplative,* 2 vols. (New York, 1853), vol. 1, pp. 236–8.

9 John Ruskin, *Modern Painters II,* in *The Works of John Ruskin,* ed. E. T. Cook and Alexander Wedderburn (London: G. Allen, 1903–12), vol. 4, pp. 132–3.

10 Sigourney's reconciliation corresponds to the narrative format of the "Sacred Marriage" distinguished by Richard Slotkin as one of the four basic types of initiation in the American wilderness. See Richard Slotkin, *Regeneration Through Violence:*

The Mythology of the American Frontier, 1600–1860 (Middletown, Conn.: Wesleyan University Press, 1973), p. 179. As Slotkin established, the pattern of the sacred marriage – "in which the human protagonist is united with a female who is both the embodiment of the god-spirit immanent in nature and the 'other half' of his own individual nature (anima)" – recurs throughout American history before the Civil War. Simms's antagonism to nature relates to the initiatory pattern that Slotkin designated as "Exorcism" – "in which the same being, components of psychology, races, or powers conceived of as the anima in the sacred marriage are treated as if they were representations of the id, being sought out and recognized only that they might be destroyed."

11 James Hammond, *Diary, 1841–1846* (May 21, 1846), Library of Congress Archives. Quoted in William W. Freehling, *Prelude to Civil War: The Nullification Controversy in South Carolina, 1816–1836* (New York: Harper & Row, 1968), p. 9. Hammond went on to record the effects of a trip he had recently taken that had destroyed his confidence in himself: "I can bear no fatigue & therefore am [word?] restrained from being a man of action. I cannot be a man of intellect for an hour's reading knocks [?] me completely. I can only drag on then – a little here a little there: when with a sound constitution I verily believe [?] I should have been a great man & I am sure I should have been a happy one – I cannot believe that even such as I am I can last long."

12 W. J. Cash, *The Mind of the South* (New York: Vintage, 1969), p. 48. Compare Hammond's awareness of the swamp with T. W. Higginson's encounter with the "miniature" swamp recounted in Chapter 2 of this text. Higginson is not threatened by the stunning bauble that he confronts merely visually. His restoration of purity to the swamp image is an act of creative perception that consciously struggles beyond conceptual thought to merge with the reverberations of childhood reminiscence.

13 See Clement Eaton, *The Mind of the Old South,* rev. ed. (Baton Rouge: Louisiana State University Press, 1967), p. 44.

14 See Clement Eaton's discussion of Hammond in ibid., pp. 44–68.

15 Drew Faust discussed Hammond's depressiveness in the context of other Southern intellectuals friendly with him (including Simms), referred to as the "Sacred Circle." Whereas the other members of the circle (including George Frederick Holmes, Edmund Ruffin, and Nathaniel Beverley Tucker) also experienced depression and a sense of isolation from Southern society at large – a condition that drew them closer together – Hammond seems to have felt them the most. Hammond and his friends identified with the Romantic doctrine of genius, which they associated with the "wan and sickly" Byronic hero who wallowed in self-pity. Faust tied this emotional syndrome not only to a sense of being isolated and unappreciated but also, especially in Hammond's case, to ambivalence about opportunity – the conflict that perversely led him to scuttle his career. See Drew Faust, *The Sacred Circle: The Dilemma of the Intellectual in the Old South* (Baltimore: Johns Hopkins University Press, 1977), especially pp. 37–44.

16 Quoted in *The Letters of William Gilmore Simms,* ed. Mary C. Simms Oliphant, Alfred Taylor Odell, and T. C. Duncan Eaves (Columbia: University of South Carolina Press, 1954), vol. 3, pp. 210–11. Hammond's letter is dated October 1, 1853.

17 Ibid., p. 254.

18 Ibid. Simms's point refers to the problem of Hamlet which, according to Ernest Lee Tuveson, John Locke had feared as "a deficiency in that immediate contact with primary impressions of reality." See Ernest Lee Tuveson, *The Imagination As a Means of Grace: Locke and the Aesthetics of Romanticism* (Berkeley and Los Angeles: University of California Press, 1960), p. 31.

Elsewhere, Tuveson commented on Locke's conviction that "the mind, like Antaeus, must constantly return to contact with the earth, with the physical world which conveys simple ideas to us. Unless we revert to this elemental experience frequently, we become weak; a sickness of the mind sets in, producing the darkness which artificial philosophy has so long mistaken for light" (pp. 23–4). Failure to respect the truth of this dictum results in "Shandyism," the solipsism of the private world. This aspect of the swamp experience assumes the relation of the landscape to an inner world that we found also in Poe and Porte Crayon. The tradition is counterbalanced by a different one which we shall explore in later chapters.

19   Quoted in Eaton, *The Mind of the Old South*, p. 47.

20   William R. Taylor, *Cavalier and Yankee, The Old South and American National Character* (Garden City, N.Y.: Doubleday, 1963), pp. 256–8. My conception of Simms is deeply indebted to Taylor's brilliant analysis, particularly with regard to Simms's preoccupation with the Hamlet figure (see especially pp. 240–78). Taylor's book traces the growth and development of the idea, which became a historical rationalization for the Civil War, that North and South represented two distinct civilizations. One was "a leveling, go-getting utilitarian society," the other "a society based on the values of the English country gentry" (p. xv). The Cavalier convention was in effect a symbolic transcendence of conditions wrought by the depredations of capitalist enterprise and bougeois values on the American self.

21   Ibid., p. 274.

22   Ibid., p. 275.

23   Ibid., p. 277.

24   Simms, *Letters,* vol. 1, p. 220.

25   Ibid., pp. 227–8.

26   From Henry Timrod, "The Cotton Boll" (1861), in *The Literature of the South,* ed. T. D. Young, F. C. Watkins, and R. C. Beatty (Chicago: Scott, Foresman, 1952), pp. 294–7.

27   At least up to the mid–1840s this understanding informed Simms's prescription for the whole country. In an essay, "Americanism in Literature," Simms adopted the position of "Young America": "The heart must be molded to an intense appreciation of our woods and streams, our dense forests and deep swamps, our vast immeasurable mountains, our voluminous and tumbling waters." See C. Hugh Holman, ed., *Views and Reviews in American Literature, History and Fiction* (Cambridge, Mass.: Harvard University Press, 1962), p. 16.

28   Annette Kolodny, *The Lay of the Land: Metaphor as Experience and History in American Life and Letters* (Chapel Hill: University of North Carolina Press, 1975), p. 118.

29   Ibid., p. 120.

30   William Gilmore Simms, *The Scout* (New York, 1854), p. 14.

31   Ibid., p. 15.

32   Quotations from William Gilmore Simms, *The Forayers* (New York, 1855), p. 12.

33   See Joseph V. Ridgeley, *William Gilmore Simms* (New York: Twayne, 1962), p. 92.

34   Ibid., pp. 107–8.

35   Ibid., pp. 96–104 and the bibliography, p. 141.

36   Porgy is what William W. Freehling described as the "low-country capitalist who often despised the painstaking care and economy which the capitalist enterprise requires." *Prelude to Civil War,* p. 34.

37   Relevant to this point is Kolodny's emphasis on Porgy's regressive asexuality, which she links to his excessive orality and his infantile, almost fetal physical

appearance. The *Lay of the Land*, p. 124. Kolodny pointed out that "psychologically, Millhouse gives external verbal expression to Porgy's own suppressed sexual energies, and simultaneously represents that aspect of necessary economic self-assertion that is denied the master who must himself remain totally passive and unassertive if he is to restore on the plantation the primal landscape of the Mother" (p. 129).

38 William Gilmore Simms, *Woodcraft* (New York, 1854), p. 212.

39 We should point out that neither Bostwick nor "Hell-Fire Dick" is totally depraved. Each shows signs of essential humanity.

40 William G. McLoughlin, *The Meaning of Henry Ward Beecher: An Essay on the Shifting Values of Mid-Victorian America, 1840–1870* (New York: Knopf, 1970). Henry Nash Smith contended, however, that Beecher's brand of transcendental Christianity was a degradation of Emerson's doctrine of symbolic perception. Above all, Beecher ignored Emerson's essential distinction between Reason and Understanding. In Beecher's view, ordinary understanding, with help from the affections – what Beecher meant by the "heart" – was all that was necessary to interpret nature religiously. See Henry Nash Smith, *Democracy and the Novel: Popular Responses to Classic American Writers* (New York: Oxford University Press, 1977), p. 66.

41 Quoted in McLoughlin, *The Meaning of Henry Ward Beecher*, p. 75.

42 Quoted in ibid., p. 68.

43 Douglas, *The Feminization of American Culture*, pp. 6–7.

44 Ibid., p. 8. With regard to "influence," Douglas suggested an intriguing connection between sentimentalism and narcissism, emphasizing the common factor of wish fulfillment. The narcissist, she noted, "is committed not only to an underestimation of the force of facts, but in Freud's words, to an 'overestimation of the power of wishes and mental processes . . . a belief in the magical virtue of dealing with the outer world – the art of magic.' Narcissism can necessitate replacement of society by the self, reality by literature." See note 11, pp. 419–20. Such a development points, of course, to the regressive nature of primitivism.

45 See Chapter 9 of this text for a discussion of the relevance of such ideas as influence to the general notion of atmospheric agency and its role in American Romantic and Victorian culture.

46 George W. Frederickson, *The Black Image in the White Mind: The Debate on Afro-American Character and Destiny, 1817–1914* (New York: Harper & Row, 1972), pp. 97–129.

47 Quoted in ibid., pp. 114–15.

48 Quoted in Forest Wilson, *Crusader in Crinoline: The Life of Harriet Beecher Stowe* (Philadelphia: J. B. Lippincott, 1941), p. 260.

49 Reference to the large numbers of slaves who hid in the Dismal Swamp of Virginia and North Carolina is made in Merl R. Eppse, *The Negro, Too, in American History* (Nashville: National Publication Co., 1943), p. 159, and in John Hope Franklin, *The Free Negro in North Carolina, 1790–1860* (Chapel Hill: University of North Carolina Press, 1943), p. 39. As early as the first part of the eighteenth century, William Byrd, referring to the Dismal Swamp, noted: "It is certain many slaves shelter themselves in this obscure part of the world. . . . " See William Byrd, "History of the Dividing Line," in *The Prose Works of William Byrd of Westover*, ed. Louis B. Wright (Cambridge, Mass.: Harvard University Press, 1966), p. 186. Other references include Charles William Janson, *The Stranger in America* (London, 1807), p. 330; Robert C. McLean, ed., "A Yankee Tutor in the Old South," *North Carolina Historical Review*, 47 (January 1970): 56; Frederick Law Olmsted, "Journey to the Seaboard States" (1856), in *The Slave States Before the*

Civil War, ed. Harvey Wish (rev. ed., New York: Putnam, 1959), pp. 83–4. See also the New Orleans legend of "Bras Coupé," an escaped slave who lived in the swamps and whose story was adopted by George W. Cable in *The Grandissimes,* recorded in B. A. Botkin, *A Treasury of Southern Folklore* (New York: Crown, 1949), pp. 328–30. Botkin also told the story of a colony of escaped slaves living on the shores of a lake secreted in the swamps between the Alabama and Tombigbee rivers and presided over by a tyrannical leader named Hal. A disaffected member of the colony notified the whites of its whereabouts, leading to the capture of the slaves (pp. 347–9). The following narratives of freedmen offer accounts of hiding in the swamp: *Narrative of the Life and Adventures of Henry Bibb, An American Slave, Written by Himself* (New York: Harper & Row, 1969; originally published, 1850), especially pp. 119–30; Solomon Northrup, *Twelve Years a Slave* (New York: Dover, 1970), especially pp. 119–31. For the account of the murder of a young white girl by two slaves who held her captive on an island in the swamp (a narrative that is obviously much rewritten and that reads like a passage by Charles Brockden Brown), see Charles Ball, *Fifty Years in Chains, or, The Life of an American Slave* (New York, 1859), especially pp. 150–92. See also Herman Melville's poem, "The Swamp Angel," in Herman Melville, *Battle-Pieces and Aspects of the War* (New York, 1866).

50 Samuel Warner's pamphlet, "Authentic and Impartial Narrative of the Tragical Scene . . ." (New York, October 21, 1831), culled largely from contemporary newspaper accounts, is reprinted in Henry Irving Trangle, ed., *The Southampton Slave Revolt of 1831: A Compilation of Source Material* (Amherst, Mass.: University of Massachussetts Press, 1971), pp. 280–300.

51 Ibid., p. 298.

52 Ibid., p. 299.

53 Ibid., p. 297. See also Byrd, *The Prose Works,* pp. 194–9.

54 Henry Wadsworth Longfellow, *The Poems of Henry Wadsworth Longfellow* (New York: Modern Library, n.d.), p. 462. The poem is part of the series "Poems on Slavery."

55 "The Great Dismal Swamp," in Cecil D. Eby, Jr., ed., *The Old South Illustrated by Porte Crayon* (Chapel Hill: University of North Carolina Press, 1959), pp. 147–9.

56 William Gilmore Simms, *The Partisan, A Romance of the Revolution* (New York, 1885), p. 259.

57 Ibid., p. 247.

58 Ibid., p. 259.

59 See ibid., pp. 325–34.

60 For instance, Forest Wilson wrote: "As a credible character . . . Dred is as divorced from human reality as the statue of an Egyptian Pharoah." *Crusader in Crinoline,* p. 415.

61 Richard Chase, *The American Novel and Its Tradition* (Garden City, N.J.: Doubleday, 1957), p. 19.

62 Harriet Beecher Stowe, *Dred, A Tale of the Dismal Swamp* (Boston, 1856), vol. 2, p. 274. Subsequent page numbers are cited in the text.

63 See Lawrence Buell, "Calvinism Romanticized: Harriet Beecher Stowe, Samuel Hopkins, and *The Minister's Wooing,*" in *Critical Essays on Harriet Beecher Stowe,* ed. Elizabeth Ammons (Boston: G. K. Hall, 1980), p. 266. Buell sees "not a rejection of Hopkins but an adaptation of a principle for which he himself stood."

64 Stowe wrote: "The camp-meeting is one leading feature in the American development of religion, peculiarly suited to the wide extent of the country, and to the primitive habits which generally accompany a sparse population. Undoubtedly its general effects have been salutary. Its evils have been only those incident to large

gatherings, in which the whole population of a country were brought together. As in many other large assemblies of worship, there are those who go for all sorts of reasons; some from curiosity, some from love of excitement, some to turn a penny in a small way of trade, some to scoff, and a few to pray. And, so long as the heavenly way remains straight and narrow, so long the sincere and humble worshippers will ever be the minority in all assemblies" (*Dred,* vol. 1, p. 280).

65 Victor Turner, *Dramas, Fields, and Metaphors: Symbolic Action in Human Society* (Ithaca, N.Y.: Cornell University Press, 1974), p. 53.

66 For a parallel example of this archetype, consider the example of Wieland in Charles Brockden Brown's novel of the same name.

67 Quoted in Barbara M. Cross, ed., *The Autobiography of Lyman Beecher,* 2 vols. (Cambridge, Mass.: Harvard University Press, 1961), vol. 2, p. 367.

68 Ibid., p. 368.

69 Mary Douglas noted that pollution beliefs are rarely the object of contemplation and speculation – as a worldview – but, instead, are pragmatic, a machinery for resolving social problems, questions of social differentiation and organization. *Purity and Danger,* pp. 90–1.

70 Erich Neumann, *The Great Mother: An Analysis of the Archetype,* trans. Ralph Mannheim (Princeton, N.J.: Princeton University Press, 1974), p. 51.

71 Ibid., p. 51.

72 In *The Daughter's Seduction: Feminism and Psychoanalysis* (Ithaca, N.Y.: Cornell University Press, 1982), Jane Gallop identified a romantic feminism (she is discussing Ernest Jones's revisions of Freud's notion of the castration complex, but the case is relevant to our view of Jung) with the "liberal, humanist tradition which always threatens to re-cover our discoveries of obscene truths [and] makes the recognition of 'castration,' of a certain unfair distribution between men and women, subject to revision in the direction of complementarity and symmetry" (p. 21). Gallop went on to build on Lacan's insights and those of other commentators in establishing the status of the phallus as signifier and tying it to the symbolic fabrication of a "subject," one that leaves the female in an alienated relationship to language. Rather than symmetry in sexual differentiation, Gallop sees a "reciprocity [that] is skewed" (p. 24). Interestingly enough for our purposes, the asymmetry of sexual differentiation is tied to a distinction between sight and smell – one relatively rational and penetrative, the other, immersive and "obscenely" physical – which has suggestive parallels with my argument in Chapters 8 and 10 concerning shifts in the focus of the sensorium and their relationship to sensibility relating to the swamp.

Chapter 4

1 Henry T. Tuckerman, *The Book of the Artists* (New York: J. F. Carr, 1966), p. 530.

2 Barbara Novak stated: "At mid-century, the artists' belief in the unity of God and nature remained undisturbed, nor was it apparently shaken by the publication of *The Origin of Species....* This attitude was consistent with the tone of pre-Darwinian science, which ingeniously rationalized each step towards Darwinism with a powerful religious idealism. The 'new science' has perhaps been read too quickly into references to organic change in pre-Civil War America." Barbara Novak, *Nature and Culture: American Landscape and Painting, 1825–1875* (New York: Oxford University Press, 1980), p. 50. See also Theodore Dwight Bozeman, *Protestants in an Age of Science: The Baconian Ideal and Antebellum Religious Thought* (Chapel Hill: University of North Carolina Press, 1977); and Herbert Hovenkamp,

Science and Religion in America, 1800–1860 (Philadelphia: University of Pennsylvania Press, 1978). Both studies see the harmonization of science and religion throughout the antebellum period within the circles of conservative Protestantism, although Hovenkamp traced the breakup of this synthesis under the onslaught of Kantian Idealism in the 1840s and 1850s, through the work of Horace Bushnell in particular. It is not clear, however, that Bushnell's influence was as widespread as Hovenkamp made it out to be.

3   David C. Huntington, *The Landscapes of Frederic Edwin Church: Vision of an American Era* (New York: Braziller 1966), discussed Humboldt's influence on Church at some length; see especially pp. 17, 20, 41–2. Huntington cited Humboldt's *Cosmos, Personal Narrative,* and *Aspects of Nature* as especially influencing Church. In the ensuing discussion of Church, I am greatly indebted to Huntington's fine analysis of Church's sources and his significance as a whole.

4   Alexander von Humboldt, *Cosmos: A Sketch of a Physical Description of the Universe* (New York, 1850), vol. 2, p. 93.

5   See Albert Ten Eyck Gardner, "Scientific Sources of the Full-Length Landscape: 1850," *New York Metropolitan Museum of Art Bulletin* 4 (1945–6): 63.

6   Humboldt, *Cosmos,* vol. 1, p. 36.

7   Ibid., p. 37.

8   Ibid., p. 40.

9   Tuckerman, *The Book of the Artists,* p. 370.

10 From Alexander von Humboldt, *Contributions to the Natural History of the United States,* 2 vols. (Boston, 1857), vol. 1, p. 9. Quoted in Hovenkamp, *Science and Religion in America,* pp. 111–12.

11 Tuckerman, *The Book of the Artists,* p. 375.

12 Ibid., p. 375.

13 See Katherine Manthorne, *Creation and Renewal: Views of Cotopaxi by Frederic Edwin Church* (Washington, D.C.: National Museum of American Art, 1985), for a discussion of Church's gradual movement away from picturesque conventions and toward sensitivity to the features of geological transformation in his series of depictions of the volcano. As Manthorne noted, the Cotopaxi series documents Church's "developing belief that the dynamic volcanic forces and molten lava within the earth's interior had formed and modified its surfaces" (pp. 9–10).

14 Louis Legrand Noble, *Church's Painting. The Heart of the Andes* (broadside) (New York, 1859), p. 13.

15 Robert Hunt, *The Poetry of Science* (Boston, 1850; first American ed.), p. 26. Quoted in Huntington, *Landscapes of Frederic Edwin Church,* p. 48.

16 *Putnam's Monthly Magazine* 5(February 1855): 133.

17 Noble, *Heart of the Andes,* p. 14.

18 See Huntington, *The Landscapes of Frederic Edwin Church,* especially pp. 1, 9, 10, 17, 34, 39.

19 Those works painted during the Civil War may be seen as expressing this theme in the context of adversity. In *Rainy Season in the Tropics,* for instance, the rainbow depicts the hope that follows a thunderstorm.

20 See Elizabeth McKinsey, *Niagara Falls: Icon of the American Sublime* (Cambridge, England: Cambridge University Press, 1985) for a discussion of the linkage between the falls as a New World image and the unique destiny of the American people (especially pp. 100–16).

21 Hunt, *The Poetry of Science,* p. 26.

22 For the remarkable popularity of the stereograph and its relation to Church's work, see Elizabeth Linquist-Cock, *The Influence of Photography on American Landscape Painting* (New York: Garland, 1977), pp. 100–1.

23 Noble, *Heart of the Andes*, p. 4. Quoted in Novak, *Nature and Culture*, p. 73.

24 Louis Legrand Noble, *The Life and Works of Thomas Cole*, ed. Elliot S. Vesell (Cambridge, Mass.: Harvard University Press, 1964), p. 145, full quotation, note 12.

25 David C. Huntington, in particular, emphasized this point about Church's work. See Huntington, *Landscapes of Frederic Edwin Church*, p. 26. For a comparison of Church's typological approach with Cole's on the one hand, and the luminists, on the other, see David C. Huntington, "Church and Luminism: Light for America's Elect," in *American Light: The Luminist Movement, 1850–1875* (exhibition catalogue) (Washington, D. C.: National Gallery, 1979), pp. 155–87. The distinction between literal-historical and allegorical typology in the Puritan context was clearly drawn by Sacvan Bercovitch in "Typology in New England: The Williams–Cotton Controversy Reassessed." *American Quarterly* 19 (Summer 1967): 166–91.

26 John Ruskin, *Modern Painters IV*, in *The Works of John Ruskin*, ed. E. T. Cook and Alexander Wedderburn (London: G. Allen, 1903–12), vol. 6, p. 110. Relevant here is Ruskin's own use of a Literal-historical typological perspective, as discussed in Chapter 7 of this text.

27 George Washington Bethune, *An Address Before the Artists' Fund Society of Philadelphia at the Opening of Their Exhibition* (Philadelphia, 1840), p. 32.

28 Tuckerman, *The Book of the Artists*, p. 371.

29 Quoted in Huntington, *Landscapes of Frederic Edwin Church*, p. 59.

30 *The Heart of the Andes*, in Theodore Winthrop, *Life in the Open Air and Other Papers* (Boston, 1863), p. 353. Subsequent page references are cited in the text.

31 Ruskin, *Modern Painters I*, in *Works*, Vol. 3, p. 427.

32 In Allston's painting, the bluish mountain in the background, visually joining heaven and earth, presides as the mediating presence and perhaps offers a visual pun as the "rock of Christ."

33 Related to this point, see John Barrell's discussion of the influence of Claudian landscape conventions on the poetry of James Thomson and the idea of "composing" a landscape in eighteenth-century England, in *The Idea of Landscape and the Sense of Place, 1730–1840: An Approach to the Poetry of John Clare* (Cambridge, England: Cambridge University Press, 1972). Barrell wrote: "The main point of this insistence on a high viewpoint is that it creates a space between the landscape and the observer, similar in its effect to the space between a picture and whoever is looking at it, so, in this passage, Thomson is able to see the landscape, not as something in which he is involved, and which is all round him, but as something detached from him, *over there:* his eye may wander over the view, but his own position is fixed, and from his viewpoint he can organize the landscape into a system of parallel bands and flat perspectives by which only can we comprehend what he sees" (p. 21).

34 Marshall McLuhan and Harley Parker, *Through the Vanishing Point: Space in Poetry and Painting* (New York: Harper & Row, 1968).

35 Tuckerman, *The Book of the Artists*, p. 530.

36 Ibid., p. 377.

37 Paul Marçoy, *Travels in South America*, 2 vols. (New York, 1875), vol. 2, pp. 103–4.

Chapter 5

1 Thomas Francis Meagher, "The New Route Through Chiriqui," *Harper's New Monthly Magazine* 22 (January 1861): 199.

2   It should be emphasized that the encounter with the tropics during the nineteenth century was not peculiar to the United States. From early in the century, English and European travelers, naturalists, and artists had explored the exciting possibilities of the Latin American landscape. Alexander von Humboldt and Paul Marçoy have already been cited. Others included Prince Maximilian of Wied-Neuwied, whose *Travels in Brazil* appeared in 1820, the German artists Johann Moritz Rugendas and Ferdinand Bellerman – both Romantics whose images of dense jungle are closely observed and spectacular – and the English artist Frederick Catherwood, who liked to depict the ruins of ancient Indian civilizations moldering amid creeping vegetation. See Hugh Honour, *The New Golden Land: European Images of America from the Discoveries to the Present Time* (New York: Pantheon, 1975), pp. 161–89. A number of works on Latin America, like Julius Froebel's *Seven Years' Travel in Central America* (London, 1859), appeared in the United States and contributed considerably to Americans' familiarity with the tropics.

3   Meagher, "The New Route Through Chiriqui," p. 204.

4   Bayard Taylor, *Eldorado, or, Adventures in the Path of Empire* (New York, 1864). Taylor's book is drawn from a collection of letters written for the *New York Tribune* in 1849.

5   N. P. Willis, *Health-Trip to the Tropics* (New York, 1853), p. 49.

6   Anonymous, "Trees in Assemblages," *Atlantic Monthly* 8 (August 1861): 139.

7   Ibid., p. 139. The lines are from *Paradise Lost,* bk. 2, line 951.

8   Anonymous, "Trees in Assemblages," p. 139.

9   *Putnam's Monthly Magazine* 12 (November 1868): 553–4. The observation is no less revealing for the fact that in the next sentence, the writer admitted: "These ideas and impression are doubtless wrong in themselves, but they are such as fill the mind of the wayfarer in trackless wilds."

10 Professor and Mrs. Louis Agassiz, *A Journey in Brazil* (Boston, 1868), p. 264.

11 Anonymous, "Trees in Assemblages," p. 140.

12 *The Crayon,* May 23, 1855, p. 396.

13 Claude Lévi-Strauss, *Tristes Tropiques* (New York: Atheneum Publishers, 1975), p. 41.

14 Dr. G. Hartwig, *The Polar and Tropical Worlds: A Description of Man and Nature* (Chicago, 1875), p. 524. Hartwig quoted Agassiz on the promising capacities of the Amazon basin: "Its woods alone have an almost priceless value. Nowhere in the world is there finer timber either for solid construction or for works of ornament. The rivers which flow past these magnificent forests seem meant to serve first as a water-power for the saw-mills which ought to be established on their borders, and then as a means of transportation for material so provided. . . . An empire might esteem itself rich in any one of the sources of industry which abounds in this valley; and yet the greater part of its vast growth rots on the ground, and goes to form a little more river-mud or to stain the waters on the shores of which its manifold products die and decompose" (p. 524). See also "Oran," "Tropical Journeyings," *Harper's New Monthly Magazine* 18 (January 1859): 145–61, which tells about the construction of the Panama Railroad; and William Lewis Herndon, *The Exploration of the Valley of the Amazon* (New York: McGraw-Hill, 1952; reprint of 1853–4 ed.). Herndon wrote: "I was now, for the first time, fairly in the field of my operations. I had been sent to explore the Valley of the Amazon, to sound its streams, and to report as to their navigability. I was commanded to examine its field, its forests, and its rivers that I might gauge their capabilities, active and dormant, for trade and commerce and make known the resources which lie in concealment there" (p. 27).

15 Lévi-Strauss, *Tristes Tropiques*, p. 41.

16 William Cullen Bryant, ed., *Picturesque America: The Land We Live In* (New York, 1872), vol. 1, p. 267.
17 *Putnam's Monthly Magazine* 12 (May 1868): 591–2.
18 *Putnam's Monthly Magazine* 13 (March 1869): 341–2.
19 *Harper's New Monthly Magazine* 12 (May 1853): 730–1.
20 Anonymous, "Adventures in the Gold Fields of Central America," *Harper's New Monthly Magazine* 8 (September 1861): 326.
21 Theodore Winthrop, *Life in the Open Air and Other Papers* (Boston, 1863), p. 350.

Chapter 6

1 *Harper's New Monthly Magazine* 5 (August 1852): 302.
2 Ibid., p. 303.
3 Charles Lanman, *Letters from a Landscape Painter* (Boston, 1845), pp. 40–1.
4 To understand the role of typology in American culture, see Sacvan Bercovitch, *The Puritan Origins of the American Self* (New Haven, Conn.: Yale University Press, 1975). The emergence of a sense of Manifest Destiny out of a typological reading of the Bible required that that reading be literal-historical, as opposed to allegorical. The literal-historical interpretation of Old Testament types, according to Bercovitch, allowed the Puritans to see their own history as a direct continuation of the history of God's chosen people. Charles Lanman, Frederic Church, and others still reflected this way of thinking in the mid-nineteenth century. The pervasive influence of typology was explored by James Collins Moore in "The Storm and the Harvest: The Image of Nature in Mid-Nineteenth Century American Landscape Painting" (Ph.D. diss., Indiana University, 1974), pp. 91–105; as well as by David C. Huntington in "Church and Luminism: Light for America's Elect," in *American Light: The Luminist Movement, 1850–1875* (exhibition catalogue) (Washington, D.C.: National Gallery, 1979).
    The general distinction between allegory and typology is most simply seen as an explicit versus an implicit type of meaning. An example of the kind of allegorical reading of nature that existed alongside the literal-typological hermeneutic can be found in an article entitled "A Coup D'Oeil of Niagara Out of Season," *The Crayon* 3 (March 1856): 76–7. "The sun shone brightly; the cloud of spray below was as white as drifted snow, and the rainbow had followed us all day. While I looked upon the rapids alone . . . the whole scene became to me an allegory. So we rush on to our goal, and as suddenly disappear in the mystery that envelopes our fall, and conceals from all eyes the dread connection of this world and the next; there is only agony and a flood of tears. No eye has ever penetrated that spectral cloud to tell us what passes behind it, and we look into it with dread and awe; but upon that very veil is painted the rainbow, and to every soul that looks up there is a separate bow of promise; it spans the fathomless abyss where all seemed lost and away down that vale of tears it follows us, until again we see the gleam of calm waters, and they tell us that there is beyond our sight a tranquil world of sunshine, soft airs and vernal showers – eye hath not seen it, but we know it must be there." This passage could almost be a gloss of the latter two panels of Thomas Cole's *The Voyage of Life*.
5 William Cullen Bryant, James Fenimore Cooper, Washington Irving, et al., *The Home Book of the Picturesque: or American Scenery, Art, and Literature* (New York: Putnam, 1852), pp. 1–2.
6 Ibid., p. 25.
7 Ibid., p. 7.
8 Charles Lanman, *Adventures in the Wilds of North America* (London, 1854), p. 225.

9   Herman Melville, *The Piazza Tales and Other Prose Pieces, 1839–1860* (Evanston, Ill., and Chicago: Northwestern University Press and the Newberry Library, 1987), p. 134.

10 Henry David Thoreau, *Cape Cod* (New York: Library of America, 1985), p. 923.

11 Theodore Winthrop, *Life in the Open Air and Other Papers* (Boston, 1863), pp. 97–8. Subsequent page numbers are cited in the text.

12 John Higham, *From Boundlessness to Consolidation: The Transformation of American Culture, 1848–1860* (Ann Arbor, Mich.: William L. Clements Library, 1969), pp. 4–5.

13 As Higham wrote: "Far from casting off all inhibitions, nineteenth-century Americans ordinarily sought release only from the material and institutional confinements that bound them to a fixed place or a given social role. In proportion as those external ties relaxed, the internalized restraints of conscience and of public opinion tightened. Thus the Age of Boundlessness combined a passion for freedom with an exceptionally strict moral code." Ibid., p. 13.

14 John Cawelti, *Adventure, Mystery, and Romance: Formula Stories as Art and Popular Culture* (Chicago: University of Chicago Press, 1976), p. 31.

15 Ibid., p. 26.

16 Henry Nash Smith, *Democracy and the Novel: Popular Responses to Classic American Writers* (New York: Oxford University Press, 1977), p. 20.

17 Ibid., p. 15.

Chapter 7

1   See, for instance, James T. Callow, *Kindred Spirits: Knickerbocker Writers and American Artists, 1807–1855* (Chapel Hill: University of North Carolina Press, 1967); William Charvat, *The Origins of American Critical Thought, 1810–1835* (New York: Barnes, 1961); Terence Martin, *The Instructed Vision: Scottish Common Sense Philosophy and the Origins of American Fiction* (Bloomington: Indiana University Press, 1961); Ralph N. Miller, "Thomas Cole and Alison's Essays on Taste," *New York History* 37 (July 1956): 281–99; Donald Ringe, "James Fenimore Cooper and Thomas Cole: An Analogous Technique," *American Literature* 30 (March 1958): 26–36; Donald Ringe, "Kindred Spirits: Bryant and Cole," *American Quarterly* 6 (Fall 1954): 232–44; Donald Ringe, *The Pictorial Mode: Space and Time in the Art of Bryant, Irving and Cooper* (Lexington: University of Kentucky Press, 1971); Charles L. Sanford, "The Concept of the Sublime in the Works of Thomas Cole and William Cullen Bryant," *American Literature* 28 (1956–7): 434–48; and Roger Stein, *John Ruskin and Aesthetic Thought in America* (Cambridge, Mass.: Harvard University Press, 1967).

2   Archibald Alison, *Essays on the Nature and Principles of Taste* (Boston, 1812): 430–1.

3   For an excellent discussion of Burke's anticipation of Coleridge and Romantic poetic theory, see J. T. Boulton, "Introduction" to Edmund Burke, *A Philosophical Enquiry into the Origin of Our Ideas of the Sublime and Beautiful* (Notre Dame, Ind.: Notre Dame University Press, 1968), especially pp. i, viii, xxviii.

4   Quoted in Charvat, *The Origins of American Critical Thought,* p. 37.

5   The connection between seeing and owning was made quite explicit, even in the early eighteenth century, by Joseph Addison in detailing "The Pleasures of Imagination" (1712): "A man of polite imagination . . . meets with a secret refreshment in a description and often feels a greater satisfaction in the prospect of fields and meadows than another does in the possession. It gives him indeed a kind of property in everything he sees and makes the most rude, uncultivated parts of nature ad-

minister to his pleasures, so that he looks upon the world, as it were, in another light and discovers in it a multitude of charms that conceal themselves from the generality of mankind." See no. 411 (Introductory); reprinted in *Essays in Criticism and Literary Theory: Addison,* ed. John Loftis (Northbrook, Ill.: AHM Press, 1975), p. 140.

    For a discussion of the role of the consuming observer in the idealized landscape, detached from the means of production, see Raymond Williams, *The Country and the City* (New York: Oxford University Press, 1973), especially chap. 12, "Pleasing Prospects." A growing body of critics have investigated the ideological dimension of seventeenth- and eighteenth-century British landscape representation. See especially John Barrell, *The Dark Side of the Landscape* (Cambridge, England: Cambridge University Press, 1980); Ann Bermingham, *Landscape and Ideology: The English Rustic Tradition, 1740–1860* (Berkeley and Los Angeles: University of California Press, 1986); David H. Solkin, *Richard Wilson: The Landscape of Reaction* (London: Tate Gallery, 1982); and James Turner, *The Politics of Landscape: Rural Scenery and Society in English Poetry, 1630–1660* (Cambridge, Mass.: Harvard University Press, 1979). For a study with a specifically feminist slant, see Carole Fabricant, "Binding and Dressing Nature's Loose Tresses: The Ideology of Augustan Landscape Design," in *Studies in Eighteenth-Century Culture,* ed. Roseanne Runte (Madison: University of Wisconsin Press, 1979), pp. 109–35.

6   Samuel F. B. Morse, *Lectures on the Affinity of Painting with the Other Fine Arts,* ed. Nicolai Cikovsky, Jr. (Columbia: University of Missouri Press, 1983; originally delivered in 1826), p. 67.

7   Henry Home, *Elements of Criticism* (New York, 1855), p. 165.

8   Martin Price, "The Picturesque Moment," in *From Sensibility to Romanticism: Essays Presented to Frederick A. Pottle,* ed. Frederick W. Hilles and Harold Bloom (New York: Oxford University Press, 1965), pp. 259–92.

9   Ibid., pp. 262–3.

10   Richard S. Moore, "That Cunning Alphabet: Melville's Aesthetics of Nature," *Costerus* 35 (1982): 29. Because of the requirements of the covenantal terms of American destiny and its primary association with American scenery during the Romantic period, Moore argued, Americans tended to assume a moral picturesque that merged with the sublime in a unified aesthetic closer to the Transcendentalists than to the Scottish associationists (see p. 31). Such an approach characteristically led to an "intrinsic contiguity of the wild and the cultivated" in American landscape paintings (p. 33).

11   Alison, *Nature and Principles of Taste,* p. 62.

12   Quoted in M. H. Abrams, *The Mirror and the Lamp: Romantic Theory and the Critical Tradition* (New York: Norton, 1953), p. 173.

13   Ibid., p. 178. Barton L. St. Armand discussed the behavioristic implications of associationism in relation to "The Fall of the House of Usher." He allied them with the rationalism of the narrator, against the irrationalism of Usher, who believes in the sentience of all things. See Barton L. St. Armand, "Poe's Landscape of the Soul: Association Theory and the 'Fall of the House of Usher,' " *Modern Language Studies* 7 (Fall 1977): 32–41.

14   As Perry Miller noted in one of his outlines for *The Life of the Mind in America: From the Revolution to the Civil War* (New York: Harcourt, Brace & World, 1965): "Little or no influence within circles of science and orthodox theology of Kantian idealism. Throughout almost all these regions 'Common Sense' metaphysics prevail, and epistemological 'realism' is untroubled. For what, historically speaking, is the mainstream of American intellectual activity the problem was not any terrible

doubt of appearances – appearances were real – but of adjusting the conception of mind to a reality which was racing dizzily through a process of transformation" (p. 318).

15 Charvat, *The Origins of American Critical Thought*, p. 6.

16 Alison, *Nature and Principles of Taste*, pp. 152–3.

17 For an extensive study of the iconography of these concerns – especially as they apply to Thomas Cole's work – and of the shift to a more optimistic and nationalistic iconography, see Angela Miller, " 'The Imperial Republic': Narratives of National Expansion in American Art, 1820–1860" (Ph.D. diss., Yale University, 1985).

18 Louis Legrand Noble, *The Life and Works of Thomas Cole*, ed. Elliot S. Vesell (Cambridge, Mass.: Harvard University Press, 1964), pp. 144–5.

19 "Westminster Abbey," for instance, is a set piece recalling the morbid meditations of the British graveyard school and offering a veritable orgy of sympathetic rapport with the storied past, in which associations pour forth from the visitor's mind in response to the memorializing surfaces and textures of this venerable pile. The theme of the "presence of the past" is carried through in the oratorical quality of Irving's language, especially in the orotund passage on the sound of the organ – an onomatopoeic binge: "Again the pealing organ heaves its thrilling thunders, compressing air into music, and rolling it forth upon the soul. What long-drawn cadences! What solemn sweeping concords! It grows more and more dense and powerful – it fills the vast pile, and seems to jar the very walls – the ear is stunned – the senses are overwhelmed. And now it is winding up in full jubilee – it is rising from the earth to heaven – the very soul seems rapt away and floated upward on this swelling tide of harmony!" Washington Irving, *History, Tales and Sketches* (New York: Library of America, 1983), p. 901. For a more elaborate discussion of this passage and the relationship among picturesque ruin, the oratorical, and the sublime, see my unpublished article, "Hawthorne, Melville, and the Undoing of the 'Moral Picturesque.' "

20 See especially Rufus Choate, "The Importance of Illustrating New England History by a Series of Romances Like the Waverley Novels. Delivered at Salem, 1833," in *The Works of Rufus Choate with a Memoir of His Life*, ed. Samuel Gilman Brown (Boston, 1862), vol. 1, pp. 319–46. For an illuminating discussion of the various constituents of the conservative Whig worldview, see Daniel Walker Howe, "Whig Conservatism" (chap. 9), in *The Political Culture of the American Whigs* (Chicago: University of Chicago Press, 1979), pp. 210–37. On the general question of oratory in New England, see Lawrence Buell, "New England Oratory from Everett to Emerson" (chap. 6), in *New England Literary Culture: From Revolution Through Renaissance* (Cambridge, England: Cambridge University Press, 1986), pp. 137–65.

21 In his "Lectures on Poetry" (1825), William Cullen Bryant epitomized the attitude: "Among the most remarkable of the influences of poetry is the exhibition of those analogies and correspondences which it beholds between the things of the moral and of the natural world. I refer to its adorning and illustrating each by the other – infusing a moral sentiment into natural objects, and bringing images of visible beauty and majesty to heighten the effect of moral sentiment. Thus it binds into one all the passages of human life and connects all the varieties of human feeling with the works of creation." *Prose Writings of William Cullen Bryant*, ed. Parke Godwin (New York: D. Appleton, 1889), p. 19.

22 See Keats's letter to his brothers George and Thomas (Sunday, December 21, 1817). Keats's idea is likely based on the passage in Coleridge's *Biographia Literaria*

in which the poet speaks of "negative faith" as what "simply permits the images presented to work by their own force, without either denial or affirmation of their real existence by the judgement" (pp. 256–7).

23 Noble, *The Life and Works of Thomas Cole*, p. 41.

24 John Muir, *A Thousand-Mile Walk to the Gulf* (Boston: Houghton Mifflin, 1916), p. 88.

25 Aldous Huxley, "Wordsworth in the Tropics," in *Life and Letters* (London: Brendin Pub., 1928), vol. 1, no. 5, p. 343. To Huxley, "The jungle is marvellous, fantastic, beautiful; but it is also terrifying, it is also profoundly sinister. . . . The life of those vast masses of swarming vegetation is alien to the human spirit . . ." (p. 343).

26 Ibid., p. 345. I am using Huxley's remarks on Wordsworth in a relative sense here, but I might as well stress the difference between Coleridge's theory of Imagination and Wordsworth's views which were, as M. H. Abrams pointed out, still essentially tied to neoclassical and associationist assumptions: in particular, Wordsworth's adoption – as opposed to Coleridge's – of the old antithesis between nature and art and his uniformitarianism and attraction to "general" nature. Abrams noted: "In Coleridge's criticism . . . the imaginative synthesis of discordant or antithetic aesthetic qualities replaces Wordsworth's 'nature' as the criterion of highest poetic value; and this on grounds inherent in Coleridge's world-view." Abrams, *The Mirror and the Lamp*, p. 119. Wordsworth's neoclassical views and his emphasis on the morally nurturant function of nature explain why he alone among the great English Romantic poets gained early and enduring favor in America.

27 John Beer, *Coleridge's Poetic Intelligence* (New York: Barnes & Noble, 1977), p. 86. Beer observed that although warmth and congeniality, according to Coleridge, promote the cooperation of primary and secondary consciousness, cold tends to separate the two levels, "leaving the individual more exposed to the 'primary' emotion of fear" (p. 88).

28 Stein, *John Ruskin and Aesthetic Thought in America*, p. 41. The first volume of *Modern Painters* was published in England in 1843, and Ruskin first began attracting attention in America around 1847.

29 John Ruskin, *Modern Painters II,* in *The Works of John Ruskin,* ed. E. T. Cook and Alexander Wedderburn (London: G. Allen, 1903–12), vol. 4, p. 64.

30 Raymond Williams sees Ruskin's notion of vital beauty as integral to his social criticism, in which he sought "the conditions of 'joyful and right exertion of perfect life' in man." Raymond Williams, *Culture and Society: 1780–1950* (New York: Harper & Row, 1958), p. 135. These conditions were implicit in the design of Typical Beauty (Ruskin had in mind an hierarchical, paternalistic society). The symbiotic relationship between Typical and Vital Beauty was based on the assumption (new with the nineteenth century) that there is a necessary relation between art and the culture that produces it. By the same token, we might say that the quality of artistic vision depends on the emotional constitution of the artist; hence the connection Ruskin drew between the pathetic fallacy in art and morbidity in the artist. The idea of beauty, founded on the concept of a divinely sanctioned order, transcended the potentially disfiguring impact of not only emotion but also anarchic social conditions (for example, democracy, the market economy) on art.

31 Ruskin, *Modern Painters II,* vol. 4, pp. 35–6.

32 See George P. Landow, *The Aesthetic and Critical Theories of John Ruskin* (Princeton, N.J.: Princeton University Press, 1971). As Landow put it: "[Ruskin's] attempt and failure to exclude all these subjectivist, variable elements of beauty indicate how conservative – and how tenuous – was his attempt to solve the problems of

romanticism in art by appealing to a metaphysical order" (p. 94). Related to Landow's point is Ruskin's declaration in *Modern Painters II*, that "it is evident that the full exercise of this noble function of the Associative faculty is inconsistent with absolute and incontrovertible conclusions on subjects of theoretic preference. For it is quite impossible for any individual to distinguish in himself the unconscious underworking of indefinite association peculiar to him individually, from those great laws of choice under which he is comprehended with all his race. And it is well for us that it is so, the harmony of God's work is not in us interrupted by this mingling of universal and peculiar principles: for by these such difference is secured in the feelings as shall make fellowship itself more delightful, by its inter-communicate character; and such variety of feelings also in each of us separately as shall make us capable of enjoying scenes of different kinds and orders, instead of morbidly seeking for some perfect epitome of the Beautiful in one" (p. 74).

33 Ruskin, *Modern Painters I*, vol. 3, p. 134.

34 *Modern Painters IV*, vol. 6, pp. 109–10. Note again the distinction between literal-historical and allegorical typology drawn by Sacvan Bercovitch with regard to the early American context, in "Typology in New England: The Williams–Cotton Controversy Reassessed."

35 Quoted in *The Crayon* 5 (3) (March 1858): 66.

36 *The Crayon*, January 3, 1855, p. 2.

37 *Modern Painters I*, vol. 3, p. 309.

38 *The Crayon*, January 17, 1855, p. 34.

39 See Theodore Dwight Bozeman, *Protestants in an Age of Science: The Baconian Ideal and Antebellum Religious Thought* (Chapel Hill: University of North Carolina Press, 1977); and Herbert Hovenkamp, *Science and Religion in America, 1800–1860* (Philadelphia: University of Pennsylvania Press, 1978). The major constituents of the Baconian philosophy, according to Bozeman, were (1) an "inductive" methodology, (2) "a strenuously empiricist approach to all forms of knowledge," and (3) "a declared greed for objective *fact*" and (4) "a corresponding distrust of 'hypothesis' and 'imagination' " (p. 3). Speaking of the "doxological" conception of science held by conservative Presbyterians in particular, Bozeman noted that "emphasis falls not upon the material benefits of scientific investigation, but upon the subjective, elevating, religious transaction between the investigator and nature" (p. 78).

40 James McCosh, for instance, wrote: "We are inclined to think that as there are eternal homologies among organic structures, so there may also be correspondences among spiritual natures, and that other intelligences, differing in many respects from man, may resemble him in this, that they also delight in these laws and patterns; while God, over all, may be conceived as rejoicing in all His works together." James McCosh, *Typical Forms and Special Ends in Creation* (New York, 1856), p. 433. In his essay "The Influence of Darwinism on Philosophy," John Dewey pointed to some of the implications of the violation, by the *Origin of Species,* of the ancient concept of species, to which formulations like McCosh's refer. Dewey saw a transfer of interest from permanency to change, from design to change, from mind to matter. After Darwin, "philosophy foreswears inquiry after absolute origins and absolute finalities in order to explore specific values and the specific conditions that generate them." John Dewey, *The Influence of Darwin on Philosophy and Other Essays in Contemporary Thought* (New York: Henry Holt, 1910).

41 McCosh, *Typical Forms and Special Ends in Creation*, p. 473.

42 Ruskin, *Modern Painters I*, vol. 3, p. 92. The passage reads in full: "But I say that the art is greatest, which conveys to the mind of the spectator, by any means whatsoever, the

greatest number of the greatest ideas; and I call an idea great in proportion as it is received by a higher faculty of the mind, and as it more fully occupies, and in occupying, exercises and exalts, the faculty by which it is received."

43 As Ruskin wrote: "The landscape painter must always have two great and distinct ends; the first, to induce in the spectator's mind the faithful conception of any natural objects whatsoever; the second, to guide the spectator's mind to those objects most worthy of its contemplation, and to inform him of the thoughts and feelings with which these were regarded by the artist himself" *Modern Painters I,* vol. 3, p. 133.

44 See the preface to *Modern Painters* (New York: 1844), in which Ruskin wrote: "The rapid and powerful artist looks with such contempt on those who seek minutiae of detail rather than grandeur of expression . . . " (p. xxxii). Ruskin had originally defended the Pre-Raphaelites, not on the basis of their faithfulness to microscopic detail but for their ability to evoke nature truthfully through the mysterious transformation of dabs of paint on the canvas when seen at a certain distance: "The true work represents all objects exactly as they would appear in nature in the position and at the distances which the arrangement of the picture supposes. The false work represents them with all their details, as if seen through a microscope." *The Works of John Ruskin,* vol. 12, p. 331. It is important to establish this distinction because it has led to a good deal of confusion among interpreters of Ruskin, not only among his contemporaries, but among recent critics as well (see, for instance, Stein, *John Ruskin and Aesthetic Thought in America,* p. 102).

45 See *The Stones of Venice III,* in The *Works of John Ruskin,* eds. E. T. Cook and Alexander Wedderburn (London: 1903–12), vol. 11, pp. 201–2.

46 *The Crayon* 5(4) (April 1858): 105.

47 *The Crayon* 5(2) (February 1858): 42.

48 For the influence of the English Pre-Raphaelites on American painting and its relation to Ruskinism, see William H. Gerdts, "The Influence of Ruskin and Pre-Raphaelitism on American Still-Life Paintings," *American Art Journal* 1 (2) (Fall 1969): 80–97.

49 The debate is discussed by Roger Stein in *John Ruskin and Aesthetic Thought in America,* pp. 152–3.

50 The prevalance of such techniques was also due to the influence on American landscape painting of the Dusseldorf school, in which artists like William Trost Richards, William Stanley Haseltine, and Albert Bierstadt were trained.

51 See Elizabeth Lindquist-Cock, *The Influence of Photography on American Landscape Painting* (New York: Garland, 1977).

52 Ruskin, *Modern Painters I,* vol. 3, p. 470.

53 Henry T. Tuckerman, *The Book of the Artists* (New York: J. F. Carr, 1966), p. 530.

54 Quoted in Linda S. Ferber, *William Trost Richards: American Landscape and Marine Painter, 1822–1905* (exhibition catalogue) (New York: Brooklyn Museum, 1973), p. 32. Ferber made the point about the surreal appearance of *In the Woods.*

55 Noble, *The Life and Works of Thomas Cole,* p. 82.

56 James Jackson Jarves, *The Art-Idea,* ed. Benjamin Rowland, Jr. (Cambridge, Mass.: Harvard University Press, 1960; originally published in 1864), p. 142.

57 Tuckerman, *The Book of the Artists,* p. 530.

Chapter 8

1 Donald Ringe, *The Pictorial Mode: Space and Time in the Art of Bryant, Irving and Cooper* (Lexington: University of Kentucky Press, 1971).

2   All quotations from Jane Gallop, *The Daughter's Seduction: Feminism and Psycho-analysis* (Ithaca, N.Y.: Cornell University Press, 1982), p. 27.

3   Ibid.

4   Alexander von Humboldt, *Cosmos: A Sketch of a Physical Description of the Universe* (New York, 1850), vol. 2, p. 96.

5   All quotations from Bayard Taylor, *Eldorado, or Adventures in the Path of Empire* (New York, 1864), pp. 14–15.

6   Henry T. Tuckerman, *The Book of the Artists* (New York: J. F. Carr, 1966), pp. 542–43.

7   Worthington Whittredge, *The Autobiography of Worthington Whittredge, 1820–1910,* ed. John I. H. Baur (New York: Arno Press, 1969), p. 42.

8   *The Crayon,* April 18, 1855, p. 242.

9   *The Crayon,* March 28, 1855, p. 210.

10 Uvedale Price, *Essays on the Picturesque, as Compared with the Sublime and the Beautiful . . .* (London, 1810), p. 116.

11 Ibid., p. 111.

12 Sir Joshua Reynolds, *Discourses on Art,* ed. Stephen O. Mitchell (New York: Bobbs-Merrill, 1965), p. 121.

13 Anton Ehrenzweig, *The Hidden Order of Art: A Study in the Psychology of Artistic Imagination* (Berkeley and Los Angeles: University of California Press, 1967). The term is used throughout the book.

14 Herbert Read, *Icon and Idea: The Function of Art in the Development of Human Consciousness* (London: Schocken, 1955), p. 73. For a similar thesis, see Marshall McLuhan and Harley Parker, *Through the Vanishing Point: Space in Poetry and Painting* (New York: Harper & Row, 1968).

15 For the rise of the penny press and its implications, see Michael Schudson, "The Revolution in American Journalism in the Age of Egalitarianism: The Penny Press" (chap. 1), in *Discovering the News: A Social History of American Newspapers* (New York: Basic Books, 1981), pp. 12–60. Brian Jay Wolf developed these implications and the general impact of an information-oriented society on antebellum American painting in "All the World's a Code: Art and Ideology in Nineteenth-Century American Painting, *Art Journal* (Winter 1984): 328–37. For an excellent account of the impact of literacy on American literature of the early national period, with conclusions of relevance to the period discussed here, see Cathy N. Davidson, *Revolution and the Word: The Rise of the Novel* (New York: Oxford University Press, 1986), especially chap. 4. Some of the general implications of the shift from oral-aural to print culture were examined by Walter Ong in *The Presence of the Word: Some Prolegomena for Cultural and Religious History* (New York: Simon & Schuster, 1970). On the question of literature's emergence as a commodity during the Mid-Victorian period, see Michael Gilmore, *American Romanticism and the Marketplace* (Chicago: University of Chicago Press, 1985); and Catherine Quoyser, "Literature as Commodity: The Fruit and Flower Festival of 1855" (chap. 1 in a forthcoming dissertation entitled "'Fugitives and Standards': Journalism and the Commodification of Literature in Antebellum America" ; Stanford University).

16 This idea was suggested to me in a conversation with Jay Fliegelman of Stanford University's English department concerning the illustrations by F. O. Darley for "Rip Van Winkle" in an edition of the story distributed by the American Art Union (1848). The illustrations are highly linear, eschewing the normal picturesque concern with light, shadow, and gradation. As Professor Fliegelman noted, they continually move beyond mere illustration of the text to offer their own implicit

commentary on what is taking place, underscoring certain points suggested by the text, complicating or subverting others. It occurred to me that such illustrations relax the relatively controlled response associated with the picturesque while making far more complex the interplay between text and illustration.

17 Read, *Icon and Idea*, p. 71. Kenneth Clark discussed this expressionist impulse in the work of the sixteenth-century German artists Grunewald and Altdorfer. Of Altdorfer's *St. George,* Clark wrote: "Trees fill every inch of the picture, not the orderly, decorative trees of tapestry landscape, with their gifts of fruit and blossom, but menacing, organic growth, ready to smother and strangle any intruder." *Landscape into Art* (New York: Harper & Row, 1976), p. 75.

18 Price, *Essays on the Nature and Principles of Taste,* p. 77.

19 Reynolds, *Discourses on Art,* p. 143.

20 Ibid., pp. 143–4.

21 John Barrell, *The Political Theory of Painting from Reynolds to Hazlitt: "The Body of the Public"* (New Haven, Conn.: Yale University Press, 1986), p. 55.

22 Quoted in James Collins Moore, "The Storm and the Harvest: The Image of Nature in Mid-Nineteenth Century American Landscape Painting" (Ph.D. diss., Indiana University, 1974), p. 143.

23 Dr. G. Hartwig, *The Polar and Tropical Worlds: A Description of Man and Nature* (Chicago, 1875), p. 515.

24 Rudolph Arnheim, *Art and Visual Perception: A Psychology of the Creative Eye* (Berkeley and Los Angeles: University of California Press, 1974), p. 417.

25 John Ruskin, *Modern Painters II* in *The Works of John Ruskin,* ed. E. T. Cook and Alexander Wedderburn (London: G. Allen, 1903–12), vol. 4, p. 96.

26 Ruskin, *Modern Painters V,* vol. 6, p. 28.

27 Ibid., p. 121.

28 Ortega y Gasset, "On Point of View in the Arts," *Partisan Review* 16 (August 1949): 824.

29 Ralph Waldo Emerson, *The Complete Works of Ralph Waldo Emerson* (centenary ed.) (Boston: Houghton Mifflin, 1903), vol. 1, p. 67.

30 Uvedale Price, *A Letter to Humphrey Repton . . .* (London, 1798), pp. 178–9.

31 The concept of luminism was pioneered by John I. H. Baur in "American Luminism," *Perspectives USA,* no. 9 (Autumn 1954): 90–8. It was further developed by Barbara Novak in *American Painting of the Nineteenth Century: Realism, Idealism, and the American Experience* (New York: Praeger, 1969), pp. 92–137. Novak attributed to luminist painting such characteristics as horizontal framing, lack of drama, homogeneous emphasis (lack of subordination of parts), high ratio of sky to ground, anonymity of the artist, and the effect of light that, rather than creating a sense of action, "produces a mirror-like plane that both disappears and assumes a glass-like tangibility" (p. 122). See also the exhibition catalogue, *American Light: The Luminist Movement, 1850–1875* (Washington, D.C.: National Gallery, 1979).

32 In *Nature,* Emerson wrote, "Things are ultimates, and they never look beyond their sphere. The presence of reason mars this faith. The first effort of thought tends to relax this despotism of the senses, which binds us to nature as if we were a part of it, and shows us nature aloof, and, as it were, afloat. Until this higher agency intervened, the animal eye sees, with wonderful accuracy, sharp outlines and coloured surfaces. When the eye of reason opens, to outline and surface are at once added grace and expression. These proceed from imagination and affection, and abate somewhat of the angular distinctness of objects. If the Reason be stimulated to more earnest vision, outlines and surfaces become transparent, and are no longer seen. . . . " Emerson; *The Complete Works,* vol. 1, pp. 49–50.

33 Katherine Manthorne sees the pressure on Church to move away from exact treatment as coming from his audience: "Gradually some of Church's critics began to voice the opinion that some element was missing from his tropical pictures: Paradise required not so much scientific illustration as dreamy, poetic evocation." "The Quest for a Tropical Paradise," *Art Journal* 44 (Winter, 1984): 380. Relevant to this tendency to shift back to a generalized, Claudian treatment on Church's part is Henry T. Tuckerman's comment: "Quite diverse from the exactitude and vivid forest tints of many of our Eastern painters, are the southern effects so remarkably rendered by Louis R. Mignot, whose nativity, temperament, and taste combine to make him the efficient delineator of tropical atmosphere and vegetation." Quoted by Manthorne, "The Quest," p. 380. The tension between the scientific and the romantic treatment of the swamp or jungle runs throughout the Mid-Victorian period and reflects the ambiguity of attitude to be expected in any period of transition. It is to some extent paralleled by the contrast between swamp and tropical discussed in the Introduction.

34 James Henry, "Pennsylvania Forest Scenery," *The Crayon*, February 28, 1855, p. 131.

35 Ibid.

36 Ruskin, *Modern Painters II,* vol. 4, p. 46.

37 *The Crayon,* February 14, 1855, p. 98.

38 *The Crayon,* January 31, 1855, p. 66.

39 Bryan Jay Wolf, in *Romantic Re-Vision: Culture and Consciousness in Nineteenth-Century American Painting and Literature* (Chicago: University of Chicago Press, 1982), argued at length for Cole's modernism on the basis of a thoroughgoing Freudian and Lacanian reading (pp. 177–236).

40 See "The Bewilderment," in Louis Legrand Noble, *The Life and Works of Thomas Cole,* ed. Elliot S. Vesell (Cambridge, Mass.: Harvard University Press, 1964), pp. 46–51.

41 H. D. Thoreau, *Walden* (New York: Library of America, 1985), p. 422.

42 Ibid.

43 Ong, *The Presence of the Word,* p. 112.

44 Thoreau, *Walden,* p. 422.

45 John Lawson, *History of North Carolina* (London, 1714; reprinted in Richmond: 1937), p. 22.

46 *Harper's New Monthly Magazine* 8 (November 1853): 771.

47 John Muir, *A Thousand-Mile Walk to the Gulf* (Boston: Houghton Mifflin, 1916), p. 90.

48 Gaston Bachelard, *The Poetics of Space,* trans. Maria Jolas (Boston: Beacon Press, 1969), p. 7.

49 Erich Neumann, *Origin and History of Consciousness,* trans. R. F. Hull (Princeton, N.J.: Princeton University Press, 1954), p. 45.

50 See George W. Fredrickson, *The Inner Civil War: Northern Intellectuals and the Crisis of the Union* (New York: Harper & Row, 1965).

51 The article is reprinted in Clarence Gohdes, ed., *Hunting in the Old South: Original Narratives of the Hunters* (Baton Rouge: Louisiana State University Press, 1967), pp. 101–112. Subsequent page numbers are cited in the text.

52 For a similar nightmarish account of being surrounded by alligators in a swamp, see William Bartram, *Travels of William Bartram,* ed. Mark Van Doren (New York: Dover, 1955), pp. 114–23.

53 Solomon Northrup, *Twelve Years a Slave* (New York: 1970), p. 39.

54 Anonymous, "The Rattle-Snake and Its Congeners," *Harper's New Monthly Magazine* 10 (March 1855): p. 473.

55 Ibid., p. 470.

56 Professor Francis DeCaro of Louisiana State University told me that among the published Louisiana folk narratives there is, on the whole, no projection of an image: "At most there may be a reference to part of the action taking place along a bayou or something of the sort." There is apparently little preoccupation with swamps in Cajun and creole songs.

57 Two popular collections of such tales are found in Hubert J. Davis, *The Great Dismal Swamp: Its History, Folklore and Science* (Murfreesboro, N.C.: 1971); and F. Roy Johnson, *Tales from Old Carolina* (Murfreesboro, N.C.: 1965). See also Margaret Davis, "'Great Dismal' Pictures," *South Atlantic Quarterly* 33 (April 1934): 171–84. In her paean to the Little Sorrowful Swamp, Marie Heriot Allan indicated the mixed fear and reverence of the folk toward this region: "The riverfolk believe in a living God who takes note of every misstep, who promises a land of milk and honey for those whose books are balanced. They believe that every bush harbors Satan, or one of his imps like the plat-ans or the boogerman. . . . One thing that never affrights a man of Little Sorrowful is the ghost of a long-dead neighbor. He is truly satisfied that, in time, milk and honey and streets of pure gold would pall upon a man from Big River." Quoted in B. A. Botkin, *A Treasury of Southern Folklore* (New York: Crown, 1949), p. 549.

58 Robert Arnold, *The Dismal Swamp and Lake Drummond* (Norfolk, Va., 1888), pp. 8–10.

59 Johnson, *Tales from Old Carolina*, p. 179.

60 See Chapter 1.

61 For instance, see item 5735 of *The Frank C. Brown Collection of North Carolina Folklore,* vol. 7 (Durham, N.C.: Duke University Press, 1964): "A light in a swamp is a wandering spirit."

62 "Snakeskin bay and toad's eye in it are worn to ward off swamp fever." Item 2306 in ibid., vol. 5. See also Johnson, *Tales from Old Carolina*, p. 230.

63 See Phyllis Allen, "Etiological Theory in America Prior to the Civil War," *Journal of the History of Medicine and Allied Sciences* 2 (1947): 492. Allen noted that the most common of the prevailing theories for the origin of various diseases "were those based on marsh miasma, atmospheric causes, chemical causes, electricity, predisposing causes in the individual, fomites and animalculae."

Chapter 9

1 All references to Herman Melville, *The Confidence-Man: His Masquerade,* are taken from The Northwestern-Newberry Edition (Evanston, Ill.: Northwestern University Press, 1984), pp. 129–30. Reference to "Yellow Jack" should speak for itself. Calvin Edson was the thin man associated with P. T. Barnum.

2 In the preceding chapter Pitch and the P.I.O. man had argued about freedom of the will and whether a "bad" boy may grow up to be a "good" man. Arminian notions of free will had come to dominate American evangelical thought by the 1850s.

3 See Richard Wightman Fox and T. J. Jackson Lears, eds., *The Culture of Consumption: Critical Essays in American History, 1880–1980* (New York: Pantheon, 1983); also Ann Douglas, *The Feminization of American Culture* (New York: Avon, 1977) for important explorations of this problem.

4 The words are those of Thomas Reid in *Essays on the Active Powers of the Human Mind* (Cambridge, Mass.: MIT Press, 1969; originally published in 1788), p. 272.

5 John Locke, *An Essay Concerning Human Understanding,* in *The Works of John Locke* (London, 1875), vol. 2, p. 3.

6 Ibid., p. 2.
7 Paul de Man, "The Epistemology of Metaphor," in *On Metaphor,* ed. Sheldon Sacks (Chicago: University of Chicago Press, 1979), pp. 11–28. De Man considered Locke's denunciation of eloquence and concluded that Locke's theory of language was in fact a theory of tropes, though the philosopher himself would have been the last to admit it (p. 13). Though attempting to ground words in things (simple ideas), Locke's theory was actually semantic rather than semiotic: It established the arbitrariness of words and sounds. The word (or mixed mode) "can be said to produce of and by itself the entity it signifies and that has no equivalence in nature" (p. 19). This leads to the abuse of language, metaphoric language gone mad ("catachresis"), which Locke feared. Ultimately, the mind or subject has no ontological grounding but is reduced to the "metaphor of metaphors" (p. 23). De Man saw Condillac and Kant as finally no more successful in establishing a workable distinction between schematic and symolic hypotheses (p. 24). This led him to the speculation that "if we assume, just for the sake of argument, that these same historians would concede that Locke, Condillac, and Kant can be read as we have here read them, then they would have to conclude that our own literary modernity has reestablished contact with a 'true' Enlightenment that remained hidden from us by a nineteenth-century Romantic and realist epistemology that asserted a reliable rhetoric of the subject or representation. A continuous line could then be said to extend from Locke to Rousseau to Kant and to Nietzsche, a line from which Fichte and Hegel, among others, would very definitely be excluded" (p. 27).

What I trace through the metaphor of infection may be seen as a subterranean line of development of this problem posed by the Enlightenment. In this context, the paronomasia characteristic of *The Confidence-Man* might be seen as a kind of "revenge of the repressed" on the Enlightenment's urge to stabilize the meaning of words, to keep intact the wall between rhetoric and philosophy.
8 Reid, *Essays on the Active Powers,* p. 267.
9 Ibid., p. 170.
10 See William Charvat, *The Origins of American Critical Thought, 1810–1835* (New York: Barnes, 1961); and D. H. Meyer, *The Instructed Conscience: The Shaping of the American National Ethic* (Philadelphia: University of Pennsylvania Press, 1972).
11 See Merrell R. Davis, "Emerson's 'Reason' and the Scottish Philosophers," *New England Quarterly* 17 (1944): 209–28.
12 As Foucault wrote: "One speaks upon the basis of the fabric of the world; one speaks about it to infinity, and each of its signs becomes in turn written matter for further discourse; but each of these stages of discourse is addressed to that primal written word whose return it simultaneously promises and postpones." Michel Foucault, *The Order of Things: An Archaeology of the Human Sciences* (New York: Vintage, 1973), p. 41.
13 Ibid., p. 43.
14 Ibid., p. 42.
15 Kenneth Burke, *A Grammar of Motives* (Berkeley and Los Angeles: University of California Press, 1969), p. 76.
16 As Burke wrote: "Distinctions, we might say, arise out of a great central moltenness, where all is merged. They have been thrown from a liquid center to the surface, where they have congealed. Let one of these crusted distinctions return to its source, and in this alchemic center it may be remade, again becoming molten liquid, and may enter into new combinations, whereat it may be again thrown forth as a new crust, a different distinction." Ibid., p. xix.

17 See Phyllis Allen, "Etiological Theory in America Prior to the Civil War," *Journal of the History of Medicine and Allied Sciences* 2 (1947): 489–520; and Charles E. Rosenberg, *The Cholera Years: The United States in 1832, 1849 and 1866* (Chicago: University of Chicago Press, 1962), especially p. 75.

18 William Gilmore Simms, *New York Mirror*, May 25, 1889. Reprinted in *The Letters of William Gilmore Simms*, ed. Mary C. Simms Oliphant, Alfred Taylor Odell, and T. C. Duncan Eaves (Columbia: University of South Carolina Press, 1954), vol. 1, pp. 142–3.

19 Julius Froebel, *Seven Years' Travel in Central America* (London, 1859), p. 18.

20 For a full account of the history of the dispute over whether the natural environment of the New World was proof of decadence or promise of superiority over the Old, which forms the background for Caldwell's remarks, see Antonello Gerbi, *Dispute of the New World: The History of a Polemic, 1750–1900*, trans. Jeremy Mayle (Pittsburgh: University of Pittsburgh Press, 1973).

21 Charles Caldwell, "An Oration on the Causes of the Difference, in Point of Frequency and Force, Between Two Endemic Diseases of the United States of America, and Those of the Countries of Europe . . . " (Philadelphia, 1802), p. 14.

22 Ibid., p. 15.

23 Ibid., p. 21.

24 Quoted in David B. Tyack, *George Ticknor and the Boston Brahmins* (Cambridge, Mass.: Harvard University Press, 1967), p. 149.

25 Charles Eliot Norton, *Letters of Charles Eliot Norton*, 2 vols. (Boston: Houghton Mifflin, 1913), vol. 1, pp. 121–2.

26 Rosenberg, *The Cholera Years*, p. 166.

27 See ibid., pp. 75–6. Rosenberg noted: "The atmospheric theory was too convenient: flexible and amorphous enough to explain the varied phenomena of the disease, it served also as a weapon against the 'antisocial' and 'antiquated' doctrine of contagion" (p. 76). In 1823, Peter S. Townsend, M. D., justifying his use of the terms *contagion* and *infection* as more or less synonymous, defined the former as "a specific poison or virus, emitted from the body of a person labouring under the disease" while attributing *infection* to "morbific exhalations derived most usually from organic substances, in a state of decomposition. . . . By Infected, I mean that condition of the atmosphere where it is charged with the matter of contagion. . . . " Peter S. Townsend, "An Account of Yellow Fever, as It Prevailed in the City of New York in the Summer and Autumn of 1822" (New York, 1823), p. ix.

28 See Angus Fletcher, *Allegory: The Theory of a Symbolic Mode* (Ithaca, N.Y.: Cornell University Press, 1964), pp. 199–200, note.

29 Quoted in David V. Erdman, *Blake: Prophet Against Empire*, rev. ed. (New York: Doubleday, 1969), p. 57.

30 William Shakespeare, *Twelfth Night*, act 3, sc. 4, line 135.

31 For a careful account of the development of the notion of sympathy among eighteenth-century thinkers, see James Engell, "The Psyche Reaches Out: Sympathy" (chap. 11), in *The Creative Imagination: Enlightenment to Romanticism* (Cambridge, Mass.: Harvard University Press, 1981), pp. 143–60. Jay Fliegelman's *Prodigals and Pilgrims: The American Revolution Against Patriarchal Authority, 1750–1800* (Cambridge, England: Cambridge University Press, 1982) includes a discussion of the rival eighteenth-century theories of sympathy and rational love and explores how a sentimentalized sympathy compromised human rational and emotional autonomy (see especially pp. 230–2).

32 Horace Bushnell, *Christian Nurture* (New Haven, Conn.: Yale University Press, 1967; reprint of 1888 ed.), p. 76.

33 Ibid., p. 71. For a different application of this notion of a pervasive silent influence, as it relates to an organic community, note the passage in Washington Irving's "The Legend of Sleepy Hollow" on the reigning atmosphere of the village that has seen no change: "It is remarkable, that the visionary propensity I have mentioned is not confined to the native inhabitants of the valley, but is unconsciously imbibed by every one who resides there for a time. However wide awake they may have been before they entered that sleepy region, they are sure, in a little time, to inhale the witching influence of the air, and begin to grow imaginative – to dream dreams, and to see apparitions." (New York: Library of America, 1983), p. 1060.

34 Ibid., p. 82.

35 The problem of sincerity in mid-nineteenth-century American culture is discussed at length in Karen Halttunen, *Confidence Men and Painted Women: A Study of Middle-Class Culture in America, 1830–1870* (New Haven, Conn.: Yale University Press, 1982). See also Lionel Trilling, *Sincerity and Authenticity* (Cambridge, Mass.: Harvard University Press, 1972).

36 See especially Robert C. Fuller, *Mesmerism and the American Cure of Souls* (Philadelphia: University of Pennsylvania Press, 1982); Maria M. Tatar, *Spellbound: Studies on Mesmerism and Literature* (Princeton, N.J.: Princeton University Press, 1978), especially chap. 2, "Salvation by Electricity: Science, Poetry and 'Naturphilosophie' "; and Robert Darnton, *Mesmerism and the End of the Enlightenment in France* (Cambridge, Mass.: Harvard University Press, 1968).

37 J. Stanley Grimes, *Etherology and the Phreno-Philosophy of Mesmerism and Magic-Eloquence* (Boston, 1850), especially pp. 28, 74.

38 *The Univercoelum and Spiritual Philosopher,* vols. 1 and 2 (New York, 1848), p. 297.

39 Horace Bushnell, *Sermons for the New Life* (New York, 1859), p. 189.

40 J. H. Jung-Stilling, *Theory of Pneumatology . . .*, ed. George Bush (New York, 1851; first American ed.), p. 28.

41 Ibid., p. 23.

42 Ibid.

43 Grimes, *Etherology*, p. 81.

44 For this background, see Barton L. St. Armand, " 'Seemingly Intuitive Leaps': Belief and Unbelief in *Eureka*," *American Transcendental Quarterly* 26 (Spring 1975): especially pp. 5–6.

45 Michael Davitt Bell, *The Development of American Romance: The Sacrifice of Relation* (Chicago: University of Chicago Press, 1930), pp. 93–4. Bell's suggestive discussion of Poe strongly influenced my own thinking.

46 Anonymous, *The Parents' Great Commission* (London, 1851), p. 113.

47 Quoted in Herbert Ross Brown, *The Sentimental Novel in America, 1789–1869* (Durham, N.C.: Duke University Press, 1940), p. 84.

48 Charles Brockden Brown, *Ormond, or The Secret Witness* (bicentennial ed.) (Kent, Ohio: Kent State University Press, 1982), p. 71.

49 Nathaniel Hawthorne, *The Marble Faun or the Romance of Monte Beni* in *Works* (centenary ed.) (Columbus: Ohio State University Press, 1968), p. 326.

50 Henry James, *Daisy Miller,* in *The Novels and Tales of Henry James* (New York: Scribner, 1909), vol. 18, p. 85.

51 Hawthorne, *The Marble Faun*, p. 237.

52 Washington Irving, "Adventure of the Mysterious Picture," in *Tales of a Traveller* (London: John Murray, 1824), p. 91.

53 Ibid., pp. 92–3.

54 Edgar Allan Poe, "The Fall of the House of Usher," in *The Complete Works of*

Edgar Allan Poe, ed. James A. Harrison (New York: AMS Press, 1965), vol. 3, p. 276.

55 Ibid., p. 274.

56 Ibid., p. 290.

57 Leo Spitzer, *Essay in English and American Literature* (Princeton, N.J.: Princeton University Press, 1968), p. 60. See also Leo Spitzer, "Milieu and Ambience," in *Essays in Historical Semantics* (New York: S. F. Vanni, 1968), pp. 179–225. Spitzer believes that "we cannot understand the achievement of Poe unless we place his concept of atmospheric within the framework of ideas concerning *milieu* and *ambiance* which were being formulated at the time" (*Essays in English and American Literature,* p. 62).

58 Harold Bloom, *Shelley's Mythmaking* (Ithaca, N.Y.: Cornell University Press, 1969), p. 159.

59 Percy Bysshe Shelley, *The Poetical Works of Percy Bysshe Shelley,* ed. Henry Buxton Forman (London: Reeves & Turner, 1876), vol. 2, pp. 267–80.

60 Allen Tate, "The Angelic Imagination," in *Essays of Four Decades* (New York: Morrow, 1968), p. 401.

61 Poe, *The Complete Works,* vol. 6, p. 142.

62 As Kenneth Burke pointed out, the word *substance* is used to designate what some thing or agent intrinsically is; "yet etymologically, 'substance' is a scenic word – literally, a person's or thing's substance would be something that stands beneath or supports the person or thing." Burke, *A Grammar of Motives,* p. 21. In other words, "though used to designate something *within* the thing, *intrinsic* to it, the word etymologically refers to something *outside* the thing, *extrinsic* to it. Or otherwise put: the word in its etymological origins would refer to an attribute of the thing's *context,* since that which supports or underlies a thing would be a part of the thing's context. And a thing's context, being outside or beyond the thing, would be something that the thing is *not*" (p. 23). As Burke concluded, "Here is a strategic moment, an alchemical moment, wherein momentous miracles of transformation can take place – for here the intrinsic and the extrinsic can change places" (p. 24). This is precisely the condition under which values exchange places in the linguistic realm we have been considering. Interestingly, Burke cited Locke on the fictional status of "substance": "The idea, then, we have, to which we give the *general* name substance, being nothing but the supposed, but unknown support of those qualities we find existing, which we imagine cannot subsist *sine re substante,* 'without something to support them,' we call that support *substantia;* which according to the true import of the word, is, in plain English, standing under, or upholding" (p. 21).

63 Carolyn Porter, *Seeing and Being: The Plight of the Participant Observer in Emerson, James, Adams, and Faulkner* (Middletown, Conn.: Wesleyan University Press, 1981), especially pp. 76–7. Porter drew on Raymond Williams for her definition of the hegemonic process of capitalism, one that is relevant here: a "dominant culture... at once produces and limits its own forms of counter culture." Raymond Williams, *Marxism and Literature* (New York: Oxford University Press, 1977), p. 114. Although Williams is specifically concerned with the role of landscape gardening, the point is relevant to the role here of the imagery of infection. The transformation it helped wreak on the conception of agency, if at one level a genuine "return of the repressed," is at a deeper level a reflection of the power of the hegemonic value structure to shape its opposition and, in this case, largely to neutralize it as a force. For the most part, the imagery we have been examining complies with the system's demands. Williams went on to acknowledge, nonetheless, that "there can be areas of experience [the hegemonic

process] is willing to ignore or dispense with; to assign as private or to specialize as aesthetic or to generalize as natural" (p. 24). Such areas demarcate the creative or liminal areas of the culture, out of which all genuinely creative and subversive imagery comes.

64 Similarly, as Henry Sussman pointed out in discussing *The Confidence-Man:* "The debunkers who arise to battle the operators' claims turn out to be fellow operators, just as the most duplicitous discoursers profess the most extreme sort of prudery." Henry Sussman, "The Deconstructor As Politician: Melville's *Confidence-Man,*" *Glyph* 4 (Baltimore: Johns Hopkins University Press, 1978), p. 39.

65 Ironically, the tradition of *ut pictura poesis,* the notion that literature and art should be seen as analogous to each other (as conceived within the empiricist tradition) supported the idea that the visual was "natural" whereas words were conventional, thus giving credence to the notion of difference between text and picture that Melville, in *The Confidence-Man,* was debunking. W. J. T. Mitchell characterized the notion of the image held by empiricists from Hobbes to Locke to Hume as "an automatic, necessary, and transparently accurate tran-scription of reality that forms the basis of ideas and, in turn, the basis of words." Mitchell also noted that "the pictorialist aesthetic of European neoclas-sicism, the claim that a poem is a 'speaking picture' in a rather strong and lit-eral sense, is grounded in the notion of the mind as a storehouse of images and language as a system of retrieving those images. The very possibility of com-munication is understood as based in the 'universal language' that underlies the local and limited languages of human speech." W. J. T. Mitchell, *Iconology: Im-age, Text, Ideology* (Chicago: University of Chicago Press, 1986), p. 121. Mel-ville, through Pitch, appears to be suggesting against this tradition that images, like language, are conventional, not natural.

66 Once again, I must express my indebtedness to Michael Davitt Bell's *The Devel-opment of American Romance: The Sacrifice of Relation* (Chicago: University of Chi-cago Press, 1980) in making this formulation.

Chapter 10

1 William Byrd, *The Prose Works of William Byrd of Westover,* ed. Louis B. Wright (Cambridge, Mass.: Harvard University Press, 1966), p. 183. Subsequent page references are cited in the text.

2 David Wagoner, "Wading in a Marsh," *Poetry Magazine* 133 (January 1979): 192–3.

3 Kenneth Burke, "The Vegetal Radicalism of Theodore Roethke," in *Language As Symbolic Action: Essays on Life, Literature, and Method* (Berkeley and Los Angeles: University of California Press, 1968), p. 254.

4 Walt Whitman, *An American Primer,* ed. Horace Traubel (San Francisco: City Lights Books, 1970).

5 Roderick Nash, *Wilderness and the American Mind* (New Haven, Conn.: Yale Uni-versity Press, 1970), p. 16.

6 Edward Johnson, *Johnson's Wonder-working Providence: 1628–1651,* ed. J. Franklin Jameson (New York: Barnes & Noble, 1967), p. 112.

7 Richard Slotkin, *Regeneration Through Violence: The Mythology of the American Fron-tier, 1600–1860* (Middletown, Conn: Wesleyan University Press, 1973), p. 218.

8 H. D. Thoreau, *The Writings of Henry David Thoreau* (New York: Houghton Mifflin, 1968), vol. 5, pp. 205–48. Subsequent page numbers are cited in the text.

9 Ralph Waldo Emerson, *The Complete Works of Ralph Waldo Emerson* (centenary ed.) (Boston: Houghton Mifflin, 1903), vol. 5, p. 288. In a journal entry dated September 13, 1837, Emerson pointed to the implications of American scenery

for American art: "The American artist who would carve a wood-god, and who was familiar with the forest in Maine, where enormous fallen pine trees 'cumber the forest floor,' where huge masses depending from the trees and the mass of the timber give a savage and haggard strength to the grove, would produce a very different statue from the sculptor who only knows a European woodland – the tasteful Greek, for example."

10 See Antonello Gerbi, *Dispute of the New World: The History of a Polemic, 1750–1900,* trans. Jeremy Mayle (Pittsburgh: University of Pittsburgh Press, 1973).

11 Horace Bushnell, *Nature and the Supernatural* (New York, 1858), p. 192.

12 See Walter Harding, *The Days of Henry Thoreau* (New York: Knopf, 1965), p. 286.

13 Sherman Paul, *The Shores of America: Thoreau's Inward Exploration* (Urbana: University of Illinois Press, 1958), p. 76.

14 It is this attitude that is behind Thoreau's assertion, in a letter to Harrison Blake: "I see less difference between a city and a swamp than formerly. It is a swamp, however, too dismal and dreary even for me, and I should be glad if there were fewer owls, and frogs, and mosquitoes in it. I prefer ever a more cultivated place, free from miasma and crocodiles. I am so sophisticated and I take my choice." *The Writings,* vol. 6, p. 185; entry dated August 9, 1850.

15 Ibid, vol. 3, p. 257.

16 Ralph Waldo Emerson, *The Journals and Miscellaneous Notebooks of Ralph Waldo Emerson* (Cambridge, Mass.: Harvard University Press, 1978), vol. 9, p. 203, letter dated May 1, 1858.

17 Quoted by Carl Bode in his introduction to *The Portable Thoreau* (New York: Viking, 1964), p. 8.

18 Emerson, *The Complete Works,* vol. 2, p. 321.

19 See F. O. Matthiessen, *American Renaissance: Art and Expression in the Age of Emerson and Whitman* (New York: Oxford University Press, 1968), especially the chapter "New England Landscapes," pp. 157–66.

20 Ralph Waldo Emerson, *Journals of Ralph Waldo Emerson,* ed. Edward Waldo Emerson and Waldo Emerson Forbes, vol. 8 (Boston: Houghton Mifflin, 1904), pp. 294–5; June 7, 1852. On another occasion (September 4, 1857), Emerson took note of "a valuable walk through the savage, fertile, houseless land, where we saw pigeons and marsh hawks, and ere we left it, the mists, which denote the haunt of the elder gods rising." *Journals,* vol. 9, p. 113.

21 *Journals,* vol. 9, p. 59.

22 Ibid., pp. 58–9.

23 Thoreau, *The Writings,* vol. 7, pp. 141–2; entry dated June 15, 1840.

24 David Porter, *Emerson and Literary Change* (Cambridge, Mass.: Harvard University Press, 1978), p. 134.

25 Carolyn Porter, *Seeing and Being: The Plight of the Participant Observer in Emerson, James, Adams, and Faulkner* (Middletown, Conn.: Wesleyan University Press, 1981), pp. 105–7.

26 Emerson, *The Complete Works,* vol. 6, p. 32. Related to this is Sherman Paul's point that for Emerson, "reason, as the faculty in which the spirit had its life, that is, as the faculty capable of self-intuition or philosophic imagination, of reading the symbol, expressed its penetration into the spirit behind objects and events by means of ideas." Sherman Paul, *Emerson's Angle of Vision* (Cambridge, Mass.: Harvard University Press, 1952), p. 47.

27 Ibid., p. 22.

28 Matthiessen, *American Renaissance,* p. 87. In his journal, Thoreau demonstrated his realization of the importance of immersion: "If we only see clearly how mean our lives are, they will be splendid enough. Let us remember not to strive upwards

too long, but sometimes drop plumb down the other way, and wallow in mean-ness. From the deepest pit we may see the stars, if not the sun. Let us have presence of mind enough to sink when we can't swim. At any rate, a carcass had better lie on the bottom than float an offense to all nostrils. It will not be falling, for we shall ride wide of the earth's gravity as a star, and always be drawn upward still . . . and so, by yielding to universal gravity, at length become fixed stars." Thoreau, *The Writings*, vol. 7, p. 146.

29 Paul, *Emerson's Angle of Vision,* pp. 63–4.
30 Emerson, *The Complete Works*, vol. 2, pp. 319–20.
31 Paul, *Emerson's Angle of Vision*, p. 101.
32 Thoreau, *The Writings*, vol. 3, p. 198.
33 Ibid., p. 200.
34 Ibid., pp. 200–1.
35 Ibid., p. 201.
36 Porter, *Seeing and Being*, p. 113.
37 Thoreau, *The Writings,* vol. 9, pp. 495–6.

Chapter 11

1 For many insights into the connection between the work of Thoreau and Heade, particularly with regard to the question of technique, I am indebted to my teacher Barton St. Armand (Brown University) and to his article, "Luminism in the Work of Henry David Thoreau: An Experiment in Cultural Transliteration," *Canadian Review of American Studies* 2 (Spring 1980): 13–30.

2 See Barbara Novak, *American Painting of the Nineteenth Century: Realism, Idealism and the American Experience* (New York: Praeger, 1969), pp. 122–3.

3 Ralph Waldo Emerson, *The Complete Works of Ralph Waldo Emerson* (centenary ed.) (Boston: Houghton Mifflin, 1903), vol. 2, p. 50.

4 Quoted in John Higham, *From Boundlessness to Consolidation: The Transformation of American Culture 1848–1860* (Ann Arbor, Mich.: William L. Clements Library, 1969), p. 6.

5 See Theodore E. Stebbins, Jr., *The Life and Works of Martin Johnson Heade* (New Haven, Conn.: Yale University Press, 1975) for an informative analysis contrasting Heade's painting with a work of the same title by John Kensett (pp. 36–9). Al-though Heade adopted essentially the same composition as the Hudson River painter did, as Stebbins pointed out, his presentation gains its disturbing quality from its tight construction, extreme clarity, excessive horizontality, and a much broader color spectrum, compared with Kensett's painting.

6 See Stebbins, *The Life and Works,* for a comprehensive compilation of what is known of the man and a sensitive analysis of his work.

7 See Higham, *From Boundlessness to Consolidation*, p. 2.

8 Martin Johnson Heade, "Exterminatory Peregrinations," *Forest and Stream,* June 10, 1899, p. 446.

9 Ibid., p. 446.

10 Francis Parkman, *The Journals of Francis Parkman,* ed. Mason Wade, 2 vols. (New York: Harper, 1947), vol. 1, p. 31. Parkman made his trip to the White Mountains and Maine in the summer of 1841.

11 Ibid., p. 52.

12 Ibid., p. 55.

13 Higham, *From Boundlessness to Consolidation,* p. 2. Parkman's La Salle, for instance, was the very type of the hunter: tough, dedicated, fearless, and alone.

14 Martin Johnson Heade, "On the Chagres River," *Forest and Stream,* September 23, 1899, p. 244.

15 Herman Melville, *Moby-Dick, or, the Whale,* ed. Charles Feidelson (New York: Bobbs-Merrill, 1964), p. 311.

16 See Erich Neumann *The Origin and History of Consciousness,* trans. R. F. Hull (Princeton, N.J.: Princeton University Press, 1954), p. 41.

17 Unless otherwise noted, Tuckerman's poems are from N. Scott Momaday, ed., *The Complete Poems of Frederick Goddard Tuckerman* (New York: Oxford University Press, 1965).

18 See Frederick Goddard Tuckerman, *Poems* (Boston, 1860).

19 For information about Tuckerman's life and a lengthy discussion of his poetry, see Samuel H. Golden, *Frederick Goddard Tuckerman* (Boston: Twayne, 1966).

20 I am here following Golden's impressionistic dating in *Frederick Goddard Tuckerman.* Eugene England, in "Tuckerman's Sonnet I, 10: The First Post-Symbolic Poem," *Southern Review* 12 (1976): 323–47, made a good case for placing this sonnet shortly after the death of Tuckerman's wife.

21 William James, *The Varieties of Religious Experience* (New York: Collier Books, 1972), p. 132.

22 Reproductions of these paintings may be found in the catalogue section of Stebbins, *The Life and Works.* They are numbered 110, 112, and 36, respectively.

23 No. 58 in Stebbins's catalogue.

24 T. W. Higginson, "My Out-Door Study," *Atlantic Monthly* 8 (September 1861): 5.

25 Gaston Bachelard, *The Poetics of Space,* trans. Maria Jolas (Boston: Beacon Press, 1969), p. 5.

26 In "Nature," Emerson wrote: "To the attentive eye, each moment of the year has its own beauty; and in the same field, it beholds, every hour, a picture which was never seen before, and which shall never be seen again. The heavens change every moment, and reflect their glory or gloom on the plains beneath. . . . The succession of native plants in the pastures and roadsides, which makes the silent clock by which time tells the summer hours, will make even the divisions of the day sensible to a keen observer." *The Complete Works,* vol. 1, p. 18.

27 T. W. Higginson, "The Procession of Flowers," *Atlantic Monthly* 10 (December 1861): 656.

28 See Erich Neumann, *The Origin and History of Consciousness,* p. 36.

Chapter 12

1 Lafcadio Hearn, "Philosophy of Imaginative Art," in *An American Miscellany,* ed. Albert Mordell (New York: 1924), vol. 2, pp. 30–2.

2 Hearn, "A Concord Compromise," in *An American Miscellany,* vol, 2. pp. 139–41.

3 Hearn, "The Great 'I Am,' " in *An American Miscellany,* vol. 2, pp. 134–5.

4 Sidney Lanier, *The Science of English Verse, in The Centennial Edition of the Works of Sidney Lanier,* ed. Paul Franklin Baum (Baltimore: Johns Hopkins University Press, 1945), vol. 2, pp. 194–5.

5 See letter to Mary Day Lanier, dated March 15, 1874, in Lanier, *Works of Sidney Lanier,* vol. 9, pp. 39–40.

6 To Bayard Taylor, Lanier wrote: "Emerson, who I have been reading all winter, gives me immeasurable delight because he does not propound to me disagreeable systems and hideous creeds but simply walks along high and bright ways where one loves to go with him." Lanier, *Works of Sidney Lanier,* vol. 1, p. 446.

7   See letter to Bayard Taylor dated February 2, 1878, in Lanier, *Works of Sidney Lanier,* vol. 10, p. 18.

8   See letter to Walt Whitman dated May 5, 1878, in Lanier, *Works of Sidney Lanier,* vol. 10, p. 40. Comparing Whitman and Lanier, E. C. Stedman wrote: "It is manifest that the two (as near and as different as Valentine and Orson) were moving in the same direction; that is, for an escape from conventional trammels to something free, from hackneyed time-beats to an assimilation of nature's larger rhythm – to limitless harmonies suggested by the voices of her winds and the diapason of her ocean billows." Quoted in Norman Foerster, *Nature in American Literature: Studies in the Modern View of Nature* (New York: 1923), p. 126.

9   See letter to Clifford Lanier dated July 21, 1873, in Lanier, *Works of Sidney Lanier,* vol. 8, p. 314.

10   Quoted by Charles R. Anderson in his notes to "The Marshes of Glynn," in Sidney Lanier, *Poems and Letters* (Baltimore: Johns Hopkins University Press, 1969), p. 81.

11   See Lanier, "Nature-Metaphors," in *Works of Sidney Lanier,* vol. 5, p. 308.

12   Ibid., p. 306.

13   Ibid., p. 308.

14   Ibid., p. 309.

15   Hearn, *An American Miscellany,* vol. 2, pp. 103–4.

16   Ibid., pp. 104–5.

17   Lanier, "The Maryland Music Festival" (1878), in *Works of Sidney Lanier,* vol. 2, p. 321.

18   Robert Penn Warren, "The Blind Poet: Sidney Lanier," *American Review* 2 (November 1933): 38; quoted in Robert H. Ross, 'The Marshes of Glynn': A Study in Symbolic Obscurity," *American Literature* 32 (January 1961): 403–16.

19   Hearn, "The Life of Stars," in *An American Miscellany,* vol. 2, p. 123. (First published in the *Times-Democrat,* February 18, 1883.)

20   Lafcadio Hearn, *Chita: A Memory of Last Island,* ed. Arlin Turner (Chapel Hill: University of North Carolina Press, 1969), p. 28.

21   Hearn, "Torn Letters," in *An American Miscellany,* vol. 2, p. 57.

22   Hearn *Chita,* p. 26.

23   Lafcadio Hearn, *Two Years in the French West Indies* (New York: 1923), pp. 47–8.

24   Ibid., p. 49.

25   In *Two Years in the French West Indies,* Hearn wrote: "There is a something unutterable in this bright Gulf-air that compels awe, – something vital, something holy, something pantheistic: and reverentially the mind asks itself if what the eye beholds is not . . . indeed, the Infinite Breath, the Divine Ghost, the Great Blue Soul of the Unknown. All, all is blue in the calm, – save the low land under your feet" (pp. 20–1).

26   Quoted in Elizabeth Stevenson, *Lafcadio Hearn* (New York: Macmillan, 1961), p. 138.

27   Hearn, "The Great 'I Am' " in *An American Miscellany,* vol. 2, p. 135.

28   Hearn, *Two Years in the French West Indies,* pp. 7–8.

29   Hearn, *Chita,* p. 17.

30   Hearn, "The Life of Stars," in *An American Miscellany,* vol. 2, p. 124.

31   Hearn, *Two Years in the French West Indies,* p. 68.

32   Lafcadio Hearn, *The Selected Writings of Lafcadio Hearn,* ed. Henry Goodman (New York: Citadel, 1949), p. 512.

33   Ibid., p. 513.

34   Ibid., p. 515.

35   Ibid., p. 516.

36 Ibid., p. 517.
37 Ibid., p. 521.

Conclusion

1 Georg Lukács, "Reification and the Consciousness of the Proletariat," in *History and Class Consciousness,* trans. Rodney Livingstone (Cambridge, Mass.: MIT Press, 1971), pp. 185–6.
2 Katherine Anne Porter. *The Collected Stories of Katherine Anne Porter* (New York: Harcourt Brace Jovanovich, 1979), pp. 298–9. Subsequent page references are cited in the text.
3 Herman Melville, *Pierre, or the Ambiguities* (Evanston, Ill., and Chicago: Northwestern University Press and the Newberry Library, 1971), p. 342. Subsequent page references are cited in the text.

Selected Bibliography

Abrams, M. H. *The Mirror and the Lamp: Romantic Theory and the Critical Tradition.* New York: Norton, 1953.

Alison, Archibald. *Essays on the Nature and Principles of Taste.* Boston, 1812.

Allen, Phyllis. "Etiological Theory in America Prior to the Civil War." *Journal of the History of Medicine and Allied Sciences* 2 (1947): 489–520.

Bachelard, Gaston. *The Poetics of Space.* Translated by Maria Jolas. Boston: Beacon Press, 1969.

Bartram, William. *Travels of William Bartram.* Edited by Mark Van Doren. New York: Dover, 1955.

Bell, Michael Davitt. *The Development of American Romance: The Sacrifice of Relation.* Chicago: University of Chicago Press, 1980.

Botkin, B. A. *A Treasury of Southern Folklore.* New York: Crown, 1949.

Bozeman, Theodore Dwight. *Protestants in an Age of Science: The Baconian Ideal and Antebellum Religious Thought.* Chapel Hill: University of North Carolina Press, 1977.

Bryant, William Cullen, ed. *Picturesque America: The Land We Live In.* 2 vols. New York, 1872–4.

Burke, Edmund. *A Philosophical Enquiry into the Origin of Our Ideas of the Sublime and Beautiful.* Edited by J. T. Boulton. Notre Dame, Ind.: Notre Dame University Press, 1968.

Burke, Kenneth. *A Grammar of Motives.* Berkeley and Los Angeles: University of California Press, 1969.

Byrd, William. *The Prose Works of William Byrd of Westover.* Edited by Louis B. Wright. Cambridge, Mass.: Harvard University Press, 1966.

Charvat, William. *The Origins of American Critical Thought, 1810–1835.* New York: Barnes, 1961.

Chopin, Kate. *The Complete Works of Kate Chopin.* Edited by Per Seyersted. Baton Rouge: Louisiana State University Press, 1969.

Coleridge, Samuel Taylor. *Biographia Literaria or Biographical Sketches of My Literary Life and Opinions.* Edited by George Watson. New York: Dutton, 1975.

Davidson, Edward H. *Poe, A Critical Study.* Cambridge, Mass.: Harvard University Press, 1957.

Douglas, Ann. *The Feminization of American Culture.* New York: Avon, 1977.

Douglas, Mary. *Purity and Danger: An Analysis of the Concepts of Pollution and Taboo.* London: Routledge & Kegan Paul, 1978.

Eaton, Clement. *The Mind of the Old South.* Rev. ed. Baton Rouge: Louisiana State University Press, 1967.

Eby, Cecil D., Jr., ed. *The Old South Illustrated by Porte Crayon.* Chapel Hill: University of North Carolina Press, 1959.

Ehrenzweig, Anton. *The Hidden Order of Art: A Study in the Psychology of Artistic Imagination.* Berkeley and Los Angeles: University of California Press, 1967.

Emerson, Ralph Waldo. *The Complete Works of Ralph Waldo Emerson.* Centenary ed. Boston: Houghton Mifflin, 1903.

   Journals of Ralph Waldo Emerson. Edited by Edward Waldo Emerson and Waldo Emerson Forbes. Boston: Houghton Mifflin, 1904–14.

Fletcher, Angus. *Allegory: The Theory of a Symbolic Mode.* Ithaca, N.Y.: Cornell University Press, 1964.

Forgie, George. *Patricide in the House Divided: A Psychological Interpretation of Lincoln and His Age.* New York: Norton, 1979.

Froebel, Julius. *Seven Years' Travel in Central America.* London, 1859.

Gerbi, Antonello. *Dispute of the New World: The History of a Polemic, 1750–1900.* Translated by Jeremy Mayle. Pittsburgh: University of Pittsburgh Press, 1973.

Halttunen, Karen. *Confidence Men and Painted Women: A Study of Middle-Class Culture in America, 1830–1870.* New Haven, Conn.: Yale University Press, 1982.

Higham, John. *From Boundlessness to Consolidation: The Transformation of American Culture, 1848–1860.* Ann Arbor, Mich.: William L. Clements Library, 1969.

Hovenkamp, Herbert. *Science and Religion in America, 1800–1860.* Philadelphia: University of Pennsylvania Press, 1978.

Humboldt, Alexander von. *Cosmos: A Sketch of a Physical Description of the Universe.* 2 vols. New York, 1850.

Huntington, David C. *The Landscapes of Frederic Edwin Church: Vision of an American Era.* New York: Braziller, 1966.

Kuklick, Bruce. "Myth and Symbol in American Studies." *American Quarterly* 24 (October 1972): 435–50.

Lanier, Sidney. *Florida.* In *The Centennial Edition of the Works of Sidney Lanier.* Edited by Philip Graham. Baltimore: Johns Hopkins University Press, 1945.

Lindquist-Cock, Elizabeth. *The Influence of Photography on American Landscape Painting.* New York: Garland, 1977.

Lukács, Georg. "Reification and the Consciousness of the Proletariat." In *History and Class Consciousness.* Translated by Rodney Livingstone. Cambridge, Mass.: MIT Press, 1971.

McKinsey, Elizabeth. *Niagara Falls: Icon of the American Sublime.* Cambridge, England: Cambridge University Press, 1985.

McLoughlin, William. *The Meaning of Henry Ward Beecher: An Essay on the Shifting Values of Mid-Victorian America, 1840–1870.* New York: Knopf, 1970.

McLuhan, Marshall, and Harley Parker. *Through the Vanishing Point: Space in Poetry and Painting.* New York: Harper & Row, 1968.

Matthiessen, F. O. *American Renaissance: Art and Expression in the Age of Emerson and Whitman.* New York: Oxford University Press, 1968.

Melville, Herman. *The Piazza Tales and Other Prose Pieces, 1839–1860.* Evanston, Ill., and Chicago: Northwestern University Press and the Newberry Library, 1987.

Mitchell, W. J. T. *Iconology: Image, Text, Ideology.* Chicago: University of Chicago Press, 1986.

Moore, James Collins. "The Storm and the Harvest: The Image of Nature in Mid-

Nineteenth Century American Landscape Painting." Ph.D. diss., Indiana University, 1974.

Muir, John. *A Thousand-Mile Walk to the Gulf.* Boston: Houghton Mifflin, 1916.

Nash, Roderick. *Wilderness and the American Mind.* New Haven, Conn.: Yale University Press, 1970.

Neumann, Erich. *The Origin and History of Consciousness.* Translated by R. F. Hull. Princeton N.J.: Princeton University Press, 1954.

Noble, Louis Legrand. *The Life and Works of Thomas Cole.* Edited by Elliot S. Vesell. Cambridge, Mass.: Harvard University Press, 1964.

Novak, Barbara. *American Painting of the Nineteenth Century: Realism, Idealism and the American Experience.* New York: Praeger, 1969.

    Nature and Culture: American Landscape and Painting. New York: Oxford University Press, 1980.

Ong, Walter. *The Presence of the Word: Some Prologomena for Cultural and Religious History.* New York: Simon & Schuster, 1970.

Peck, H. Daniel. *A World by Itself: The Pastoral Moment in Cooper's Fiction.* New Haven, Conn.: Yale University Press, 1977.

Poe, Edgar Allan. *The Complete Works of Edgar Allan Poe.* Edited by James A. Harrison. New York: Crowell, 1965.

Porter, Carolyn. *Seeing and Being: The Plight of the Participant Observer in Emerson, James, Adams, and Faulkner.* Middletown, Conn.: Wesleyan University Press, 1981.

Price, Uvedale. *A Letter to H. Repton, Esq. on the Application of the Practice as Well as the Principles of Landscape-Painting to Landscape Gardening.* London, 1798.

Read, Herbert. *Icon and Idea: The Function of Art in the Development of Human Consciousness.* London: Schocken, 1955.

Reynolds, Sir Joshua. *Discourses on Art.* Edited by Stephen O. Mitchell. New York: Bobbs-Merrill, 1965.

Ringe, Donald. *The Pictorial Mode: Space and Time in the Art of Bryant, Irving and Cooper.* Lexington: University of Kentucky Press, 1971.

Ruskin, John. *The Works of John Ruskin.* Edited by E. T. Cook and Alexander Wedderburn. London, 1903–12.

Simms, William Gilmore. *The Letters of William Gilmore Simms.* Edited by Mary Simms Oliphant, Alfred Taylor Odell, and T. C. Duncan Eaves. Columbia: University of South Carolina Press, 1954.

Slotkin, Richard. *Regeneration Through Violence: The Mythology of the American Frontier, 1600–1860.* Middletown, Conn.: Wesleyan University Press, 1973.

Smith, Henry Nash. *Democracy and the Novel: Popular Responses to Classic American Writers.* New York: Oxford University Press, 1977.

Stein, Roger. *John Ruskin and Aesthetic Thought in America.* Cambridge, Mass.: Harvard University Press, 1967.

Stowe, Harriet Beecher. *Dred, A Tale of the Dismal Swamp.* 2 vols. Boston, 1856.

Taylor, William R. *Cavalier and Yankee: The Old South and American National Character.* Garden City, N.Y.: Doubleday, 1963.

Thoreau, Henry David. *The Writings of Henry David Thoreau.* Boston: Houghton Mifflin, 1906.

Tuckerman, Henry T. *The Book of the Artists.* New York: J. F. Carr, 1966; first published in 1867.

Turner, Victor. *Dramas, Fields, and Metaphors: Symbolic Action in Human Society.* Ithaca, N.Y.: Cornell University Press, 1974.

Wilmerding, John, et al. *American Light: The Luminist Movement, 1850–1875.* Exhibition catalogue. Washington, D.C.: National Gallery, 1979.

Winthrop, Theodore. *Life in the Open Air and Other Papers.* Boston, 1863.

Index

Abbott, Jacob, *Memoirs of the Holy Land*, 125
Abraham, 100
Acheron, 50
Adams, Henry, 72
Agassiz, Louis, 109, 118
Agassiz, Mrs. Louis, 120
Alison, Archibald, 133, 135–7, 159, 161; Alisonian associationism, 133, 143; *see also* associationism
Allston, Washington, 112; *Elijah in the Wilderness*, 112; *Moonlit Landscape*, 172
American Medical Association, 191
American Revolution, 44, 192
American romance tradition, 196–9
Andes mountains, 107, 124, 126
animal magnetism, 15, 196
Ariel, 47
Arnheim, Rudolph, 161
Arnold, Robert, 182
Arriola, Fortunato, 72; *Moon over Lake Nicaragua*, 172; 176; *Tropical Landscape* (1870), 74
Arts and Crafts movement, 75
associationism, 133, 135–6, 143
Atchafalaya basin, 64
Atlantic Monthly, 1, 51, 52, 120, 129, 216
Atlantis, 216

Bachelard, Gaston, 4, 5, 52–3, 77, 179, 237; Bachelardian sense, 151
Bachofen, J. J., 15
Baconian ideal, 145
Bailey, Gamaliel, 90
Baker, Page, 252
Bancroft, George, 191
Barrell, John, 160
Bartram, William, 6; *Travels*, 50
beautiful, the, 133
Beecher, Henry Ward, 89, 96; *Norwood*, 89
Beecher, Lyman, 90
Beer, John, 141
Beethoven, Ludwig van, 246–7; *see also* Lanier, Sidney, "From Bacon to Beethoven," 246
Belch, Sir Toby, 192

Beowulf, 47
Bethune, George Washington, 111
Blair, Hugh, 133, 139, 190
Bloom, Harold, 199
Boston, Mass., 230
Bozeman, Theodore Dwight, 145
Bradford, William, 51
Brahma, 239–40
Brazil, 120, 155, 224
Bresdin, Rodolphe, 81; *Eclaircie dans la Foret*, 82
British empirical school, 133
Brooks, Preston, 96
Brown, Brownlee, 146
Brown, Charles Brockden, 125, 196–7; *Edgar Huntly*, 125, 189, 196; *Ormond*, 197
"Brown Decades," 72
Bryant, William Cullen, 59, 126, 136, 140; *Thanatopsis*, 138
Buck, William, 6; *Louisiana Swamp*, 6, 7
Buell, Lawrence, 97
Bunyan, John, 7, 49–50, 262
Burke, Edmund, 10, 109, 133, 140; *Burkean sublime, 134 (see also* sublime); Burkean theory, 135
Burke, Kenneth, 189, 209; "grammar of motives," 201
Bush, Norton, 72; *Misty Day in the Tropics*, 73
Bushnell, Horace, 136, 196; *Christian Nurture*, 192–3; concept of "unconscious influence," 193; *Nature and the Supernatural*, 215; "Unconscious Influence," 194
Butler, James: *Fortune's Foot-ball*, 197
Byrd, William, 18, 36, 92; *History of the Dividing Line*, 207–8, 210–14

Cain, 92
Cairo, 184
Caldwell, Charles, 190
Caliban, 47
Carlyle, Thomas, 49
Cash, W. J., *The Mind of the South*, 82
Casilear, John, 140
Catskill mountains, 125, 139, 174

Cavalier myth, 71, 103; character, 84; legend, 84; type, 104
Cawelti, John, 130
Chagres River, Panama, 119, 154, 190, 227
Chamber's Edinburgh Journal, 37
Champney, J. Wells, 68
Channing, Ellery, 219
Channing, William Ellery, 225
Chapman, John Gadsby: engraving after *View of the Dismal Swamp*, 30, 31, 38, 183
Charleston, S.C., 83, 84, 190
Charvat, William, 136
Chase, Richard, 96
child rearing, 192, 196
Chiriqui, volcano of, 119
Choate, Rufus, 140
Chopin, Kate: *At Fault*, 45–6
Church, Frederic, 72, 107–17, 118, 124, 126, 129, 130, 140, 163, 224; *Chimborazo*, 110, 115; *Cotopaxi*, 110; *Deep Jungle Foliage*, 116; *Evening in the Tropics*, 165, 167; *The Heart of the Andes*, 107–109, 111, 112–13, 115; *Jungle Scene*, 117; *Morning in the Tropics* (1856), 115; *Morning in the Tropics* (1876), 113–17; *Niagara*, 110; *Rainy Season in the Tropics*, 110; *Tropical Scenery at Night*, 172, 175; *Vale of St. Thomas, Jamaica*, 115
Civil War, 1, 2, 3, 9, 10, 45, 51, 53, 56, 68, 72, 81, 129, 136, 179, 194, 201; pre-Civil War period, 148
Claudian, 165, 167
Cole, Thomas, 11, 111, 136, 140, 148, 173–4, 194, 224, 225, 237; "The Bewilderment," 174; *The Course of Empire*, 138, 140, 172; "Desolation," 172; *The Garden of Eden*, 11; *Landscape with a Dead Tree*, 138–9, 137; *The Voyage of Life*, 11
Coleridge, Samuel T., 5, 7, 49, 50, 133, 136, 141; Coleridgean: Imagination, 140, 142; theory, 159; theory of Imagination, 195
Colombia, 107
Committee on Practical Medicine and Epidemics, *see* American Medical Association
contagion, 192–3, 196, 198; *see also* infection
Cooper, James Fenimore, 126, 136, 140; *The Crater*, 138; *The Pioneers*, 136
Costa Rica, 118
Coulon, George A., *350 Miles in a Skiff Through the Louisiana Swamps*, 64
Crayon, The, 121, 140, 157, 167; "Natural Scenery in Jamaica," 121

Darwin, Charles, 107, 247; Darwinian science, 18; Darwinian struggle for survival, 10, 250; Darwinian view of nature, 249; Darwin's theory, 242; *On the Origin of Species*, 107
Davidson, Edward H., 42
De Man, Paul, 186
"desert" landscapes, 1, 45, 211–12, 224, 237, 239, 255, 262
Dickens, Charles, *Bleak House*, 190
Dickinson, Emily, 15, 16, 18, 153, 256, 261;

"By My Window Have I for Scenery," 266; "Further in Summer than the Birds," 256, 264–6
"Didymus" (Doubting Thomas), 225
Dismal Swamp, 29, 35, 36–7, 38, 41–2, 44, 45, 95, 157, 207; *see also* Great Dismal Swamp of Virginia
Dodge, Julia E., 65
Dom Pedro, Emperor of Brazil, 155
Don Giovanni, 26
Dore, Gustave, 65
Douglas, Ann, 8, 79; "feminization of American culture," 89
Douglas, Mary, 78
Drummond, 38
Durand, Asher B., 140, 237; *The Beeches*, 169, 170; *In the Woods*, 169, 170; "Letters on Landscape Painting," 144–5, 157, 167–8

Eaton, Clement, 83
Eaton, Walter Prichard: "The Real Dismal Swamp," 38
Ehrenzweig, Anton, 158
Eliot, George, 68
Emerson, Ralph Waldo, 18, 72, 129, 139, 187, 201–2, 218–23, 225, 243; "Circles," 219; *The Conduct of Life*, 220; doctrine of correspondence, 225; Emersonian idealism, 89; Emersonian Transcendentalism, 142, 225; *English Traits*, 214–15; journal, 218; *Nature*, 162, 220; "Self-Reliance," 225
Enceladus, 263
epidemiology, 188, 190
ethic of the strenuous life, 179
Eurydice, 43
Every Saturday Magazine, 57, 59
Ezekiel, 47

Fairchild, Hoxie, 44
Falstaff, 87
Federalists, 191
Feidelson, Charles, 78
Fenn, Harry: *Ascending the Ocklawaha River at Night*, 62; *A Florida Swamp*, 64; *A Sudden Turn in the Ocklawaha*, 61; *Waiting for Decomposition*, 63
Field, Erastus Salisbury: *The Garden of Eden*, 11
Figuier, Louis: *The World Before the Deluge*, 122
Fisher, Flavius: *Dismal Swamp*, 38, 39
Fiske, John, 241
Fletcher, Angus, 5, 191
Florida, 13, 50–1, 53, 60, 68, 69, 141, 172, 178, 224, 227, 244
folklore of the swamp, 182
Forest and Stream Magazine, 226–7
Forgie, George, 45
Fort George's Island, 65
Foucault, Michel, 187–8
Fountain of Youth, 28
Frederickson, George W., 89

French Huguenot settlers, 51
Freud, Sigmund, 26, 152–3; Freudian analysis, 173; "the omnipotence of thought," 154; "the uncanny," 24, 257, 258, 266
Friedrich, Caspar David, 156; *Oak Tree in Snow*, 156
Froebel, Julius, 190
Frost, Robert, 37

Galapagos Islands, 127–8
Gallop, Jane, 152–3
Geertz, Clifford, 3–4
Georgia, 50, 53, 71
German Idealism, 136
Gifford, Sanford, 140
Gignoux, François Régis: *Sunset in a Swamp*, 167–8
Gilpin, William, 135
Gospel of John, 185
"Great Dismal," 26, 212
Great Dismal Swamp of Virginia, 1, 18, 23, 90, 181–2
Great Mother archetype, 103, 152
Grendel, *see Beowulf*
Grimes, J. Stanley, 194–5
Guiana, 252

Hallam, Arthur, 52
Halttunen, Karen, 34
Hamilton, James, 32; *Bayou in Moonlight*, 32, 33, 172
Hamlet, problem of, 84
Hammond, James, 82–4, 88
Hampton, Wade, 83
Harper's Monthly, 1, 28, 38, 59, 123, 125, 131, 153, 173, 181
Harper's Weekly, 38, 57, 123
Hartman, Geoffrey, 44
Hawthorne, Nathaniel, 104, 131, 189; *The Blithedale Romance*, 196; *The Marble Faun*, 197
Heade, Martin Johnson, 13, 15, 18, 124, 129, 150, 159, 172, 194, 224–8, 232–7, 238; *Approaching Storm: Beach near Newport*, 233, 234, 236, 237; *Brazilian Forest*, 165, 237; *The Great Florida Marsh*, 14, 172; *Lake George*, 225, 226; *Low Tide*, 232; marsh scenes, 237; *Orchids and Hummingbird*, 155; *Salt Marshes, Newport, Rhode Island*, 235, 237; *South American River Scene*, 172, 173; *Thunderstorm over Naragansett Bay*, 232; *Twilight, Spouting Rock Beach*, 232; *View from Tree-Fern Walk, Jamaica*, 165, 166
Hearn, Lafcadio, 18, 72, 240, 241–3, 246–7, 249–53; *Chita*, 250; "The Eternal Feminine," 253; "The Garden of Paradise," 246; Review of "The Life of Stars," 249; "Torn Letters," 250; *Two Years in the French West Indies*, 251
"heart of darkness," 228, 262
Hegel, G. W. F., 205; Hegelian critical standards, 148

Hemingway, Ernest: "Big Two-Hearted River," 214
Henry, James, 167
Hercules, 212
Herzog, Herman: *Moonlight in Florida*, 172, 174
Hesperides, 216
Higginson, Thomas Wentworth, 18, 52–3, 138, 181, 224, 237–8; *Army Life in a Black Regiment*, 53–6; "My Out-Door Study," 52; "A Night in the Water," 54–6; "Water-Lillies," 53
Higham, John, 129, 227; *From Boundlessness to Consolidation*, 129
Home Book of the Picturesque, 59, 126
Homer, Winslow, 179, 228; *Homosassa Jungle*, 229; *In the Jungle, Florida*, 229
Hopkins, Samuel, 97
Hotspur type, 84
Houston, John Adam: "The Fugitive Slave," 91
Hovenkamp, Herbert, 145
Hudson River School, 1, 127, 140, 167, 171, 194, 262
Humboldt, Alexander von, 107, 109–10, 154; *Cosmos*, 110
Hunt, Robert: *The Poetry of Science*, 110
Huntington, David, 11, 110
Huxley, Aldous, 141
Hyperion, 112
hypnotism, 196

"Ibis Shooting in Louisiana," *Harper's Monthly*, 173, 179–81
infection, infectious atmosphere, 13, 184–8, 190, 191 (*see also* miasma); metaphor of infection, 13, 187–8, 190, 196–204, 255
Inferno (Dante's), 65
influenza epidemic, 256
Inman, Henry: engraving after *The Great Dismal Swamp*, 33, 38
Inness, George, 146
Irving, Washington, 28, 126, 140, 197; "The Devil and Tom Walker," 51; Geoffrey Crayon, 28; *Tales of a Traveller*, 197–8; "Westminster Abbey," 139
Israelites, 79, 211

Jackson, Andrew, 129
James, Henry: *Daisy Miller*, 197
James, William, 223, 231; "stream of thought," 223; "the sick soul," 231
Japan (and Lafcadio Hearn), 253
Jarves, James Jackson, 146–7, 149, 155, 237
Jefferson, Thomas, 187
Johnson, David: *Brook Study at Warwick*, 148, 171
Johnson, Edward: *Wonder-Working Providence*, 211–12
Jones, Howard Mumford, 72
Judah, 47
Jung, C. G., 15, 103, 153; Jungian notion of individuation, 175

Jung-Stilling, J. H., 194; *Theory of Pneumatology*, 195

Kames, Henry Home, Lord, 133–4, 139
Keats, John, 49; "negative capability," 140; "Ode to a Nightingale," 177
Keatsian, 230
Kensett, John, 140
King, Edward: *The Great South*, 62–3, 68
Knight, Richard Payne, 135
Kolodny, Annette, 85–6

Lacanian: psychoanalysis, 103; sexual differentiation, 152
LaFarge, John, 72
Lake Drummond, 23, 25, 29, 30, 34–5, 37, 41, 44, 183
Landow, George P., 143
Lane, Fitzhugh, 163, 194
Lanier, Sidney, 18, 60, 71–2, 241, 242–6, 247–9, 250, 251; "The Cloud," 242, 244; "Corn," 243; *Florida*, 71–2, 244; "From Bacon to Beethoven," 246; *Hymns to the Marshes*, 247; "The Marshes of Glynn," 242, 244, 247–9; *Science of English Verse*, 243; "Sunrise," 245, 247
Lanman, Charles, 125–9, 139, 227; *Letters from a Landscape Painter*, 125–6; *Adventures in the Wilds of North America*, 127
LaSalle, Robert, 51
Latin America, 1, 110, 228
Lawson, John: *History of North Carolina*, 177
Lazarus, 261, 264
Lears, T. J. Jackson, 56, 75; "crisis of bourgeois values," 75; "therapeutic culture of consumption," 75
Lévi-Strauss, Claude, 121–2
Lewis, C. S., 48
Lincoln, Abraham, 210
Linnaean categorization of species, 161
Locke, John, 186–7, 195, 198
Longfellow, Henry Wadsworth, 32, 92; "Evangeline," 32; "The Slave in the Dismal Swamp," 92
Longinus: *On the Sublime*, 139
Louisiana, 57, 179, 246
Lowell, Percival, 72
Ludlow, Fitzhugh, 60
Lukacs, Georg, 255
luminism, luminist, 128, 225, 229; painting, 194, 237

McCosh, James, 133, 145
McLoughlin, William G., 89
McLuhan, Marshall, 113
Magnolia, The, 30, 84
Magoon, E. L.: *Scenery and Mind*, 127
Maine, 218, 223
Malvolio, 192
Manifest Destiny, 110, 111, 126, 225
Manthorne, Katherine, 11
Marcoy, Paul: *Travels in South America*, 115–16
martial ideal, 75

Martinique, 253
Masque of Poets, A, 242
Marxist perspective, 72, 255
Matthiessen, F. O., 219, 221
medievalism, 75
Meeker, Joseph Rusling, 68; *Bayou Teche*, 69; *Swamp on the Mississippi*, 70, 187
Melville, Herman, 2, 5, 11, 15, 18, 131, 189–93, 201–4, 221; Ahab, 16; *The Confidence Man*, 11, 13, 15, 154, 184–6, 188, 202, 264; *The Encantadas*, 127; Ishmael, 16, 228; Ishmael's "insular Tahiti", 237; Ishmael, "The Spirit-Spout", 228; *Moby Dick*, "The Whiteness of the Whale", 104, 225, 261; "Mount of the Titans," *Pierre*, 15, 256, 262–4, 266; *The Piazza*, 15, 43, 264; *Pierre, or the Ambiguities*, 13–15, 16, 262
mesmerism, mesmeric, 192, 193–4, 195, 196; medium, 196, 199; trance, 194–5
Mexico, 72
miasma, 183, 190–9; etymology of, 191; miasmic atmosphere, 255; *see also* infectuous atmosphere
Mignot, Louis R., 11
Mill, John Stuart, 136
Milton, John: *Paradise Lost*, 48
Mississippi River, 60, 68, 122
Mississippi Valley, 50
Montrelay, Michele, 153
Moore, Richard S., 135
Moore, Thomas, 27, 29, 30, 35–6, 37, 38, 41, 43, 44; "The Lake of the Dismal Swamp," 27, 29–30, 37, 44
Moran, Thomas, 65; *Slaves Escaping Through the Swamp*, 92, 94, 172
Morris, Gouverneur, 192
Morse, Samuel F. B., 134
Moses, 126
Mound Builders, 30
Mount Katahdin, 128–9
Mount Sinai, 126
Muir, John, 141, 178
Muybridge, Eadweard: *Las Nubes, Delia Falls*, 163, 164

Nash, Roderick, 211–12
National Era, 90
National Magazine (1853), 50
Native Americans, 223
Neumann, Erich, 15, 103, 179; mandala, 239; uroboros, 140, 239
New England, 50, 51, 84–5, 89, 91, 139, 187; settlers, 211
New Orleans, 6, 13, 53, 63, 250, 253
New Orleans *Times-Democrat*, 241, 249, 252
New Path, The, 146
New York, 107, 109
New York Mirror, 190
Newburyport, Mass., 237
Newport, R.I., 236, 237
Niagara Falls, 30
Nicolson, Marjorie Hope, 48
Nietzsche, Friedrich, 15
Noble, Louis Legrand, 110–11

North Carolina, 90, 207, 211
Northrup, Solomon, 181
Norton, Charles Eliot, 111, 191

Ocklawaha River, Fla., 60
Ohio River, 90
Old Testament, 1, 126, 128, 139; symbols, 128
Ong, Walter, 176
O'Reilly, John Boyle, 30
Orpheus, 43
Ortega y Gasset, José, 162
Ossa, 263

Paley, William, 195
Panama, 119, 154, 190; isthmus of, 72
Panofsky, Erwin, 6; iconography, 6, 8; iconology, 6, 8, 9
Parents' Great Commission, The (1851), 196
Parker, Harley, 113
Parkman, Francis, 31–2, 224, 227; The Pioneers of the New World, 179
Paul, Sherman, 217, 222
Pelion, 263
Pennsylvania, 123
Perkins, Granville, 67, 124; Florida Landscape (1888), 67, 172
photography, 148; photographic accuracy, 147; photographic realism, 148
"pictorial mode," 151
picturesque, 1, 11, 31, 126, 128, 157–8, 159, 161; delineation of objects, 52; description, 140; language, 139; mode, 158; moral picturesque, 135; tradition, 224
Picturesque America, 59–62, 122, 126
Poe, Edgar Allan, 11, 24, 28, 30, 35, 41, 44, 189, 198–200, 201–2, 250; "The Domain of Arnheim," 41; Eureka, 243; Fall of the House of Usher, 11, 24, 41, 136, 157, 189, 195; "The Lake: To . . . ," 41; "Mesmeric Revelation," 195; Narrative of A. Gordon Pym, 11; "The Philosophy of Furniture," 30; "The Power of Words," 195, 200–1; "Ulalume," 41–2, 43
Poe, Virginia, 41
Pollock, Jackson, 159
Porte Crayon, 15, 23–9, 34–5, 37, 38, 41, 44, 46, 92, 124, 157; see also David Hunter Strother
Porter, Carolyn, 72, 201, 220, 223
Porter, David, 220
Porter, Katherine Anne, 16, 18, 153, 256, 264, 266; "The Grave," The Old Order, 261, 267–8; "Old Mortality," 259; "Pale Horse, Pale Rider," 256–62, 263, 264, 267, 268
Pre-Raphaelites, 146; Pre-Raphaelite credo, 149, 169; Pre-Raphaelitism, 150
Price, Martin, 135
Price, Uvedale, 135, 157–8, 163
Prince, Morton: The Nature of Mind and Human Automatism, 241
Prospero, 47
Puritan, 49; chaste "Puritan" maiden, 197;

community, 79; distrust, 51; heritage, 89; quest for salvation, 49; restraint, 69; self-discipline, 103; "that old genius of Puritanism," 84–5; tradition, 193
Puritans, 211–2, 223
Putnam's Monthly, 1, 110; "The Unexplored Regions of Central America," 120, 122; "Wonders of the Deep," 122

Quidor, John: The Devil and Tom Walker, 51
Quito, Peru, 107

Radcliffe, Ann, 36
Reed, Herbert, 158–9
Reconstruction, 68
Reid, Thomas, 133; Essays on the Active Powers of the Human Mind, 186
reification, 72, 134, 220, 222, 255
republican institutions, 75; Republicanism as moral influenza, 192
Reynolds, Sir Joshua, 143, 158, 159–60
Richards, T. Addison: "The Landscape of the South," 59, 123
Richards, William Trost, 148; Ferns in a Glade, 149; In the Woods, 147, 148
Ridgeley, Joseph V., 86
Ringe, Donald, 151
Rocky Mountains, 30
Roethke, Theodore: "greenhouse poems," 209
Roheim, Geza, 25
romance tradition in America, 196–9
Romantic attitudes toward death, 32–4
romantic racialism, 89
Rosa, Salvator, 93; Salvatoresque, 172
Rosenberg, Charles E., 191
Rousseau, Henri, 258
Rowe, Anne, 68
Rudolph, Harold: Bayou Sunset, 65
Ruskin, John, 80–1, 111–12, 135, 142–8, 161, 162, 168, 224; Modern Painters, 111, 142–8; "pathetic fallacy," 141, 143, 247, 257, 266; Typical Beauty, 143, 147; Vital Beauty, 143, 147
Ruskinism, 169
Ruisdael, Jacob van, 168
Rydal, 141

St. Armand, Barton L., 34; "Sentimental Love Religion," 32
St. John's River, Florida, 60, 62, 65
St. Louis, 68
St. Louis River, 127
San Francisco, 72, 172
Sands, Robert C., 32
Sarpedon, 26
Sartre, Jean-Paul, 5
Scottish Common Sense school, 133, 184; philosophy, 193; theory, 136
Scribner's (The Century), 65, 68
"Sentimental Love Religion," 32
"Sentimental Years," 44
sentimentalism, 30–4; sentimental culture, 135
Shaftesbury, Third Earl of, 48–9

Shakespeare, William: Lear's fool, 266; *The Tempest*, 259

Shattuck, Aaron Draper, 150

Shelley, Percy Bysshe, 49; "The Sensitive Plant," 199–200

Sigourney, Lydia, 78–9, 81; "The Father," 79, 81; "The Patriarch," 78–9, 81

Silver, Reverend Abiel, 161

Simms, William Gilmore, 18, 77, 81–8, 93, 102–4, 190; "The Edge of the Swamp," 80–1; *The Foragers*, 85, 86, 88; "The Moral Character of Hamlet," 84; *The Partisan*, 93; *The Scout (The Kinsman)*, 86; "The Sword and the Distaff," 87; *Woodcraft*, 86–7

Sister Arts: doctrine, 134, 188, 204; ideal, 137

slave in the swamp, 90–4

Slotkin, Richard, 212

Smillie, James, engraving after Thomas Cole's *Garden of Eden*, 12

Smith, Henry Nash, 131

Social Darwinism, 1, 179

South Carolina, 54, 82, 83, 85, 88, 96, 190

Southern Agrarians, 249

Spencer, Herbert, 129, 243, 244, 246; Spencerian view of nature, 249

Spenser, Edmund, 162

spiritualism, 192, 194

Spitzer, Leo, 198

Spofford, Harriet Prescott: "The Amber Gods," 106

Stebbins, Theodore, 225

Stein, Roger, 142

Stewart, Dugald, 133

Stowe, Harriet Beecher, 3, 13, 18, 77; *Dred*, 3, 15, 56–7, 68, 90–1, 93–102, 104; *The Minister's Wooing*, 97; *Palmetto Leaves*, 68; *Pink and White Tyranny*, 89; *Uncle Tom's Cabin*, 86, 90, 93

Stowe, Thomas, 101

Strain, Lieutenant, 123

Strauss, Meyer, 124; *Bayou Teche*, 66

Strother, David Hunter, 23, 28, 29, 35, 45, 93 (see also Porte Crayon); *The Barge*, 24; *Lake Drummond*, 27; *Osman*, 93

Styx, 50; Stygian, 217

sublime, 11, 31, 133, 136, 139, 140, 157, 162; language, 139; moral sublime, 135

Sumner, Charles, 96

Symplegades or clashing rocks, 27

Talisman, The, 35, 38

Tate, Allen, 200

Taylor, Bayard, 72, 119, 126, 154–5, 243

Taylor, Edward, 231

Taylor, William R., 84

Têche country, 246

Tennyson, Alfred, Lord, 52, 230

Thompson, Lawrence, 37

Thoreau, Henry David, 5, 11, 15, 17, 18, 104, 129, 130, 201–2, 224, 238, 256; "Allegash and East Branch," 218; *Cape Cod*, 127–8, 232, 250; *Walden*, 175–6, 177; *Walking, or the Wild*, 11, 214–18, 220–3

Ticknor, George, 191

Tilton, Theodore, 89

Timrod, Henry, 85

Transcendentalism, 225; Transcendentalists, 11, 136, 187

Tucker, Beverly, 84

Tuckerman, Frederick Goddard, 15, 18, 224, 228–30, 237, 238; "The Cricket," 230, 233–7; "A Sample of Coffee Beans," 228–230; Transcendental correspondence, 230; Transcendental faith, 228; "Twilight," 230

Tuckerman, Henry T., 107, 113; *Book of the Artists*, 109, 147, 148–9, 155

Tundalus, Vision of, 47

Turner, James Mallord William, 68, 146

Turner, Nat, 95; rebellion, 90

Turner, Victor, 3, 4; "communitas," 98

Unitarian, 82, 187

Univercoelum, and Spiritual Philosopher, 194

ut pictura poesis, 16, 133

Verplanck, Gulian, 38–41

Vesey, Denmark, 95

Virginia, 23, 90, 207

Volney, Constantin: *Ruins*, 139

Wagoner, David, 18; "Wading in a Marsh," 18, 208–9, 213–24; "Walking in a Swamp," 105

Warner, Samuel, 90–1

Warren, Robert Penn (and Southern Agrarians), 249

Washington, George, 44

Watts, Isaac, 35

Waud, A. R., 57–9; *Bear Hunt in a Southern Canebrake*, 123; *Cypress Swamp on the Opelousas Railroad, Louisiana*, 58; *On Picket Duty in the Swamps of Louisiana*, 59

Webster, Daniel, 10, 140

Webster, Noah: *First American Dictionary*, 9, 124

Weir, Robert Walter, 42

Whigs, 10; Conservative Whigs, 191

Whitman, Walt, 5, 201, 214, 221, 243–4; *Calamus*, 209; *Children of Adam*, 209; *Leaves of Grass*, 243; "O Magnet South," 60; "Out of the Cradle Endlessly Rocking," 209–10; "I Sing the Body Electric," 208–9; "This Compost," 210; "When Lilacs Last in the Dooryard Bloomed," 210

Whitmanesque, 239

Whittredge, Worthington, 157; *The Old Hunting Grounds*, 169, 171

wilderness, 211

Willis, N. P.: *American Scenery*, 39, 119

Winthrop, Theodore, 112, 124; *Life in the Open Air*, 128–9

Wirt, William, 36–7

woman's influence, 188

Woolson, Constance Fenimore, *East Angels*, 69

Wordsworth, William, 135, 141, 148

Wordsworthian, 43, 44, 243; poetry, 49, 50;
    visionary gleam of youth, 228
World War I, 256

Yankee, 85, 87, 88, 103, 104, 215
Young Lady's Offering, A, 78

Cambridge Studies in American Literature and Culture

Editor
Albert Gelpi, Stanford University

Charles Altieri, *Painterly Abstraction in Modernist American Poetry: The Contemporaneity of Modernism*

Douglas Anderson, *A House Undivided: Domesticity and Community in American Literature*

Steven Axelrod and Helen Deese (eds.), *Robert Lowell: Essays on the Poetry*

Sacvan Bercovitch and Myra Jehlen (eds.), *Ideology and Classic American Literature*

Mitchell Breitweiser, *Cotton Mather and Benjamin Franklin: The Price of Representative Personality*

Lawrence Buell, *New England Literary Culture: From the Revolution to the Renaissance*

Patricia Caldwell, *The Puritan Conversion Narrative: The Beginnings of American Expression*

Peter Conn, *The Divided Mind: Ideology and Imagination in America, 1898–1917*

Michael Davidson, *The San Francisco Renaissance: Poetics and Community at Mid-Century*

George Dekker, *The American Historical Romance*

Stephen Fredman, *Poet's Prose: The Crisis in American Verse*

Albert Gelpi (ed.), *Wallace Stevens: The Poetics of Modernism*

Paul Giles, *Hart Crane: The Contexts of* The Bridge

Richard Gray, *Writing the South: Ideas of an American Region*

Alfred Habegger, *Henry James and the "Woman Business"*

David Halliburton, *The Color of the Sky: A Study of Stephen Crane*

Susan K. Harris, *19th-Century American Women's Novels: Interpretive Strategies*

Margaret Holley, *The Poetry of Marianne Moore: A Study in Voice and Value*

Lothar Hönnighausen, *William Faulkner: The Art of Stylization*

Lynn Keller, *Re-making It New: Contemporary American Poetry and the Modernist Tradition*

Anne Kibbey, *The Interpretation of Material Shapes in Puritanism: A Study of Rhetoric, Prejudice, and Violence*

Robert Lawson-Peebles, *Landscape and Written Expression in Revolutionary America: The World Turned Upside Down*

Robert S. Levine, *Conspiracy and Romance: Studies in Brockden Brown, Cooper, Hawthorne, and Melville*

John Limon, *The Place of Fiction in the Time of Science: A Disciplinary History of American Writing*

Jerome Loving, *Emily Dickinson: The Poet on the Second Story*

Elizabeth McKinsey, *Niagara Falls: Icon of the American Sublime*

John McWilliams, *The American Epic: Transformations of a Genre, 1770–1860*

David Miller, *Dark Eden: The Swamp in Nineteenth-Century American Culture*

Warren Motley, *The American Abraham: James Fenimore Cooper and the Frontier Patriarch*

Brenda Murphy, *American Realism and American Drama, 1800–1940*

Marjorie Perloff, *The Dance of the Intellect: Studies in Poetry in the Pound Tradition*

Karen Rowe, *Saint and Singer: Edward Taylor's Typology and the Poetics of Mediation*

Barton St. Armand, *Emily Dickinson and Her Culture: The Soul's Society*

Eric Sigg, *The American T. S. Eliot: A Study of the Early Writings*

Tony Tanner, *Scenes of Nature, Signs of Man: Essays in 19th and 20th Century American Literature*

Brook Thomas, *Cross-Examinations of Law and Literature: Cooper, Hawthorne, Stowe, and Melville*

Albert von Frank, *The Sacred Game: Provincialism and Frontier Consciousness in American Literature, 1630–1860*

David Wyatt, *The Fall into Eden: Landscape and Imagination in California*

Lois Zamora, *Writing the Apocalypse: Ends and Endings in Contemporary U.S. and Latin American Fiction*